Extracting Promises

Indigenous Peoples, Extractive Industries
&
the World Bank

Tebtebba
Indigenous Peoples' International Centre for
Policy Research and Education

Forest Peoples Programme (FPP)

4

Extracting Promises:
Indigenous Peoples, Extractive Industries and the World Bank
Tebtebba Foundation

Copyright © TEBTEBBA FOUNDATION, 2003

Published by
TEBTEBBA FOUNDATION
No. 1 Roman Ayson Road
2600 Baguio City
Philippines
Tel: 63 74 4447703   Tel/Fax: 63 74 4439459
E-mail: tebtebba@skyinet.net
Website: www.tebtebba.org

FOREST PEOPLES PROGRAMME
1c Fosseway Business Centre, Stratford Road
Moreton-in-Marsh GL56 9NQ
United Kingdom
Tel: 44 01608 652893   Fax: 44 01608 652878
E-mail: info@fppwrm.gn.apc.org

Edited by Marcus Colchester, Ann Loreto Tamayo, Raymundo Rovillos,
Emily Caruso

Cover design and lay-out by Raymond de Chavez

Maps by Jack Gilbert L. Medrana

ISBN 971-92846-1-7

Printed in the Philippines
by Capitol Publishing House, Inc.

Extracting Promises

Indigenous Peoples, Extractive Industries
&
the World Bank

ACKNOWLEDGEMENTS

The publishers would like to thank Conrad Feather, Tom Griffiths, John Nelson, Mara Stankovitch, Tony Laviña, Joji Cariño, Vicky Tauli-Corpuz, Roger Moody, Matilda Koma, Augustine Hala, Jacklyne Membup, Rodion Sulyandziga, Vladimir Botcharnikov, Vlad Peskov, Catalino Corpuz, Raymundo Rovillos, Peter Duyapat, Armando Valbuena, Gladys Jimeno, Cecilia Mattos, Mabel Otolora, Didier Amougou , Jeanne Nouah, Joachim Gwodog, Bineet Mundu, Philan Horo, Yuyun Indradi, Pak Pius, Adriana Sri Adhiati, Liz Chidley, Tricia Feeney, Ingrid MacDonald, Gisele Morin-Labatut, Nur Hidayati, Catriona Bass, Sara Asadullah, Dr Emil Salim, Chandra Kirana, Julia Grutzner, Robert Goodland, Saleem Ali, Stuart Kirsch, Kathryn MacPhail, Stan Peabody, Clive Armstrong for their contributions to the workshop and for providing help and advice.

This work has been funded by grants from the Extractive Industries Review, the International Development Research Centre of Canada and the Moriah Fund. Additional funding for the research and writing by Forest Peoples Programme staff and for translation and publication of the results has come from the Finnish government, the Charles Stewart Mott Foundation and the Ford Foundation. We are very grateful for all this support. None of these are responsible for the views and information presented in this report.

CONTENTS

FOREWORD

For many indigenous peoples throughout the world, oil, gas and coal industries conjure images of displaced peoples, despoiled lands, and depleted resources. This explains the unwavering resistance of most indigenous communities with any project related to extractive industries.

The bad historical record of extractive industries explains the skepticism of many indigenous peoples and non-government organizations regarding the World Bank's Extractive Industries Review (EIR). We (in Tebtebba) have always agreed with the civil society criticism that the EIR process was unduly dominated and therefore controlled by the World Bank. Still, we participated in this independent study together with the Forest Peoples' Programme (FPP) because we wanted to formally present the voices of the indigenous peoples into the process.

Indigenous participants in the seven (7) case studies have once again proven that they can use their human agency even in arenas that are supposed to be dominated by powerful institutions like the world bank. Directly engaging the World Bank in its own forum has been helpful in the case of indigenous peoples who presented their written and oral testimonies in the presence of representatives of the World Bank. They felt a sense of relief just being able to articulate their issues and concerns in the global sphere.

Before we even considered participating in this project, we did not have any illusion that the World Bank will consider all the findings and recommendations of the study. At any rate -- I believe that the opportunity to document and disseminate the impact of extractive industries on indigenous peoples could be seen as an end in itself.

The indigenous peoples have spoken. The majority of the case studies presented in this book reveal that indigenous peoples want the World Bank to stay out of the Extractive Industries Sector. This conclusion is based not only on our negative experiences with extractive industries on the ground. We have also had frustrating experiences with the World Bank's inability to properly implement its own instruments, such as its Indigenous Peoples' Policy. It should also be noted that this policy, along with other policies on forests and resettlement, are being weakened in the revision process.

Let us welcome this book as an affirmation of the growing self-awareness and empowerment of indigenous peoples. With the help of non-government organizations, indigenous researchers and activists who contributed to this modest project are saying that they can speak for themselves. They are also transcending the "victimhood" discourse about themselves. In fact, as this book portrays, they can be active participants in the long-term process of protecting their ancestral territories from unwanted extractive industries.

Indeed, indigenous peoples' movements to protect their land and resources go beyond the EIR process.

Victoria Tauli-Corpuz
Executive Director, Tebtebba

INTRODUCTION

Mining, oil and gas development poses one of the greatest of the many threats facing indigenous peoples and the lands, territories and the resources that they depend on. As the global economy expands, pressure on indigenous lands to yield up these resources is intensifying. Historically, the huge transnational corporations spearheading these enterprises have paid little attention to indigenous peoples' rights. Today these same companies talk about "best practice" and extol the virtues of participation and self-regulation. What can an institution like the World Bank, which is meant to promote poverty alleviation and 'sustainable development, do to ensure that the rights of indigenous peoples are not compromised by oil, gas and mining development?

This independent study was compiled as a contribution to the World Bank's *Extractive Industries Review* (EIR). The EIR process has been criticised by many indigenous peoples and non-governmental organisations for being unduly controlled by the World Bank. It remains to be seen whether contributions, such as this one, are taken seriously by the review and, if so, whether the recommendations will be heeded by the World Bank itself. The study builds on an extensive literature review and legal analysis, seven specially commissioned case studies carried out by indigenous peoples of their experiences of the World Bank and extractive industries and a two-day workshop at which these various contributions were presented and discussed.

Indigenous peoples are now accepted to be a self-identified category of peoples in the Americas, Africa, Asia and the Pacific. International human rights law and associated jurisprudence recognises that indigenous peoples, like all other peoples, enjoy rights to self-determination and sovereignty over their natural resources. States also claim these rights and assert the right to control sub-surface resources and to develop them in the national interest.

These competing rights are not easily reconciled. However, it is a norm of international law that the promotion of national development should not be carried out at the expense of human rights. Existing human rights laws recognise the rights of indigenous peoples to the ownership and control of their lands, territories and natural resources and to free, prior and informed consent over developments proposed on their lands. The forced relocation of indigenous peoples to make way for development is expressly prohibited. These assertions of the rights of indigenous peoples have become so general that they may be considered to have become part of customary international law: there is a general acceptance that indigenous peoples should control developments that may affect their fundamental rights, which include their rights to their lands, territories and natural resources.

World Bank policies, however, make little mention of human rights. The Bank's "safeguard" policies on indigenous peoples and involuntary resettlement seek only to mitigate the impacts of destructive development schemes. They permit forced resettlement. However, in order to lessen the consequences for vulnerable social groups, specific plans are required during project preparation which, in the case of indigenous peoples, are meant to secure their lands and ensure participation in Bank-funded projects. The indigenous peoples policy was developed without the participation of indigenous peoples and have since been strongly criticised by them.

Moreover, successive reviews show that these safeguard policies are routinely flouted in practice. The World Bank's own studies show that only more than one third of World Bank projects that impact indigenous peoples have not applied the safeguard policy in any way at all. Even in the projects that did apply the policy, 14% had the required "Indigenous Peoples Development Plan"and then only on paper. Case studies presented to the workshop from India and the Cameroon reveal the shocking consequences of this negligence for the indigenous peoples themselves.

The World Bank is currently reviewing its policy on indigenous peoples. The revision has been repeatedly repudiated by indigenous peoples, both for the manner in which the associated consultations have been carried out, and for the fact that the revised draft policy fails to uphold their rights and is indeed weaker than the previous policy which it is designed to replace. In resisting indigenous demands for a policy which respects their rights, the World Bank claims that it is prohibited from addressing human rights by its Articles of Agreement and it argues that it cannot require its borrowers or clients to observe even those human rights agreements to which they are party. This argument, while legally questionable, is routinely deployed by Bank staff and can be said to be part of the culture of the Bank. In an era when discourse about "rights-based development" has become routine, the World Bank Group appears out of date and out of touch.

World Bank Group interventions in the extractive industries sector have negatively impacted indigenous peoples in manifold ways. In pursuit of national development through trade liberalisation, structural adjustment and the promotion of foreign direct investment, the World Bank has routinely advised countries to rewrite national mining codes to facilitate large-scale mining by foreign companies. These revised mining codes have been pushed through without the participation of indigenous peoples and without taking into account the interests and rights of indigenous peoples.

The case studies from Colombia and the Philippines show how the revised mining codes have intensified pressure on indigenous lands and weakened or overridden the legal protections previously enjoyed by indigenous peoples. In Colombia, mineral, oil and gas reserves are exploited by unaccountable companies, which enjoy legal impunity while regularly violating national laws and using severely repressive measures to overcome local resistance. In Ecuador, the World Bank has also promoted national minerals surveys, again without taking the rights of indigenous peoples into account or assessing the likely consequences of intensified minerals extraction.

The synthesis paper and case studies also document the way the World Bank Group, through its various arms -- the International Bank for Reconstruction and Development, the International Development Association, the International Finance Corporation and the Multilateral Investment Guarantee Agency -- has directly supported mines, oil and gas ventures without adequate assessment of the social and environmental consequences and without taking heed of the lack of good governance and institutional or regulatory capacity in project areas or countries.

In the case of the Chad-Cameroon Pipeline, the World Bank's Board voted to go ahead with the project even when the forest-dwelling Bagyéli and supporting NGOs had clearly demonstrated the risks and even though Board members admitted that the Bank's safeguard policy on indigenous peoples has not been properly applied. The IFC has even supported mining in war-torn countries like the Democratic Republic of the Congo by companies with bad track records: projects that have been condemned by the United Nations.

The impacts of Bank-facilitated mining ventures have been severe, not just in terms of the direct social and environmental impacts of the mines or wells themselves but also in terms of spills of poisonous chemicals such as cyanide and mercury, ruptured oil pipes, breached tailings dams and long term pollution through acid mine drainage. The case study from Papua New Guinea reveals World Bank support for the use of the highly controversial technique of submarine tailings disposal – "out of sight is out of mind" -- without consideration for the long term implications for marine ecosystems and the livelihoods that depend on them.

World Bank employees, assessors and consultants, working with mining companies in the name of the IFC and the World Bank's Business Partners for Development have been party to, or have endorsed, processes that have engineered consent or have coopted communities into untransparent and manipulated decision-making. In some cases, as in Russia, the World Bank's involvement in specific projects may have temporarily mitigated some of the worst impacts of oil extraction but overall the World Bank's involvement in the sector has intensified pressure on indigenous lands which remain unsecured.

The Cameroon case also illustrates how the application of the World Bank's Natural Habitats policy, which requires the funding of compensatory conservation measures to "offset" habitat destruction, has negatively impacted indigenous peoples by excluding them from the national parks set up in their forests. They thus suffer a double jeopardy, losing rights in the area impacted by the Bank-funded oil pipeline and in the GEF-funded conservation zones.

The study reveals that underlying these problems lies a flawed process of decision-making within the World Bank in which the pressure to lend overwhelms other objectives and objections. By prioritising its direct clients and the interests of large-scale private sector enterprises, the Bank is overriding its commitment to sustainable development. Corruption is knowingly tolerated and governance failures routinely overlooked. Staff who question loans being made under these circumstances are penalised. Currently, in the name of "efficiency", lower "transaction costs" and "country ownership", the Bank is systematically weakening its safeguard policies, in order to 'panel proof' them against complaints by civil society to the Inspection Panel.

Given the weakness of its safeguards, its institutionalised opposition to invoking binding human rights standards and the way it rou-

tinely flouts its own procedures, the study concludes that the World Bank should not be involved in the Extractive Industries sector.

Moreover, the study recommends that the World Bank should radically revise its social policies and its safeguard policy on indigenous peoples. It should adopt a rights-based approach to development, recognise indigenous peoples' rights to the ownership and control of their lands, territories and natural resources, proscribe the forced relocation of indigenous peoples, and uphold the principle that development projects should only go ahead in areas owned or used by indigenous peoples subject to their free, prior and informed consent. Such changes in approach should be applied to the whole World Bank Group, should be complemented with new, legally binding systems of accountability and should be accompanied by an acceptance that the promotion of development through the private sector requires, first of all, the promotion of good governance, real accountability, effective regulatory mechanisms and strong institutional capacity.

Marcus Colchester
Director, Forest Peoples' Programme

SYNTHESIS REPORT:
Indigenous Peoples, Extractive Industries and the World Bank

Emily Caruso, Marcus Colchester,
Fergus MacKay, Nick Hildyard & Geoff Nettleton

They promised us jobs. They took everything from us. They took our land. They took our forest. They took our water.

Sama Bailie of South West Cameroon
speaking of the Chad-Cameroon Oil Pipeline Project.

Land is our life. Land is our physical life – food and substance. Land is our social life, it is marriage, it is status, it is security, it is politics. In fact, it is our only life. Tribesmen would rather die to protect their traditional land… When you take our land you cut away the heart of our existence… Big multinational foreign companies being from an alien culture would neither understand nor grasp the significance of this. For them land is a commodity to be bought or sold. They just treat it as an exploitable resource…. Why would a genuine funding organisation like the World Bank Group fund culprit industries and their government cronies to violate lesser indigenous communities' rights to exist?

Augustine Hala presenting the Papua New Guinea
Case Study to the Workshop

Mining, oil and gas exploitation are among the most serious threats to the territories and livelihoods of indigenous peoples. For peoples who have already been pushed to the margins by colonialism, nation-building and cultural discrimination, the pressures of the mining, oil and gas industries can be hard to resist. Denied secure rights and with many nation States claiming sovereign rights over the resources which lie under their territories, indigenous peoples face an unequal struggle when confronted by highly capitalised companies backed by voracious global markets.

In developing countries, pressure on indigenous territories from the oil, gas and mining sectors has increased dramatically in the past forty years. Export-led development models, structural adjustment programmes and massive growth in foreign direct investment, have all favoured the expansion of the oil, gas and mining sectors. The World Bank has been a world leader promoting development along this path.

Yet, the mining industry also has concerns about indigenous peoples. Dealing with communities with unclear property rights, poorly understood political processes, in areas where the national administration may have little influence and the rule of law is weak, makes investment risky. Neither are mining companies immune to public criticism nor devoid of ethics. Mining industries are thus also in search of ways of dealing with indigenous peoples, that can assure predictable and legally secure outcomes, and avoid conflict and costly litigation.

As a development agency, the World Bank has a responsibility to find means to reconcile the interests of these two players. Indeed for more than twenty years the World Bank has adopted policies designed to cushion "tribal" and indigenous peoples from the worst impacts of the development process. It is also currently in the midst of an extended process of reviewing its indigenous peoples policy.

This study is part of a piece of independent 'focused research' that will contribute to the World Bank's "Extractive Industries Review". It is complemented by seven case studies elaborated by indigenous peoples themselves which set out their own experiences and views of extractive industries and the World Bank's involvement. Taken together this "focused research" seeks answers to a number of key questions.

- ❑ What are the rights of indigenous peoples in relation to extractive industries?
- ❑ What is the World Bank's policy on indigenous peoples? Has it been effective in securing these rights and protecting indigenous peoples against the negative impacts of extractive industries? What are indigenous peoples de-

manding of a revised policy?

❏ What is the World Bank's record of support for the extractive industries? How have these investments performed in terms of indigenous peoples' rights, cultures and livelihoods?

❏ If there are deficiencies in the way standards are set and applied in World Bank projects and programmes, what are the underlying reasons for these institutional and practical shortcomings?

❏ What are industry and indigenous peoples proposing as "best practices", which might form the basis for new industry and development agency standards in the future?

❏ Given the answers to the above, what can be concluded about the World Bank's involvement in the extractive industries sectors? What recommendations should the Extractive Industries Review make to the World Bank?

This synthesis report offers answers to these questions. It is designed as a benchmark contribution to the final report of the Eminent Person, Professor Emil Salim, who is leading the Extractive Industries Review, and who is to present his report to the World Bank in December 2003.

THE EXTRACTIVE INDUSTRIES REVIEW

Growing global consumption demands ever greater supplies of energy and raw materials, meaning increasing fossil fuel and mineral consumption and thus the need to explore and exploit the world's subterranean resources. Whilst previously untouched areas are prospected and opened to exploration, and forest frontiers are advancing ever further, financial globalisation and deregulation of trade create space for unfettered private investments and ventures. The increasing devastation caused by these forces has provoked a growing global voice campaigning against the unsustainable and destructive nature of such exploitation. In 2000, prompted by a Friends of the Earth campaign urging International Financial Institutions to phase out their investment in oil, mining and gas ventures, the World Bank responded by promising a "World Commission on Mines" similar to the then ongoing World Commission on Dams (WCD). In the event, the World Bank's "Extractive Industries Review" (EIR), which was launched by the World Bank in late 2001, turned out to be a very different kind of process to the WCD.

The World Commission on Dams, which was jointly established by the World Bank and World Conservation Union in 1997, was composed of a panel of commissioners -- a set of independent experts drawn from the various "stakeholder" groups with an interest in dam building: industry, government, engineering, environment, development NGOs, dam affected groups, indigenous peoples etc. They reviewed the experience with large dams, held extensive consultations, contracted independent researchers and organisations to carry out thematic reviews and then jointly authored a consensus-based report independent of the World Bank. The WCD recommendations address the entire large dams sector. Although not without its problems, the WCD has been viewed by many as a credible process which made sincere efforts to develop standards in line with the ideals of "sustainable development".[1]

By contrast, the Extractive Industry Review is being chaired and authored by a single Eminent Person, is largely staffed by seconded World Bank employees and is limited to a review of World Bank engagement in the Oil, Gas and Mining sectors. The Eminent Person is to report his findings, based on a series of hearings, focused research and field visits, directly to the World Bank President, James Wolfensohn and the World Bank's Board of Directors, at the end of the 3 year review period. Four regional workshops, consisting of discussions and presentations made by the various interest groups will provide information and evidence, on which the Eminent Person will draw to develop his final report. Complementary evidence will be delivered by project visits and a continual input of documentation from civil society and academics, as well as two independent focused research papers.

This report is the preliminary result of one such piece of focused research, and comprises a study commissioned by the EIR from the Tebtebba Foundation and the Forest Peoples Programme. The study assesses the past and present impacts of World Bank projects in the oil, gas and mining sectors on indigenous peoples worldwide [*See Box 1, p.22 for details*].

At its commencement, concerns surrounding the organisation and administration of the EIR process were raised by the civil society organisations that were tracking it.[2] Due to its financial link to the World Bank, concerns were raised over the independence, inclusiveness, transparency and comprehensiveness of the process, and the faith of civil society in a just and accurate outcome was limited. At the outset therefore a number of changes were demanded:

- ❑ The revision of the Terms of Reference to ensure an open and inclusive enquiry and not a pre-judged outcome and which should provide real independence for the Eminent Person (EP).

- ❑ The EP was called upon to establish an advisory group drawn from the various interest groups to share the burden of the work and ensure greater representation and independence.
- ❑ The EP and advisory board should be supported by a team of writers and rapporteurs to capture all the testimony and ensure a fair report.
- ❑ The EP and advisers should visit impacted communities.
- ❑ The EIR Secretariat should not be housed in the International Finance Corporation on the same floor as the WBG Mining Department nor staffed by World Bank employees.
- ❑ The EP should control the full budget and not allow over half to be controlled by the WBG.
- ❑ Regional workshops should be open to all observers, provided with good preparatory documents in the right languages and allow time for testimonies to be presented. Sponsored participants should be self-selected.
- ❑ WBG staff should participate as observers not 'stakeholders' in regional workshops.
- ❑ The time frame of the review should be extended.
- ❑ There should be time for EIR to take on board the results of the internal review of the sector being carried out by the WBG Operations Evaluation Department and Group.
- ❑ The operations of the Multilateral Investment Guarantee Agency should be included in the Extractive Industries Review purview.
- ❑ The "Management Recommendation", to be made by the WBG staff to the Bank's Executive Directors after receipt of the EP's report, should be made available to review participants in draft form for comments before being finalised.

Although some changes in the process were made in response to these demands, many NGOs and indigenous peoples' organisations (IPOs) feel that these have been tokenistic. In February 2003, the EIR secretariat posted an interim "Compilation Report" on its website which prematurely set out the main findings of the review, including a conclusion that the World Bank should "remain involved but change -- because extractive industries can be a tool for reducing poverty, and the World Bank Group can be a leader in tackling these issues".[3] This caused dismay among civil society groups, as it confirmed their suspicions that

Box 1: *Indigenous Peoples, Extractive Industries and the World Bank*

The aims of the process are to:

- Assess the experience of indigenous peoples with World Bank-financed projects and policy interventions in the oil, gas and mining sectors.
- Promote a direct dialogue between World Bank operational staff, the extractive industries and indigenous peoples spokespersons.
- Develop concrete recommendations for the World Bank, specifically with regard to indigenous peoples, in respect of future engagement in the oil, gas and mining sector.

The activities entailed are:

- Gathering relevant indigenous experiences and recommendations through an email consultation.
- Sub-contracting indigenous peoples' organisations to write up "case studies" outlining their experience with World Bank-financed activities in the sector. These case studies were selected from the following main regions: Latin America, Africa, South Asia, South East Asia, Pacific, and Russian Federation.
- Carrying out a detailed literature review on the theme.
- Drafting a synthesis paper, which would include the findings from the email consultation, the literature review and the case studies.
- Holding an international workshop at which the case studies and synthesis paper would be presented and discussed with the participation of other indigenous spokespersons, representatives of the extractive industries, the World Bank and the Eminent Person and other advisers to the EIR.
- Present a final report, which will take into account the issues raised in the international workshop and which will include: the case study papers; the synthesis paper; the recommendations made by indigenous peoples to the EIR.

the review was not genuinely independent but was drawing conclusions even before important hearings on indigenous peoples and in the Asia-Pacific were held. In mid-March 2003, many NGOs and IPOs sent a further letter to the Eminent Person expressing their continued frustration with the process and its apparent lack of independence and calling again for a more inclusive and independent process. In April, a large number of NGOs and IPOs attending the Asia-Pacific regional consultation staged a walk-out to express their indignation with the process.

However, this piece of "focused research", while 40% financed by the EIR, is nevertheless substantially independent of World Bank influence. Nor has there been any suggestion of editorial control being exerted over this research document by the EIR.

DEFINITIONS OF INDIGENOUS PEOPLES

In 1986, the United Nations' Working Group on Indigenous Populations adopted the following working definition to guide its work:

> *Indigenous communities, peoples and nations are those which, having a historical continuity with pre-invasion and pre-colonial societies that developed on their territories, consider themselves distinct from other sectors of the societies now prevailing in those territories, or parts of them. They form at present non-dominant sectors of society and are determined to preserve, develop and transmit to future generations their ancestral territories, and their ethnic identity; as the basis of their continued existence as peoples, in accordance with their own cultural patterns, social institutions and legal systems.[4]*

Since 1984 the Working Group, which has met annually, has heard presentations from thousands of indigenous spokespersons from all over the world. Many of these spokespersons are from countries in Asia and Africa that were either never colonised by European powers (such as China, Thailand and Japan) or from which colonial settlers mainly withdrew following decolonisation (such as India and Malaysia). Nevertheless the "aboriginal" or "tribal" peoples in these countries, whose territories have been administratively annexed by emerging independent nation states, experience discrimination and a denial of their rights. They thus equate their situation with that of other indigenous peoples in settler states and demand the same rights and consideration.[5]

Summing up the deliberations of years of work, the Chairperson of the UN's Working Group has concluded:

In summary, the factors which modern international organisations and legal experts (including indigenous legal experts and members of the academic family) have considered relevant to understanding the concept of 'indigenous' include:

a) priority in time with respect to the occupation and use of a specific territory;

b) the voluntary perpetuation of cultural distinctiveness, which may include aspects of language, social organisation, religion and spiritual values, modes of production, laws and institutions;

c) self-identification, as well as recognition by other groups, or by State authorities, as a distinct collectivity;

d) and an experience of subjugation, exclusion or discrimination, whether or not these conditions persist.[6]

The International Labour Organization's Convention No.169 applies to both indigenous and tribal peoples. It ascribes both the same rights without discrimination. Article 1(2) of ILO Convention No. 169 notes:

Self-identification as indigenous or tribal shall be regarded as a fundamental criterion for determining the groups to which the provisions of this Convention apply.

In its General Recommendation No. VIII, the Committee on the Elimination of Racial Discrimination made the important statement that membership in a group "shall, if no justification exists to the contrary, be based upon self-identification by the individual concerned."[7] Logically, if individual members of a group may self-identify, they may also collectively self-identify as a group, nation or people, indigenous or otherwise. The Committee confirms that this is the case:

C. Concerns and recommendations: 18. The Committee reiterates its previous concern regarding the delay in resolving the claims of the Inughuit with respect to the Thule Air Base. The Committee notes with serious concern claims of denials by Denmark of the identity and continued existence of the Inughuit as a separate ethnic or tribal entity, and recalls its general recommendation XXIII on indigenous peoples, general recommendation VIII on the application of article 1 (self-identification) and general recommendation XXIV concerning article 1 (international standard).[8]

The principle of self-identification has been strongly endorsed by indigenous peoples themselves and has been adopted in Article 8 of the

United Nations Draft Declaration on the Rights of Indigenous Peoples. The Draft Declaration is now being reviewed by another special working group of the UN's Human Rights Commission, with the objective of it being adopted during this current "International Decade of Indigenous People". Although disputes between governments about definitions have absorbed a disproportionate amount of time at this Working Group, many international lawyers agree with indigenous peoples that there is no need for an external definition of the term 'indigenous peoples'. Indeed they note that this is hardly possible, especially as the component term "peoples", which is fundamental to the constitution of the United Nations, is itself undefined.[9] The Commission on Human Rights Special Rapporteur on the Rights and Fundamental Freedoms of Indigenous People, for instance, states:

> As regards individual membership, indigenous communities usually apply their own criteria, and whereas some States do regulate individual membership, it has become increasingly accepted that the right to decide who is or is not an indigenous person belongs to the indigenous people alone. Nevertheless, it must be recognized that membership in indigenous communities implies not only rights and obligations of the individual vis-à-vis his or her group, but may also have legal implications with regard to the State. In the design and application of policies regarding indigenous peoples, States must respect the right of self-definition and self-identification of indigenous people.[10]

Meanwhile there has been growing acceptance that the term "indigenous peoples" applies in Asia and Africa. The newly established United Nations Permanent Forum on Indigenous Issues, for example, includes representatives of indigenous peoples from Africa and Asia on its panel. Likewise, the African Commission on Human Rights has recently established a working group on indigenous peoples. The working group takes the view that there are indigenous peoples in Africa, based on the principle of self-identification, among others, as expressed in Convention 169.[11]   Likewise, the African Commission on Human Rights has recently established a working group on indigenous peoples. The Asian Development Bank has adopted a policy on indigenous peoples and a number of Asian governments, such as the Philippines, Nepal and Cambodia have accepted that the term 'indigenous peoples' applies to marginalized ethnic groups in their countries. This report thus accepts that the term "indigenous peoples" has widespread applicability in all the major developing and transition countries in which the World Bank operates and the term has been used in this inclusive sense throughout this report.

INDIGENOUS PEOPLES' RIGHTS AND RESOURCE EXPLOITATION

Threats to indigenous peoples' rights and well-being are particularly acute in relation to resource development projects, be they state- or corporate-directed. These projects and operations have had and continue to have a devastating impact on indigenous peoples, undermining their ability to sustain themselves physically and culturally. It is therefore no coincidence that the majority of complaints submitted by indigenous peoples to intergovernmental human rights bodies involve rights violations in connection with resource development.

Over the past 50 years, the World Bank has been involved in financing resource development and associated infrastructure projects affecting indigenous peoples. Indeed, the Bank's first policy on indigenous peoples -- Operational Manual Statement 2.34 Tribal People in Bank-Financed Projects — was adopted in response to "internal and external condemnation of the disastrous experiences of indigenous groups in Bank-financed projects in the Amazon region."[12] Moreover, these violations are not confined to the past; as the UN Special Rapporteur comments:

> ...resources are being extracted and/or developed by other interests (oil, mining, logging, fisheries, etc.) with little or no benefits for the indigenous communities that occupy the land. Whereas the World Bank has developed operational directives concerning its own activities in relation to these issues ... and some national legislation specifically protects the interests of indigenous communities in this respect, in numerous instances the rights and needs of indigenous peoples are disregarded, making this one of the major human rights problems faced by them in recent decades.[13]

On this subject, the UN Special Rapporteur on indigenous land rights observes that:

> The legacy of colonialism is probably most acute in the area of expropriation of indigenous lands, territories and resources for national economic and development interests. In every sector of the globe, indigenous peoples are being impeded in every conceivable way from proceeding with their own forms of development, consistent with their own values, perspectives and interests.

Much large-scale economic and industrial development has taken place without recognition of and respect for indigenous peoples' rights to lands, territories and resources. Economic development has been largely imposed from outside, with complete disregard for the right of indigenous peoples to participate in the control, implementation and benefits of development.[14]

International human rights law places clear and substantial obligations on states in connection with resource exploitation on indigenous lands and territories. The UN Human Rights Committee has stated that a state's freedom to encourage economic development is limited by the obligations it has assumed under international human rights law;[15] the Inter-American Commission on Human Rights has observed that state policy and practice concerning resource exploitation cannot take place in a vacuum that ignores its human rights obligations,[16] as have the African Commission on Human and Peoples' Rights[17] and other intergovernmental human rights bodies.[18] In other words, states may not justify violations of indigenous peoples' rights in the name of national development. The basic principle, reaffirmed at the 1993 Vienna World Conference on Human Rights is that, "[w]hile development facilitates the enjoyment of all human rights, the lack of development may not be invoked to justify the abridgement of internationally recognized human rights."[19]

While the obligations incumbent on states have traditionally been the focus of international human rights law, there is strong evidence in contemporary law that obligations to respect human rights can apply to non-state actors including multinational corporations.[20] This issue aside, states have affirmative obligations to take appropriate measures to prevent and to exercise due diligence in response to human rights violations committed by private persons, including corporate entities.[21] Additionally, international financial institutions, such as the World Bank, are, as subjects of international law, unquestionably bound to respect customary international law norms and general principles of international law, including those pertaining to human rights.[22] The International Court of Justice specifically referred to such obligations in the WHO Agreement Case.[23]

International financial organizations are also bound to ensure that they neither undermine the ability of other subjects of international law, including their member states, to faithfully fulfill their international obligations nor facilitate or assist violation of those obligations.[24] The World Bank, as a specialized agency of the United Nations, also has obligations derived from the human rights provisions of the Charter of the United Nations and authoritative interpretations of the Charter, such as the Universal Declaration of Human Rights, the Covenants and other UN human rights instruments.[25]

The following sections describe the rights of indigenous peoples that limit and condition resource exploitation and the involvement of international financial institutions therein.

Rights to Lands, Territories and Resources

For indigenous peoples, secure, effective collective property rights are fundamental to their economic and social development, to their physical and cultural integrity, to their livelihoods and sustenance. Secure land and resource rights are also essential for the maintenance of their worldviews and spirituality and, in short, to their very survival as viable territorial and distinct cultural communities.[26] These rights are almost always collective in nature and often involve rights and duties held of and owed to previous and future generations. According to the UN Rapporteur on indigenous land rights:

> i.   A profound relationship exists between indigenous peoples and their lands, territories and resources;
> ii. This relationship has various social, cultural, spiritual, economic and political dimensions and responsibilities;
> iii. The collective dimension of this relationship is significant; and,
> iv. The intergenerational aspect of such a relationship is also crucial to indigenous peoples' identity, survival and cultural viability.[27]

This multifaceted nature of indigenous peoples' relationship to land, as well as the relationship between development and territorial rights, was emphasized by United Nations High Commissioner for Human Rights, Mary Robinson, in her December 2001 Presidential Fellow's Lecture at the World Bank. She states that, for indigenous peoples:

> *economic improvements cannot be envisaged without protection of land and resource rights. Rights over land need to include recognition of the spiritual relation indigenous peoples have with their ancestral territories. And the economic base that land provides needs to be accompanied by a recognition of indigenous peoples' own political and legal institutions, cultural traditions and social organizations. Land and culture, development, spiritual values and knowledge are as one. To fail to recognize one is to fail on all.[28]*

In short, without secure and enforceable rights to lands, territories and resources indigenous peoples' means of subsistence are permanently threatened. Their lands and territories are their resource base and "food basket". Land and territory are also the source of, *inter alia*, medicines, construction materials and household and other tools and implements. Loss or degradation of land and resources results in deprivation of the basics required to sustain life and to maintain an adequate standard of living. The UN Special Rapporteur on indigenous land rights concurs, stating that failure to guarantee indigenous peoples' property rights substantially undermines their socio-cultural integrity and economic security: "[i]ndigenous societies in a number of countries are in a state of rapid deterioration and change due in large part to the denial of the rights of the indigenous peoples to lands, territories and resources …"[29]

In recognition of the preceding, international law requires that indigenous peoples' ownership and other rights to their lands, territories and resources traditionally owned or otherwise occupied and used be legally recognized, respected and guaranteed, which includes titling, demarcation and measures to ensure the integrity and sustainability of those lands and territories. These rights are protected in connection with a variety of other rights, including the general prohibition of racial discrimination, the right to equal protection of the law, the right to property, the right to cultural integrity and as part and parcel of the right to self determination.

Indigenous peoples' rights to lands, territories and resources have been addressed a number of times by intergovernmental bodies under human rights instruments of general application. Concerning the territorial and economic aspects of self-determination, the UN Human Rights Committee (HRC), stated that:

> *The right to self-determination requires, inter alia, that all peoples must be able to freely dispose of their natural wealth and resources and that they may not be deprived of their own means of subsistence (article 1(2)). … The Committee also recommends that the practice of extinguishing inherent aboriginal rights be abandoned as incompatible with article 1 of the Covenant.*[30]

Article 27[31] of the International Covenant on Civil and Political Rights (ICCPR),[32] protects linguistic, cultural and religious rights and, in the case of indigenous peoples, includes, among others, land and resource, subsistence and participation rights.[33] These rights are held by individuals, but exercised "in community with other members of the group," thereby providing some measure of collectivity.

The HRC has interpreted article 27 to include the "rights of persons, in community with others, to engage in economic and social activities which are part of the culture of the community to which they belong."[34] In reaching this conclusion, the HRC recognized that indigenous peoples' subsistence and other traditional economic activities are an integral part of their culture, and interference with those activities can be detrimental to their cultural integrity and survival. The HRC further elaborated upon its interpretation of article 27 in 1994, stating that:

> With regard to the exercise of the cultural rights protected under Article 27, the committee observes that culture manifests itself in many forms, including a particular way of life associated with the use of land resources, specifically in the case of indigenous peoples. That right may include such traditional activities as fishing or hunting and the right to live in reserves protected by law. The enjoyment of those rights may require positive legal measures of protection and measures to ensure the effective participation of members of minority communities in decisions which affect them.[35]

In July 2000, the HRC added that article 27 requires that "necessary steps should be taken to restore and protect the titles and interests of indigenous persons in their native lands ..." and; "securing continuation and sustainability of traditional forms of economy of indigenous minorities (hunting, fishing and gathering), and protection of sites of religious or cultural significance for such minorities ... must be protected under article 27...."[36]

Article 30 of the UN Convention on the Rights of the Child contains almost identical language to that found in ICCPR article 27, therefore, the points made above are also relevant to the rights of indigenous children under that instrument.[37] Article 30 and ICCPR article 27 embody one manifestation of the general norm of international law relating to the right to cultural integrity.[38]

The Committee on Economic, Social and Cultural Rights has highlighted state obligations to recognize and respect indigenous peoples' land and resource rights under the International Covenant on Economic, Social and Cultural Rights (ICESCR).[39] In 1998, the Committee stated that:

> The Committee views with concern the direct connection between Aboriginal economic marginalization and the ongoing dispossession of Aboriginal people from their lands, as recognized by RCAP,

and endorses the recommendations of RCAP that policies which violate Aboriginal treaty obligations and the extinguishment, conversion or giving up of Aboriginal rights and title should on no account be pursued by the State Party.[40]

It then recommended that the state party "take concrete and urgent steps to restore and respect an Aboriginal land and resource base adequate to achieve a sustainable Aboriginal economy and culture."[41] In the case of Panama, the Committee expressed its concern "that the issue of land rights of indigenous peoples has not been resolved in many cases and that their land rights are threatened by mining and cattle ranching activities which have been undertaken with the approval of the State party and have resulted in the displacement of indigenous peoples from their traditional ancestral and agricultural lands."[42]

Under the Convention on the Elimination of All Forms of Racial Discrimination (CERD) state parties are obligated to recognize, respect and guarantee the right "to own property alone as well as in association with others" and the right to inherit property, without discrimination.[43] These provisions of CERD are declaratory of customary international law.[44] In its 1997 *General Recommendation on Indigenous Peoples, the UN Committee on the Elimination of Racial Discrimination* contextualized these rights to indigenous peoples. In particular, the Committee called upon states-parties to "recognize and protect the rights of indigenous peoples to own, develop, control and use their communal lands, territories and resources and, where they have been deprived of their lands and territories traditionally owned or otherwise inhabited or used without their free and informed consent, to take steps to return these lands and territories."[45] While this General Recommendation is technically non-binding, it is nonetheless "a significant elaboration of norms" and corresponding state obligations under the Convention.[46]

Similar conclusions about indigenous peoples' rights have been reached under inter-American human rights instruments, specifically the American Convention on Human Rights (1969) and the American Declaration on the Rights and Duties of Man (1948). It is well established in the inter-American system that indigenous peoples have been historically discriminated against and disadvantaged and therefore, that special measures and protections are required if they are to enjoy equal protection of the law and the full enjoyment of other human rights. These special measures include protections for indigenous languages, cultures, economies, ecosystems and natural resource base, religious practices, "ancestral and communal lands," and the establishment of an institutional order that facilitates indigenous participation through their freely chosen representatives.[47] The Inter-American Commission of Human Rights (IACHR) characterized the preceding as "human rights also essential to the right to life of peoples."[48]

According to the IACHR, indigenous peoples' property, including ownership, rights derive from their own laws and forms of land tenure, their traditional occupation and use, and exist as valid and enforceable rights absent formal recognition by the state.[49] It has related territorial rights on a number of occasions to cultural integrity, thereby recognizing the fundamental connection between indigenous land tenure and resource security and the right to practice, develop and transmit culture free from unwarranted interference. In 1997, for instance, the IACHR stated that:

> The situation of indigenous peoples in the Oriente [affected by petroleum exploitation] illustrates, on the one hand, the essential connection they maintain to their traditional territories, and on the other hand, the human rights violations which threaten when these lands are invaded and when the land itself is degraded. ... For many indigenous cultures, continued utilization of traditional collective systems for the control and use of territory are essential to their survival, as well as to their individual and collective well-being. Control over the land refers to both its capacity for providing the resources which sustain life, and to 'the geographical space necessary for the cultural and social reproduction of the group.'[50]

The IACHR reiterated this conclusion in its *Second Report on the Human Rights Situation in Peru*, stating that "[l]and, for the indigenous peoples, is a condition of individual security and liaison with the group. The recovery, recognition, demarcation and registration of the lands represents essential rights for cultural survival and for maintaining the community's integrity."[51]

The Inter-American Court on Human Rights in the *The Mayagna (Sumo) Indigenous Community of Awas Tingni v. the Republic of Nicaragua Case* confirmed that indigenous peoples' territorial rights arise from traditional occupation and use and indigenous forms of tenure, not from grants, recognition or registration by the state. The latter simply confirm and guarantee pre-existing rights. In its judgment, issued in September 2001, the Court observed that:

> Among indigenous communities, there is a communal tradition as demonstrated by their communal form of collective ownership of their lands, in the sense that ownership is not centered in the individual but rather in the group and in the community. By virtue of

the fact of their very existence, indigenous communities have the right to live freely on their own territories; the close relationship that the communities have with the land must be recognized and understood as a foundation for their cultures, spiritual life, cultural integrity and economic survival. For indigenous communities, the relationship with the land is not merely one of possession and production, but also a material and spiritual element that they should fully enjoy, as well as a means through which to preserve their cultural heritage and pass it on to future generations.[52]

Finding that "[t]he customary law of indigenous peoples should especially be taken into account because of the effects that flow from it. As a product of custom, possession of land should suffice to entitle indigenous communities without title to their land to obtain official recognition and registration of their rights of ownership;"[53] the Court held, among others, that "the State must adopt measures of a legislative, administrative, and whatever other character necessary to create an effective mechanism for official delimitation, demarcation, and titling of the indigenous communities' properties, in accordance with the customary law, values, usage, and customs of these communities."[54]

Most recently, in the *Mary and Carrie Dann Case*, citing numerous international standards jurisprudence, the IACHR stated that "general international legal principles applicable in the context of indigenous human rights" include:

- the right of indigenous peoples to legal recognition of their varied and specific forms and modalities of their control, ownership, use and enjoyment of territories and property;
- the recognition of their property and ownership rights with respect to lands, territories and resources they have historically occupied; and
- where property and user rights of indigenous peoples arise from rights existing prior to the creation of a state, recognition by that state of the permanent and inalienable title of indigenous peoples relative thereto and to have such title changed only by mutual consent between the state and respective indigenous peoples when they have full knowledge and appreciation of the nature or attributes of such property;
- This also implies the right to fair compensation in the event that such property and user rights are irrevocably lost.[55]

In this case, it interpreted the American Declaration on the Rights and Duties of Man to require "special measures to ensure recognition of the particular and collective interest that indigenous people have in the occupation and use of their traditional lands and resources ...."[56]

International Labour Organisation Convention No 169 contains a number of provisions on indigenous territorial rights.[57] These provisions are framed by article 13(1) which requires that governments recognize and respect the special spiritual, cultural and economic relationship that indigenous peoples have with their lands and territories and especially "the collective aspects of this relationship." Article 14 requires that indigenous peoples' collective "rights of ownership and possession ... over the lands which they traditionally occupy shall be recognized" and that states "shall take steps as necessary to identify" these lands and to "guarantee effective protection of rights of ownership and possession." Article 13(2) defines the term "lands" to include "the concept of territories, which covers the total environment of the areas which the peoples concerned occupy or otherwise use."

The preceding provisions on land rights must be read in connection with article 7(1), which provides that "[t]he people concerned shall have the right to decide their own priorities for the process of development as it affects their lives, beliefs, institutions and spiritual well-being and the lands they occupy or otherwise use, and to exercise control, to the extent possible, over their own economic, social and cultural development." This provision recognizes that indigenous peoples have the right to some measure of self-government with regard to their institutions and in determining the direction and scope of their economic, social and cultural development (the latter is limited by reference to other provisions of the Convention).

ILO 169's predecessor, ILO 107 adopted in 1957, also provides that "[t]he right of ownership, collective or individual, of the members of the population concerned over the lands which these populations traditionally occupy shall be recognized." The ILO Committee of Experts has held that the rights that attach under article 11 also apply to lands presently occupied irrespective of immemorial possession or occupation. The ILO Committee stated that the fact that the people has some form of relationship with land presently occupied, even if only for a short time was sufficient to form an interest and, therefore, rights to that land and the attendant resources.[58]

The African Charter on Human and Peoples' Rights is also relevant here. Property rights are guaranteed under article 14 and the right to equal protection of the law, both for individuals and peoples (articles 3 and 19), and the prohibition of discrimination (article 2) are also recognized. If UN and IACHR jurisprudence are relied upon, these provisions read together will amount to a recognition of indigenous property rights based upon traditional occupation and use.

Recent normative developments relating to indigenous lands, territories and resources are expansive, requiring legal recognition, restitution and compensation, protection of the total environment thereof, and various measures of participation in and consent to extra-territorial activities that may affect subsistence and resource rights and environmental and cultural integrity. Article 26 of the UN Draft Declaration, for instance, provides that:

> *Indigenous peoples have the right to own, develop, control and use the lands and territories, including the total environment of the lands, air, waters, coastal sea, sea-ice, flora and fauna and other resources which they have traditionally owned or otherwise occupied or used. This includes the right to the full recognition of their laws and customs, land-tenure systems and institutions for the development and management of resources, and the right to effective measures by states to prevent any interference with, alienation or encroachment upon these rights.*

The OAS Proposed Declaration also provides a substantial measure of protection (Art. XVIII):

1. Indigenous peoples have the right to the legal recognition of the various and specific forms of control, ownership and enjoyment of territories and property.
2. Indigenous peoples have the right to the recognition of their property and ownership rights with respect to lands and territories they have historically occupied, as well as to the use of those to which they have historically had access for their traditional activities and livelihood.
3. i) Subject to 3.ii.), where property and user rights of indigenous peoples arise from rights existing prior to the creation of those States, the States shall recognize the titles of indigenous peoples relative thereto as permanent, exclusive, inalienable, imprescriptible and indefeasible.
   ii) Such titles may only be changed by mutual consent between the state and respective indigenous peoples when they have full knowledge and appreciation of the nature or attributes of such property.
   iii) Nothing in 3.i.) shall be construed as limiting the right of indigenous peoples to attribute ownership within the

community in accordance with their customs, traditions, uses and traditional practices, nor shall it affect any collective community rights over them.

4. The rights of indigenous peoples to existing natural resources on their lands must be especially protected. These rights include the right to the use, management and conservation of such resources.

The Convention on Biological Diversity (CBD), a binding international environmental treaty is also of relevance. Article 10(c)of the CBD provides that states shall "protect and encourage customary use of biological resources in accordance with traditional cultural practices that are compatible with conservation or sustainable use requirements." Although the precise scope and meaning of this article have yet to be formally articulated, it certainly includes indigenous agriculture, agroforestry, hunting, fishing, gathering and use of medicinal plants and other subsistence activities. This article, by implication, should also be read to include protection for the land base, ecosystem and environment in which those resources are found. These observations on article 10(c) are supported by the analysis of the Secretariat of the CBD in its background paper entitled 'Traditional Knowledge and Biological Diversity'. In that paper, the Secretariat said the following about the language "protect and encourage" found in 10(c):

> In order to protect and encourage, the necessary conditions may be in place, namely, security of tenure over traditional terrestrial and marine estates; control over and use of traditional natural resources; and respect for the heritage, languages and cultures of indigenous and local communities, best evidenced by appropriate legislative protection (which includes protection of intellectual property, sacred places, and so on). Discussions on these issues in other United Nations forums have also dealt with the issue of respect for the right to self-determination, which is often interpreted to mean the exercise of self-government.[59]

Sub-Surface Resources

The basis for state (public) ownership of natural, including subsoil, resources in international law is territorial sovereignty.[60] The basis for peoples' rights to natural resources is the right of permanent sovereignty over natural resources and the concomitant right to freely dispose of natural wealth and resources. The latter was developed and elaborated upon by a series of UN General Assembly resolutions, the first adopted in the 1950s.[61]   In the first instance, the right to permanent sovereignty over natural resources was (somewhat ambiguously) vested in "peoples and nations" and was intimately related to decolonization and self-determination.[62] As colonial peoples became independent, the right, with some notable exceptions, was increasingly expressed as a right of developing countries and then as a right of states.[63] It has subsequently been incorporated, as a right of states, into a number of multilateral treaties, for instance, the Convention on Biological Diversity.[64]

The content of the right of states is widely acknowledged to include the right to possess, use and dispose of natural resources, to determine freely and control prospecting, exploration and exploitation, to manage and conserve natural resources, to regulate foreign investors and to nationalize or expropriate property.[65] However, as with sovereignty in general, state sovereignty over natural resources is not absolute but is subject to other principles and rules of international law.[66] As a consequence, an increasing number of duties are associated with this right. In particular and among others, the duty to exercise permanent sovereignty in the interest of national development, ensuring that the entire population benefits, the duty to have due care for the environment, and the "duty to respect the rights and interests of indigenous peoples...."[67]

The two core international human rights instruments adopted by the UN in 1966 -- the ICCPR and the ICESCR — both contain a major limitation on and exception to states' rights to natural resources. Common article 1 of the Covenants states, in pertinent part for our purposes, that:

1. All peoples have the right to self-determination, by virtue of that right they freely determine their political status and freely pursue the economic, social and cultural development.
2. All peoples may, for their own ends, freely dispose of their natural wealth and resources.... In no case may a people be deprived of its own means of subsistence.

Articles 47 of the ICCPR and 25 of the ICESCR describe the right set forth in sub-paragraph 2 -- the human right of peoples, including indigenous peoples, to permanent sovereignty over natural resources[68] -- as "the inherent right of peoples."[69] Its importance to indigenous peoples was eloquently stated by Ted Moses, Grand Chief of the Grand Council of the Crees:

When I think of self-determination, I think also of hunting, fishing and trapping. I think of the land, of the water, the trees, and the animals. I think of the land we have lost. I think of all the land stolen from our people. I think of hunger and people destroying the land. I think of the dispossession of our peoples of their land. ... The end result is too often identical: we indigenous peoples are being denied our own means of subsistence. ... We cannot give up our right to our own means of subsistence or to the necessities of life itself. ... In particular, our right to self-determination contains the essentials of life – the resources of the earth and the freedom to continue to develop and interact as societies and peoples.[70]

A leading commentator on the right to self-determination states that "Article 1 common to the Covenants addresses itself directly to peoples" and "[p]eoples are thus the holders of international rights to which correspond obligations incumbent upon Contracting States ...."[71] These rights are not restricted to peoples in classic colonial situations only, but are vested in "all" peoples.[72] Consistent with this, the UN Human Rights Committee (HRC), the body charged with monitoring state compliance with the ICCPR, has applied article 1 to indigenous peoples.[73] In its Concluding observations on Canada's fourth periodic report, the HRC stated that:

With reference to the conclusion by the [Royal Commission on Aboriginal Peoples] that without a greater share of lands and resources institutions of aboriginal self-government will fail, the Committee emphasizes that the right to self-determination requires, inter alia, that all peoples must be able to freely dispose of their natural wealth and resources and that they may not be deprived of their own means of subsistence (article 1(2)). The Committee recommends that decisive and urgent action be taken towards the full implementation of the RCAP recommendations on land and resource allocation. The Committee also recommends that the practice of extinguishing inherent aboriginal rights be abandoned as incompatible with article 1 of the Covenant.[74]

The HRC reached similar conclusions -- that the state implement and respect the right of indigenous peoples to self-determination, particularly in connection with their traditional lands and resources -- in its Concluding observations on the reports of Mexico and Norway issued in 1999 and Australia in 2000.[75] In its complaints-based jurisprudence, the HRC has also related the right to self-determination to the right of indigenous peoples to enjoy their culture under Article 27 of the ICCPR.[76]

The Committee on Economic, Social and Cultural Rights has also referred to the rights of indigenous peoples in connection with article 1.

In 2002, the Committee stated: "[t]aking note of the duty in article 1, paragraph 2, of the Covenant, which provides that a people may not 'be deprived of its means of subsistence', States parties should ensure that there is adequate access to water for subsistence farming and for securing the livelihoods of indigenous peoples."[77]

While most attention has focused on the rights of indigenous peoples as set forth in article 1(2), the first sub-paragraph is also highly relevant because resource exploitation directly affects indigenous peoples' right "to freely determine their economic, social and cultural development." Indeed, it is a mistake to disaggregate the various components of the right to self-determination as they are, in sum, a complex of inextricably related and interdependent rights. In this context, note article 1(2) of the 1986 UN Declaration on the Right to Development, which provides that "[t]he human right to development also implies the full realization of the right of peoples to self-determination, which includes, subject to the relevant provisions of both International Covenants on Human Rights, the exercise of their inalienable right to full sovereignty over all their natural wealth and resources."[78]

The African Charter on Human and Peoples Rights (1981)[79] is another human rights treaty that contains a provision guaranteeing the right of peoples to freely dispose of their natural wealth and resources.[80] Whether this provision applied to the constituent peoples of a state or only to its entire population has been a bone of contention for many years.[81] However, in May 2002, the African Commission on Human and Peoples' Rights unambiguously applied the right to the Ogoni people,[82] one of the constituent peoples of Nigeria:

> Contrary to its Charter obligations and despite such internationally established principles, the Nigerian Government has given the green light to private actors, and the oil companies in particular, to devastatingly affect the well-being of the Ogonis. By any measure of standards, its practice falls short of the minimum conduct expected of governments, and therefore, is in violation of Article 21 of the African Charter.[83]

The Commission noted in general that:

> At a primary level, the obligation to **respect** entails that the State should refrain from interfering in the enjoyment of all fundamental rights; it should respect right-holders, their freedoms, autonomy, resources, and liberty of their action. With respect to socio economic rights, this means that the State is obliged to respect the free use of resources owned or at the disposal of the individual alone or in any

form of association with others, including the household or the fam-
ily, for the purpose of rights-related needs. And with regard to a
collective group, the resources belonging to it should be respected, as
it has to use the same resources to satisfy its needs.[84]

Attempts by the United Nations to regulate the activities of multi-national corporations with respect to human rights have also addressed this issue. The *Proposed Draft Human Rights Code of Conduct for Companies* for instance, provides, under the heading "Respect for National Sovereignty and the Right of Self-Determination" that "[c]ompanies shall recognize and respect the national laws, regulations, administrative practices, and authority of the State to exercise control over its national resources in the countries in which the companies operate in so far as these laws, regulations, practices, and authority do not conflict with international human rights standards;" and, "[c]ompanies shall respect the rights of indigenous communities and minorities to own, develop, control, protect, and use their lands and cultural and intellectual property; indigenous communities and minorities may not be deprived of their own means of subsistence."[85]

In addition to relying on textual expressions of the right to self-determination and the right to freely dispose of natural wealth in human rights instruments, discussed above, indigenous peoples' rights to resources, including those of the subsoil, may also be said to derive from the general international law of self-determination and related law pertaining to permanent sovereignty over natural wealth and resources.[86] This is the case because the preceding rights remain vested in peoples notwithstanding international instruments that also vest permanent sovereignty in states.[87] The initial stage of an UN study on this issue concludes that it is apparent that this basic principle of permanent sovereignty over natural resources applies as well to indigenous peoples for the following reasons, among others:

a. Indigenous peoples are colonized peoples in the economic, political and historical sense;
b. Indigenous peoples suffer from unfair and unequal economic arrangements typically suffered by other colonized peoples;
c. The principle of permanent sovereignty over natural resources is necessary to level the economic and political playing field and to provide protection against unfair and oppressive economic arrangements;
d. Indigenous peoples have a right to development and ac-

tively to participate in the realization of this right; sovereignty over their natural resources is an essential prerequisite for this;

e. The natural resources originally belonged to the indigenous peoples concerned and were not freely and fairly given up.[88]

This last point raises an important issue in connection with the rights of indigenous peoples in and to their lands, territories and resources traditionally owned or otherwise occupied and used discussed in the preceding section. These rights exist absent formal recognition by the state, are in large measure determined by indigenous peoples' laws, customs and usages, and unilateral extinguishment has been determined to violate, among others, the right to self-determination and the prohibition of racial discrimination.[89]

Note that in all the formulations used in the various international instruments and jurisprudence, the term 'resources' is used without explicit qualification or explanation. In the absence of evidence to the contrary — see, ILO 169, article 15(2), for instance, which provides for "cases in which the State retains the ownership of mineral or sub-surface resources" — "resources" should presumptively be understood to include subsoil resources. This is especially the case in states where private ownership of minerals is recognized in domestic law: discrimination against indigenous peoples is not permitted where non-indigenous citizens can own minerals.

In common law jurisdictions -- much of the British Commonwealth -S- in the absence of valid extinguishment or expropriation, surface rights include rights to base, subsoil minerals.[90] The same has also been held to be the case, again subject to valid extinguishment, for rights of indigenous peoples under native/aboriginal/Indian title jurisprudence in Australia, Canada and the United States.[91] In *Delgamuukw v. British Columbia*, for example, Lamer CJ of the Canadian Supreme Court stated that "aboriginal title also encompass [sic] mineral rights, and lands held pursuant to aboriginal title should be capable of exploitation in the same way...."[92] Indigenous ownership of subsoil resources within reserves and reservations is also recognized in the United States and Canada. This recognition even extends to the so-called "royal minerals", gold and silver, which is not the case for non-indigenous surface owners under common law.[93]

In conclusion, with respect to the nature of the rights held by indigenous peoples in general to natural resources, including those of the subsoil, a leading scholar concludes that, the "rights of indigenous peoples to the natural resources of their lands are at first glance similar to those of States (to be) derived from the principle of permanent sovereignty.... Yet, the essential difference is that indigenous peoples are still an object rather than a subject of international law; at best they can be identified as an emerging subject of international law."[94] Without discussing the object versus subject issue, existing international human rights norms and jurisprudence provide ample support for this conclusion.[95] Moreover, at least in the case of natural resources, classification as an object or subject of international law does not impede the rights of indigenous peoples under existing and emerging international human rights law nor does it diminish the duties of states and certain non-state actors to respect, protect and fulfill those rights.

Free Prior and Informed Consent as an Accepted Principle

In contemporary international law, indigenous peoples' have the right to participate in decision making and to give or withhold their consent to activities affecting their lands, territories and resources or rights in general. Consent must be freely given, obtained prior to implementation of activities and be founded upon an understanding of the full range of issues implicated by the activity or decision in question; hence the formulation, free, prior and informed consent.

Observing that indigenous peoples have and continue to suffer from discrimination, and "in particular that they have lost their land and resources to colonists, commercial companies and State enterprises,"[96] the Committee on the Elimination of Racial Discrimination called upon states-parties to "ensure that members of indigenous peoples have equal rights in respect of effective participation in public life, and that no decisions directly relating to their rights and interests are taken without their informed consent."[97] The Committee later recognized indigenous peoples' right to "effective participation . . . in decisions affecting their land rights, *as required under article 5(c) of the Convention and General Recommendation XXIII of the Committee*, which stresses the importance of ensuring the 'informed consent' of indigenous peoples" (emphasis added).[98]

The IACHR has found that Inter-American human rights law requires "special measures to ensure recognition of the particular and collective interest that indigenous people have in the occupation and use of their traditional lands and resources and their right not to be deprived of this interest except with fully informed consent, under conditions of equality, and with fair compensation."[99] In the same vein, the Commission emphasized that:

Articles XVIII and XXIII of the American Declaration specially oblige a member state to ensure that any determination of the extent to which indigenous claimants maintain interests in the lands to which they have traditionally held title and have occupied and used is based upon a process of fully informed and mutual consent on the part of the indigenous community as a whole. [100]

Similarly, finding that Nicaragua had violated the right to property, judicial protection and due process of law by granting logging concessions on indigenous lands without taking steps to title and demarcate those lands, the IACHR held that:

The State of Nicaragua is actively responsible for violations of the right to property, embodied in Article 21 of the [American] Convention, by granting a concession to the company SOLCARSA to carry out road construction work and logging exploitation on the Awas Tingni lands, without the consent of the Awas Tingni Community. [101]

Additionally, the IACHR stated that "general international legal principles applicable in the context of indigenous human rights" include the right to:

where property and user rights of indigenous peoples arise from rights existing prior to the creation of a state, recognition by that state of the permanent and inalienable title of indigenous peoples relative thereto and to have such title changed only by mutual consent between the state and respective indigenous peoples when they have full knowledge and appreciation of the nature or attributes of such property. [102]

In addition to prohibiting unilateral extinguishment of indigenous peoples' land and resource rights, the property and user rights governed by this principle clearly include subsoil minerals.

Further, in 2001, the UN Committee on Economic, Social and Cultural Rights noted "with regret that the traditional lands of indigenous peoples have been reduced or occupied, without their consent, by timber, mining and oil companies, at the expense of the exercise of their culture and the equilibrium of the ecosystem."[103] It then recommended that the state "ensure the participation of indigenous peoples in decisions affecting their lives. The Committee particularly urges the State party to consult and seek the consent of the indigenous peoples concerned ...."[104]

While not strictly requiring consent, ILO 169 requires that states "establish or maintain procedures through which [they] shall consult these peoples" to determine the extent to which indigenous peoples' "interests would be prejudiced" prior to engaging in, or allowing resource exploitation (art. 15(2)). This provision should be read consistently with article 6(2)'s general requirement that consultation be undertaken "in good faith . . . in a form appropriate to the circumstances, with the objective of achieving agreement or consent." Respect for indigenous peoples' right to give their free and informed consent is still required if a state party has ratified one of the instruments noted above because, pursuant to article 35, application of ILO 169 "shall not adversely affect the rights and benefits of the peoples concerned pursuant to other Conventions and Recommendations, international instruments, treaties or national laws, awards, customs or agreements."

Emerging standards also require free and informed consent. Article 30 of the UN draft Declaration, for instance, provides that:

> *Indigenous peoples have the right to determine and develop priorities and strategies for the development or use of their lands, territories and other resources, including the right to require that states obtain their free and informed consent prior to the approval of any project affecting their lands, territories and other resources, particularly in connection with the development, utilization or exploitation of mineral, water or other resources.*

The approach adopted by the respective instruments above is consistent with the observations of the UN Centre for Transnational Corporations in a series of reports that examine the investments and activities of multinational corporations on indigenous territories.[105] The fourth and final report concluded that multinational companies' "performance was chiefly determined by the quantity and quality of indigenous peoples' participation in decision making" and "the extent to which the laws of the host country gave indigenous peoples the right to withhold consent to development...."[106]

A recent UN workshop on indigenous peoples and natural resources development reiterated and elaborated upon this conclusion, stating in its conclusions that the participants:

> *recognized the link between indigenous peoples' exercise of their right to self determination and rights over their lands and resources and their capacity to enter into equitable relationships with the private sector. It was noted that indigenous peoples with recognized land and resource rights and peoples with treaties, agreements or*

other constructive arrangements with States, were better able to enter into fruitful relations with private sector natural resource companies on the basis of free, prior, informed consent than peoples without such recognized rights.[107]

Finally, as discussed in detail in the next section, both general and treaty-based international law require indigenous peoples' free and informed consent in connection with relocation.

Forced Relocation

Involuntary or forcible resettlement "is considered a practice that does grave and disastrous harm to the basic civil, political, economic, social and cultural rights of large numbers of people, both individual persons and collectivities."[108] This is also recognized in a World Bank study on resettlement, which states that "[t]he potential for violating individual and group rights under domestic and international law makes compulsory resettlement unlike any other project activity. … Carrying out resettlement in a manner that respects the rights of affected persons is not just an issue of compliance with the law, but also constitutes sound development practice."[109]

For indigenous peoples, forcible relocation can be disastrous, severing entirely their various relationships with their ancestral lands.[110] As observed by the UN Sub-Commission, "where population transfer is the primary cause for an indigenous people's land loss, it constitutes a principal factor in the process of ethnocide;"[111] and, "[f]or indigenous peoples, the loss of ancestral land is tantamount to the loss of cultural life, with all its implications."[112]

Due to the importance attached to indigenous peoples' cultural, spiritual and economic relationships to land and resources, international law treats relocation as a serious human rights concern. In international instruments, strict standards of scrutiny are employed and indigenous peoples' free and informed consent must be obtained.[113] Relocation may only be considered as an exceptional measure in extreme and extraordinary cases. The implicit statement contained in these standards is that forcible relocation is prohibited as a "gross violation of human rights."[114]

The report of the Representative of the UN Secretary General on this issue concluded that "an express prohibition of arbitrary displacement is contained in humanitarian law and in the law relating to indigenous peoples"[115] and, "[e]fforts should be made to obtain the free and informed consent of those to be displaced. Where these guarantees are absent, such measures would be arbitrary and therefore unlawful. Special protection should be afforded to indigenous peoples, minorities, peasants, pastoralists and other groups with a special dependency on and attachment to their lands."[116] Another UN report found that, with regard to relocation, the principle of consent has obtained the status of a binding general principle of international law.[117] Finally, the IACHR concluded that "[t]he preponderant doctrine" holds that the principle of consent is of general application to cases involving relocation.[118]

Again, given the fundamental physical, cultural, spiritual and other relationships that indigenous peoples have with their lands and resources, forcible resettlement amounts to a gross violation of a series of human rights. In the jurisprudence of the IACHR, forcible relocation amounts to a violation of human rights "essential to the right to life of peoples."[119] It certainly constitutes a violation of article 27 of the ICCPR and article 30 of the Convention on the Rights of the Child in that, in most cases, it amounts to a *denial* of the right of indigenous persons and children, respectively, to enjoy their culture.[120] Addressing this issue, the HRC stated that:

> *the Committee is concerned by hydroelectric and other development projects that might affect the way of life and the rights of persons belonging to the Mapuche and other indigenous communities. Relocation and compensation may not be appropriate in order to comply with article 27 of the Covenant. Therefore: When planning actions that affect members of indigenous communities, the State party must pay primary attention to the sustainability of the indigenous culture and way of life and to the participation of members of indigenous communities in decisions that affect them.*[121] (emphasis added)

The Committee on Economic, Social and Cultural Rights frequently expresses concern about forcible relocation and has urged states to abandon the practice as incompatible with the obligations assumed under the Covenant.[122] In its *General Comment on the Right to Adequate Housing*, the Committee stated that it "considers that instances of forced eviction are prima facie incompatible with the requirements of the Covenant and can only be justified in the most exceptional circumstances, and in accordance with the relevant principles of international law."[123] As discussed above, in the context of indigenous peoples, the relevant principles of international law include the right to free and informed consent. Concern has also been expressed about forcible relocation in connection with mining on a number of occasions. In its Concluding observations on Bolivia in 2001, for instance, the Committee highlighted its concerns about "the incidence of forced evictions with respect to peasants and indigenous populations in favour of mining and lumber concessions ...."[124]

In General Comment No. 7, which exclusively addresses forced evictions, the Committee noted that indigenous peoples suffer disproportionately from the practice of forced eviction.[125] Observing that forcible relocation often occurs in relation to "largescale development projects, such as dambuilding and other major energy projects,"[126] the Committee further stated that it:

> is aware that various development projects financed by international agencies within the territories of State parties have resulted in forced evictions. In this regard, the Committee recalls its General Comment No. 2 (1990) which states, inter alia, that 'international agencies should scrupulously avoid involvement in projects which, for example ... promote or reinforce discrimination against individuals or groups contrary to the provisions of the Covenant, or involve largescale evictions or displacement of persons without the provision of all appropriate protection and compensation. Every effort should be made, at each phase of a development project, to ensure that the rights contained in the Covenant are duly taken into account.'[127]

From the preceding, it is clear that, in the case of indigenous and tribal peoples, both general and conventional international law require that consent be obtained prior to resettlement. It is also clear that international law accords indigenous and tribal peoples, given their unique connection with their lands and resources, a higher standard of protection than applies to others. This higher standard in part entails a substantial, if not complete, limitation on the exercise of eminent domain powers by the state, at least to the extent that relocation is involved. For these reasons, the European Union, the Inter-American Development Bank and the World Commission on Dams also prohibit relocation without indigenous peoples' consent.[128]

Indigenous Peoples' Rights in Customary International Law

Indigenous peoples' rights to lands and resources have crystallized into norms of customary international law binding on all states and most intergovernmental organizations. This is confirmed by no less than the Inter-American Commission on Human Rights. In the *Mary and Carrie Dann Case*, the IACHR stated that "general international legal principles[129] applicable in the context of indigenous human rights" include:

❑ the right of indigenous peoples to legal recognition of their
varied and specific forms and modalities of their control,
ownership, use and enjoyment of territories and property;

❑ the recognition of their property and ownership rights with
respect to lands, territories and resources they have historically occupied;

❑ where property and user rights of indigenous peoples arise
from rights existing prior to the creation of a state, recognition by that state of the permanent and inalienable title of
indigenous peoples relative thereto and to have such title
changed only by mutual consent between the state and
respective indigenous peoples when they have full knowledge and appreciation of the nature or attributes of such
property;

❑ This also implies the right to fair compensation in the event
that such property and user rights are irrevocably lost[130]

This conclusion is supported by a number of scholars.[131] Profes-
sors Anaya and Williams, for instance, state that "the relevant practice
of states and international institutions establishes that, as a matter of
customary international law, states must recognize and protect indigenous peoples' rights to land and natural resources in connection with
traditional or ancestral use and occupancy patterns."[132] Professor
Siegfried Wiessner concludes that state practice and *opinio juris* permit
the "identification of specific rules of a customary international law of
indigenous peoples." These rules relate to the following areas:

> First, indigenous peoples are entitled to maintain and develop their
> distinct cultural identity, their spirituality, their language, and their
> traditional ways of life. Second, they hold the right to political,
> economic and social self-determination, including a wide range of
> autonomy and the maintenance and strengthening of their own sys-
> tems of justice. Third, indigenous peoples have a right to demarca-
> tion, ownership, development, control and use of the lands they have
> traditionally owned or otherwise occupied and used. Fourth, gov-
> ernments are to honor and faithfully observe their treaty commit-
> ments to indigenous nations.[133]

Additionally, Anaya persuasively asserts that much of ILO 169
reflects customary international law.[134] This assertion is supported by
Lee Swepston, head of the Equality and Human Rights Branch of the
ILO, who describes the influence of the Convention on state practice,
including non-ratifying states, and intergovernmental organizations.[135]

Finally, indigenous land and resource rights are already protected under customary international law in connection with the principal provisions of CERD[136] and article 27 of ICCPR.[137]

Environmental Rights

This section provides a brief overview of rights related to environmental protection.[138] As discussed above, the understanding that protection of indigenous peoples' cultural integrity is closely linked to recognition of and respect for rights to lands, territory and resources and to protection and preservation of their physical environment is firmly entrenched in the normative structure of existing and emerging international human rights instruments. As one scholar states:

> *There can be little room for doubt that there exists today a general consensus among states that the cultural identity of traditional indigenous peoples and local communities warrants affirmative protective measures by states, and that such measures be extended to all those elements of the natural environment whose preservation or protection is essential for the groups' survival as culturally distinct peoples and communities.[139]*

A major United Nations study on the intersection of human rights and the environment reached the same conclusion. Determining that, given indigenous peoples' unique relationship with their lands and territories, "all environmental degradation has a direct impact on the human rights of the indigenous peoples dependent on that environment,"[140] the Special Rapporteur proposed the following principle for inclusion in a Declaration of Principles on Human Rights and the Environment:

> *Indigenous peoples have the right to control their lands, territories and natural resources and to maintain their traditional ways of life. This includes the right to security in the enjoyment of their means of subsistence.*
> *Indigenous peoples have the right to protection against any action or course of conduct that may result in the destruction or degradation of their territories, including land, air, water, sea-ice, wildlife or other resources.[141]*

The IACHR has also stated, and reaffirmed numerous times, that "indigenous peoples maintain special ties with their traditional lands, and a close dependence upon the natural resources therein -- respect for which is essential to their physical and cultural survival."[142]

ILO 169, while not declaring a right to environment, is the first international instrument to exclusively relate environmental concerns to indigenous peoples. Article 4(1), for instance, requires states to take "special measures" to protect the environment of indigenous peoples. These special measures include environmental impact studies of proposed development activities (art. 7(3)), recognition and protection of subsistence rights (art. 23), safeguarding of natural resources (art. 15(1)), and measures to protect and preserve the territories of indigenous peoples (art. 7(4)). Article 7(1) contains one of the most important principles of the Convention, providing that "[t]he people concerned shall have the right to decide their own priorities for the process of development as it affects their lives, beliefs, institutions and spiritual well-being and the lands they occupy or otherwise use, and to exercise control, to the extent possible, over their own economic, social and cultural development." This article is one of the general principles of the Convention and provides a framework within which other articles are to be interpreted.

Indigenous peoples' rights in relation to the environment have also been addressed under instruments of general application. In Ominayak and the *Lake Lubicon Bank v. Canada*, the HRC found that oil and gas exploitation and pollution generated thereby threatened the way of life and culture of the Band and therefore constituted a violation of article 27 of the ICCPR.[143] In 1985, the IACHR examined the rights of the Yanomami people in the context of the construction of the Trans-Amazonia highway in Brazil, invasion of their territory by small-scale gold miners, environmental degradation and devastating illnesses brought in by the miners. The highway forced a number of Yanomami communities located near the construction path to abandon their communities and means of subsistence. The IACHR found, due to Brazil's failure to take "timely measures" to protect the Yanomami, that violations of, *inter alia*, the right to life and the right to preservation of health and well-being under the American Declaration on the Rights and Duties of Man had occurred.[144]

The IACHR re-visited the Yanomami situation in its 1997 *Report on the Situation of Human Rights in Brazil*.[145] It concluded that although the Yanomami people have obtained recognition of their right to ownership of their land, "[t]heir integrity as a people and as individuals is constantly under attack by both invading prospectors and the environmental pollution they create. State protection against these constant pressures and invasions is irregular and feeble, so that they are constantly in danger and their environment is suffering constant deterioration."[146] It recommended that Brazil "institute federal protection measures with regard to Indian lands threatened by invaders, with particular attention to those of the Yanomami … including an increase in controlling, prosecuting and imposing severe punishment on actual perpetrators and architects of such crimes, as well as state agents who are active or passive accomplices."[147]

In its *Ecuador Report*, the IACHR again relates the right to life to environmental security stating that "[t]he realisation of the right to life, and to physical security and integrity is necessarily related to and in some ways dependent upon one's physical environment. Accordingly, where environmental contamination and degradation pose a persistent threat to human life and health, the foregoing rights are implicated."[148] With regard to implementation of state obligations concerning resource exploitation, the IACHR "considers that the absence of regulation, inappropriate regulation, or a lack of supervision in the application of extant norms may create serious problems with respect to the environment which could translate into violations of human rights protected by the American Convention."[149]

Building upon principles adopted at the United Nations Conference on Environment and Development and various articles of the American Convention, the IACHR highlighted the right to participate in decisions affecting the environment.[150] An integral part of this right is access to information in an understandable form. Emphasizing procedural guarantees and state obligations to adopt positive measures to guarantee the right to life, the IACHR stated that, "[i]n the context of the situation under study, protection of the right to life and physical integrity may best be advanced through measures to support and enhance the ability of individuals to safeguard and vindicate those rights. The quest to guarantee against environmental conditions which threaten human health requires that individuals have access to: information, participation in relevant decision-making processes, and judicial recourse."[151]

The African Commission also found that the right to life had been violated in connection with environmental pollution in the Ogoni case:

> *The pollution and environmental degradation to a level humanly unacceptable has made living in the Ogoni land a nightmare. The survival of the Ogonis depended on their land and farms that were destroyed by the direct involvement of the Government. These and similar brutalities not only persecuted individuals in Ogoniland but also the whole of the Ogoni Community as a whole. They affected the life of the Ogoni Society as a whole.*[152]

It also found a violation of article 24 of the African Charter, which guarantees the right of peoples to a healthy environment. The Commission stated that article 24 "imposes clear obligations upon a government" and "requires the State to take reasonable and other measures to prevent pollution and ecological degradation, to promote conservation, and to secure an ecologically sustainable development and use of natural resources."[153] Among the measures proposed to remedy violations, the Commission recommended "a comprehensive cleanup of lands and rivers damaged by oil operations."[154]

Economic, Social and Cultural Rights

A range of economic, social and cultural rights are implicated and may be adversely affected by resource exploitation. As is apparent from the preceding and as illustrated below, indigenous peoples' enjoyment of economic, social and cultural rights is fundamentally related to recognition of and respect for rights to own and control their lands, territory and resources traditionally owned or otherwise occupied and used. Also, while it is correct to say that economic, social and cultural rights are subject to progressive realization determined by availability of resources, it is incorrect to argue on this basis that states have no obligations in relation to these rights. On the contrary, "a minimum core obligation to ensure the satisfaction of, at the very least, minimum essential levels of each of the rights is incumbent upon every State party."[155]

In the Ogoni case, the African Commission found Nigeria in violation of the right to housing and protection against forced eviction — a "right enjoyed by the Ogonis as a collective right"[156] — the right to health and the right to food: "[w]ithout touching on the duty to improve food production and to guarantee access, the minimum core of the right to food requires that the Nigerian Government should not destroy or contaminate food sources. It should not allow private parties to destroy or contaminate food sources, and prevent peoples' efforts to feed themselves."[157]

The Committee on Economic, Social and Cultural Rights has also raised the issue of violations of the right to health, to food and to culture:

> The Committee notes that, in indigenous communities, the health of the individual is often linked to the health of the society as a whole and has a collective dimension. In this respect, the Committee considers that development-related activities that lead to the displacement of indigenous peoples against their will from their traditional territories and environment, denying them their sources of nutrition and breaking their symbiotic relationship with their lands, has a deleterious effect on their health.[158]

The Committee deplores the discrimination against indigenous people, particularly with regard to access to land ownership, housing, health services and sanitation, education, work and adequate nutrition. The Committee is particularly concerned about the adverse effects of the economic activities connected with the exploitation of natural resources, such as mining in the Imataca Forest Reserve and coal-mining in the Sierra de Perijá, on the health, living environment and way of life of the indigenous populations living in these regions.[159]

The Committee has also observed that indigenous peoples are especially vulnerable to violations of the right to food in cases where "access to their ancestral lands may be threatened."[160] In this respect, and in similar terms to those employed by the African Commission,[161] Asbjorn Eide, whose work has had enormous influence on economic, social and cultural rights, states that:

> In light of evolving practice at the international level, there is now a broad consensus that human rights impose three types or levels of obligations on state parties: the obligations to **respect**, to **protect** and to **fulfil**. ... States must, at the primary level, respect the resources owned by the individual, her or his freedom to find a job of preference and the freedom to take the necessary actions and use the necessary resources – alone or in conjunction with others – to satisfy his or her own needs. With regard to the latter, **collective** or group rights can become important: the resources belonging to a collective of persons, such as indigenous populations, must be respected in order for them to be able to satisfy their needs. Consequently, as part of the obligation to respect these resources the state should take steps to recognise and register the land rights of indigenous peoples and land tenure of smallholders whose title is uncertain.[162]

The right to food enjoys a privileged status among economic, social and cultural rights and is the only right labelled "fundamental" under the ICESCR.

The IACHR has also addressed indigenous peoples' economic, social and cultural rights on a number of occasions. A general principle, as stated in a report on human rights in Mexico, is that "[i]t is the obligation of the State of Mexico, based on its constitutional principles and on internationally recognized principles, to respect indigenous cultures and their organizations and to ensure their maximum development in accordance with their traditions, interests, and priorities."[163] This language clearly indicates that development efforts must be consistent with indigenous traditions, interests and priorities, all of which presuppose and require a substantial measure of indigenous participation in and agreement with development activities.

Discussing environmental degradation, the IACHR's 2001 report on Paraguay observes that "[t]he environment is being destroyed by ranching, farming, and logging concerns, who reduce [indigenous peoples'] traditional capacities and strategies for food and economic activity."[164] It then recommended that Paraguay "[a]dopt the necessary measures to protect the habitat of the indigenous communities from environmental degradation, with special emphasis on protecting the forests and waters, which are fundamental for their health and survival as communities."[165]

In the same report, noting the inadequacy of Paraguay's efforts to resolve indigenous peoples' land and resource rights, the IACHR stated that:

> The process of sorting out territorial claims, to which the Paraguayan State committed itself more than 20 years ago, to benefit the indigenous communities, is still pending. This obligation is not met only by distributing lands. While the territory is fundamental for development of the indigenous populations in community, it must be accompanied by health, education, and sanitary services, and the protection of their labor and social security rights, and, especially, the protection of their habitat.[166]

Consequently, not only must sufficient lands and resources be legally recognized or otherwise transferred to indigenous peoples, a measure fundamental to indigenous development, the environmental integrity of those lands must be guaranteed and the state must ensure that indigenous peoples enjoy adequate health, education and sanitary services, presumably of at least the same quality as those enjoyed by non-indigenous persons.

In its 2000 report on human rights in Peru, the IACHR condemned the severe impact of resource extraction operations on the indigenous communities of the Amazon region, observing that "The actions of the lumber and oil companies in these areas, without consulting or obtaining the consent of the communities affected, in many cases lead to environmental degradation and endanger the survival of these peoples."[167] To mitigate the negative impact, it recommended that Peru "improve access to the public services, including health and education, for the native communities, to offset the existing discriminatory differences, and to provide them dignified levels in keeping with national and international standards."[168] It also recommended "[t]hat it help strengthen the role of the indigenous populations so that they may have options and be able to retain their cultural identity, while also participating in the economic and social life of Peru, with respect for their cultural values, languages, traditions, and forms of social organization."[169]

Finally, various economic, social and cultural rights are also addressed in other binding treaties.[170] Article 24 of the Convention on the Rights of the Child, for instance, obliges states to recognize "the right of the child to the enjoyment of the highest attainable standard of health" and to provide all children with "adequate nutritious foods and clean drinking-water, taking into consideration the dangers and risks of environmental pollution." Article 14(2)(h) of the Convention on the Elimination of Discrimination Against Women (CEDAW) obliges states to "ensure to women the right to enjoy adequate living conditions, particularly in relation to housing, sanitation, electricity and water supply ...."[171]

Article 12 of CEDAW requires states to eliminate discrimination in provision of health care so as to ensure that women are able to meet their health goals and needs. In this context, the UN Committee on the Elimination of Discrimination Against Women has advised states that "special attention should be given to the health needs and rights of women belonging to vulnerable and disadvantaged groups, [including] … indigenous women."[172]

THE WORLD BANK'S POLICY ON INDIGENOUS PEOPLES

Responding to widespread criticism from civil society and certain borrower governments regarding the social and environmental damage caused by its projects, in early 1981 the World Bank began developing what have come to be called "safeguard policies" designed to protect vulnerable peoples and environments against such damage. The first policy, on involuntary resettlement was established in 1980, and the first operational directive on indigenous people, then known as OMS 2.34, was written in 1982. The current safeguards constitute *minimum standards* that have been developed through actual experience. They are not idealised regulations, but rather essential preconditions for sustainable development. Without adherence to safeguard policies, the basic function of development aid and the Bank's mandate are liable to be negated, especially if project implementation is not in accordance with target communities' needs and aspirations.

Strong, unambiguous and mandatory safeguard policies are important to civil society because they constitute the only mechanism available to citizens and project beneficiaries to hold the World Bank and its clients accountable for their operations. The safeguard policies are the principal instruments the World Bank has to ensure that its projects and programmes are consistent with international human rights and environmental law [*See The World Bank and Human Rights, p. 62*]. They also provide an agreed basis upon which to lay loan negotiations with borrowers and clients. In addition, the World Bank's safeguard policies provide benchmark norms and standards upon which other development actors in the international community base their investment and strategies. And the Bank concurs that "[the Bank's Safeguard Policies] have become internationally recognised references"[173]. In this light, it is essential that the World Bank maintain safeguards that accurately reflect the needs and aspirations of the communities where it is operating.

In 1999, and steadily growing since, 58% of the Bank's portfolio was composed of structural and programmatic lending.[174] Today much of it is linked to so-called "Poverty Reduction Strategy Papers" (PRSPs) and, to these types of loans, most of the safeguard policies do not apply. As the Bank now moves to apply its "Comprehensive Development Framework", which seeks to encourage all borrower countries to develop national development visions aimed at poverty reduction, it is expected that more and more lending to borrower governments will be "programmatic" loans and credits from the two sections of the World Bank Group which deal with governments, the International Bank for Reconstruction and Development (IBRD) and the International Development Association (IDA). At the same time specific projects, it is predicted, will increasingly be funded by the private sector arm of the Bank, the International Finance Corporation (IFC), or provided with political risk insurance through the Bank's Multilateral Investment Guarantee Agency (MIGA). Consequently, it is essential that safeguard policies apply to such lending as well, and that appropriate mechanisms are set in place to assure their implementation.

The World Bank's Indigenous Peoples' Policy, Operational Directive 4.20

The Indigenous Peoples Policy, first known as the OMS 2.34, was first revised in 1991 to become the Operational Directive (OD) 4.20, and is now undergoing a second process of revision to become the OP/BP 4.10. The purpose of the OD 4.20, which is currently in force, is to ensure "*that the development process fosters full respect for their dignity, human rights and cultural uniqueness*". In sum, OD 4.20 ensures that in World Bank assisted projects, borrower governments commit to securing indigenous rights, legal mechanisms are set in place to secure land tenure and resource rights, indigenous peoples are protected from adverse effects during the development process, that the economic and development benefits received from the project are culturally appropriate and that projects where negative impacts cannot be adequately ameliorated are not approved by the Bank.

OD 4.20 also includes the fundamental provision that all investment projects affecting indigenous peoples should include an "Indigenous Peoples Development Plan" (IPDP)[175]. This plan or component must, first and foremost "be based on the full consideration of the options preferred by the indigenous people affected by the project", and it must "*anticipate adverse trends* likely to be induced by the project". Crucially, OD 4.20 stresses that the IPDP requires long lead times and extended follow-up and that local cultural beliefs and systems must be taken into account.

The IPDP must also involve:

- An assessment of the national legal framework regarding indigenous peoples;
- Compilation of baseline data about the indigenous peoples to be affected;
- A mechanism for the legal recognition of indigenous peoples' rights, especially tenure rights;
- Sub-components on health care, education, legal assistance and institution building;
- Capacity-building of the government agency dealing with indigenous peoples;
- A clear schedule for fitting actions related to indigenous peoples into the overall project, with a clear and adequate budget.[176]

Problems with OD 4.20

The Bank's 1991 Indigenous Peoples Policy has significant deficiencies such as its failure to make explicit reference to ILO Convention 169 and its disregard for the right to prior informed consent. Despite these serious problems, and although it is insufficient as it stands, if implemented properly, OD 4.20 can help safeguard the rights of indigenous communities affected by World Bank projects.

The problems of OD 4.20 lie largely in the fact that it was not designed with the participation of indigenous people, even though, prior to its publication, some indigenous peoples' organisations, such as the Amazonian indigenous alliance, COICA, made specific demands as to the content of the policy:

- Inclusion of the recognition of indigenous peoples' rights

as set out in international law;
- ❑ Elaboration of the policy in direct consultation with indigenous peoples;
- ❑ Prior consent of indigenous peoples be mandatory before implementation of a World Bank project;
- ❑ Participation of indigenous peoples throughout the project cycle;
- ❑ Establishment of tripartite commissions, including funders, government representatives and indigenous peoples' representatives to oversee project implementation;
- ❑ Prioritisation of indigenous peoples' development needs and aspirations.[177]

None of these demands were provided for in the OD 4.20, rendering it an unsuitable protection of the livelihoods and requirements of indigenous peoples under World Bank operations.

Indigenous Peoples' Development Aspirations and OD 4.20

Although the World Bank and bilateral development agencies tend to argue that people of the developing world aspire to the lifestyle of the western world, and that NGOs opposing the market-based development model are "anti-development", it is not so simple. Local communities and indigenous peoples have witnessed the human distress and ecological imbalance that the western development model has led to, and they are often unwilling to choose this model for themselves. Indigenous peoples are often vocally opposed to unsustainable development programmes, such as those promoting the extractive industries, as a model for poverty alleviation.

Their close physical, spiritual, cultural and religious ties to their land make them unwilling to proceed with development likely to break the fragile equilibrium of the ecosystems they rely on. In the words of Western Shoshone tribal member, Berenice Lalo:

> Our people will be here, because according to our traditions in this valley, this is where we came. This is where we exist, and when mining comes, it's a form of genocide ... a systematic destruction of a race of people. And when this comes in, this mining comes in, it is a destruction of our way of life.

Indeed, the sheer number of indigenous global anti-mining and anti-oil campaigns is evidence of this fact. Sustainable development in the true sense, where the future of the earth and its inhabitants is foremost, is the aspiration of most indigenous peoples, and the Kimberly Declaration of September 2002 is a testimony to this. The World Bank ignores this aspiration: (i) by not including international standards of human rights in OD 4.20, and (ii) by failing to respect the principle of self-determination, thereby foregoing the most appropriate method for ensuring that targeted peoples and communities fully benefit from proposed development projects.

Problems with Implementation of OD 4.20

Despite these serious failings, OD4.20 is considered to be an improvement of the Bank's previous policy on Indigenous Peoples (OMS 2.34). Unfortunately, the quality of implementation of OD 4.20 in the 1990s has been patchy and often poor[178.]

The most important shortcoming of the OD 4.20 is that it has rarely, if ever, been implemented to its full extent. A participatory study carried out by Forest Peoples Programme in 1999[179] and 2000, found that implementation of the safeguards by Bank staff and borrower countries was weak. In many projects, most of the fundamental issues regarding indigenous people were seriously overlooked or swept under the carpet. Indigenous Peoples Development Plans were rarely included, or were severely lacking in adequate provisions.

This report prompted the World Bank to initiate its own review process, and in 2000, the Operations Evaluation Department began reviewing implementation of the OD 4.20 by Bank staff. A recent report of the OED review confirms the poor pattern of compliance reported by studies and surveys conducted by NGOs. Its survey of 89 closed projects that had affected indigenous peoples during the period 1992-2001 found, for example, that only 58% had applied the OD and that just twelve projects (14%) had self-standing Indigenous Peoples Development Plans as required under OD 4.20.[180] The same review found that the participation of indigenous peoples in decision-making in Bank projects affecting them was "low" and that just 20% of projects had included clear benchmarks for monitoring to measure impacts on indigenous communities[181].

These shortcomings are equally apparent in oil, gas and mining projects. This research has identified a large number of projects and interventions, where the World Bank seems unable to implement its safeguard policies and fails to address fundamental problems that need to be tackled before projects are approved. In India for example, none of the environmental and social problems of existing National Thermal

Power Corporations (NTPC) operations were "fully addressed prior to negotiations"[182], and no safeguard policy was implemented before operations started. The World Bank's answer to these serious failings was the preparation of various retroactive Environmental and Social Action Plans in the Singrauli area, and yet even these do not consider "the impact on the broader social environment" and do not "foresee socio-economic studies on the fate of the earlier project affected people, and resettlement and rehabilitation action plans"[183]. In addition, by the time these action plans were initiated in 1998, 85% of the new loan was already disbursed. If the safeguard measures put in place by the Bank are to be of any use and profit for the sustainable development of the communities benefiting from its loans, at a minimum they must be applied and adhered to in a timely manner.

Examples of World Bank projects not complying with the institution's own policies abound, and recent examples can be found in the Inspection Panel report on the Coal India Social and Environmental Mitigation Project, as well as that on the Chad portion of the Chad-Cameroon Pipeline. In Cameroon also, the indigenous Bagyéli pygmies, who are directly affected by the construction of the pipeline, were not adequately involved in the development of an Indigenous Peoples Development Plan, which is now tardily being designed and implemented piecemeal and in a retroactive way after the social impacts of pipeline construction have already been felt.

In Bolivia, the construction of two pipelines, the Cuiabá and the Bolivia-Brazil Gas Pipeline, led to post-project implementation of inadequate IPDP's, which did not even provide the fundamental (and OD 4.20-required) legal land demarcation processes to the "beneficiary" indigenous populations. To varying extents, non-compliance to the minimum (and in the main, deficient) standards set out in its safeguard policies is the norm, as evident in the recent OED implementation review of OD 4.20.

Revision of OD 4.20

Over the past few years, the World Bank has undertaken a systematic "conversion" of its safeguard policies, which has largely resulted in the release of weakened and watered down versions of the policies' predecessors [*See Box 19, p. 135 for a discussion on the revision process*]. In line with this revision process, the OD 4.20 was converted into the draft OP/BP 4.10 in 1998.

Two consultations with indigenous organisations were undertaken, in 1998/99 and 2001/02[184] . However this process has been roundly condemned for being rushed, for lacking informed and representative indigenous participation, and for failing to meet the Bank's own guidelines on meaningful public consultation.[185]

OP 4.10 has been refuted by the indigenous peoples' organisations[186], as it is a severely weakened version of OD 4.20, and does not take into account their fundamental demands, which are the following:

- To be based on a thorough participatory *implementation review* of the existing policy (OD4.20) to ensure that any revisions are derived from practical lessons based on the actual experience of indigenous peoples with World Bank operations.
- To address the concerns and priorities of indigenous peoples.
- To adopt the indigenous right to "self-identification" in accordance with the principles set out in Article 8 of the UN Draft Declaration on the Rights of Indigenous Peoples.
- To further specify that securing indigenous land and resource rights be an essential precondition for project appraisal and approval with concrete benchmarks to ensure compliance.
- To require "effective" participation by indigenous peoples affected by Bank loan operations throughout the project cycle.
- To prohibit involuntary resettlement of indigenous peoples. Resettlement may only take place with the full, prior, free and informed consent of affected indigenous communities.
- To recognise the indigenous right to "prior, free and informed consent" to any developments proposed on their lands and territories as specified under Article 30 of the UN Draft Declaration on the Rights of Indigenous Peoples.
- To include an environmental audit in baseline studies that properly values indigenous peoples' resources and territories. Any use of indigenous knowledge in such studies must incorporate adequate intellectual property rights safeguards and benefit sharing mechanisms.
- To ensure consultations include traditional leaders as well as local indigenous organisations.
- To require the involvement of affected indigenous peoples in negotiations between the World Bank and the client gov-

ernment regarding loan agreements.

❑ To include requirements for involving local, national and regional indigenous organisations in active tracking and monitoring of World Bank operations through the whole project cycle.

❑ To require the proactive circulation of information in local languages to indigenous organisations and communities affected by Bank loan operations.

By inadequately addressing the human rights issues of indigenous peoples, especially with regards to land and resource rights, by failing to comply with the Bank's obligations under international law, and by failing to ensure that borrowers do not violate their own obligations under international human rights standards, the OP 4.10 is at odds with the World Bank's professed mandate for effective poverty reduction and its mission to promote good governance and rule of law in developing countries.[187]

THE WORLD BANK AND HUMAN RIGHTS

The World Bank has no formal, written policy on human rights, either in terms of the Bank's role, or lack thereof, in promoting and requiring respect for human rights in its operations or internally in terms of its policies. OD 4.20 on Indigenous Peoples of 1991 is the only operational policy that explicitly mentions human rights and the Bank has never officially stated its understanding of the term "human rights" in that directive.

Whether the World Bank has legal obligations to respect human rights turns a) largely on the legal interpretation given to the Bank's Articles of Agreement (its Constitutional instrument) and its Relationship Agreement with the United Nations and; b) an examination of the status of the Bank in the international legal system and whether a duty to respect human rights attaches to that status. In other words, two fundamental questions are: (i) is the Bank prohibited from or limited in some way from addressing and accounting for indigenous peoples' and other human rights by its Articles and; (ii) is the Bank a subject of international law bound by its norms?

The Bank has long maintained that it is not required to respect and promote all human rights in its operations and policies. Similarly, it also maintains that it cannot require that its borrowers respect human rights in connection with Bank-funded projects.

There are two main arguments the Bank makes to support these positions:

a. The Bank's Articles of Agreement is the highest law applying to the Bank, prohibits it from interfering in the political affairs of its members and requires that all of its decision-making must be based solely on economic considerations, and;

b. Its borrowers are sovereign states and, therefore, the Bank may not require that they account for and respect human rights in Bank-funded projects because this would be illegitimate interference in the internal affairs of their borrowers.

The prevailing interpretation within the Bank of its Articles leads to a classification of human rights issues as either economic or political; those that can be classified as economic, social or cultural rights are legitimate and cognizable, those classified as political rights are beyond the jurisdiction of the Bank. For this reason, the Bank has often highlighted what it perceives to be its contribution to furthering economic, social and cultural human rights through poverty alleviation, while disregarding the majority of civil and political rights[188]: "For the World Bank, protecting and advancing human rights means helping the world's poorest people escape poverty."[189]

The counter argument made by numerous scholars, lawyers and UN experts states, on the first point, that interpretation of the term "political affairs" must occur in the context of contemporary international law. This position is supported by the International Court of Justice, which stated that "an international instrument has to be interpreted and applied within the framework of the entire legal system prevailing at the time of its interpretation."[190] In contemporary international law, human rights are considered to be of international concern rather than the domestic political affairs of states. As Judge Weeramantry of the International Court of Justice observed:

> In its ongoing development, the concept of human rights has long passed the stage when it was a narrow parochial concern between sovereign and subject. We have reached the stage, today, at which the human rights of anyone, anywhere, are the concern of everyone, everywhere. [191]

The UN Charter has a similar provision prohibiting interference in internal political affairs.[192] However, it is standard and accepted practice within the UN that this provision does not apply to human rights, which are deemed of international concern and therefore not solely within the internal sovereign or political sphere of states.[193]

With regard to the term "only economic considerations", it is well documented that human rights have economic implications and therefore such rights can also be characterized as economic considerations. For instance, World Bank studies show that countries with good human rights records have greater success in implementing Bank-funded economic development projects and receive higher levels of investment than countries with bad records.[194] Similarly, World Bank publications have recognized the economic costs of discrimination against indigenous peoples.[195] James Wolfensohn, the current President of the Bank, goes further stating unequivocally that "Without the protection of human and property rights, and a comprehensive framework of laws, no equitable development is possible."[196]

On the second point, the vast majority of the Bank's members have voluntarily committed themselves to abide by human rights standards through ratification of international conventions, through the formation of international customary human rights norms and, in some cases, by assenting to UN and other declarations.[197] In doing so, they have accepted international obligations to promote, respect, protect and fulfill human rights and, in many cases, international oversight of their compliance with these obligations. As stated by Judge Weeramantry of the ICJ, "there is not even the semblance of a suggestion in contemporary international law that [human rights] obligations amount to a derogation of sovereignty.[198]

Integration of human rights issues into Bank policy setting and operational activities would, in the majority of cases, merely restate aims, objectives and obligations to which the vast majority of its members have already subscribed. In states with a monist legal system[199] — a significant number of Bank members — these international obligations are an integral part of their domestic law; in dualist states[200] they have been incorporated, or are required to be incorporated, into domestic law.[201]

The Legal Obligations of the Bank to Respect Human Rights

The preceding shows that there are strong legal arguments that the Bank's Articles cannot prohibit attention to and respect for all human rights and that state sovereignty is not a valid excuse for not requiring that borrowers respect human rights in Bank-funded operations. However, it does not address the more fundamental issue of whether the Bank has a legal *obligation* to respect, promote and protect human rights.

The Bank has legal obligations to respect human rights and to account for these rights in its safeguard policies and operations for four reasons:

    a. The Bank is a subject of international law bound by its rules and norms;

    b. The Bank, as a general principle and as a Specialized Agency of the United Nations, has obligations derived from the human rights provisions of the Charter of the UN and international human rights instruments interpreting and elaborating upon those provisions;

    c. The Bank is an international organization created by and comprised of states, each of which has an obligation to promote and respect human rights both individually and through collective action; the Bank is one place such collective action is required; and

    d. The Bank is required by general international law not to interfere with or facilitate violations of its borrowers international obligations, including those pertaining to human rights.

A subject of international law is an entity capable of possessing international rights and duties as well as the capacity to enforce these in international tribunals. The Bank is regarded as a subject of international law by scholars and the Bank itself. As a subject of international law, the Bank has rights and duties, separate from and in addition to its member states, defined by international law.

Neither the Bank nor its Articles are above the law; as the International Court of Justice observed, "international organizations are bound by any obligations incumbent upon them under general rules of international law...."[202] These general rules include principles of customary international law, *jus cogens* norms, such as the right to self-determination, the right to life and the prohibition of systematic racial discrimination, and international obligations *erga omnes*. The latter are duties owed by states "towards the international community as a whole...,"[203] and derive from, among others, the prohibition of genocide and "from the principles and rules concerning the basic rights of the human person, including protection from slavery and racial discrimination."[204] Based in part on this statement, the International Law Institute has supported the proposition that the general obligation to respect human rights is itself an obligation *erga omnes*.

Concerning treaties, the general rule of international law is that third parties are not bound by treaties without their express consent.[205] The Bank is not party to any human rights conventions and therefore is not directly bound. This does not mean however that these instruments are irrelevant to the Bank's obligations: they may restate or inform the content of binding rules of customary international law,[206] they set out the obligations of most Bank members, and they elaborate upon the human rights provisions of the UN Charter, a source of obligations for both the Bank and its members.

The UN Charter and the Bank as a Specialized Agency

Both the Bank and its members have obligations under the UN Charter that supercede the provisions of the Bank's Articles.[207] Article 103 of the Charter states unequivocally that: "In the event of a conflict between the obligations of the Members of the United Nations under the present Charter and their obligations under any other international instrument, their obligations under the present Charter shall prevail." Article 1(3) of the UN Charter defines one of the primary purposes and principles of the UN to be "promoting and encouraging respect for human rights and fundamental freedoms for all without distinction as to race, sex, language or religion." Under the heading "International Economic and Social Cooperation," Article 55 of the Charter requires the UN to promote "universal respect for, and observance of human rights and fundamental freedoms for all …." The UN Charter's provisions on human rights are therefore directly relevant to the larger issue of the Bank's responsibility towards human rights.

The Bank is also a Specialized Agency of the UN. Its status as a specialized agency of the UN, and the nature of the relationship between the Bank and UN, is based upon and defined by a treaty known as the Relationship Agreement.[208] Article 4(3) of the Relationship Agreement stresses that the Bank is an independent organization and recognizes that:

> action to be taken by the Bank on any loan matter is to be determined by the independent exercise of the Bank's own judgment in accordance with the Bank's Articles of Agreement. The United Nations recognises, therefore, that it would be sound policy to refrain from making recommendations to the Bank with respect to particular loans or with respect to the terms or conditions of financing by the Bank.

While this provision provides for a much looser association between the UN and the Bank than exists between the UN and other specialized agencies, it relates only to UN involvement in Bank-decision making processes rather than any larger responsibility the Bank may have under the UN Charter or international law in general. Skogly observes that, "part of the reasoning behind bringing these organizations [specialized agencies] into a formalised relationship with the UN must have been to grant them, both legally and practically, rights and obligations in relationship to the UN ...."[209] These obligations, at a minimum, include respect for the principles and purposes of the UN. Therefore, as a specialized agency of the UN, the Bank has obligations derived from the UN Charter, in particular to act in conformity with the Charter.[210] This means that the Bank's policies, internal and external, and operations must be formulated and implemented in accordance with the Charter's provisions related to human rights.

The Charter's provisions dealing with human rights are very basic. Other than self-determination, the only right explicitly mentioned is the prohibition of discrimination. Partly for this reason, in 1948, the UN General Assembly adopted the Universal Declaration of Human Rights to elaborate upon and specify the Charter's human rights provisions and obligations. The Universal Declaration, wholly or in part, is widely considered to express general principles of international law and binding norms of customary law despite its non-binding status when adopted.[211] Subsequent codification of human rights by the UN, the International Covenants and CERD in particular, has also further clarified ambiguities in the meaning of the Charter's provisions. Professor Sohn observes that, although the Covenants:

> resemble traditional international agreements which bind only those who ratify them, it seems clear that they partake of the creative force found in the Declaration and constitute in a similar fashion an authoritative interpretation of the basic rules of international law on the subject of human rights which are embodied in the Charter of the United Nations. ... Consequently, ... they are of some importance ... with respect to the interpretation of the Charter obligations of the non-ratifying states.[212]

Presumably this would also apply to the Charter obligations of non-ratifying subjects of international law, especially members of the UN system such as the Bank. The jurisprudence of the UN bodies, such as the Human Rights Committee and the Committee on the Elimination of All Racial Discrimination, charged with monitoring state compliance with human rights instruments is also important in this context. Their interpretations of the human rights instruments not only inform the obligations of state-parties, they also develop greater understanding of the nature of Charter-based obligations.

The conclusion that can be drawn from the preceding is that the Bank has obligations towards human rights derived from the UN Charter, both as a general principle of international law and as a Specialized Agency. These obligations also extend to at least the core rights set forth in the Universal Declaration and UN human rights treaties, as these instruments are simply interpretations of the Charter's human rights provisions.

The obligations of the Bank's members are relatively straightforward. As members of the UN, Bank members are legally bound by the UN Charter "to take a joint and separate action in cooperation with the Organisation for the achievement of the purposes set forth in Article 55".[213] This obligation also requires that states act in conformity with human rights guarantees in their conduct within and with the Bank, for instance, as members of the board, as policy setters and as borrowers.

While the Bank has rights and duties separate from and in addition to its member states, the obligations of its members states are not irrelevant. On the contrary, the Bank is obliged, as is any other subject of the law, to ensure that it neither undermines the ability of other subjects, including its members, to faithfully fulfill their international obligations nor facilitates or assists violation of those obligations.[214] This duty is binding on all subjects of international law. This adds an extra dimension to the obligations of the Bank and requires that its policies and operations account for and respect the obligations of its members under ratified human rights conventions, regional as well as universal, and other sources of law binding on them.

As parties to UN and regional human rights instruments, the Bank's members are obligated to respect, ensure and fulfill the rights set forth in those instruments. What this means in practice will vary depending on the specific obligations of the various members of the Bank and how those obligations are implicated in Bank-financed activities. On a policy level, the Bank is obliged to ensure that policy formulation and implementation account for and respect its members' human rights obligations. Bradlow and Grossman concur: "in general, it is safe to assume that the IFIs should perform their functions in a way which supports the fundamental rights of individuals and peoples."[215]

Finally, it is relevant in this context to note that the Bank's Operational Policy 4.01 on Environmental Assessment clearly states that "the Bank takes into account ... the obligations of the country, pertaining to project activities, under relevant international environmental treaties and agreements. The Bank does not finance project activities that would contravene such country obligations, as identified during the EA" (para. 3). If this is possible with regard to environmental obligations, is there a compelling reason why human rights obligations should not be accorded equal status?[216]

THE WORLD BANK EXPERIENCE

The purpose of this section is to highlight some of the experience of indigenous peoples at the hands of extractive industries projects and particularly look at the contribution the Bank has made to this experience. This draws therefore from both the experiences presented in the case studies discussed at the workshop and other documented experiences.

The mining industry has long been subject to criticism for its lasting detrimental impacts on the environment and the communities affected by its operations. Abuses have taken various forms as is illustrated in some of the cases cited. Scrutiny and protest have increased in recent years and have reached a point where they can and have led to the cancellation of some funding and projects, including projects involving the Bank.

Impacts on Indigenous Peoples

Indigenous peoples have always carried a disproportionately high burden of extractive industries projects within their territories. This is even true in the USA, Canada and Australia where the mining industry is long established, and is increasingly so in developing States, which are served by the World Bank Group. Indeed the Bank has actively promoted this expansion despite the widespread negative experiences of indigenous peoples affected by Extractive Industries (EI) projects. It is predicted that "the majority of current big mines, and those planned for the next fifteen years, are located on indigenous territory - where the human and environmental consequences of mining are usually much more serious than in established extractive zones. . ." [217]

Given the sustained negative experiences of many indigenous peoples at the hands of extractive sector projects, a key question considered herein is whether it is appropriate for the Bank to have financed and promoted Extractive Industries' development on indigenous lands. Particularly, where, as is common, the basic rights of indigenous peoples to control the development of their lands and culture are denied. Additionally, evidence suggests that even where legal frameworks have been established with the stated objective of improving the protection of affected communities' rights, this may not in practice improve the situation adequately, if at all. While indigenous rights are gaining increased recognition within some nations and the international community, this is not yet adequately represented in the practices of mining companies or even in the guidelines of the industry or International Financial Institutions (IFIs) including the World Bank. Indigenous peoples do find ways, however, to effectively assert their rights and aspirations. In the process they have become a major factor in decisions concerning the development of EI projects.

A common understanding of the nature of past experiences of indigenous peoples and other local communities affected by EI projects is essential to the aim of this review. This should provide the context for the assessment of any current or future prospects for EI investment. It is important to recognise however that, as a result of past experience, there is a very low level of trust in communities concerning industry claims of community benefits or environmental protection. At the very least it is clear that any such claims of benefit cannot, as is too often current practice, be assumed.

The history of the expansion of the EI around the world is inextricably linked to colonialism and its exploitative processes. It is little surprise therefore that historically indigenous communities, and other affected communities and nations, have suffered invasion of their territories without consultation or consent, and that their cultural practices and indigenous economy have been overwhelmed through militarization, coercion, violent displacement, introduction of disease and the generation of a legacy of lasting environmental degradation. This is a shared global experience.

Accounts indicate that most mining has been suffered by indigenous peoples and other affected communities as a form of "development aggression". EI projects have in some cases, according to accounts from all regions, caused impoverishment, environmental degradation, cultural disintegration and other physically and socially negative effects. Some of these cases are extremely grave in their destructive impact. Researchers have particularly pointed to the heightened severity of the intrusion of EI projects where indigenous communities subsisting off the land are involved. The reduction of land access and the degradation of land and water resources that inevitably accompanied an EI project can impoverish both materially and culturally. The relationship between the Extractive Industries and indigenous peoples is therefore viewed by the affected peoples primarily as a matter of human rights and their abuse. This explains the primacy of their sustained demand for the recognition and respect for their collective and individual rights.[218]

There have even been attempts by some companies and institutions to interfere politically and through the courts to thwart or hold back emerging recognition of indigenous rights including land rights. This inevitably has engendered hostility and mistrust. One of the most notorious historical examples of such obstructive approaches were the efforts of Australian Mining Industry Council spearheaded by the Western Mining Company's CEO Hugh Morgan, through the so-called media misinformation "black hands campaign" of 1984, to portray recognition of indigenous rights as a threat to the State and its development.[219]

Examples of such subversive efforts by mining industry interests continue. The legal challenge to the Indigenous Peoples Rights Act in the Philippines is another example. In Indonesia, mining interests have exerted pressures resulting in the breach of former prohibitions on mining in protected areas.[220] In a number of cases including around the Yanacocha mine in Peru, investors and even sections of the Bank have sought to deny the presence of indigenous peoples despite local peoples' self-identification as indigenous peoples.[221] This denial seems motivated by the desire to avoid the extra scrutiny and safeguards this identification might require.

Within the mining industry there is a growing recognition of the need to acknowledge the existence of shameful incidents of past abuse of community rights and environmental values. Sir Robert Wilson Chair, of Rio Tinto, has urged others in the industry to "accept that [the industry leaders] have made mistakes and to actively engage with, and listen to [their] critics…"[222] Leon Davies, a former CEO of Rio Tinto, has also gone on record to acknowledge specifically the mistakes that his company made which generated the environmental destruction and civil conflict resulting from the operations of the Panguna mine on the island of Bougainville. Some companies, including Rio Tinto, have been active more recently in initiatives that are seeking a new image and improved community relations for the mining industry. Some leading oil companies have also launched similar initiatives. Companies are however not the only factor.

Some States, according to indigenous reports to the UN Working Group on Indigenous Populations, have been complicit in such abusive approaches, and even promote mineral development within ancestral land. Indeed, some indigenous organisations have accused States of consciously prioritising natural resource extraction in indigenous areas over other areas as part of a policy of discrimination against indigenous peoples.

The conflict between States' obligations to respect basic indigenous peoples' human rights under international law, and their aspiration to proceed with projects promising national economic benefits, which are thought to require sacrifice in and around the project site, is a fundamental problem for the World Bank. While the Bank is required to respect international law, it is the representatives of States that both govern the Bank and are the major recipients of its loans, and thus wield substantial power over its investments. Currently, States which deny or fail to fully respect the rights of indigenous peoples remain acceptable recipients of Bank loans. States are frequently major beneficiaries of mining investment, and even operate as shareholding partners in mining projects that have adverse impacts on indigenous peoples. They also receive income from imposed taxes and duties, and therefore may be reticent to respect international law obligations that might affect revenue flows. This conflicting role of the State as both beneficiary and regulator of World Bank funding is perceived as a serious flaw by indigenous communities who experience that Governments holding shares in mines make poor regulators and poor prosecutors of infractions by the companies . [*See for example, Box 6: Omai - The Poisoned Chalice, p. 89*]

Lack of Trust

The past experience of limitations, failures and abuse has bred a deep mistrust of mining companies and, by extension, their financiers. Combined with the magnitude of the potential impacts, this mistrust is the basis of the widely articulated demand for tighter legally binding regulation of mining operations supported by effective independent monitoring and enforcement.

Affected communities, including indigenous groups, assert that abuse has been, and remains, the norm rather than the exception. The Philippine Mining Code for example offers nominal legal protections for indigenous peoples, including the right to free prior informed consent (FPIC) to any and all development on indigenous lands. Nonetheless, reports from communities [*See for example, Box 14 for the Philippine Case Study, p. 116*] reveal that in virtually all cases where companies assert having secured FPIC, such claims are in effect fraudulent and acquired by misrepresentation, bribery, fraud or coercion, even where these assertions are endorsed by government agencies[223]. It is most disturbing to note this conflict of claims extends even to the case of the community of Didipio where the IFC consultant endorsed the company's version of a satisfactory consultation [*See Philippine case study*]:

> *In approving the plan, the IFC consultant stated that the acceptance*

by the host community of the development plan represented the best case of prior informed consent he had ever witnessed.[224]

This, despite vehement denials by the affected community.[225]

Many NGOs and IPOs call upon the EIR to recommend a halt to Bank funding and support for mining, oil, and gas projects. As a minimum prior condition, they seek a rights regime that promises, and delivers protection of international human rights standards that ensure sufficient control of indigenous communities over the development of their land. This further requires any such development to be consensual, beneficial and based on informed processes free from duress. It is difficult to identify regimes where this is currently the case, hence the widespread call for a moratorium on the development of new mining projects as manifest in numerous conference resolutions. [226]

The World Bank and Mining

The Bank has a long involvement in extractive industry projects, dating back more than 40 years. Between 1955 and 1990, the Bank financed nearly 50 mining or mineral processing projects, granting loans and credits totalling nearly US$2 billion, of which nine (around 20%) were disbursed in the period 1988-1990 alone. These disbursements covered five areas: mining sector reform and rehabilitation; new "greenfield" mine construction; mineral processing; technical assistance; and engineering work.

Bank involvement has grown in more recent years[227]. Bank spending on EI projects in the last 5 years alone has been in excess of US $5 billion. Through time Bank-supported projects have included a disturbing stream of those failing to operate to safe standards and have been the subject of protest and complaint from affected communities. Increasingly, projects are delayed or prevented by such protests. Allegations of abuses are also increasingly finding their way to court as "victims" of mining projects seek redress from companies and even from the Bank.

Policy Reform, Technical Funds and Dialogue

Traditionally project finance has been the main focus of Bank activities. Since the late 1980's however, the Bank has chiefly emphasised, and exerted its greatest influence in, financing policy "reform", through liberalisation of regulations concerning mining investment, promotion of dialogue initiatives, and generation of guidelines. In 1988 the Bank's Mining Unit conducted a survey of opinions of multinational mining companies. Forty-five companies (with combined mineral sales of US$ 40 billion that year) informed the Bank of their requirements regarding the future behaviour of selected specific countries. They demanded "higher rates of return than in developed countries", expressed a "strong preference" for the "stable environment of countries with proven track records", and required "payback" (i.e. rate of return, or IRR) of between 20% and 25% over 2-4 years. Such demands partially explain the heavy dependence of companies on precious gems and gold projects in their overseas exploration activities. In contrast they willingly accepted IRR of only 13% to 17% in industrialised countries, with a payback of up to six years. The perceived risks of asset appropriation, adverse exchange fluctuations, community disruptions and general conflict allegedly accounted for this discrepancy between developing and developed countries[228].

Although Chile, Botswana and Papua New Guinea were at the time reckoned to be the most attractive countries for mineral investment, this was not particularly because they offered better entry conditions than others. Indeed, as the Bank pointed out, these three favoured countries had, at the time, relatively high tax rates once mining was underway[229]. More important was a state's financial and political stability, while "mandatory majority local participation, either public or private" carried a strong negative rating.[230]

The canvassed companies gave "greatest importance" to the Bank's "work with individual countries to update and reform [existing] mining investment codes" which would open prospective regions to exploration, guarantee security of investment, and introduce generous tax holidays to protect the early years of exploitation. Addressing other problems identified by the industry, the Bank placed importance on job cuts and restriction of workers' rights:

> allow[ing] for the reduction of personnel, and even mine closure in
> response to economic reasons [sic], and to regulate the right of strike
> in order to avoid unnecessary conflicts where confrontations could
> be avoided. [231]

It is important to note that while the Bank actively solicited the wishes of mining companies and acted strongly in support of the emerging demands, no similar consultation with indigenous peoples, or other directly affected "victims/beneficiaries" of mining, was realised at this time or later. In 1991, the World Bank set out its table, based on these industry demands, justifying finance for the mining sector. Public sector reform, under which state companies would be subjected to "market discipline", alongside the encouragement of investment in exploration and development by "qualified firms"[232], was to become the order of the day. The Bank pledged to work to streamline investment legislation, foreign exchange regulations, taxation and labour legislation in mining-dependent countries of the South, and "improve" mining codes "where issues refer to the access by the investors to mining rights, the politics (sic) with respect to mining rights and the role and scope of the state owned enterprises".

It is clear that the Bank's role in this area of policy reform has been hugely influential. The Mining Codes of more than 70 countries[233] have been changed within the last 20 years, in line with a package of recommendations from the Bank. Some have responded to the atmosphere of competitive reform even without significant financial intervention by the Bank. The thrust of Bank policy in this area has even provided direction to the policies of other institutions, including the overseas aid agencies of countries such as Canada where mining has a strong base, the regional development Banks, and other UN agencies including UNDP.

While project finance now requires consultations with communities and affected Peoples, under the World Bank policies OD 4.20 on Indigenous Peoples, OD 4.12 on Involuntary Resettlement, and OP 4.36 on Forestry, these are not required for structural adjustment loans, nor for the influence exerted through the conduct of trainings and seminars, policy dialogue and the placement of consultants that have in practice been major vehicles of "reforms'. Reform measures including influence to liberalise mining codes are however potentially more far-reaching in their effect than project financing, yet these reform interventions do not appear in practice to be scrutinised with regards to the WBG safeguard policies framework.

Ecuador: Undermining Protected Areas

In Ecuador, the Mining Development and Environmental Control Technical Assistance Project, PRODEMINCA, was approved in 1993. It funded a project for the prospecting, surveying and mapping of mineral wealth within the Cotacachi-Coyapas Ecological Reserve. This project was criticised[234] as, according to a local NGO, DECOIN, the project would disturb traditional agricultural activities as well as some of the world's most critical and endangered habitat regions. DECOIN filed an official complaint with the World Bank's Inspection Panel, maintaining that the Bank violated its policies on environmental assessment, wildlands, projects supervision and indigenous peoples.

Despite the content of the complaint, the Inspection Panel Report did not analyse the impacts on local communities or indigenous peoples. It did however find that the Bank was in relative compliance with its policies on wildlands and supervision, whilst identifying severe flaws in its environmental assessment, including the inadequacy of consultation. It was concluded that although mapping and surveys are not environmentally destructive actions per se, they can be means to a destructive end. The World Bank argued that such surveys would have no environmental consequence since Ecuadorian law prohibits extractive activities in protected areas.

This defence was effectively undermined when Article 27 of the law prohibiting mining in protected areas was repealed during the Bank project's operation. According to the Inspection Panel, no link between PRODEMINCA and this change was found. Affected groups claim the Bank financed a project which increased the threat to protected areas and to the subsistence base of indigenous communities. The Bank claim was that the mineral survey did not imply mineral development. However in a developing country with limited resources it is difficult to comprehend how the academic survey of mineral wealth, without an intention to exploit such wealth, could be defined as a priority for financing over other potential sources of investment. Indeed the President of the IBRD had written earlier that:

> The two major objectives of the project are: (a) attract new private mining investment and support the systematic development of increased, yet environmentally sound mineral production; and (b) arrest mining related environmental degradation and mitigate the damage that results from the use of primitive and inadequate technology by informal miners.

Many other countries[235] have received some form of advice, technical or structural support, or pressure originating from the World Bank, recommending the liberalisation of mining, petroleum and gas laws.

These revisions in mining codes can and do clash with recent constitutional provisions for the safeguard of land tenure and ownership rights — which are fundamental to indigenous peoples. Law reforms relating to mineral development have been identified by indigenous groups as among the gravest current threats to their lives and culture[236]

In Peru, the reforms have been the basis of the creation of new governmental structures set up to deal with environmental assessments and indigenous peoples[237]. In practice these will most probably merely provide increased opportunities for fixers and middlemen to take advantage of their specialist knowledge of a rapid and complex process. Of general concern arising from the specific Peruvian experience is that the new minerals-related laws and the new Constitution in Peru have no mechanism for respecting the rights and wishes of indigenous peoples who are in voluntary isolation, i.e. those peoples who choose not to interact with the State or other agencies. These groups are effectively denied the political space within the country's legal framework to choose isolation. This problem is exemplified by the situation in the Nahua/ Kugapakori state reserve, where Pluspetrol, an Argentinean oil company is drilling for gas with the aim of constructing a pipeline to the ocean, on the reserve lands of the Nahua, the Kugapori (otherwise known as the Nanti) and the Matsigenka, who are only in the incipient stages of direct interaction with national society.

This situation has brought to light significant problems regarding the interpretation of the notion of community consultation and free prior and informed consent. Companies have been allowed to interpret non-participation in consultation as acquiescence and therefore consent rather than rejection. This clearly is a perverse and self-serving interpretation of the conscious act of avoidance practiced by these indigenous groups. This highlights the need for the drafting of comprehensive laws, and Bank procedures and requirements to prevent the continuation of such an inappropriate interpretation. It is one of the recommendations of groups involved in this workshop that a policy of voluntary isolation pursued by a community should clearly be viewed as a rejection of all forms of economic exploitation of natural resources within their area.

It is also clear that for any indigenous community, the decision-making processes require adequate access to information, which, given the predominantly oral nature of most indigenous societies, will and should inevitably require direct participation in public meetings as a minimum basis for claiming social acceptability. The Didipio case also highlights the absence of trust between companies and communities and therefore the need for credible independent monitoring agencies that enjoy the confidence of affected communities. [*See Box 2 next page*]

Papua New Guinea: Low Standards and Development Failures

Papua New Guinea is a country in which the Bank has invested. PNG combines an extremely rich mineral endowment with massive developmental needs. It is generally acknowledged that Bank influence in the country is substantial. Technical assistance for the reform of the extractive sector has been a major form of World Bank investment for Papua New Guinea for the past two decades. The Petroleum Exploration Technical Assistance Project (1982), the Petroleum Exploration and Develop-

Box 2: *The Philippines: Engineering Consent*

The World Bank directly and with and through other agencies including UNDP, and ADB championed reform of mining legislation in the Philippines and the formulation of the Mining Act of 1995. Philippine government representatives have been prominent participants in numerous international seminars and training programmes. The Philippines' acceptance of the reform package has itself been projected through such meetings. The Philippine Mining Code 1995 closely follows the Bank template (c.f. the Philippines Case Study). The Bank also chose to project Western Mining Company (WMC) as a best practice company for their approach to investment in the Philippines. WMC was, at the time, a major backer, and the first beneficiary, of the mining code and was actively involved in its formulation.[238]

When enacted, the law was described by the Mining Journal as "among the most favourable to mining companies anywhere". Applications for exploration flooded the Mining Department[239]. This rapid expansion of mining was and remains opposed by Indigenous Peoples all across the Philippines, who based their negative response on past experience.

Mining has a long history in the Philippines, particularly in the Cordillera region, which is also the ancestral land of the largest concentration of indigenous peoples in the country. Mining companies have operated on Igorot lands for 100 years. They have dispossessed indigenous peoples not only of their mineral wealth (some Igorots are traditionally miners) but through mineral claims even of their surface rights to land and livelihood. No mine site in the region has been adequately restored and every mine in the region has experienced at least one serious tailings dam breach. The majority of these tailings dams have collapsed with catastrophic impacts downstream. Mining has seriously degraded the quality of all the major rivers flowing out of the Cordillera mining districts.

This negative analysis of the Philippine mining industry is shared even by industry and government consultants. Dr Allen Clark of the East West Centre in Hawaii observed, in a 1994 Asian Development Bank commissioned report, "We have never seen a mining industry with a poorer environmental record."[240]

Legal provisions have been developed in the Philippines for the protection of indigenous rights in decisions about mineral development within ancestral lands. These are contained both in the Indigenous Peoples Rights Act 1997 (IPRA) and the 1995 Mining Code. The framework of these laws could and should have provided a significant protection for the rights of indigenous peoples. However in practice according to numerous accounts[241] these provisions have been honoured more in the breach than the observance. Substantiated accounts of breach of the provisions of IPRA and the Mining Code in relation to FPIC and or other important issues come from many areas.

The decisions allowing or rejecting mining are momentous ones which require communities to be fully informed, well advised and possess sufficient time to conduct their own decision making processes. The implementing practice of the Mining Code and the IPRA is currently not allowing this. Implementing rules and regulations of the IPRA law have been repeatedly changed, following mining industry pressure, to further deprive communities of effective means of legally defending their rights. The time for lodging appeals has been reduced while no improvements have been made in transparency to allow communities to ascertain company claims regarding the achievement of FPIC. One unintended consequence of improvement of legislation concerning the protection of the rights of indigenous peoples is that new and sometimes illegal and coercive pressures are being applied to indigenous communities to secure by all means their "consent"

Different communities report militarization of isolated communities as a recurring element in engineering consent. There is grave concern at the conscious and successful effort of mining companies to introduce factionalism, divide communities and promote individuals who may have no traditional authority as leaders to represent the presence of FPIC where it does not exist. Reports suggest traditional leaders may be ignored or displaced where they oppose mining. Communities report the widespread use of bribes and gifts and unregulated and questionable patronage by companies over prominent individuals/decision-makers within their communities. Practices that, if applied to a local government official, might constitute an offence against graft and corruption laws are openly practiced to traditional leaders and others. The repeated accounts of collaboration by representatives of government agencies in such processes are particularly disturbing.

There is therefore a widespread scepticism in the processes of the 1995 Mining Code. Its repeal has been called for by the Catholic Bishops Conference of the Philippines, the National Council of Churches of the Philippines, the Dapitan Initiative, and the National Mining Consultation, Baguio 2003.

> Mining conflicts have already led to acts of civil disobedience, protest and violence. Legitimate protests have been branded subversive and mining sites increasingly maintained by militarization. Every indication is that mining related conflict is on the rise, and it seems inevitable that indigenous peoples will be the victims.
>
> These experiences reveal that even where legislation exists nominally to protect indigenous rights, and even where Bank identified "best practice" companies operate, we still cannot assume effective implementation or adequate safeguards. Without effective credible independent monitoring, abuses may reasonably be assumed to continue.

ment Technical Assistance Project (1983), the Gas Development and Utilisation Technical Assistance Project (2000), and the Mining Sector Institutional Strengthening Technical Assistance Project (2000) were all generally geared towards increasing private sector investment in extractive operations and increasing government capacity to encourage this investment and monitor it. Most of these projects have been classified under environmental categories C or B, which do not require environmental impact assessments, and do not trigger the scrutiny of the safeguard measures.

Research, including the OED report for this EI review, show that EI projects, while generating income for companies and central government (in 2001, the extractive sector accounted for two thirds of total exports), have mostly failed to reach the communities in improved services or benefits[242]. Indeed the extremely high externalised costs of mining in PNG leave a heavy burden on the mine-affected regions and peoples. The World Bank's own OED report for the EI Review identifies this PNG experience as illustrative of the reality that good governance is an essential prerequisite of positive outcomes for Bank projects.

In PNG, some environmental standards for mine operations are shamefully deficient, and despite the substantial influence of the Bank, are below international best practice in important areas. Indeed in relation to mine waste management PNG, supported by the Bank, allows the controversial practice of submarine tailings disposal, which is currently barred in the USA, Canada and Australia. In the case of the Lihir mine, supported by MIGA, STD is being applied on a small island where its impacts are, as a consequence, likely to be more severe for the local population in impacts on fisheries, coastal impacts, and health. The practice of direct dumping of mine waste into rivers is practiced by major inter-

Box 3: *New Technology Brings Heightened Misery*[243]

During the 1990s, Benguet Corporation, the Philippines oldest mining company, developed an open pit mine at the site of their former underground operation at Antamok Itogon within Ibaloi ancestral lands. They destroyed the community of Antamok with its school, clinic, and churches, to make way for the open pit, they also mined lands including indigenous burial sites, water sources, traditional settlements, and farms amongst others. The area has been severely depopulated as a consequence. The company incorporated in their operations the traditional surface ore deposits previously worked by indigenous miners. As a result of the shift to open pit mining they reduced their workforce from more than 6000 in the 1970s to less than 600 working the open pit and processing plant.

The ore deposit, which had been worked by indigenous miners for at least 1000 years and by the company continuously for more than 80 years, was by open pit methods worked out and closed within 7 years, finally closing in 1997, with a loss of all remaining jobs save a skeleton security staff. In the same period a large proportion of the 20000-24000 Igorot peoples in the area, engaged in or dependent upon small scale mining, had their livelihoods abruptly terminated by the expansion of company mining. An area noted for its prosperity and stable indigenous communities has become another area of hardship and out migration.

This area has seen no effective restoration, and the Antamok mine site is still bare and dusty. The run-off of silt and heavy metal-rich material into the Itogon River continues. A cyanide rich tailings pond, which was constructed adjacent to the pre-existing indigenous community of Loakan, lingers as a health and environmental hazard. The fumes from the pond pervade the air. The company continues to exercise its "rights" over the land, which has not been and, according to the company will not be restored to its original indigenous owners.

national companies in PNG but not in their operations elsewhere. The impact of this on the river and marine environment has been severe.

"Best Practice" from "Bad Actors"

Despite the widespread clamour for strict regulation of the extractive

Box 4: *WMC and Best Practice*

The Bank chose to highlight Western Mining Company (WMC) as a best practitioner, specifically in relation to the Tampakan project in the Philippines, because of the company's stated commitment and structural efforts, i.e. the formation of an indigenous peoples department, and the development of an Indigenous Peoples Plan within the Tampakan project. The company emphasised its approach to indigenous issues at Tampakan as being the project on which it sought to be judged. WMC did make efforts to inform and negotiate with communities, organised exposures to other mines, and entered agreements with tribal leaders, amongst other activities. However welcome these developments might seem on paper the promotion of WMC as a best practitioner was unacceptable to many, both historically and for its actual practice in Tampakan.

In the past, Hugh Morgan, CEO of WMC, has been one of the most vociferous critics of environmentalists and indigenous rights campaigners. The involvement of Morgan and WMC in the racist "Black Hands campaign" was unforgettable and unforgivable to many indigenous rights campaigners. The company also continues to have serious unresolved issues in relation to projects on indigenous lands particularly in South Australia. The practice of WMC within the Tampakan project has also been both well documented[244] and the subject of severe criticism both from local organisations and development agencies and church groups in the Philippines and Australia. WMC stand accused of dividing communities against themselves, making payments to leaders to secure their support, giving gifts and organising junkets for indigenous leaders/ decision makers in order to influence their decisions including outings to night clubs and bars away from the community, and along with government agencies rushing indigenous leaders into signing agreements without adequate preparation or understanding (too short notice, inadequate consultation, failure to explain the full complexity of the agreements, absence of legal advice, version only presented in English.) According to Muntz, the Tribal Principal Agreements in particular contained a gross imbalance of benefit for the company:

> *The fundamental issue with these Tribal Principal Agreements (TPAs) was the unequal nature of the commitments involved by each party. They committed the communities*

*irrevocably to allow mining on their land for the duration of the process, from exploration to mining to rehabilitation of the mine site at the end. In return the agreements required the company to make various financial commitments to community development programs in the tribal communities, but left it with **absolute discretion** about almost everything else. The company had achieved what every business craves, total certainty over at least one aspect of its operation. But the communities gained no certainty whatsoever about any of the crucial social and environmental parameters of mining, only the financial compensation for mining damage, and the royalties from it.[245]*

Despite its efforts, WMC failed to secure the support of many in the local communities. Eventually WMC withdrew from the project. However despite WMC's stated commitment to "best practice" at Tampakan, in the face of sustained opposition they sold their rights to other mining interests. This left the local B'laan peoples with a deep uncertainty over commitments entered into by WMC.

industries, the World Bank has, in the EI sector, focused its efforts on various non-binding efforts to promote "best practice". The Bank has chosen to do this by the projection of certain leading companies. It has partnered their initiatives and funded their projects. In mineral extraction however, many companies and many projects have been accused of serious violations of rights. A problem therefore has been finding companies whose own record is adequate to the exposure.

The perpetrator of the destructive and irresponsible mine waste management system at the notorious Ok Tedi mine in PNG was BHP, now BHPBilliton, the world's largest mining company. In the case of Ok Tedi the damage to the river and environment has already had a direct negative impact on the subsistence activities, livelihood and health of people living along the Fly River. Further, the silt, acid and heavy metals build-up from the tailings deposited in the Ok Tedi and Fly rivers has resulted in the severe reduction of river life and biodiversity and in die back of forest cover.

This condition is still deteriorating and it is predicted to continue to do so for many years to come.[246] Community representatives have filed legal cases against BHP (now BHPB), which was the main owner and operator of Ok Tedi, in an attempt to force the company to acknowledge liability. In efforts to prevent local ancestral land holders from pursuing their case against BHP in the Australian courts, the company engaged in interference in the political process in PNG. Following initial denial, BHP was forced to confess that it had helped draft a PNG law seeking to outlaw the legal process followed by the landholders. The purpose was clearly to silence the landholders and prevent their case coming to court. This strategy failed when the Australian court ruled the company in contempt when their involvement in this skulduggery was revealed.

The company was eventually forced to enter an out of court settlement promising to pay damages and undertake management improvements. In practice the company has so far failed to honour the settlement and the ancestral land-holders have returned to court. Meanwhile BHPB have exited the project after first pressuring local people and the Government to agree to a final settlement package that once again seeks to undermine the ongoing legal action. The deal offers a cheap and finite settlement to a pollution problem that is currently continuing to expand and whose final costs are likely to be many times more.[247]

BHPBilliton have therefore, at Ok Tedi and other projects [See Box 7, p.92], a track record of environmental and social failures, deviousness, and manipulation yet the Bank continues to cooperate with the company and finance its projects.

Substantiated cases of environmental or social abuses have been cited against many other companies that still are seen as acceptable partners by the Bank. In the case of AMF the company was indicted by a UN panel of experts into illegal activities in the Congo shortly before it became an IFC partner [See Box 5, p.85]

The wilful breach of existing standards and even legal requirements perpetrated by a range of companies argues that good faith or best practice cannot be presumed even from leading EI companies. Where mines exist there is the need for independent, adequately resourced, rigorous and frequent monitoring of mines and mining company activities to safeguard the interests of affected communities and the wider society, if only for the reason that the consequences of failures in EI projects can be so serious. Much evidence reveals that where indigenous rights are not adequately protected in law and practice then abuses by companies tend to continue to occur.

Dialogue, Conciliation

The Bank has been subject to strong criticism particularly from indigenous peoples and organisations for its sustained support for unacceptable mining projects. So far the Bank response, rather than concentrate

Box 5: *The UN indicts while the IFC invites*

In February 2003, America Mineral Fields Inc. (AMF) signed an agreement with the IFC and South Africa's Industrial Development Corporation to participate in a new copper-cobalt tailings treatment scheme at Kolwezi in the Democratic Republic of Congo (DRC), formerly operated by the state mining company, Gecamines. The agreement includes the right of IFC to buy equity in AMF.[249]

AMF and its founder, and chief shareholder, Jean-Raymond Boulle, are notorious. As bloody conflict over resources raged in Zaire during the nineties, AMF became the chief vehicle by which Boulle expanded into Africa. Boulle has been described, as "a man who can manoeuvre as a privileged and powerful player in several regions and markets. In environments of chaos, state collapse and economic decay, a powerful private player with access to significant amounts of money, raw materials, military technology and even a private rapid reaction force, can deviously pursue his own private agenda."[250] Jean-Raymond Boulle has now obtained control of a substantial portion of DRC's strategic minerals. Boulle first acquired the valuable Kolwezi workings five years ago, in return for loaning then-rebel leader Kabila his private jet and donating US$1 billion to Kabila's anti-Mobutu campaign[251].

Now registered in London, AMF started life as a petroleum company in 1979. From 1995, under Boulle, it expanded in Africa, in DRC, Zambia and Angola. Boulle had been De Beer's "diamond czar" in the Congo/Zairean capital, Kinshasha, when the country was in fief to Mobutu.[252] AMF has been accused by authoritative researchers of having been linked in the recent past with IDAS (International Defence and Security), a spin-off of the notorious Executive Outcomes mercenary force, and the British-based Defence Systems Ltd, another band of paramilitaries active in securing mineral resources in conflict areas, also based in London[253]. IFC is now supporting AMF in the DRC. Astonishingly, their deal followed shortly after the indictment of AMF (along with several other companies) by a UN panel of experts inquiring into illegal activities in the Democratic Republic of Congo: the company was accused of violating the OECD Guidelines for Multinational Enterprises.[254]

on the specific concerns and wishes of affected communities, has instead developed general programmes like Business Partners for Development, which has failed even within its own terms.[248] BPD was to be a multistakeholder initiative to seek to explore new means to resolve disputes. The BPD had an Extractive Industries sector within it. Yet in practice even the claims of multistakeholder participation are rather threadbare. An assessment of the EI cluster project reports that only one Government (the United Kingdom) and one NGO (CARE International) participated. The companies involved expressed disappointment that BPD was not able to address their central concerns. BPD made attempted interventions in several projects including the Kelian mine run by Rio Tinto in Indonesian Kalimantan and which was a place of conflict and protest by indigenous peoples throughout the 1990s. [See Box 13, p. 114]

The Bank has also responded to critics by developing the Compliance Advisor Ombudsman (CAO) and the Inspection Panel mechanisms. While these mechanisms offer the prospect of recognising and investigating complaints there has been strong criticism that even here the emphasis is on conciliation and amelioration whatever the nature of the complaint [See Box 9, p. 105].

The Bank has prepared documents, videos and also organised seminars, including in Quito and Madang on the subject of "Mining and the Community", which have provided a forum for the presentation of Bank ideas and a dialogue among participants on issues of community relations. Such seminars have, as with so many other initiatives, tended to be dominated by participants from the Bank, government departments and mining companies, with the attendance of some NGOs. This was the case for the above, despite their topic being focused upon improving community relations. However communities and indigenous organisations, particularly those in dispute with companies, have been seriously under-represented. Nonetheless publications from such seminars have made some information and opinions more widely available.

Multistakeholder Dialogue

The Bank is increasingly using multistakeholder dialogues to address the concerns of its critics. Such efforts abound, the Extractive Industries Review being but one example. However while multistakeholder dialogues are seen to carry a credibility, which is absent from internal review, there is growing concern about the abuse of this credibility resulting in its diminution.

There are, as yet, no standards applied to the adequacy of the participation or quality of access and control within such processes. There are no standards to assure the independence and credibility of the processes. Consequently, even these processes are being discredited by over-zealous claims or cynical manipulation. The World Commission on Dams (WCD), in which the Bank was involved, set new standards of participation, independence of management and process, and consensual outcomes that might be reasonably assumed to form a minimum for future initiatives. Sadly this has been far from the case. Despite its role in the formation and financing of the WCD, the Bank has failed to respond adequately to its recommendations.

The EIR, which originally was characterised by Bank President Wolfensohn to civil society groups as an activity in the mould of WCD, has a significantly different structure. The shortcomings of the structure and process mean it clearly fails to maintain the standards set in the WCD process in governance and process. This has inevitably affected its credibility and will erode the authority of the conclusions. Civil society groups highlighted these shortcomings at the outset and have reiterated them at every stage[255].

Global Mining Initiative/ MMSD

The Bank has also endorsed other controversial processes that have tended to generate more suspicion than harmony. The Global Mining Initiative, and particularly its Mining, Minerals, and Sustainable Development project, launched by the mining industry is a case in point. This initiative was set up by the industry to address issues seen as critical to its future credibility. As with the EIR, the central question concerned the potential role of mining in sustainable development. Yet the industry unilaterally imposed the definition of problems, the management structure, the selection of a host for the project, even the selection to the MMSD process monitoring committee. The major source of all funding was the industry, which provided $7 million.

Given the deep suspicion that exists in the sector, generated in part by the industry's regrettable history of one-sided initiatives and self-declared and "self regulated" codes of conduct, such an approach inevitably led to suspicion among civil society groups and indigenous organisations[256]. There is a widespread concern that industry's willingness to sign up to binding agreements on generalised issues concerning improved standards has been more directed at improving the poor image of mining rather than in improvements in on-site practice.

A number of groups directly involved in mine monitoring wrote early on in the MMSD process to appeal for, among others, a restructuring of MMSD project control and a broadening of its central goal to incorporate the priority concerns of mine-affected communities[257]. When this was rejected the majority of civil society groups, indigenous organisations and affected communities who knew of the initiative chose to boycott the process[258]. This has been repeated by some with regard the EIR process. For most of the period of the MMSD project, the assurance group had no participation from any indigenous representation. Low attendance at indigenous workshops revealed a widespread scepticism. Indigenous organisations who attended one such event also report that they did so only due to misrepresentation. For example, among the indigenous participants in an indigenous workshop concerning the project, some attended unaware of the links to MMSD[259].

Despite the widespread rejection of MMSD and its commitments to the contrary, the project and the associated Toronto conference "Resourcing the Future" were subsequently represented as a credible multi-stakeholder dialogue. The mining industry has been particularly enthusiastic in hailing this failed process as a mandate for their interventions in the WSSD processes.

The World Bank uncritically accepted the legitimacy of the MMSD. It acted as one of the few non-industry sponsors of the project and contributed to its financing. The MMSD and the Bank held joint workshops within the process where the multistakeholder claims for the project were uncritically endorsed.

ENVIRONMENTAL GUIDELINES

The World Bank Group has developed and promoted environmental guidelines with the purpose of ensuring adequate safeguards in relation to environmental protection.

These guidelines have also been the subject of criticism. Critics have pointed to the severe damage caused by the environmental impacts of mining and mine-related management failures and deficiencies as evidence for the need to both substantially raise environmental safeguard standards in mining and effectively uphold such standards. The Bank therefore has been criticised for pitching its environmental standards too low. In some significant aspects including marine disposal of mine waste, riverine disposal, and minimum standards for tailings dams the Bank has identified standards below those that already apply in active mining economies in the north including the USA and Canada. This has been maintained despite serious negative experience by the Bank of environmental damage caused even within Bank-supported projects including the Omai mine in Guyana, Freeport mine in West Papua, Kumtor mine in Kyrgyzstan and Lihir mine in PNG.

Box 6: *Omai - The Poisoned Chalice*

At close to midnight on August 19th 1995, the tailings dam of the Omai gold mine in Guyana, burst its bounds, propelling around four billion cubic litres of mine effluent into a local creek and then into the country,s main waterway, the Essequibo river. What the country's then president, Cheddi Jagan, called "the country's worst environmental disaster" has been the subject of numerous articles and several major reports. The World Bank, through MIGA along with Canada's EDC provided critical political risk insurance covers for the Omai partners, Cambior and Golden Star Resources (both Canadian) and the Guyana government itself.

MIGA dismally failed to properly assess the standards of mine construction. Although the company claimed to have observed North American standards, these were ones set in Quebec rather than higher ones followed in Ontario or by the US EPA. The partners failed to line the tailings dam with HDPE covers and to protect groundwater resources. Worse, they permitted the dam wall to rise far above limits set in the original EIA almost certainly the key factor in ensuring that wastes would overwhelm the dam's capacity to contain them.

As the scenario for disaster developed during late 1994 and early 1995, several observers pointed out that a collapse was virtually inevitable[261]. There had in fact been three "spills" already over the previous six months, when cyanide poisoned the river's fish. These, combined with an admission by Cambior that the dam was filling to its brink, led Omai to petition the government to be allowed to discharge treated wastes directly into the river. The government refused on environmental grounds, but the mine continued to operate until the dam's collapse in August that year. Throughout this critical period, MIGA failed to monitor mine safety, let alone insist on a precautionary closure of its operations. The United Nations Development Programme (UNDP) concluded that the "baseline and continuous monitoring at Omai have largely been inadequate".

The mine was allowed to re-open in 1996, albeit with several new technological improvements, but before a parliamentary sub-commission on the disaster had delivered its final report. The World Bank, from its early promotion of Guyana's "structural adjustment" - based inevitably on privatisation - had regarded Omai as a tangible example of the large-scale minerals-related investment which must be imposed upon a highly indebted country. It was certainly not going to argue that the disaster proved the mine was unacceptable. Indeed, two months after the dam collapse, Gerald T West, MIGA's Senior Advisor for Guarantees, offered his opinion that the damage had been grossly overestimated. According to a Guyanese member of parliament, MIGA told the ensuing Omai inquiry that, if the government imposed any new environmental regulations on the mine, the agency would consider this "tantamount to nationalisation" compelling it to pay compensation to Cambior and Golden Star[262.]

The Bank guidelines therefore are seen as being insufficient to raise mining environmental safeguards to more acceptable levels.

The worst nightmare faced by any mining company is perhaps for its tailings containment facility to collapse, pouring thousands, if not millions of gallons of cyanide and/or heavy metals-laced sludge into neighbouring streams and rivers. At least one such disaster has occurred each year over the past thirteen years.[260] The industry's International Commission on Metals and Mining (ICMM) points to 1-3 per annum. Among the worst disasters ever to have occurred have been mines supported and assessed by the World Bank.

One problem that derives from the existence of the guidelines, but contrary to its stated intentions, is the proliferation of claims by companies to be adhering to "Best International Standards" represented by the Bank guidelines. Clearly the claim by such companies is misleading since the Bank guidelines do not currently represent international best practice in certain key respects. Secondly, companies who are not funded or scrutinised by the Bank in any way are increasingly making such claims to add credibility and the seeming authority of Bank backing to their proposed plans. TVI Pacific for example, a company that has met with strong local opposition to its operations from the Subanen people in the Philippines, has announced that it intends to operate to "Best International Standards" which it defines itself as compliance with Bank guidelines.

The same company has also claimed that its proposed mine will be part of a World Bank-supported regional development for the area. Despite research efforts it has not been able to verify the validity of these claims. There is no record of the Bank having involvement in this project. It is the consequence of the current Bank approach however that there is no mechanism to regulate or prevent such questionable claims. TVI is a company accused of abuses and environmental mismanagement by the Subanen. Company claims regarding adherence to Bank standards only tend to reflect badly on the Bank. However in the absence of effective monitoring and enforcement, such claims are becoming commonplace. Currently no one is in a position to assess their relationship to actual practice and the overall effect is to undermine the credibility of all regulatory frameworks.

The IFC

The emphasis placed in the Bank on development through privatisation, mobilising private capital for direct investment and expanding the reach of the global economy have all tended to strengthen the relative role of the IFC in project financing. Its pivotal role in the funding of extractive projects has been highly controversial in a number of cases, including the Chad-Cameroon Oil Pipeline Project, implemented by ChevronTexaco-ExxonMobil consortium, the Yanacocha Gold Mine in Peru, which is owned by Newmont, and the BP-owned Baku-Ceyhan Oil Pipeline in Georgia and Azerbaijan, and most recently its support for gold mining development in Laos and diamond mining in Botswana. [*See Box 7, p. 92*]

The IFC is notorious for long having operated to lower standards of rigour on environmental and social standards than other parts of the Bank. In addition there are instances where the IFC has misclassified projects or misrepresented the local situation to avoid rigorous scrutiny and particularly the application of Bank safeguards. Throughout the Bank it has proved difficult to get any branch of the institution to accept the legitimacy of questions concerning allegations of bad practice in projects it is funding. In the case of IFC it holds significant numbers of shares in some projects and has proved, as a result, to be even more reticent to acknowledge the validity of criticism.

The IFC has long stood by "bad actor" countries as well as companies. It invested in Chile by purchasing equity in the vast Escondida copper mine while the country suffered under the iron fist of the Pinochet military regime. Recently (2001) in Laos, which is governed by an undemocratic regime widely recognised as abusing human rights, the IFC has bankrolled Oxiana Resources (OR) and OR's own chief financier, Rio Tinto. The IFC has even used the status of the regime and the reticence of other investors as a justification, maintaining that "political and regulatory uncertainties" have "dissuaded the world's larger companies from investing in the country".[263] The Sepon mine will, in the IFC's own words "require the relocation of two [Indigenous] villages

Box 7: *IFC and BHPBilliton in Botswana*

In its current decision to support the activities of
BHPBilliton in Botswana the IFC has broken its own investment criteria. BHPB are seeking to explore for diamonds on San
bushman territory. Despite an IFC policy not to fund exploration activity, this case has been made an exception. Here as
elsewhere (e.g. Yanacocha) the IFC has unilaterally decided to
question the indigenous status of the affected communities,
presumably in a conscious effort to circumvent Bank requirements concerning projects affecting indigenous peoples.

Kalahari Diamonds Ltd is an (as yet) unlisted company,
set up only in March 2003 to explore great tracts of Botswana,
many of which are traditional lands of the San hunter-gatherer
peoples. The company currently has an impressive capital base
of more than twenty million dollars ($US 21 million), raised
from a group of influential backers including Antwerp diamond merchants -- headed by the world's biggest mining
company, BHPBilliton (20%), and the IFC (10%). [*Mining Journal*
21/3/2003.] The plan is to register the company on London-
based AIM (Alternative Investment Market) over the next 2-3
years.

Although Botswana is the most successful diamond-
mining nation on the planet (thanks to extremely high quality
output), BHPBilliton will now investigate new diamondiferous
kimberlite pipes over no less than 30% of the country's prospective terrain. The Botswana government has the right to buy an
interest in any future mine, but BHPB may also buy back up to
60% of Kalahari's interest in any newly located mineral deposit.

The IFC defends its involvement with KDL as, *inter alia*,
"making [the company] a leader in sustainable mining development initiatives [and] in defining the principles for support and
improvement of local communities". [264]

But the IFC also acknowledges that its role "is likely to
come under close scrutiny from civil society and the media",
since a third of KDL's exploration licences fall within the
Central Kalahari Game Reserve, home to the indigenous Gana
and Gwi San Bushmen". [265]

Extraordinarily, while identifying the London-based
Survival International as a vociferous opponent of such exploration, the IFC's appraisal mission "did not identify any groups
in Botswana opposed to the project or the IFC's involvement".[266]

A cursory glance at Survival's website reveals a very different picture. Not only have several San spokespeople vigorously opposed such trespass on or over their territory; so have Botswanan human rights workers[267].

It's unusual for the IFC to invest at such an early stage in a mining project and regrettable given the clear local opposition by local people. Apart from profit motive it is difficult to see why the World Bank has entered at this stage. The IFC confesses that its experience in "early entry" mining projects has been "mixed"[268].

A successful outcome of KDL's exploration would, according to the IFC, "bring in new foreign exchange and fiscal receipts for the government, providing an important engine for growth and implicitly a source of financing to support the social sector, especially HIV/AIDS projects, economic diversification, infrastructure development and poverty reduction programmes". But much of this contention is both moot and speculative. Botswana has an average growth rate of 7% a year, making it the highest in the developing world[269] as well as high internal liquidity and foreign exchange reserves which will cover another two and a half year of imports[270].

While Botswana's status as a lower middle-income country could clearly be improved one may wonder why -- as the world's biggest diamond producer -- profits have failed so far to be better distributed as development benefits among its poorer citizens. Nor is there a compelling reason to jeopardise the precarious livelihoods of its indigenous people, when the existing diamond pipes at Orapa and Jwaneng (itself bringing in annual revenues of US$1.5 billion) are as the IFC itself agrees -- of "exceptional size and host resources that will support mining operations for over 20 [more] years"[271]. In fact, according to the IFC, Janeng is "the most profitable mine anywhere, enjoying production costs lower than 6% of revenue"[272].

It is difficult to understand how the investment can be prioritised in development terms. BHPBilliton, as the world's largest mining company, is one of the last companies on earth actually to need IFC finance. It looks increasingly that the IFC involvement is to provide some credibility to a project already under severe attack for its violation of Indigenous rights and that for IFC the pay off is the speculation that they will hold a share in a major diamond mine and their most profitable investment to date.

The Botswana government's protestations last year that

the San had not been removed from the Central Kalahari game reserve (as they were until 2001) in order to facilitate the entry of mining companies, are now looking increasingly thread-bare[273]. IFC's spurious contention that, since all Botswanans are "indigenous" the San cannot claim special status, exposes a wilful ignorance among IFC staff and the use of self-serving denial of status to indigenous peoples. Despite the IFC denial of the San special status it reports contradictorily that KDL will "ensure that all project affected peoples receive culturally compatible social and economic benefits in compliance with WB OD 4.20 Indigenous Peoples policy"[274]. This misses the central point that at least some San groups do not want the project and certainly oppose removal, especially forced re-moval, from their lands. Also, as the Botswana government is accused of forcibly resettling the San, not to protect their livelihoods but the opposite, there seems no basis for optimistic assumptions of benefit for the affected peoples.

BHPB is faced with a public relations problem. It has involved the IFC in its Botswana adventure on the basis of promises of "sustainable development" initiatives and Impact Benefits Agreement packages introduced at its Ekati mine in Canada. This, even though it had experienced stiff and pro-longed opposition from many in the Dene nation, and even though its 1996 compensation agreement with 30,000 villagers affected by its mismanagement of the Ok Tedi gold/copper mine in Papua New Guinea has still not been properly imple-mented and is certainly the opposite of sustainable develop-ment.

(120 people) -- if only to an area fairly close to their existing homes." It is difficult to image how the rights or wishes of the affected communities are assured in such a process within the current Laotian state.

The Chad-Cameroon Pipeline Project (CCP), Africa's largest devel-opment project, was approved in June 2000, after a lengthy and well-founded campaign against it, supported by far-reaching environmental and human rights NGOs. The CCP starts in the Doba oil fields at the southern tip of Chad, splits Cameroon in two along 670 miles, and ends at Kribi on the South-west coast of Cameroon. It traverses some of the most important rainforest remaining in the Congo basin, and cuts through the lands of the Bagyéli (pygmy) peoples. Promoted by the World Bank as a unique opportunity for "[it] to play a significant complementary role in reducing poverty in one of Africa's poorest regions", this project would not have been commenced without the benediction and funds of the Bank. It has been hailed by global development players as a "defining moment in World Bank history", and "a prism through which the world views the institution and, it is likely, development assistance more broadly."

Clearly, the World Bank needs to prove that local communities and countries will truly benefit from this project in a lasting and sustainable way. This, unfortunately, is far from being the current reality. Even prior to construction, human rights abuses, repression and violence had occurred. Now, with construction roaring ahead, and due to be completed ahead of schedule, it is a tragedy. Violence and abuse have escalated in Chad, and the very survival of the Bagyéli in Cameroon is at risk. The latter depend almost entirely on the forest and forest products to provide for their subsistence-based lifestyle; increased logging, the high demand for bushmeat, loss of water resources, in-migration and social upheaval brought by the pipeline have left them with little to survive upon, and under severe cultural attack.

The World Bank's safeguard policy framework has remained largely unimplemented, and the current plight of the Bagyéli peoples is a violation of their human rights under significant and diverse human rights instruments[275]. In addition, in order to partially address the environmental problems caused by the pipeline project, the World Bank has, through the GEF, established two national parks in southeastern Cameroon, which arc now denying the traditional access rights to the Bagyéli population in that region. The IFC's involvement in this project has brought poverty, hunger and social collapse to the local communities.

The IFC has a key role in the Yanacocha mine in Peru, owned and controlled by US-based Newmont mining. It was a critical catalyst for the provision of private loans and owns 5% of the shares itself. In 2000, the IFC facilitated an $80 million loan for the further expansion of the mine. This was opposed by many locals including the local authority. The mine location coincides with a number of important rivers and tributaries upon which the city of Cajamarca and the surrounding rural communities depend. These have already been severely polluted by the mine's operations, and remain unusable for a large part.

Since its inception, a failure to respect the wishes of the local campesino community or effectively protect the surrounding environment has been observed, and a complaint was filed by FEROCAFENOP and Project Underground, a US based NGO, with the Compliance Advisor Ombudsman (CAO) of the IFC [See Box 9, p. 105]. The IFC's Environmental Impact Survey here denies the indigenous roots of the campesino communities, despite most of them only speaking their native language, Quechua, and themselves self-identifying as indigenous peoples[276]. The refusal of IFC to recognise this indigenous status exempted the Bank from having to provide an indigenous peoples development plan and from adhering to the Operational Directive OD 4.20 on indigenous peoples.

It also gives it greater leeway with respect to resettlement, to which 226 families were subject. Resettlement was however termed "relocation" because according to IFC specialists, the people involved were merely temporary or seasonal land owners, thus exempting the IFC from the need to prepare any resettlement plans. This claim nevertheless contravenes OP 4.12 on Involuntary Resettlement which covers "(i) relocation or loss of shelter; (ii) loss of assets or access to assets; or (iii) loss of income sources or means of livelihood, *whether or not the affected person must move to another location;…*" (emphasis added) which renders the IFC's assertions invalid.[277]

One of the most significant local concerns in the Cajamarca area is the contamination of the sources of water, a scarce and vital resource in the uplands, which is used for drinking, cooking, bathing, irrigation and for animal husbandry. Ongoing monitoring has led to reports citing dewatering (Newmont acknowledges it has depleted water levels in 4 out of 6 lakes in the region – this results in less irrigation water for local subsistence farmers), water contamination (Yanacocha gold mine is breaching WHO standards for drinking water, through leaching of cyanide solution, iron, sulfates and copper; the Yanacocha gold mine has contaminated 4 rivers, the only water source for many campesinos), fish and endemic frog species die-off (also found by the Peruvian Ministry of Fishing), air pollution, loss of biodiversity, including medicinal plants and frogs.

In addition, on June 2, 2000, a truck spilled over 300 pounds of mercury in Choropampa, a rural village, and although the IFC claims that adequate consultation was held with the community, no one was aware of the dangers of mercury, and when the truck was struck down, many campesinos picked up the little balls of mercury and brought them home with them believing it was valuable, resulting in serious illness for over 400 people[278].

The locals are steadily being forced to move to the town of Cajamarca, and as a result the close family and kinship ties are being lost, as men have to move away to find work in order to pay the rent. Traditional arts and crafts are being lost as the people are removed from their land and cultural base[279]. This results in the total disarticulation of the social economy, upon which the continuance of the culture is based.

The Federation of Las Rondas Campesinas (LRC), a constitution-ally recognised organisation has set up an office in Cajamarca where they deal with social issues, including problems surrounding the Yanacocha mine, the rights of women and indigenous crafts. Yanacocha has provided the most work for them for the past few years. Family-related problems (non-recognition of children, abandonment of fami-lies, failure to pay child support, domestic abuse) have all been on the rise since the mine was started (from 8% to 25% of the problems LRC was dealing with, before and after mining began, respectively). Debt prob-lems have sky-rocketed from 2% in 1986-88 to 44% in 1995-97, which increase the feeling of inadequacy and resentment within the popula-tion, specifically the men.

The Multilateral Investment Guarantee Agency (MIGA)

In 2001, MIGA issued the following statement in rebuttal of NGO ex-pressions of concern about its guarantees:

> *MIGA's activities do not promote or subsidize poor corporate behaviour at the expense of people and the environment. The broad statements made in the report that MIGA's activities are anti-envi-ronmental and fail to promote economic growth or alleviate poverty are untrue. And there is no evidence to support the claims that MIGA's clients have poor environmental and human rights records. On the contrary, the agency supports only projects that have a positive developmental impact, sponsored by corporate clients who operate by the guiding principle that 'good corporate citizenship is good business'.[280]*

The Multilateral Investment Guarantee Agency was set up by the World Bank at the beginning of the 1990s for the provision of political risk insurance loans to private companies wishing to invest in develop-ment projects undertaken in developing countries where alternative cover was difficult to obtain due to political instability. The formation of MIGA was one concrete response to the demands of international companies for guarantees to protect investments in the South. MIGA is a significant contributor to World Bank activities in extractive industries sector, and some of the projects it supports have had far-reaching social and envi-ronmental implications.

However, MIGA, like IFC, operates as a commercial enterprise and according to commercial standards. When information disclosure con-cerning these projects is sought, the MIGA frequently invokes company privacy clauses inhibiting it from providing operation information, rendering this branch of the World Bank both opaque and lacking in accountability. In 1999, the MIGA elaborated its own reduced set of safeguard policies, namely a policy on Environmental Assessment and one on Information Disclosure. The latter however still does not appear to operate in many cases.

The MIGA has provided guarantees for projects in Papua New Guinea and West Papua among others, because these two countries are said to have an inherently unstable political and economic record. Indeed the first mining project insured by MIGA was the giant Freeport mine in West Papua. The irony of this is that the instability of West Papua is closely associated with and largely caused by this mine. The Grasberg mine is the world's largest copper and gold mine owned by Freeport McMoran of the USA and Rio Tinto UK; it is also one of the world's most notorious mining projects.

MIGA also extended support to the Lihir mine in Papua New Guinea, a project of Rio Tinto. Although widely broadcast as a pioneering project in terms of community participation, the Lihir mine has generated many problems. The MIGA guarantee was provided conditionally to a controversial structural adjustment programme (SAP) being accepted by the PNG government. This SAP required the government to cut public sector employment, abolish price controls of basic foodstuffs and minimum wages, introduce hospital fees and render obligatory the registration of customary land tenure[281]. Since 97% of PNG's land is owned by indigenous people through customary tenure, necessary registration would break the age-old accepted system and ultimately threaten loss of land rights to many.

On the island of Lihir, the people have suffered severe cultural and economic disruption as a direct result of the mine. Local lay and church leaders have complained of the breakdown of communal values, rise in gambling, drinking and other vices, damage to sacred sites and lasting damage to the land and sea. The project will destroy one of the most revered religious sites in Lihir, as well as graveyards and culturally important hot springs, all of which violate World Bank safeguard policies on Indigenous Peoples, Natural Habitats and Cultural Property. All were associated with the introduced cash economy overpowering and displacing the pattern of local subsistence economy.

MIGA gave its approval to Lihir despite the use by the company of experimental and dangerous technologies. The mine operates on a small island. Best practice in the mining industry suggests that mining on small islands, especially where inhabited, should be avoided because of the disproportionately large impact especially from the waste. In addition the Lihir mine adopted Submarine Tailings Disposal (STD). The processing of millions of tonnes of ore over the 40 years of mine lease is estimated to result in 341 million tonnes of waste rock[282]. It is expected that 1,800 tonnes of toxic sodium cyanide will be used annually to separate the gold ore from the body of the rock[283]. Residues of the cyanide and other toxics in the ore will be discharged into the sea. This disposal mechanism will severely affect the biodiversity-rich coastal environment, and have fundamental knock-on effects on the livelihoods of subsistence fishers from the coastal areas. According to local fisherfolk this has already occurred. The company has in fact been brought to court by Greenpeace in 2002, accusing them of dumping levels of pollutant vastly exceeding internationally set standards, established under the London Convention on Sea Dumping.[284]

Guaranteeing Disaster

In 1992, MIGA issued two reinsurance contracts totalling $49.8 to the Canadian mining companies, Cambior Montreal in partnership with Golden Star, to mine gold in the Omai mine in Guyana [*see Box, p. 89*]. In 1995, in one of the most serious environmental disasters in Guyana's history, a faulty tailings dam ruptured, releasing 3 to 4 cubic metres of cyanide, and toxic heavy metal-laced sludge into the Omai and the Essequibo rivers. The spill resulted in the loss of drinking water and domestic water, as well as the temporary loss of livelihood for 23,000 indigenous and local communities, who depend almost entirely on the river for their day-to-day subsistence needs and whose lives were severely and disproportionately affected by the spill. In 1997, Lecherches Internationales Québec, a Canadian NGO, filed a motion to authorise a class action law suit on behalf of the victims of the spill, but the suit was dismissed in Canada on the grounds that it should be heard in Guyana. Yet within Guyana the government is a shareholder in the mine and attempts at legal redress have not prospered. Many people remain to this day without adequate compensation and living a life of continued deprivation.

Despite the fact that many indigenous families, living along the banks of the Essequibo, alleged they had suffered major losses of their fish, pollution of their crucial freshwater supplies, and adverse health effects, they were never adequately compensated. Attempts to bring claims against the company and the Bank are continuing. [285]

In August 2000, more than seventy Russian and international NGOs called on the World Bank not to support environmentally sensitive projects including mining operations in the wake of the new President, Vladimir Putin's abolition of the country's main environmental agency.

Box 8: *Comsur and World Bank in Bolivia*

The year following Omai, a tailings dam in the Bolivian mining region of Potosi, operated by the country's largest private mining enterprise, Comsur, collapsed twice. Locally based scientists believe that up to 400,000 tonnes of sludge, loaded with iron sulphides, lead, zinc, cadmium, copper and arsenic, cascaded into the El Porco river[287] (The Company itself came up with a figure of 180,000 tonnes[288]). Three hundred square kilometres of river and farmland, tilled by some 50,000 indigenous campesinos, was contaminated[289] and wastes reached as far as the Pilcamayo basin[290].

Comsur was part-funded by the IFC in 1994 just after its owner, Goni Lozado, won the Bolivian presidential elections for the first time on a "neo-liberal" ticket. Comsur had been recapitalised in 1992 by Rio Tinto (then RTZ), which bought up a third of its equity, thus undoubtedly providing the imprimatur of "good actor" as ostensibly required by the Bank.

One savage irony is that, not only were the Omai and Comsur mines managed by high profile mining companies but that almost every major tailings disaster since 1991 has been directly attributable to the irresponsibility of companies which are viewed by the Bank as precisely "its kind of player."[291]

Despite this, MIGA went ahead in granting a US$27.2 million political risk cover to an untried company called New Arian Resources, a subsidiary of Bema Gold based in Canada, for the construction of the 79%-owned Julietta underground gold and silver mine in Magadan, an indigenous part of Russia's Far East Region[286]. No information on the project or its social and environmental impacts was released by MIGA before issuing the guarantee. How did the agency justify this critical failure? It said the project was approved before its disclosure policy went into effect in July 1999, so it was not required to divulge the vital information.

MIGA defended the project in an August 2000 letter to the Pacific Environment and Resources Center. The mine would "have a positive development impact on the Russian economy" while MIGA involvement "should also provide comfort to all concerned that compliance with the World Bank Group's environmental guidelines and Russian environmental law will be monitored carefully"[292].

But, according to a technical expert who visited the project in February and March 2001, Bema had already violated good practice principles. The tailings dam is located on an area "far larger than needed" which had been "stripped down to the permafrost level [with] the insulating and moisture-absorbing layers of soil, tundra and organic material removed ... the dam is less than 50 yards from a stream and two kilometres from a major river which could be affected by seepage or a larger cyanide spill"[293].

The Bank's lack of oversight in the case of the Julietta project is all the more culpable given its record over the past five years in the case of the huge Kumtor mine in Kyrgyzstan, operated by another Canadian company — Cameco. This too is located under permafrost and threatens the surrounding glacial environment. But whereas a "failure" has yet to occur at Julietta, several disasters have already afflicted Kumtor. The worst of these happened in 1998 when a truck carrying sodium cyanide slithered off an inadequate approach road, dumping part of its cargo into the river.

Global Environment Facility

The Global Environment Facility was established in 1992 nominally in order to provide a global fund for environment projects which affect the planet as a whole, such as climate change and fishery depletion, although it also provides grants to single states. It is financed through the World Bank and the UNDP, and its programmes and projects operated by both these "Implementing Agencies". The UNDP and the World Bank operate different types of grants however, the former being in charge of small grant projects, whilst the latter financing the larger scale international grants. The GEF is linked to the Bank, through staff and funding mechanisms, and its offices are found within the Bank's buildings in Washington.

Since its inception the World Bank has essentially used the GEF as a mechanism for externalising the accumulation of environmental debt it accrues through the polluting and destructive projects it finances. The World Bank provides large amounts of grant money to GEF projects, has control over how they are implemented, and is accused of using it to paint a veneer of environmental concern over its most harmful activities. In addition, the large and costly GEF programmes supported by the Bank have suffered many failures.

An example of the World Bank's use of the GEF to secure a green-tinted censure-defusing asset is that of the establishment of two national parks in southeast Cameroon (the Campo Ma'an National Park and the Mbam Djerem National Park) as biodiversity-offset areas to compensate for the loss of biodiversity due to the construction and implementation of the Chad-Cameroon Oil Pipeline.

The government foundation set up to provide grants for the implementation of the Chad-Cameroon Indigenous Peoples Plan has largely spent the sum reserved for the management of the park on field staff, and has selected two international conservation NGOs, WWF and Wildlife Conservation Society, for park management activities. In Campo Ma'an, Bagyéli communities worry that their rights to practice their subsistence livelihoods will be under increasing threat from the new protection measures currently under consideration by WWF, who have so far failed to consult with local communities[294]. To add insult to injury, although the park supposedly restricts hunting and logging within its boundaries, they have failed to stop logging and destructive extraction activities in the forests, the effects of which will be felt by the local traditional forest users.

Mechanisms of Redress

In the wake of two highly critical and devastating reports on the World Bank's inability and unwillingness to comply to its safeguard policies (the Morse Commission Report, 1992 and the Wapenhans Report, 1992), and continued international environmental and human rights critics, on September 21st, 1993, the Bank's Executive Directors passed a resolution creating an inspection panel. The stated aim was to increase accountability and compliance within the Bank's often obscure and destructive projects. The panel would be composed of functionally independent staff appointed by the Bank President however; and as a body, it is not strictly independent, since the Board of the Bank has the power to veto requests for inspection.

The fundamental issue is whether the Bank management acts on the inspection panel reports and recommendations in reality, since the Inspection Panel has no authority over the Bank's remedial action. The World Bank president, James Wolfensohn, stated in 1998 that the Inspection Panel is a "bold experiment in transparency and accountability that has worked for the benefit of all concerned". Indeed, it has been a positive instrument in cases such as the China Western Poverty Reduction Project, and the Arun Dam Project in Nepal, where the investigation led to the cancellation of the projects before they had begun implementation[295]. If the project is underway however, the Inspection Panel has little power over the actions taken as a result of its efforts. Following the report on the NTPC power plant in Singrauli, no income restoration has been achieved; the social and environmental situation there remains woefully poor.

Currently, the Inspection Panel is involved in investigating the Cameroon social and environmental policy implementations for the Chad-Cameroon Pipeline Project. It published the Chad Investigation Report in November 2002, finding serious violations of the World Bank's policies, such as consultations being carried out in the presence of armed forces. It also stressed the unacceptability of only 5% of the revenues from the project being invested directly into the oil-producing region of Doba, with no adequate measures in place to effectively provide poverty alleviation, such as delays in capacity-building projects and insufficient attention being brought to the governance and human rights problems in Chad. The Bank's responses to the report were weak and unsatisfactory. It tried to shift the blame and responsibilities to the consortium and the government of Chad, whilst claiming credit for various "successes". The Investigation Panel is also in the final stages of preparing an Investigation Report for the Cameroon side of the Chad-Cameroon Oil and Pipeline Project.

In December 2002, the Inspection Panel released the report on the investigation of the Coal Sector Environmental and Social Mitigation Project. The report is highly damning of the project's compliance to World Bank operational policies, finding non-compliance with virtually every section of the policies on resettlement, environmental assessment and indigenous peoples, as well as those on monitoring and information disclosure. The report finds the attitudes towards resettlement particularly lacking: "management's failure to ensure that the original Resettlement Action Plan (RAP) reflected reality on the ground resulted in many problems."

Many of the displaced Project-Affected Persons (PAPs) have not been and are not being compensated at full replacement cost, with the result that many have suffered and continue to suffer harm." It found that this is due to the lack of transparency in the measurements of existing land and housing, the failure to realistically value the existing land and housing, offer a wide choice of resettlement locations, and provide adequate jobs and income-generation schemes. The Panel made many recommendations for amelioration of the current situation, including the establishment of an Independent Monitoring Committee with the mandate to keep up to speed with social and environmental issues on the ground. Since the Inspection Panel has no authority over the Bank's implementation of its recommendations, the claimant NGO, Chotanagpur Adivasi Sewa Samiti (CASS), has drawn up an Action Plan which it hopes the Bank's Board will endorse [*See Box 12, p. 112 for further details*].

On the whole, the Inspection Panel is a mechanism which may allow some instances of the World Bank's social and environmental malpractice to be exposed, but the findings rarely fuel any real change within the Bank's practice on the ground.

The IFC and MIGA's Compliance Advisor/Ombudsman

In 1998, President Wolfensohn approved the creation the Compliance Advisor/Ombudsman (CAO) to fulfil a role similar to that of the Inspection Panel for the IFC and MIGA, although these two institutions also require the services of the Inspection Panel, since the CAO only has an advisory and informal problem-solving role, and one individual is responsible for investigating a claim. The CAO is also appointed by the president of the World Bank.

Experience with the CAO is thus far not very extensive, but within the extractive sector, has been highly criticised, in the Yanacocha mine in Peru [*See Box 9, p. 105*], and in the MIGA-guaranteed Bulyanhulu Mine in Tanzania.[296]

The International Advisory Group

The International Advisory Group (IAG) was set up in 2001 to monitor the Chad-Cameroon Pipeline project's compliance with the World Bank's social and environmental safeguards. It was established in the wake of an international outcry against the World Bank's approval of the financing of this environmentally and socially destructive project. Initially, it was to be the Independent Advisory Group, but the World Bank modified it, maintaining a portion of control over the process. The IAG has produced two highly critical reports since its creation, and has been commended by the NGO movement for doing so. Nevertheless, it has been criticised for skirting round issues of corruption and violence, and avoided those relating to human rights and in this respect needs to broaden its mandate[297].

In its latest report, the IAG noted, amongst others, that the only occasion upon which structured social dialogue took place was on its own rare visits; that the public dissemination concerning Chad-Cameroon Pipeline project documents was still not adequate; that there has been no capacity building for governmental monitoring of the project; that the pipeline construction speed was not being matched by the speed of implementation of social and environmental measures; and that the health concerns due to dust emissions and sexually transmitted disease are severely affecting the population[298].

Box 9: *The Yanacocha Gold Mine
and the Compliance Advisor Ombudsman of the IFC*

The Yanacocha mine has caused a number of devastating environmental and social problems of its own ranging from severe water contamination and a major mercury spill to an upsurge in prostitution, alcoholism and domestic violence. In short, the mine has had and is having severe negative impacts on the way of life of thousands of indigenous campesinos and has impacted the health and safety of the entire *Cajamarquino* community. The mine was opposed locally before its entry. The experience of mining has strengthened opposition in some quarters. There is a strong movement to prevent the further expansion of the operations of the company supported not only by indigenous groups and NGOs but by the local government in Cajamarca.

In March, 2001, Project Underground, a USA-based NGO, and the Rondas Campesinas, a local community organisation filed a complaint with the Compliance Advisor Ombudsman (CAO) of the IFC. The complaint alleges numerous violations of IFC and World Bank social and environmental safeguard policies in the mine project, most notably the mine's failure to consult with the affected community as part of the environmental impact assessment process and its refusal to recognize the affected communities as indigenous people entitled to special protection under the World Bank Policy on Indigenous Peoples.

The filing of the complaint was for the communities an expression of their grave concern and deep dissatisfaction with the role of the mine in entering and operating in their region without their consent. Bringing the complaint was a desperate strategy entered into in the absence of any other more satisfactory means of raising their opposition or gaining redress. Newmont mining company exerts enormous power in the local area both directly through its presence and economic domination and also through its ability to influence government and other support. Many attempts to protest the failures of the mine have been blocked or ignored or delayed by officials. It is fundamental to an understanding of the need for effective means of redress that the concerned communities are able to complain about disregard for their wishes and concerns. In this way they can further express their concern at their marginalisation in the processes of mine development and decision making. The CAO or any process that might offer effective redress would need to actively address this power imbalance to hope to contribute positively to satisfying the concerns of the affected peoples.

In this case the CAO accepted the complaint. Since September, 2001, the CAO has sponsored a "stakeholder" mediation process called the *"mesa de diálogo"* or "dialogue table." Mesa participants represent many sectors of *Cajamarquino* civil society, including the mine, the Rondas, the municipality, government agencies, the university and, until their withdrawal from the process, non-governmental organizations. The CAO hired a team of private mediation consultants to facilitate and oversee the *mesa de diálogo*.

In April, 2002, Project Underground facilitated a campesino community evaluation of the mesa. They have produced an account of their findings[299] which argues that the CAO has in practice not addressed the fundamental problems of the local people, as expressed in their original complaint, but instead has operated as an extension of company efforts to pacify the local community by improving the quality of the social interaction rather than addressing the central substance of their complaints.

The community complainants had a clear and substantial priority list of specific issues that needed addressing. These included the failure of the company and particularly the IFC to recognise the affected communities as being indigenous peoples entitled to the protections of Indigenous peoples within a Bank-supported project. They also called specifically for an urgent medical study of the victims of the mercury contamination in Choropampa caused by mining company negligence. They further called for an independent study of the impacts on flora and fauna and a further study on air pollution. Of central importance to the affected communities was their opposition to further mining development in the Cerro Quilish watershed. These and other concerns were identified in the first meeting.

Despite this prioritisation, the process has not effectively addressed these issues. Discussion of the Cerro Quilish issue was excluded from the process against the wishes of the affected communities and in line with the wishes of the company, who, on this issue, have refused community consultation and are pursuing their claim through the courts. The expert investigations on biodiversity and air pollution, after being deferred, were eventually ruled out as beyond the budget of the process. A main activity of the mesa has been the conduct of capacity building workshops seeking through role play in hypothetic situations to better understand constructive conflict resolution. These have been led by consultants hired for the purpose.

However these have been criticised for failing to address the power imbalance that exists between company and community. Indeed community and NGO representatives observed a bias towards the company and its high-tech presentations while community speakers are strictly time limited in their inputs. Project Underground staff, which in accordance with IFC CAO procedures jointly filed the complaint, have found themselves excluded from the exchange of communications on its status. The mediators also stand accused of cultural insensitivity in relying heavily on abstract concepts and written materials, which marginalize or exclude the peasant participants.

In addition the mediation team have consistently failed to address the substance of the supposed breaches of Bank guidelines. It is suggested that these may not even be understood by the mediation team. In particular the mediation team has not addressed the crucial issue of the rights of the people as Indigenous. The CAO is claimed to be a mechanism for IFC accountability to the communities affected by projects it finances; however the CAO stands accused here as failing to address or even fully understand the accusations of breaches of Bank IFC policies. In the assessment of their experience with the CAO Project Underground are scathing:

> *The CAO team has fostered the notion that the mesa de diálogo is a substantive achievement, an end in and of itself rather than a means to an end. The fact that parties in conflict sit in one room and talk politely to each other is heralded as a substantive achievement, regardless of the content of the dialogue or its outcome.*
>
> *The mesa is premised on the assumption that environmental protection and economic development are common ground for dialogue. This assumption glosses over the fundamental issue of whether the mine should continue to be the pillar of the Cajamarquiño economy and whether the mine has a social license to operate in Cajamarca at all. At no point during the mesa has there been a space in which to discuss the short and long term political, social and environmental implications of the mine's domination of the local economy. At no point*

> *during the mesa has there been any acknowledgement of the incompatibility of the mine with the campesino way of life or the promotion of sustainable development in the area. If these more fundamental themes were broached, issues such as mine expansion and duration and alternative models for economic and social development would be discussed. Instead, the discussion is limited to mitigation of the harmful effects caused by the mine and how the mine's development foundation will allocate its resources.*

The IAG suffers similar limitations to other internal monitoring bodies in that while it may make strong recommendations in its reports, it remains powerless as to their implementation. The IAG has called for detailed reports and action plans to address the environmental and social impacts of the pipeline construction, but the task of mitigating risk and ensuring corrective and capacity-building measures are consistently delayed by the Bank[300].

Case Studies

The case studies that accompany this synthesis paper provide a graphic picture of some of the problems generated for indigenous peoples by Bank financing for the EI sector. Summaries of the case studies are also provided to highlight some key findings.

Overall the picture presented by this review of Bank experience is of the potential and realisation of severe negative impacts for indigenous peoples, and a lack of care and due diligence in the Bank. In addition it is important to record that such abusive relationships with indigenous peoples have historically been commonplace in the dealings of EI companies with indigenous peoples.

Together these case studies argue the need for greater transparency and tighter regulation of EI industry development, and of any Bank involvement in it, as part of a package of necessary protections for vulnerable communities and threatened environments. The widespread scepticism of indigenous peoples faced with promises of reform or reviews of practice is well founded on past negative experience. And at least until measures including confidence building measures begin to be seen to deliver improvements in clean up, prevention of abuse and other raising of standards, most indigenous organisations will remain opposed not only to Bank involvement in EI projects on their land but to all EI company incursions.

Box 10: *Cameroon - Case Study on the Chad Cameroon Pipeline (CCP) and its Impacts on the Indigenous Bagyéli Peoples*

Background
Benefiting from 2 WBG loans, the CCP traverses Cameroon from the border with Chad, to the ocean, cutting through some of Africa's most pristine old growth tropical rainforest, and through the villages of Bagyéli (pygmy) communities in the south. Sixty-six percent of Bagyéli villages (comprising 229 people) are located less than 1 km from the pipeline route, and the pipeline's impact on the environment and subsistence of the Bagyéli peoples has been considerable.

Consultation, Participation and False Promises
Consultation processes were shamefully deficient, baseline socio-cultural studies were extremely poor and participation was tokenistic — in all, the way in which these were dealt with on the ground is insulting to the Bagyéli peoples. The "Fondation pour l'Environnement et le Développement du Cameroon" (FEDEC) was established by the pipeline consortium to ensure social and environmental issues were dealt with. It has so far been completely ineffective. Less than 5% of affected Bagyéli people were employed on the pipeline, even for unskilled labour, which they consider ought to be theirs. The Bagyéli have been promised health facilities, improved education for their children, identity cards, land titles, and built houses. They only received insignificant consumer goods such as small agricultural tools and food-stuffs. Medication has been placed at the sparse medical centres of the region, but it had to be paid for and the Bagyéli have little access to money. No adequate compensation was made to the Bagyéli: the Bantu, their neighbours, misrepresented that the land around the pipeline was theirs and falsely claimed compensation for it. The Bagyéli have been left landless.

Negative Impacts of the Pipeline
- Disturbance of their hunting grounds: the Bagyéli have to travel much further in order to find game.
- Loss of important non-timber forest products, including a sacred tree, the "Neeng", which has a great deal of power.
- Destabilisation of the Bagyéli's health.
- Destruction of property with no compensation.

Recommendations
- The Bagyéli should be given equal rights, including land titles, as any other Cameroonian.
- The FEDEC should be the product of the real needs and interests of the Bagyéli community.
- The Bagyeli should oversee projects directed at their needs and development.
- All promises should be fulfilled: land titles, building houses, supplying national identity cards, assistance with education, medical assistance, and agricultural extension services provided, etc.
- The consultation system should be more relevant.

Box 11: *Colombia - the World Bank's Influence on Mining Legislation*

Background

- Colombia is a country at war: between an abusive right wing government and paramilitaries and the left wing guerrillas.
- Indigenous peoples find themselves in the middle of this conflict, simply trying to defend their legally recognised territories and their ways of life. More than 300 leaders have been assassinated in recent years, because of their attempts to bring justice for indigenous peoples.
- The WBG supports OGM as a viable option for "sustainable development" in Colombia: through its Country Assistance Strategy and other technical assistance loans to Colombia.
- Democracy is nonexistent, and the state has impunity on corruption, which is a fundamental disease in Colombia's governance.
- Fiftytwo percent of extractive industries revenue is lost to corruption in Colombia, so the WBG's support of OGM is supporting corruption.
- The influence of cash creates a slave-like relationship between communities and mining companies.

The mining code and poverty reduction

- The mining code was elaborated with no participation from indigenous peoples, it was elaborated entirely by corporations, based upon the World Bank's policy of liberalisation, deregulation, free-market, low taxes and payment of minimal royalties.
- The current Colombian constitution is very progressive regarding the human rights of indigenous peoples, and yet the new mining code directly encroaches upon these rights. How can such legislation be unconstitutional and yet upheld?
- Mining activities are becoming more and more illegal, in many areas there is no government control on company activities, and indigenous peoples' communities are being pressured to leave, through violent and abusive methods.
- The WBG is merely enhancing Colombia's current debt servitude to the West through providing more loans and permitting all revenues to escape the country through corruption and unfettered trade.

Conclusion

- The Bank is complicit in the corruption and abuse through its continued funding.
- There is no adequate governance so investment inevitably fuels corruption and abuse.

Recommendations

- IFIs should withdraw funds from companies which have abused human rights.
- The Mining Code should be scrapped and rewritten with full participation and consultation with indigenous peoples.
- There should be a moratorium on all mining and all exploration on Indigenous Lands, since these disrupt local livelihoods.
- Those companies that don't comply with the law should be brought to justice.

Box 12: *India - Coal Sector Environmental and Social Mitigation Project. Case Study from East Parej*

Background

The extractive industries, such as coal mining, have both indirect and direct impacts on Adivasi (indigenous peoples) livelihoods. The latter affects indigenous lives through loss of land, water and forest resources of important subsistence value; the former affects them through the influx of a cash economy, discrimination from national society, the break down of social structures, debt bondage, land alienation, the collapse of self-sufficiency and the erosion of Adivasi identity.

East Parej is one of three open pit coal mines operated by Central Coalfields Ltd (CCL), a subsidiary of Coal India Ltd (CIL), in Jharkhand. The objective of the Coal Sector Environmental and Social Mitigation Project (CSESMP) was to assist CIL in making coal production more environmentally and socially sustainable. It followed on from the World Bank's previous loan: the Coal Sector Rehabilitation Project, whose aim was to rehabilitate old coal mines and establish new ones in order to bring India to the forefront of coal production. The World Bank loans were cancelled before the due closure date.

World Bank, Government, and Private Sector Consultations and Dealing with Affected Communities

The CSESMP was due to resettle 290 families in this area. Consultations regarding this resettlement were a travesty: some of the consultations were made with people unaffected by the mines; alleged consultations made with people who had died years before; consultations were punctuated by misinformation, as well as intimidation, aggression and threats. Those families who refused to agree to the terms of resettlement were forcibly evicted from their homes.

Implementation of the WBG's Safeguard Policy Framework: the Inspection Panel

Following a request for inspection submitted by a local IPO, the WBG Board approved inspection in September 2001. The Inspection Panel's report is damning: it found 31 points of non-compliance with WBG Safeguard policies, including the

OD 4.10 on Environmental Assessment, the OD 4.30 on Involuntary Resettlement, the OD 4.20 on Indigenous Peoples, and various items of the policies on Forestry, Cultural Property, and Natural Habitats. It also points to a severe lack of foresight, humanity and will to ensure the people are not damaged by the project.

Outcomes of the Project for Indigenous Peoples

- Indigenous peoples were offered no land-for-land compensation programmes, but rather were given cash, which is an unsustainable medium, completely alien to indigenous peoples.
- Traditional land rights were not recognised and titles not provided, leaving many of the oustees landless as a result.
- No effective income generation and restoration schemes were offered; inappropriate self-employment opportunities generally failed.
- The lack of effective transparency and participation of indigenous peoples left them feeling frustrated, marginalised and unable to voice their genuine needs and concerns.

Conclusions

Even where safeguards exist there is currently no effective control over the standard of implementation or outcomes.

Recommendations

- Viable livelihoods need to be restored to the affected peoples, indigenous land titles need to be established and given to the people, and health, education and water amenities need to be addressed by the project management; livelihoods need to be restored in a fully participatory and consultative manner.
- Compensation must be fair and just, and fully negotiated and agreed upon by the affected peoples.
- Rehabilitation of the mine sites must be effected immediately.

Box 13: *Indonesia - the Closure of Kelian Gold Mine and the Role of the Business Partnership for Development/World Bank*

Background

Kelian Equatorial Mining, a gold mining venture situated in East Kalimantan, is 90% owned by the mining company Rio Tinto Plc. It started production in 1991, and the mine is due to close in 2004. Gold had been discovered years before, and had been mined artisanally by the locals since then. The indigenous (Dayak) communities in the area depend on agroforestry, farming, non timber forest products and bushmeat for subsistence.

Kelian Equatorial Mining and the Local Community

When KEM was established, the locals were forbidden mining, agroforestry and agriculture on the lands within the KEM concession, and became poorer as a result. The water and air pollution resulting from the mine have killed off fish and created serious medical conditions. KEM's guards harassed, beat up and shot at local people mining around the Kelian concession, despite the regional governor issuing an edict permitting artisanal mining within 50 metres of the river bank.

In addition, people have been evicted from their lands with no prior consultation, graves have been destroyed, local women have suffered sexual harassment such as rape from the KEM staff, high placed officials included, and there have been repeated cases of arbitrary arrest and detention.

The local people made many demands from the company, including compensation for land which the company never paid, compensation for land where the payments were inadequate, compensation for the loss of miner's livelihoods, compensation for the destruction of homes and shelters, reduction of the dust pollution, measures to tackle environmental problems, measures to end and redress all human rights violations, and honouring of promises made by KEM at the outset regarding drinking water, electricity, site rehabilitation etc. The community went through lengthy and time-consuming processes, including letters, travelling to the provincial capital, taking grievances to Jakarta, campaigning in Australia, and the UK.

Closure of KEM mine

The mine established a Mine Closure Steering Committee (MCSC) to prepare for closure in 2004. LKMTL (the Foundation for the Mining Community's Livelihoods and Environment - the community organisation), which has been at the forefront of the community's struggle for redress, was involved in the MCSC. Business Partnerships for Development, a World Bank initiative to address conflict issues in community relations, was brought in to help resolve the situation. The KEM case was brought to BPD by Rio Tinto, although the community knew nothing of this.

The problem with BPD and the MCSC is that there is an imbalance in the dialogue in favour of government and industry, who collude representing a stronger voice than the community. The community feels the whole case was being used by Rio Tinto as propaganda for other mining operations, and so LKMTL withdrew from negotiations in March 2003. There is a profound difference between the long-term views of the community and the short-term impact-mitigation view of KEM. The community feels it is not being heeded as it should.

Conclusions and Recommendations

- Indigenous peoples have rights to natural resources as well, and must not be treated as mere bystanders in their own development.
- The existence of a mechanism for dialogue involving indigenous communities, governments and industry does not always mean it is fair or balanced. The Kelian community has experienced such dialogue negatively.

Box 14: *Philippines - The Impact of the Mining Act of 1995 on Indigenous Peoples*

Background

- ◻ The Philippines is very rich in mineral resources, although the mining industry suffered a crisis of investment from 1985, when mineral production suddenly dropped.
- ◻ The ADB attributed this to lack of foreign investment and a bad investment climate.
- ◻ The World Bank promoted policies of liberalisation, free-market and increased export featured largely in government, industry and IFI dialogues at the time; many such seminars were sponsored by the WBG.

The Mining Act of 1995

The law mandates the state to manage, control and supervise exploration, development and utilisation of mineral resources. It offers a vast array of financial and legal incentives for foreign private companies to invest in mining in the Philippines. As a result, exploration and exploitation applications now cover most of the Philippines. Many mining permits have been issued. The law allows mining on indigenous lands, although free prior and informed consent (FPIC) is required. There was no indigenous consultation regarding the Mining Code, nor were the potential impacts researched.

Impact of the Mining Act of 1995

There has been a severe lack of appropriate consultation and participation of indigenous communities. They are often a sham, seriously wanting in real substance. The use of manipulative tactics, such as divide-and-conquer, deception and bribery by the companies to obtain "FPIC" has caused severe social disruption in once peaceful communities. Militarization has become the norm, with an evident and unacceptable tie-up between companies and the military, a concern which was expressed by the UN Special Rapporteur on the Human Rights of Indigenous Peoples, at the time of his trip to the Philippines in December 2002. Indigenous peoples have been forcibly relocated and displaced from their lands, and land ownership and access struggles have escalated. There is a serious lack of adequate protection for indigenous peoples, and the biodiversity they utilise, through EIA process.

Following a nationwide massive protest against this Mining Code, exploration and new permits have been held up, although there is no indication that this will remain the case.

Conclusion

- ◻ Both directly and indirectly, the World Bank has influenced the crafting of many national mining codes and the policies of other IFIs and agencies all over the world, which promote privatisation, deregulation and liberalisation.
- ◻ These reforms have had massive adverse impacts on indigenous communities greater than those of specific projects.
- ◻ Indigenous peoples all over the Philippines are vehemently opposed to mining on their ancestral lands, and know from their experience that there is no such thing as "sustainable mining".

Recommendations

- ◻ The Mining Code should be scrapped.
- ◻ There should be a moratorium on all mining projects until a new mining law is passed.
- ◻ This new law and its implementation should: uphold indigenous peoples' rights, declarations for mining free zones, right to determine all developments within their lands; ban open pit mining, submarine tailings disposal, mining where ecosystems are fragile, licensing of permits to foreign companies, especially those with bad records; and implement confidence building measures including addressing legacy issues.
- ◻ Mechanisms of support for indigenous women should be established.
- ◻ If WBG is really interested in promoting the development of indigenous peoples, then it should not support mining, since indigenous peoples do not and have never benefited from mining.

Box 15: *Papua New Guinea - Case Study on the Multilateral Investment Guarantee Agency's involvement in the Lihir Gold Mine.*

Background

PNG is a culturally and biologically diverse country, with a 100% indigenous population, and 95-97% of land is customarily owned. It is geologically highly prospective, so mining is considered an integral part of the country's economy. It is home to some of the most notoriously controversial mining projects such as Panguna, Porgera, Ok Tedi, and Misima.

Papua New Guineans are becoming more aware of the issues and problems surrounding the extractive industries, and have become vocal on benefit distributions and compensation for the negative impacts it has on their lands. The complexity of land tenure in PNG makes compensation a thorny issue, and benefit distribution from the extractive industries is fraught with injustices. The WBG has been deeply involved in policy changes regarding the extractive industries in PNG through various technical assistance loans to the PNG government.

Lihir Gold Mine

The WBG's MIGA provided a political risk guarantee of $50 million to Rio Tinto, the Lihir Gold Mine operating company, in 1997. The US Overseas Private Investment Corporation declined financing this mine on environmental grounds. Lihirians are shareholders in the mine, yet were unaware of WBG monitoring processes which had been ongoing since its inception, and in March 2003, 100% of Lihirians interviewed did not know of the WBG's involvement in the mine.

Unequal wealth distribution, with startling differences in salaries, facilities, amenities, general well-being, and even in prices, is observed on Lihir. The mine is pumping 110 million m3 of waste into the ocean each year through a pipeline using a submarine tailings disposal system, and dumping 20 million tonnes of rock waste into Luise Harbour every year. The environmental monitoring however is not independent, and is paid for by the company. The environmental consultations have been all but transparent.

The rivers have been polluted, the sea is polluted, the most revered sacred site has been destroyed, and the game depended upon by Lihirians has all but disappeared. Relocation has not taken into account the complexity of land tenure in PNG, leaving many individuals frustrated, worse off and in very difficult positions regarding theirs and their children's future. The sudden transition from a subsistence-based existence to a cash-based one has proven complex, as indeed has coping with the large influx of foreigners.

Lihirians are deeply concerned about the future of their culture, and the society their children will inherit. The traditionally matrilineal Lihirian society has been undermined, and the imposition of Western sexist politics has greatly inhibited the Lihirian women's voice. This imposition has also skewed the traditional land inheritance process, which the incomers treated as patrilineal, leaving many families landless.

Recommendations

- The WBG should ensure that any review, development or changes in legislation concerning the extractive industries should be fully consultative and participatory.
- The mining department and the WBG should conduct forums and meetings for discussion of regulatory framework modifications with Papua New Guineans.
- Social, environmental and economic concerns should always be considered in the legal framework.
- WBG should fund research into problem projects they have been a party to, and thus fund the independent monitoring of the Lihir mine project.
- No new mines should be permitted until the basic rights of indigenous peoples have been ensured, and the industry has committed to halt submarine and riverine tailings disposal.

Box 16: *Russia - World Bank Group Projects and the Indigenous Peoples of the North, Siberia and Far East of Russia*

Background

◻ The cultural survival of indigenous peoples in Siberia and the Russian North is extremely fragile due to a difficult environment and governmental process of assimilation: oil development increases the threat to their survival.

◻ Indigenous Peoples are already a minority within their own territories.

◻ The Russian budget is entirely dependent on oil and gas, yet law implementation is poor.

◻ Alongside the European Bank for Reconstruction and Development, the World Bank Group's political and economic influence is considerable in Russia.

◻ Can the World Bank's involvement improve the lives of indigenous peoples and contribute to sustainable development?

Consequences of Oil Extraction in Siberia and the Russian Far East

The environmental destruction caused by past oil and gas operations is immeasurable, and yet oil development is being encouraged once more. As oil is being redeveloped in Siberia, this old infrastructure is being reused, leading to catastrophic spills, such as that in Komi, where 100,000 tons of crude oil was released over 6 months (The IFC's Polar Lights project was using that pipeline). Most large oilfields are located in the remote northern areas of Russia, where environmental recovery is extremely slow.

These are also the areas inhabited by the last reindeer herding tribes and indigenous peoples of Siberia. The culture and values of temporary oil workers collide with the values of indigenous peoples, resulting in severe losses for the indigenous traditional lifestyles and subsistence.

An example amongst many is the case of the Evenks: their sacred places were defiled, the spawning grounds of the fish they rely upon were destroyed, their hunting grounds were emptied of game, their hunting structures, winter huts and traps were looted and destroyed. The discovery of oil on their land led to utter desolation and breakdown of social structure.

The Polar Lights Project of the IFC in the Nenets Autonomous Okrug

- The positive outcomes of having the WBG involved are: improved ecological and technological standards, in comparison to Russian standards which are severely deficient.
- Negative impacts: lack of IPDP, lack of information; post-project consultation; the company refused to cooperate with the local herdsmen communities.
- The company is in conflict with the local administration, and there are allegations of corruption, although the local population are left in the dark.
- High level jobs depend on high level qualifications. These are available within the companies but not much to local people because of their limited qualifications.

Recommendations

- A moratorium on all new OGM projects affecting indigenous territories should be established.
- Recognition of international law, human rights standards and indigenous peoples' rights should be effected.
- Partnerships should be developed with indigenous peoples, and involve them at all stages of the project cycle.
- The WBG should encourage national governments to implement national rights and legislation.
- A system of credible monitoring and protection is urgently required.
- Transparency of consultations should be ensured, which in turn guarantees indigenous peoples their right to veto extractive projects.
- Indigenous peoples should be fully involved in WBG development strategies and indigenous peoples Development Plans.
- The UN Decade of Indigenous Peoples theme "Partnership in Action" should be endorsed.

A RECORD OF INSTITUTIONAL FAILURE

Where benefits have accrued from the World Bank to affected communities, they have rarely come through the project developers' design but as a result of concessions being won through organised opposition or advocacy work, such as at the Lihir mine in Papua New Guinea. Taken case by case, the projects that have caused such immiserations can (all too easily) be dismissed as aberrations — one-off failures from which useful lessons can be learned but which do not cast doubt on the activities and social desirability of the OMG sector as a whole. Taken together, they portray a sector whose aims, practices and policies are fundamentally at odds with the aspirations and rights of Indigenous Peoples.

That the World Bank has, from its inception, been a major backer of the divisiveness, impoverishment and environmental destruction wrought on indigenous peoples through the OMG sectors raises major questions about the Bank's internal policies, its commitment to indigenous peoples' rights and its claimed ability to influence the outcome of projects in a beneficial way.

As this paper shows, internal Bank safeguard policies have often been routinely ignored or flouted; projects and programmes have been railroaded, despite clear evidence of their adverse impacts on indigenous peoples, the environment and poverty alleviation. Recommendations for internal reform have been blocked, watered down or sidelined.

Critically this pattern of serial institutional failure is not restricted to the OMG sector: it emerges as consistent theme in reviews of the Bank's performance across the board. Unsurprisingly, the Bank is now viewed with grave distrust by many project-affected communities, particularly indigenous groups.

Regaining (or, more accurately, gaining) the trust of such communities is a *sine qua non* of successful project implementation. Indeed, the extent to which the EIR recognises the structural breakdown in trust between the Bank and its intended beneficiaries is likely to prove a major yardstick against which the credibility of its final report will be judged.

Nonetheless, the conviction is growing among many observers that the Bank will never be able to gain such trust, if indeed it once existed.

The Pressure to Lend

The World Bank has a draft of policies which, if implemented, could contribute to reducing the social and environmental impacts of its projects. Such policies, however, are routinely flouted [*See Box 17, p. 124*]

Why is this the case? Why is indigenous participation in assessment so unacceptably low? It is at least partly because indigenous communities mistrust the Bank's procedures, based on years of experience of not having their views taken seriously. The right to free, prior and informed consent by mining-affected peoples is not particular in IFC and MIGA projects: vital information has been denied on grounds of "commercial confidentiality". And, as we shall see, the Bank's recently diluted policy on indigenous peoples appears to violate safeguards supposedly built into its other policies and guidelines.

Internal investigations into the consistent failure of World Bank staff to implement operational directives on issues such as resettlement, environment and indigenous peoples have also repeatedly highlighted the "pressure to lend" as a major reason for non-compliance. This pressure is compounded specifically in the case of IFC and MIGA , by the requirement that the Bank's private arms should loan at commercial rates and make a profit where possible (certainly not operate at a loss). This appears to be the IFC's main motive behind this year's financing of KDL in Botswana. In respect of political risk insurance, MIGA attempts to avoid claims at all costs. This led the agency into deriding the full impact of the Omai tailings dam collapse in 1995 and making the reprehensible decision to continue insurance cover, even when the underlying technical causes of the disaster had not been properly addressed, and thousands of local people had been denied full compensation for their losses.

As a 1992 report by the World Bank's Portfolio Management Task Force, led by Willi Wapenhans, makes clear, the Bank's "pervasive preoccupation with new lending" takes precedence over all other considerations.[301] According to the Task Force, "a number of current practices -- with respect to career development, feedback to staff and signals from managers -- militate against increased attention to project performance management."[302] In the subculture which prevails at the Bank, staff appraisals of projects tend to be perceived "as marketing devices for securing loan approval (and achieving personal recognition)", with the result that "little is done to ascertain the actual flow of benefits or to evaluate the sustainability of projects during their operational phase."[303] Little or no effort is made to take the borrowing government's implementation capacity into account when calculating economic rates of return; "poor policy environments", "institutional constraints", lack of "sustained local commitment" — these considerations are often simply ignored in the rush to push projects through and keep them going.

The Bank's institutional priorities and management structures have thus encouraged staff to flout internal policy directives and borrower governments to ignore loan conditions. Unsurprisingly, the "credibility

Box 17: *Guidelines? What Guidelines?*

Existing World Bank policies are not only flawed but rarely implemented in full or in a timely manner. In India for example, none of the environmental and social problems of NTPC operations (at Singrauli) were "fully addressed prior to negotiations". The World Bank's answer to these serious failings was the preparation of various Environmental and Social Action Plans for Singrauli and yet, as the Berne Declaration points out, even these did not consider "the impact on the broader social environment" nor "foresee socio-economic studies on the fate of the earlier project-affected people, and resettlement and rehabilitation action plans". In addition by the time these action plans were initiated in 1998, 85% of the new loan was disbursed.

Likewise, in Bolivia, the construction of two pipelines, the Cuiabá and the Bolivia-Brazil Pipeline, led to post-project implementation of inadequate Indigenous Peoples' Development Plans (IPDPs), which did not even provide the fundamental (and OD 4.20-required) legal land demarcation processes to the "beneficiary" indigenous populations.

Other examples of World Bank projects not complying to the institution's own policies abound. Recent examples can be found in the Inspection Panel report on the Coal India Social and Environmental Mitigation Project. The Chad-Cameroon Oil Pipeline Project is also illustrative: although the project directly impacts the indigenous Bagyéli pygmies, no Indigenous Peoples Development Plan (IDDP) was drawn up as required under the Bank's Indigenous Peoples' policy.

The Chad-Cameroun pipeline and last year's apparent disagreements between the IFC and Bank top echelons over disbursements to the Rosia Montana mine in Romania also demonstrate clear divisions within the Bank over what criteria are critical, the real "meaning" of those criteria, and the degree to which the risks within the project design may or may not be diminished on implementation.

Source:
Bosshard, P., 1999. Energy from Dante's Inferno. Berne Declaration. http://www.ecb.ch.

(of loan agreements) as binding documents has suffered"[304] and "evidence of gross non-compliance (with Bank legal covenants) is overwhelming."[305] When borrowers disregard loan conditions, the typical response of Bank management has been to look the other way or waive the relevant requirement, unless public pressure forces them to do otherwise. As Patrick Coady, an ex-Executive Director of the World Bank, has remarked: "No matter how egregious the situation, no matter how flawed the project, no matter how many policies have been violated, and no matter how clear the remedies prescribed, the Bank will go forward on its own terms."[306]

Since 1992, the Bank has introduced a number of initiatives intended to address the problems identified by Wapenhans. However, far from remedying the problems, they have in many respects made them worse, not least by streamlining business procedures in order to speed up loan approvals and by introducing new rewards for staff, who move projects through the approval process at a faster place, rather than for those who comply with policy.[307] Indeed, a succession of internal reports has continued to criticise the culture of loan approval — where staff are rewarded above all for pushing money — as a major cause of project failure and "leakage" (the Bank's euphemism for graft).[308] [309] In at least one instance, the full findings of one critical report — a 1997 review of the Bank's project portfolio by the Quality Assurance Group — were never officially shared with Board members. Significantly, the report concluded:

> *The lessons from past experience are well known, yet they are generally ignored in the design of new operations. This synthesis concludes that institutional amnesia is the corollary of institutional optimism.*[310]

The prime beneficiaries of the Bank's failure to address the problems identified by Wapenhans and others are bank staff (for whom "projects through the door" are steps climbed on the ladder to promotion) and, of course, project developers. Those who lose are the project-affected communities and, where corruption is involved, both national governments and the population at large [*See Box 18, p. 127*].

"Clientitis"

Like the "pressure to lend", the Bank's desire to keep lending to its client governments — "clientitis", in the words of Bruce Rich, International Program Director at Environmental Defense, a US non-governmental organisation[311] — has also been identified as a major cause of poor loans being approved by the Bank. This is another problem that the Bank's management and Board have singularly failed to address, exacerbating the problem of corruption and poor project quality. Even when Bank staff have been well aware of corruption in loans, they have frequently ignored it in order to maintain the flow of lending.

The Bank's relationship with Indonesia during the Suharto era illustrates the point. In a February 1999 study of lending to Indonesia, for example, the Bank's own Operations Evaluations Department (OED) noted:

> *Warning signals were either ignored or played down by senior managers in their effort to maintain the country relationship. Some staff feared the potential negative impact on their opportunities that might result from challenging mainstream regional thinking.*[312]

Significantly, the Bank's reluctance to fall out with a major borrower led it to downplay major problems which internal reports had revealed in the Indonesian banking system, with the result that the "Bank's readiness to address the subsequent financial crisis in Indonesia was seriously impaired."[313] In this instance, what went right for Bank staff and Indonesia's then kleptocracy went wrong not just for the Indonesian people but for the entire South East Asian region.

The Bank's Executive Directors are, it would seem, as amenable to *clientitis* as its staff. Internal World Bank documents and external reports by the US Government and others now provide plentiful evidence that the World Bank's Board, which is responsible for ensuring that loans are spent as intended, has approved loans to countries with a known record of corruption, despite such countries failing to comply with the Bank's own anti-corruption regulations and despite warnings that the loans were likely to be misspent.

In the Summer of 1997, for example, *Business Week* alleged that at least US $100 million from a US $500 million Russian coal sector loan was either misspent or could not even be accounted for.[314] A little over a year later, the *Financial Times* estimated the amount stolen in the coal sector loan to be much higher, as much as US $ 250 million.[315]

Perhaps worse, the World Bank's programme in the sector has resulted in potentially high-grade coal reserves not being exploited, even while it has been closing down supposedly uneconomic pits. In the Vorkuta region, between 1995 and 2001, half the coal mines were closed down on the Bank's recommendation, because of high transport costs, and over-supply. But, according to Vladimir Tushkovskty, head of the

Box 18: *What went Wrong (or rather Right) - The Lesotho Highlands Water Project*

The Bank-funded and -promoted Lesotho Highlands Water Project, involving the construction of a series of dams and water diversion schemes, illustrates how project developers have benefited from the Bank's failure to address the pressure on staff to get projects up and running -- even at the expense of local people.

Leaked correspondence between the World Bank and the Lesotho government suggests that the Bank knew of corruption allegations against Masupha Sole, the former director of the Lesotho Highlands Development Authority, as early as 1994. The Bank's reaction, however, was to berate the Lesotho authorities for having suspended Sole from his post pending an investigation into the project's accounts. Their reason: it would interfere with project construction timetables and could lead to costly overruns.

In a letter to Mr Pekeche, Principal Secretary at the Ministry of Natural Resources, Praful Patel of the Bank's Southern Africa Department, gripes: "While the undertaking of a management audit may be normal practice, the suspending of key management staff in order to conduct such an audit is most unusual. In our view, the absence of key members of senior staff from the project during this critical time could seriously jeopardize the progress of the project."

Instead of picking up the ball and immediately suspending the companies pending a corruption inquiry - the minimum that the Lesotho authorities' audit should have prompted - the Bank effectively turned a blind eye to the corruption charges. Yet again, what went wrong for civil society -- the institutional pressure to push ahead with the project regardless of evidence of corruption - went right for the companies. Had suspensions been instituted at this stage in the proceedings, many of the companies might not have been awarded contracts for the second phase of the project -- constructing the Mohale Dam.

It now emerges that, despite previous assertions to the contrary, the Bank -- and the South African authorities -- knew full well of the corruption charges at the time that Mohale was approved. Nonetheless, the Bank pushed to have Mohale built immediately, rather than in a decade's time when the water may be needed in South Africa, because the contractors were in place and it would therefore be cheaper than waiting.

Vorgashorskaya coal miners' union, one major mine contains high-quality reserves which, in spite of several million dollars' of investment in its infrastructure during the late 1980s and early 1990s, was never exploited. "The World Bank said 'you don't need so much coal' so we never opened it", commented Tuskkovskty in mid-2001. "[The Bank] is an enemy of the people", he concluded.[316]

In the Ukraine, too — where the Bank asserted it was making more efficient, environmentally sound processes and working to defined codes — large scale unemployment and social discord have resulted, while the country continues to hold one of the world's worst records for mine-based fatalities and serious injuries.

In Indonesia, according to a 1997 internal World Bank study known as the Dice memorandum,[317] some 20 to 30 per cent of all development funds, totaling several billion dollars, have been systematically diverted through corruption. These figures accord closely with estimates by other experts, such as former Indonesian Finance Minister Sumitro Djodjohadikusomo and Jeffrey Winters of Northwestern University. Winters alleged in July 1997 that shoddy accounting practices by the World Bank had allowed the misappropriation of as much as US\$ 8 billion dollars of World Bank lending to Indonesia over the past 30 years.[318]

Jeffrey Winters' most sensational revelations were of corrupt dealings between the Suharto clan and Freeport (later Freeport—Rio Tinto) in promoting the Grasberg mine in West Papua. Although the Bank did not bankroll the mine, MIGA provided crucial political risk insurance from 1991 until the company itself cancelled the cover in September 1996. Interviewed in early 1997, MIGA's senior counsel, Lorin Weisenberg, admitted that the Bank had been rattled in 1995, when accusations of human rights atrocities by the Indonesian military, and huge environmental degradation (caused by the mine throwing its tailings directly into the Ajkwa river system) began to circulate around the world. "We had a meeting with Freeport in the US", said Weisenberg. "We knew of the company's bad reputation and were prepared for a battle. Initially we considered Freeport President, Jim-Bob Moffett, to be a buffoon. However by the end of our meeting he was running rings round some of our own people".[319]

The fact that OPIC, the US government political risk insurance agency, had cancelled its insurance on human rights and environmental grounds in 1995 (though under pressure from Henry Kissinger, a Freeport director, it later reinstated it) cut no ice. "We were satisfied with the World Bank's monitoring of the Grasberg mine", declared Weisenberg. "And the WB had given a relatively clean bill of health to the project".

As with the Russian loans, the Bank continued to pour money into Indonesia during the 1990s, despite the findings of the Dice report and the allegations building against the Grasberg mine operation in particular. In the 15 months after the report was written, the Bank committed and disbursed over US $1.3 billion more to Indonesia without any effective measures to address the problems identified by Dice. In October 1998, with plans to commit and disburse two billion dollars more over the next nine months, a second Bank mission, headed by Jane Loos, recorded the following:

> *Our mission confirms earlier reports on corruption in Indonesia: that it is pervasive, institutionalised and a significant deterrent to overall growth of the economy and effectiveness of the Bank's assistance . . . Despite apparent compliance with World Bank guidelines and documentation requirements for procurement, disbursement, supervision and audits, there is significant leakage from Bank funds . . . Bank procedures/standards are not being applied uniformly . . . The [World Bank] auditing requirements have been allowed to deteriorate into a superficial exercise; even an agency with overdue audits was not excluded from receiving new loans.*[320]

Bank staff themselves admit that the Bank has for years been reluctant to address corruption risks openly and directly with borrowers but argue that the it is now taking the issue seriously.[321] Nonetheless, a full five years after the Bank first adopted "internationally accepted standards of effective management control",[322] and four years after the Bank's President committed the Bank "to fight the cancer of corruption",[323] its own rules continue to be flouted.

Rubber Stamping

The failure of the Bank's board to exercise proper oversight over projects is also a constant theme of external reviews of the Bank's performance. Again the beneficiaries are those project developers whose applications would be rejected if the its procedures were properly observed.

As the US General Accounting Office (GAO) reported in a major study of the Bank's fiscal management control, published in April 2000, the Board continues to approve many projects which fail to meet the Bank's minimal financial management requirements.[324]

Of 12 projects in "corruption-prone" countries randomly selected by the GAO, "six . . . did not meet the Bank's minimal financial management requirements at the time that the Board approved the projects".[325]

The report continues:

> *Our review of 12 randomly selected projects approved by the Bank since November 1998 identified 5 projects in which the borrowers' implementing agencies had little or no experience managing development projects, according to Bank records and staff . . . Furthermore, for 3 of the 12 projects, the Bank determined that the borrowers' implementing agencies had particularly weak capacity for carrying out procurement in accordance with Bank rules . . . For four projects, the implementing agencies were not yet functioning and did not have key staff or operating procedures in place.*[326]

As a result of these and other deficiencies:

> *"The Board may not have had sufficient information to assess the borrower's capacity when approving these loans."*[327]

Disturbingly, in six of eight projects where Bank staff "had flagged weak management capacity, corruption, or political interference as a critical risk", the project appraisal documents "did not describe what specific supervisory actions the Bank planned to take to mitigate the risks."[328] It is not known whether or not the Board requested such measures when it approved the projects.

The GAO also notes that the Bank's new anti-corruption procedures only apply to "about 208, or 14 per cent, of the Bank's 1500 projects" and that "Bank studies indicate that management weaknesses persist in ongoing projects."[329] Recent procurement audits, for example, "show a lack of understanding of and non-compliance with Bank procurement rules among many (17 of 25) borrowers subject to these audits."[330]

Although the GAO review notes that the Bank has made "significant progress" in introducing anti-corruption measures, it concludes, "further action will be required before the Bank can provide reasonable assurances that project funds are spent according to the Bank's guidelines."[331] Given the huge sums that have been disbursed since the Bank began operating over 50 years ago — some US $170 billion[332] — this criticism, which is echoed by a succession of internal Bank reports dating back to the early 1990s, is profoundly disturbing.[333]

Meanwhile, the Executive Directors of the Bank — and Bank staff -- remain protected from legal proceedings against them for any failure to abide by the Bank's own rules. Yet again, what has "gone wrong" from the point of view of good governance has clearly "gone right" for those responsible for the identified governance failures.

Penalising Staff Integrity

World Bank staff are frequently reluctant to raise questions that might slow down a loan, fearing that by doing so, it will adversely affect their career. Internal Bank memoranda and reports have identified this as a major problem in addressing the Bank's "culture of loan approval" and, indeed, corruption. In its 1999 report on Indonesia, for example, the OED notes that staff who had drawn attention to major problems in the Indonesian banking sector were perceived to have suffered "unjustified penalties to their career prospects."[334]

One UK consultant similarly recalls the Bank's reaction to his discovery of evidence suggesting that one of the world's largest accountancy companies had submitted false information as part of its bid to win a World Bank contract in Kazakhstan. As he recalls:

> *When I showed [the evidence] to World Bank's Task Manager, I was told that I had not shown [the] document to him, because if I did so show it to him, the World Bank would have to stop [the company] bidding for a 3 year minimum.*[335]

Conversely, investigations reveal that management failure on the part of World Bank staff is rarely penalised. In 2002, for example, the Lawyers Environmental Action Team (LEAT) requested the MIGA's Compliance Advisory Ombudsman (CAO) to investigate MIGA's due diligence procedures with respect to the Bulyanhulu mine in Tanzania, prior to approving an investment insurance guarantee for the mine.

The LEAT complaint drew attention to serious flaws in the process and outcome of the social and environmental impact assessments that had been submitted to MIGA by Barrick Gold, the Canadian company seeking the MIGA guarantee. LEAT argued that these studies should have been carried out before artisanal miners were forcibly removed from the site in 1996 (by Sutton Resources, the company Barrick acquired along with the Bulyanhulu project):

> *That was not done. Instead, the companies waited until the Bulyanhulu communities were driven off from the area then purported to undertake an EIA. Even then the information based on these studies that Barrick Gold submitted to MIGA was materially inaccurate, erroneous and misleading. And MIGA, without first carrying out a thorough and competent due diligence investigation to establish the veracity of this information and the soundness of its conclusions, approved millions of dollars in political risk guarantees for the Bulyanhulu mine.*[336]

In its response to the LEAT complaint, the CAO acknowledges that a mission carried out by the International Finance Corporation (IFC) had found that the EIA for the Bulyanhulu project failed to meet the World Bank Group's requirements with respect to "issues of resettlement and compensation related to the pipeline, the tailings dam and the mine...." In addition, that EIA "did not address past issues of land clearance."[337] Without providing any details, the CAO states that the IFC team "noted in detail the remedies that would be required to bring the project into compliance with IFC policies and notes the reputational issues in the 1996 alleged incidents. The IFC recommended an addendum to the EIA be prepared detailing what would be required along the themes outlined above."[338]

The CAO also acknowledges that MIGA was made aware of these concerns after Barrick Gold approached it for guarantee. However, and crucially, "beyond this, the CAO has been unable to find any correspondence from MIGA to Barrick Gold or to ascertain from MIGA or Barrick staff that the issues raised in the IFC back-to-office report had been acted on by MIGA."[339] It is also clear from the CAO's Report that MIGA did not carry out any due diligence investigation on these issues. LEAT notes:

> MIGA never carried out a site visit nor did it ever send any environmental or social specialist to visit the area! By all accounts, it seems, all MIGA did was to be 'comfortable' with Barrick's assurances that all was well at Bulyanhulu.[340]

For its part, the CAO concluded that MIGA's due diligence efforts had been unsatisfactory: "At issue ... is whether MIGA sought to or felt it should seek independent verification of critical issues surrounding the viability of a Category A project for guarantee. The purpose and intent of environmental and social due diligence in the World Bank Group is to provide that independent verification, precisely so that the Group is not left to 'trust' the sponsor."[341] The CAO also rejected the notion that the IFC mission amounted to a due diligence investigation: a back-to-office report, it said, "cannot qualify as 'due diligence' and IFC made clear to MIGA its status."[342]

No action was proposed against the staff that allowed the MIGA guarantee to be issued despite these governance failures. Nor, as LEAT notes, did CAO draw the obvious conclusion: namely, that "the guarantee should never have been approved, bearing in mind that the IFC mission had found the project wanting with regard to the World Bank Group policies."[343]

Avoiding Binding Commitments

The Bank's reaction to many of the governance failures identified by Wapenhans and others has been to argue that its safeguard policies are too complicated for staff to implement and should therefore be streamlined. Other arguments have been mustered to support "simplifying" the guidelines. Chief amongst these is the claim that the guidelines impose unjustifiably high transaction costs. This view has become commonplace amongst other multilateral banks and bilateral development agencies. As a recent joint statement by such institutions puts it:

> We in the donor community have been concerned with the growing evidence that, over time, the totality and wide variety of donor requirements and processes for preparing, delivering, and monitoring development assistance are generating unproductive transaction costs for, and drawing down the limited capacity of, partner countries.[344]

As non-governmental organisations have repeatedly pointed out, such arguments ignore the very real financial and development **gains** that result from ensuring projects conform to the highest standards; they also ignore the high costs that result from poorly planned projects or projects that generate public opposition. [345]

Nonetheless, the Bank has recently undertaken revisions of a number of its safeguard policies. As documented earlier, the revisions -- undertaken in the name of improving development effectiveness -- have resulted in a serious weakening of the ability of civil society to hold Bank staff accountable for problems and failures in implementation. In the case of the Bank's Operational Policy 4.10 on Indigenous Peoples, the proposed revisions seriously undermine the Bank's social standards. The new version does not require Bank staff and borrowers to take action to safeguard the internationally recognised rights of indigenous peoples to own, control and manage their lands, it merely notes that the borrowers are required to "pay particular attention" to these issues.

The proposed new guidelines also fail to apply the test of self-identification as the trigger for the policy; they do not recognize the right to free, prior and informed consent; they do not address many issues related to property rights; and they fail to prohibit the involuntary resettlement of indigenous peoples. In addition, the new policy does not apply to full structural adjustment loans, which can have serious negative impacts on indigenous peoples; it lacks a requirement for detailed baseline studies to determine indigenous peoples' priorities and concerns, despite many Bank publications identifying the absence of such studies as a major cause of projects having adverse effects on local communities; it does not contain any provisions for the monitoring, tracking and evaluation of projects by indigenous peoples themselves; and it only requires a social assessment in cases when the Bank's staff unilaterally decide that a project may have adverse impacts.

Other safeguard policies have suffered a similar fate [*See Box 19, p. 135*]. By contrast, no steps have been proposed for making the financial guidelines that apply to Bank project more "flexible" (*read:* "less stringent"). The revision process is restricted to the Bank's social, environmental and development policy guidelines, clearly signalling that quality control in these areas is less important than ensuring borrowers pay up.

The losers in this process are indigenous peoples and other project- and programme-affected communities. The winners are Bank staff for whom the new guidelines now provide greater protection from being held to account.

Favouring Vested Interests

Many of the problems described above reflect deep-seated cultural patterns within the Bank and its partners in government and industry. Put simply, the World Bank and other funding agencies are institutionally predisposed to behaviour that "makes-things-go-WRONG-for-civil-society-and-RIGHT-for-the-corporations-and-governments-that-benefit-from-the-projects-they-finance-or-underwite".

This is not surprising. The bulk of Bank staff come from a similar political and economic background and are enmeshed in the social networks that link the Bank to government and industry. They drink in the same clubs, participate in the same training courses, share the same circle of friends and seek the same job vacancies. Even if not born to this world, they have come to participate in it and to endorse its values and aspirations. Moreover, the steady stream of Bank staff that passes through the revolving doors between the Bank, governments and companies that seek its assistance, is a clear indication of how the careers of Bank staff are intertwined with those of their "clients" outside of the Bank. The unwillingness of World Bank staff to "rock the boat" ultimately reflects this shared institutional culture.

Indeed, the World Bank has, throughout its history, assiduously sought to cultivate a sympathetic technical and political elite within governments and industry that share its view of "doing development". In 1955, for example, it established its Economic Development Institute specifically to train a technocratic elite through whom it could work in

---

Box 19: *"Panel-Proofing" the Safeguard Policies*

Over the past few years, many of the World Bank's original safeguard policies — designed to minimise the adverse social and environmental impacts of projects — have been compromised, or are not implemented.

The revision programme is intended to make policies less rigid and more amenable to decentralisation, country "ownership" in line with the Bank's new "learning approach" to development. Bank policy makers assert that clearer and more flexible guidelines will raise the standard of policy implementation and so improve development effectiveness. However, it appears that in the name of "clarity" and "flexibility", the Bank's policies are -- as Bank staff put it -- being made "panel-proof": that is to say, by making the guidelines less precise and binding, staff are protected from criticism should affected communities make a complaint to the Bank's Inspection Panel.

The original aim of clarifying the directives for staff, and reducing "policy overload" — in the words of one staff member "distinguish[ing] between the 'bottom line' of what is mandatory and the 'would it not be nice to have' statement of intentions" -- was subverted however. Under the revised safeguards, the old mandatory guidelines have been whittled down and divided into two categories: a set of new Operational Policies (OPs), whose provisions are mandatory and Bank Procedures (BP) which are non-binding. In the process, the mandatory guidelines have been reduced to a bare minimum. This weakening of Bank project implementation standards has been compounded by weaker language and the outright removal of fundamental aspects of the policies.

In other words, policies are being made so flexible that staff or borrowers can never be accused of having contravened them and therefore never held to account for problems and failures in implementation.

There are four basic reasons why the erosion of standards through the weakening of the safeguard policies is of extreme concern to civil society.

□ Eroded policies will further undermine the already limited accountability of the World Bank Group.
□ Enfeebled policies will limit the Bank's capacity to avoid or mitigate adverse development impacts.
□ Diluted safeguards will widen the growing discrep-

ancy between international social and environmental legal precepts and the standards of the World Bank.
- Any weakening of the Bank's safeguard policies will send the wrong signal to other development donors, development agencies and the private sector who may view the content and application of the Bank's operational policies as examples of best practice to be adopted in their own operations.

As we have seen, the proposed revisions to the Bank's Indigenous Peoples' policy have seriously eroded the already weak protection granted by the Bank to indigenous communities. Other World Bank policies directly relevant to indigenous peoples have also been drastically watered down. The new Operational Policies on Involuntary Resettlement and Forestry are illustrative:

- OP 4.12 on Involuntary Resettlement.
The conversion of this policy was finalised in 2001, much to the dismay of civil society and NGOs. It was completed without the participation of communities affected or likely to be affected, such as indigenous peoples. The new policy permits resettlement of indigenous peoples even if this would have "significant adverse impacts on their cultural survival", and it contains provisions which permit the curtailment of the traditional resource rights of indigenous peoples in legally recognised national parks and protected areas. Fundamentally, there is no requirement that standards of living or livelihoods are improved by the resettlement programme, and there are no provisions ensuring free prior and informed consent for indigenous peoples. These omissions weaken the protections afforded affected communities and limit their options to obtain redress through the Inspection Panel.

- OP 4.36 on Forests
The revised version of this policy was adopted in October 2002, and has been widely and bitterly criticised, primarily because it lifts the 1991 proscription on World Bank-funded logging of old growth forests. Many indigenous peoples eke out a living in such forests all over the world, and lifting this ban could have severe consequences for their continued sustenance and survival. In addition, OP 4.36 only requires borrowers to secure the tenurial rights of forest peoples in

logging projects, but not in conservation, plantation or non-forestry projects affecting forests and forest peoples' livelihoods. There are no clear provisions requiring civil society or indigenous peoples participation in national level forest policy interventions and PROFOR activities.

The new forests policy thus leaves the provisions for the needs of forest-dependent peoples to the discretion of the borrower, creating huge space for abuses of all kinds, from illegal eviction to forcible changes in traditional management practices. Although the policy explicitly states that the *Bank does not finance projects that contravene applicable international environmental agreements*, the Bank refused to include a comparable phrase requiring borrowers to comply with applicable international human rights agreements as well. As it stands, the World Bank's OP 4.26 on Forests is weak and riddled with gaps which will inevitably lead to the further destruction of remaining old-growth forests and the abuse of forest-dwellers' human rights.

the South. In the Philippines, when the IMF's efforts to persuade the government to adopt structural adjustment in the late 1970s were blocked by nationalist factions within the Philippine Central Bank, the baton was handed over to the World Bank.

As Robin Broad records, by turning to Bank-trained allies in the Ministry of Industry and Finance, the World Bank was able to bypass nationalist factions within the Central Bank and put in place a US$200 million structural adjustment loan package, "tied not to a specific project but to a set of policy stipulations consolidating an export-led course for the Philippine industrial sector".[346] In the wake of the agreement, free trade zones were established "with generous incentives to transnational corporations to exploit low-cost Filipino labour", tariffs on imports were slashed and domestic small-scale industries (textiles and the like) restructured to cater for the export market."[347]

Such is the common culture that has emerged amongst Bank staff, and their counterparts in the government ministries with which the bank deals, that one staff member has described the Bank as having an "internally cloned system of thinking".[348] In particular, staff tend to approach the problems of poverty and environmental degradation as an essentially managerial problem, rather than as problems that arise from inequitable power relations.

Typically, environmental and social problems are primarily ascribed to *insufficient capital* (solution: increase Northern investment in the South); *outdated technology* (solution; open up the South to Northern technologies); a *lack of expertise* (solution: bring in Northern-educated managers and experts); and *faltering economic growth* (solution: push for increased growth). The key questions of whether money can solve the environmental crisis, of *who* benefits from capital and technology transfers, and of *whose* environment is to be managed, by *whom* and on *whose* behalf, are simply sidelined.

Accompanying this "mindset" is a set of assumptions about decision-making that eschew process in favour of *engineering consent* or the *naked exercise of power*. The prevailing attitude is encapsulated in the remarks of Jayme Porto Carreiro, a Bank Senior Energy Planner, who was recently seconded to Electricité de France (EDF under the Bank's "Share" scheme), a programme enabling employee sharing between multinational corporations and the World Bank:

> *I was to drop everything and manage the purchase of London Electricity (LE), a large power distribution company in England. [Facing a need to get approval from the EU's competition commission] my experience as Bank staff proved invaluable. I did what any of my colleagues would have done. I instructed the lawyers to tell the European Commission to change its laws.*

Lack of accountability compounds the anti-democratic tendencies inherent in the "Masters-of-the-Universe" approach of many Bank staff. Neither individual project staff nor the Bank itself are in any real sense accountable to the local communities affected by Bank projects, policies and programmes. Large-scale OMG projects tend to be implemented over decades but, typically, staff in government institutions, private companies, consultancies and banks, may only work on any one project for a few years or even a few months — often only a few weeks or days in the case of consultants on short-term contracts to assess issues such as social impacts. Yet the contents and consequences of their reports and decisions may not show up until months or years later.

This grave deficiency might be ameliorated if the institutions themselves were in some way legally obligated to the affected communities but in fact, grievance procedures are often unwieldy or absent, opportunities for legal redress tortuous, and responsible institutions remote. Enforceable contracts between OMG project developers and affected communities, whether indigenous or not, are the exception not the rule.[349]

This problem is likely to become more, not less, acute as the financing, building and operation of infrastructure projects generally moves to the private sector.[350] Already many private sector-funded projects are eschewing support from the main lending windows of agencies, such as the World Bank, because the environment and development standards required by the Bank are considered too onerous. Instead, companies are turning to publicly backed Export Credit and Investment Insurance Agencies (ECAs) to guarantee their investments and thus ease the task of raising private sector financing. A major attraction for industry of such ECAs is that, with rare exceptions -- the US Export-Import (Ex-Im) Bank and the US Overseas Private Investment Corporation (OPIC) being cases in point -- they have no mandatory human rights, environmental and development standards; they also have a secretive institutional culture.[351]

Drawing Conclusions

Where does all this lead us? What immediate conclusions might we draw from the growth of institutional norms referred to earlier?

First, and most obvious, that the problems identified in this report are unlikely to be addressed by new regulations *unless* and *until* the well-documented structural and institutional barriers to their rigorous implementation are addressed.

Second, that addressing those institutional and structural barriers will require root-and-branch overhaul of the mission, management and culture of institutions such as the World Bank. Institutions which act so consistently to the detriment of openness, accountability and democratic decision-making processes do not do so because of minor, easily remedied institutional failures. Their delinquency is far deeper-seated. Combating the pressure to lend, for example, requires more than mere exhortation to take seriously the World Bank's guidelines. It requires radical changes in incentives, severe career penalties for those who flout the rules, and legally enforceable means of redress for those who suffer the consequences.

Third, such radical change is unlikely to come about through the goodwill of the institutions under scrutiny. Public pressure is essential if change is to be achieved.

But some observers believe that the Bank, whatever changes might be instituted, is structurally incapable of addressing the demands for self-determination of indigenous peoples, and is not willing to do so. Hence it will never honour as it should the basic precept of "fully-informed prior consent" before extractive resource projects are adopted by the Bank. Not only will the required information not be fully imparted (especially in the case of IFC and MIGA funded projects — the Sepon project is a recent example), participation in fundamental local decision-making will never take precedence over financial parameters; and the prerogative of vetoing a project will never be entertained.

While it is true that the Bank has, over the past decade, refused to fund a number of mines (such as Rio Tinto/QMM's mineral sands venture in Madagascar) or grant political risk insurance (as it has with regards to Cambior's Gros Rosebel gold project in Suriname), these decisions have usually been taken because of inadequate design criteria. Meanwhile projects involving forced or unjustified resettlement (as with Sierra Rutile in Sierra Leone or KDL in the Kalahari) and the employment of dubious technology (Submarine Tailings Disposal at Lihir) have been waved through.

Above all, however, what many critics increasingly believe is that the Bank has, without foundation and adequate research, merely adopted the extractive industries' contention that OGM projects contribute directly to sustainable community development, so long as they can make a profit.

Instead of challenging this notion from the outset, the Bank has consistently upheld it. Indeed, it has been the prime agent in reforming state mining codes in favour of foreign private capital, and dismantling many state-owned mining companies instead of seeking to make them more efficient, democratically accountable and environmentally secure. In the process, many thousands of mineworkers have lost their jobs, manifestly self-serving companies have been allowed to usurp indigenous and national patrimony, and — instead of creating the basis for community sustenance -- Bank-supported mines have created social divisions and exacerbated communal conflicts.

FROM "BEST PRACTICE" TO BINDING STANDARDS

Over the past thirty years, industry attitudes towards indigenous peoples have changed substantially, both as a result of pressure from indigenous peoples and because of major advances in the recognition of the rights of indigenous peoples at the international and national levels. Indigenous rights groups emphasise that:

◻ Mining is a privilege not a right.
◻ Extractive Industries negatively impact the environment and therefore limit alternative development options.
◻ Current standards and practices in the EI sector are generally inadequate to protect the environment and fail to minimize negative environmental and social impacts. There is

a need to substantially raise standards of protection.
- ◻ Some current practices including marine dumping, river dumping and all off-site dumping of waste need to be banned.
- ◻ Some areas including those with protected area status within ancestral lands should be excluded from all EI development.

Given the profound and disruptive impact of Extractive Industries projects there should be a basic precautionary approach based on a presumption against such development. The onus in each project should therefore be on the proponent companies to justify and argue the need and value of the particular project, in all aspects so that the costs and benefits are reviewed in a critical manner. The current widespread presumption in favour of EI projects provides a framework that has clearly failed to safeguard affected communities and encourages speculative and non-viable projects

Successive reviews of the experience of indigenous peoples in many parts of the world suggest that the following standards should be observed as a minimal framework to guard against the negative effects of mining, oil and gas projects:

- ◻ Government policies and laws should be adopted and applied which recognise indigenous peoples' rights and promote cultural diversity, territorial management and self-governance, including recognition of the rights of indigenous women.
- ◻ Clear recognition of indigenous peoples' rights over their lands and territories and their rights to the use and access of the natural resources that they depend on.
- ◻ Effective protection of subsistence activities and the environment and other resources necessary to sustain such activities.
- ◻ Acceptance of the principle of free, prior and informed consent (including the right of local communities to say "no" to developments on their customary lands).
- ◻ For communities living in voluntary isolation, or where free, prior and informed consent is not given to the satisfaction of indigenous peoples and independent monitors who enjoy the confidence of local communities, then it should be assumed that consent has not been given.
- ◻ Recognition of the peoples' own representative institutions.

- Clear and mutually accepted mechanisms for the participation of indigenous peoples in decision-making.
- Acceptance that indigenous peoples are rightsholders and not just "stakeholders".
- Acceptance of the need to work in a human rights framework.
- Timely provision of information in culturally appropriate forms and in locally accepted languages.
- Full disclosure of company plans and risks.
- Identification of "bad actor" companies and governments and their exclusion from future projects.
- Recognition of the right of communities to conduct an independent audit of mines plans and operations, and the provision of resources for such.
- Provisions for the costs of indigenous peoples obtaining independent legal counsel and independent technical advice of their choice on social and environmental issues related to proposed mining.[352]
- Detailed, open and participatory environmental and social impact assessments, which should include respect for and use of indigenous knowledge, establishment of sound and agreed baseline data and open consultations with all affected groups.
- Culturally appropriate mechanisms to ensure the participation of marginalised groups within indigenous societies such as women and children, the elderly and those who are illiterate.
- Inclusiveness should be the guiding principle for negotiations and should include the involvement of groups living downstream and adjacent to proposed mine sites.
- Early and iterative negotiations between developers and affected peoples, providing time and respect for community decision-making processes.
- Negotiations to take place in indigenous peoples' territories or communities and not in far-off locales like capital cities nor in secret.
- Respect for communities' consensual decision-making processes. Industries and government agencies should not try to extract decisions as this may divide communities and create dissent.
- Agreements which provide enforceable contracts, mechanisms for the arbitration of disputes, and joint implemen-

tation and remedial measures, without demanding the surrender of rights.

- Agreements which include financial mechanisms for dealing with the costs resulting from both foreseen risks and unforeseen developments resulting from mines development.
- Establishment of parallel local citizens' oversight committees to assess progress and activate redress mechanisms when necessary.
- Full protection of key religious and cultural sites and areas vital to subsistence.
- Compensation with land for land.
- Joint monitoring and evaluation making full use of indigenous knowledge.
- No forced relocation.
- Resettlement and impact mitigation plans, which ensure that those affected end up better off than before the project.
- Benefit sharing options including revenue sharing or joint ownership schemes.
- Mechanisms to ensure the transparent and equitable administration of funds for community benefit.
- Capacity building of indigenous peoples' institutions.
- Mutually agreed, legally binding and enforceable reclamation plans to restore lands and habitats after mine closure, including credible and full financing, to ensure that the mine sites are left safe and stable.
- Companies should be required to post adequate bonds to cover restoration and guard against disasters and damage: the "polluter pays" principle should operate.
- Establishment of independent regulatory oversight mechanisms that include local participation and enjoy local confidence to ensure compliance.
- Mutually accepted arbitration processes for the resolution of ensuing disputes.
- Guarantees not to use private armies or repressive security forces. No physical force, coercion or bribery should be applied.
- Mutually agreed, formal and legally enforceable contracts, binding on all parties and enforceable through the national courts.[353]

Companies vary greatly in the extent to which they have adopted any of these principles as corporate practice. Certainly it is true to say that an overall shift in the industry towards an acceptance of greater community participation is discernible.[354] Some multinational companies have begun to accept that their mining and oil and gas operations should, at least, comply with the provisions of the International Labour Organisations Convention 169 even in countries which have not ratified the convention. However, as the North-South Institute of Canada notes, after carrying out a very comprehensive review of the consultation and participation procedures within the mining sector:

> *To date there is not one company that has enshrined the concept of free, prior and informed consent in its corporate responsibility or Aboriginal policy.*[355]

Studies make clear that reliance on codes of conduct and self-regulation are not enough to secure the rights of indigenous peoples. In the absence of binding regulations and legally enforceable agreements and contracts, the powerful interests of the extractive industries all too easily override local concerns. The history of mining is indeed, to a large extent, a history of breached agreements, bad faith consultations and consequent social and environmental damage.

Socially and environmentally acceptable mining can only be achieved within a strong and adequate framework of law, which secures full respect for human rights including the rights of indigenous peoples, and which is backed up by credible sanctions for violations and enforced through independent monitoring. The time for reliance on voluntary standards is passed. Binding national regulations, enforceable international standards and clear contracts between miners and affected peoples are the only way forward.

CONCLUSIONS AND RECOMMENDATIONS

A preliminary conclusion of the World Bank's own internal review of extractive industries is that:

> *Increased investment in the EI [Extractive Industries] sector has the potential to bring important development benefits but it is not a universal good. In fact, the evidence suggests that it is more likely to lead to bad development outcomes when governance is poor. Because of the Bank's focus on poverty, and the links between poverty and poor governance, this means that increased EI investment is likely to lead to bad development outcomes for many if not most of*

Box 20: *Mining and Indigenous Peoples - Emerging Standards*

International agencies such as the International Finance Corporation (the private sector arm of the World Bank), Bread for the World (Germany), the International Labour Organisation and Conservation International, have not yet accepted such clear principles. They propose the following for improving the relations between indigenous peoples and the mining, oil and gas industries:

Establish a Consultation Mechanism from the Beginning
- Clear process for information sharing in appropriate languages.
- Early, open disclosure of information.
- Effective public consultations and two-way communications
- Recognition of peoples' own representative institutions.
- Demonstrable mechanisms which allow peoples' views to influence decision-making.

Carry out a Detailed Environmental Impact Assessments
- Establish sound baseline data making use of indigenous knowledge.
- Identification of risks and elaboration of a mitigation plan.
- Identification of remedial measures to restore degraded areas after mines closure.

Carry out a Detailed Social Impact Assessment
- Scoping to assess parameters.
- Involvement of local "stakeholders".
- Use of indigenous knowledge.
- Pay special attention to livelihood, health and cultural issues.

Institute a Monitoring and Evaluation Process
- Involve local people in M&E.
- Make use of local knowledge and Participatory Rapid Rural Appraisal methods.
- Agree on a Community Development Plan.
- Benefit sharing plan.
- Establishment of independently managed community trust funds.
- Compensation plan.

□ Appoint Community Liaison Officer.

Recognise the Rights of the Indigenous Peoples
□ Regularise tenure and recognise the rights of customary owners.

Establish Clear Regulatory Frameworks
□ Regularise land ownership and demarcate indigenous territories.
□ Revise laws and regulations through participatory processes.
□ Transform voluntary guidelines into required best practice.
□ Provide mechanisms by which citizens can gain redress through the courts.
□ Allow affected groups to sue foreign companies in the courts in their home countries.
□ Promote international regulatory bodies and international courts.[356]

the Bank's clients.[357]

These conclusions derive from a macro-level analysis of developing countries' economic performance. However, the conclusion is also relevant to local situations, where indigenous peoples are concerned. In these situations, "poor governance" can be taken to mean lack of respect for indigenous peoples' right to self-determination and self-governance.

Where there is a lack of respect for human rights and in particular the rights of indigenous peoples, where there is an absence of the rule of law, and where there is little sensitivity to cultural differences, then large-scale extractive industry projects are very likely to have serious negative impacts on indigenous peoples.

Extractive industry projects are only likely to operate to the benefit of indigenous peoples if the "best practice" standards set out in the previous section are scrupulously adhered to and if binding mechanisms are available to enforce these standards and hold those who violate them to account.

To date the World Bank has refused to accept these standards in dealing with indigenous peoples.

□ The Bank has refused to make borrower countries' adherence to the international human rights treaties, that the countries themselves have subscribed to, as a condition for funding.

◻ The Bank has refused to make recognition of indigenous peoples' land rights a pre-condition for its funding.

◻ The Bank has refused to incorporate the principle of free, prior and informed consent into its safeguard policies. It has refused to accept the proposed standards on indigenous peoples put forward by the World Commission on Dams.

◻ The Bank has refused to adopt standards to ensure that indigenous peoples should not be involuntarily removed from their lands to make way for development.

Moreover, as successive studies have shown and this review has substantiated further, the Bank routinely fails to adhere to those (lower) standards which it has incorporated into its safeguard policies. These compliance failures result from institutional and incentive structures within the Bank, which give low priority to human rights and community concerns and which, instead, prioritise and reward the interests of big business and rapid capital investment.

Given these realities it is hard to avoid the conclusion that, unless there are dramatic changes in the World Bank's policies and performance, **the World Bank should not support, either directly or indirectly, extractive industries that may affect indigenous peoples**.

Recommendations

Ultimately, responsibility to respect, protect and uphold the rights and interests of indigenous peoples rests with the governments of the countries in which these peoples reside. However, in countries with poor governance and where indigenous rights are not respected, development agencies mandated to alleviate poverty **must** seek to make up the "democratic deficit" by working to higher standards that make real development in indigenous areas possible. To do otherwise is to continue to accept that the rights and interests of indigenous peoples should be sacrificed in the name of 'progress'.[358]

If the World Bank is to operate as a responsible development agency, and not just as another bank in competition with other lenders with low social standards, then the World Bank will have to revise its policy on indigenous peoples. Key revisions must include the following:

- ❏ The Bank must require borrowers' and clients' adherence to international human rights standards.
- ❏ Recognition of indigenous peoples' rights to their lands, territories and resources must be made a precondition of Bank funding.
- ❏ The Bank must proscribe its support for projects that require the resettlement of indigenous peoples without their consent.
- ❏ The Bank should not support any developments that may negatively affect culturally important or sacred sites.
- ❏ Bank support for developments that may affect, directly or indirectly, indigenous peoples' lands, territories and resources should be subject to the free, prior and informed consent of the peoples concerned.
- ❏ New mechanisms of accountability must be developed at project, country and international levels to allow affected peoples redress for their grievances and to secure compensation for losses.
- ❏ These policy and procedural reforms must apply to the whole World Bank Group -- IBRD, IDA, GEF, IFC, MIGA and ICSID -- and must apply to technical assistance projects, grants, loans, credits, investments, equity arrangements, guarantees and other forms of development support, including sectoral and structural adjustment support and programmatic lending.
- ❏ Indigenous peoples must also be involved in integrated prior "upstream" planning of development schemes to ensure that proposed developments complement and do not undermine alternative livelihood development strategies.
- ❏ The World Bank should support civil society and indigenous peoples' calls for binding "Code on Corporate Accountability".
- ❏ The EIR should also promote indigenous demands for a "good practice" seminar on Extractive Industries under auspices of the Office of the High Commissioner on Human Rights.

However, as authors of this document, we doubt that these reforms, by themselves, are enough, given the poor record of the Bank in complying with its own standards. Even if the Bank does adopt these standards, what are the chances that it will actually adhere to them in the future? Changes will also be required in internal accountability procedures and incentive structures to ensure that Bank staff are rewarded and not penalised for taking time and care to comply with policies. This will require both "carrots and sticks" -- positive rewards for effective performance and tangible penalties for lack of due diligence. The Bank will also have to accept that these tightened procedures and higher standards will imply far higher "transaction costs", in the preparation of projects and programmes, and for effective implementation and monitoring.

It is only once and if such reforms of standards and procedures have been accepted by the Bank and demonstrably applied that the World Bank Group should consider getting involved in partnering "dirty industries". Until then the Extractive Industries sector should be a "no-go zone" for the Bank.

The central component of this "focused research" was a workshop held in Oxford on 14 -15 April 2003. At this workshop the indigenous participants presented a declaration on extractive industries which provides the best possible conclusion to this work.

Endnotes

[1] Navroz K Dubash, Mairi Dupar, Smitu Kothari and Tundu Lissu, 2001, *A Watershed in Global Governance? An independent assessment of the World Commission on Dams*, World Resources Institute, Lokayan and Lawyers' Environmental Action Team, Delhi.

[2] Marcus Colchester, 2002, The World Bank's Extractive Industries Review: a credible and independent review of World Bank engagement in the Mining, Oil and Gas Sectors? *Indigenous Perspectives* 5(1):96-105.

[3] Extractive Industries Review Working Paper: Compilation of Consultation Inputs, February 4 2003.

[4] E/CN.4/Sub.2/1986/7.

[5] AITPN, 1999, .

[6] Irene Daes, 1996, Supplementary Report of the Special Rapporteur on the Protection of the Heritage of Indigenous Peoples, United Nations Sub-Commission on Prevention of Discrimination and Protection of Minorities, forty-eighth Session, E/CN.4.Sub.2/1996/22.

[7] *General Recommendation VIII concerning the interpretation and application of article 1, paragraphs 1 and 4 of the Convention (1990)*.

[8] *Concluding Observsation of the Committee on the Elimination of Racial Discrimination. Denmark21/05/2002.*

[9] Andrew Gray, 1995, The Indigenous Movement in Asia. In: Barnes, R H, Gray, A and Kingsbury, B (Eds) *Indigenous Peoples of Asia*, The Association

for Asian Studies Inc, Michigan 35-59. Patrick Thornberry, 1996, Indigenous Peoples: A short note on concept and definition. Statement to the UN Working Group on Indigenous Populations, ms; Benedict Kingsbury, 1995, Indigenous Peoples as an International Legal Concept. In: Barnes, R H, Gray, A and Kingsbury, B (Eds) *Indigenous Peoples of Asia*, The Association for Asian Studies Inc, Michigan:13-35; 1998 "Indigenous Peoples" in International Law: a constructivist approach to the Asian controversy, *American Journal of International Law*, 92(3):414-457.

[10] *Report of the Special Rapporteur on the situation of human rights and fundamental freedoms of indigenous people, Mr. Rodolfo Stavenhagen, submitted pursuant to Commission resolution 2001/57.* UN Doc. E/CN.4/2002/97, at para. 100.

[11] *Conceptual Framework Paper (2nd draft) by the Working Group on the Rights of Indigenous Peoples/Communities in Africa of the African Commission on Human and Peoples' Rights*, 20 December 2002, 6-7.

[12] B. Kingsbury, Operational Policies of International Institutions as Part of the Law-Making Process: The World Bank and Indigenous Peoples. In, G.S. Goodwin-Gill & S. Talmon (eds.), *The Reality of International Law: Essays in Honour of Ian Brownlie*. Oxford: Clarendon Press (1999), at 324.

[13] *Report of the Special Rapporteur on the situation of human rights and fundamental freedoms of indigenous people, Mr. Rodolfo Stavenhagen, submitted pursuant to Commission resolution 2001/57.* UN Doc. E/CN.4/2002/97, at para. 56.

[14] *Indigenous people and their relationship to land. Final working paper prepared by Mrs. Erica-Irene A. Daes, Special Rapporteur.* UN Doc. E/CN.4/Sub.2/2001/21. at paras. 49-50.

[15] *I. Lansman et al. vs. Finland (Communication No. 511/1992)*, CCPR/C/52/D/511/1992, 10.

[16] *Report on the Situation of Human Rights in Ecuador.* OEA/Ser.L/V/II.96, Doc. 10 rev. 1 1997, 89.

[17] *Communication No. 155/96, The Social and Economic Rights Action Center and the Center for Economic and Social Rights / Nigeria*, at para. 58 and 69 (hereafter 'Ogoni Case') – "The intervention of multinational corporations may be a potentially positive force for development if the State and the people concerned are ever mindful of the common good and the sacred rights of individuals and communities."

[18] Among others, see, UN Committee on the Elimination of Racial Discrimination, *General Recommendation XXIII (51) concerning Indigenous Peoples.* Adopted at the Committee's 1235th meeting, 18 August 1997. UN Doc. CERD/C/51/Misc.13/Rev.4.; and, UN Committee on Economic, Social and Cultural Rights, General Comment No. 7, The Right to Adequate Housing (Art. 11(1) of the Covenant): forced evictions (1997). In, *Compilation of General Comments and General Recommendations Adopted by Human Rights Treaty Bodies.* UN Doc. HRI/GEN/1/Rev.5, 26 April 2001, pps. 49-54, at para. 18 (hereafter 'General Comments/Recommendations Compilation').

[19] *Vienna Declaration and Programme of Action*, adopted by the World Conference on Human Rights on 25 June 1993, Part I, at para. 10. UN Doc. A/CONF.157/23, 12 July 1993.

[20] Among others, see, *Rio Declaration on Environment and Development*,

UN Doc. A/CONF.151/26 (Vol. 1) (1992); *Copenhagen Declaration and Programme of Action*, UN Doc. UN Doc. A/CONF. 166/9 (1995); G.A. Res. 42/115, 11 February 1988, The Impact of Property on the Enjoyment of Human Rights and Fundamental Freedoms; Commission on Human Rights Resolutions 1987/18 and 1988/19; *Principles relating to the human rights conduct of companies. Working paper prepared by Mr. David Weissbrodt*. E/CN.4/Sub.2/2000/WG.2/WP.1, 25 May 2000; M. Addo (ed.), *Human Rights Standards and the Responsibility of Transnational Corporations*. The Hague: Kluwer Law International (1999); J.R. Paul, Holding Multinational Corporations Responsible Under International Law 24 *Hastings Int'l. and Comp. Law Rev.* 285 (2001); Patrick Macklem, Indigenous Rights and Multinational Corporations at International Law, *24 Hastings Int'l. and Comp. Law Rev.* 475 (2001); and, B. Frey, The Legal and Ethical Responsibilities of Transnational Corporations in the Protections of International Human Rights, 6 *Minn. J. Global Trade* 153 (1996).

[21] Inter-American Court on *Human Rights, Velasquez Rodriguez Case, Judgment of 29 July 1988*, Ser. C No. 4, para. 172 – "An illegal act which violates human rights and which is initially not directly imputable to a State (for example, because it is the act of a private person or because the person responsible has not been identified) can lead to international responsibility of the State, not because of the act itself, but because of the lack of due diligence to prevent the violation or to respond to it as required by the Convention;" - Inter-American Commission on Human Rights, *Case 7615 (Brazil)*. OEA/Ser.L/V/II.66, doc 10 rev 1 (1985), 33; UN Human Rights Committee, Communication Nos. 161/1983, Annual Rep. Of the HRC 1988, 197 and 181/1984, Annual Rep. of the HRC 1990 (Vol. II), 37; Ogoni Case, at para. 58 and; European Court of Human Rights, *Sunday Times Case, Judgment of 26 April 1979*, E.C.H.R., Ser. A, (Vol. 30), 318.

[22] Among others, C.F. Amerasinghe, *Principles of the Institutional Law of International Organizations*. Cambridge: Cambridge University Press (1996), 240; H.G. Schermers and N.M. Blokker, *International Institutional Law: Unity within Diversity* (3rd Rev. Ed.) Martinus Nijhoff: The Hague (1995), 824 & 988; S. Skogly, *The Human Rights Obligations of the World Bank and IMF*. Cavendish: London, (2001), 84-87; P. Sands & P. Klein (eds.), *Bowett's Law of International Institutions* (5th Ed.), London: Sweet & Maxwell (2001), 458-59; and, F. Morgenstern, *Legal Problems of International Organizations*. Cambridge: Grotius Publications (1986), 32.

[23] Interpretation of the Agreement of 25th of March 1951 between WHO and Egypt. International Court of Justice, *Reports of Judgments, Advisory Opinions and Orders* (1980), 89-90.

[24] Among others, D. Bradlow & C. Grossman, Limited Mandates and Intertwined Problems: A New Challenge for the World Bank and the IMF. 17 *Human Rights Q.* 411, 428 and; F. MacKay, Universal Rights or a Universe Unto Itself? Indigenous Peoples' Human Rights and the World Bank's Draft operational Policy 4.10 on Indigenous Peoples, 17 *American University International Law Review* 527, 568-70.

[25] Among others, see, *Bowett's Law of International Institutions*, *supra* note 11, 458-59 and; *Human rights as the primary objective of international trade, invest-*

ment and finance policy and practice. Working paper submitted by J. Oloka-Onyango and Deepika Udagama, in accordance with Sub-Commission resolution 1998/12. UN Doc. E/CN.4/Sub.2/1999/11, para. 33.

[26] *Report of the Special Rapporteur, supra* note 2, paras. 39-40. See, also, *Indigenous people and their relationship to land, supra* note 3.

[27] *Indigenous peoples and their relationship to land,* id, at para. 20.

[28] *Bridging the Gap Between Human Rights and Development: From Normative Principles to Operational Relevance.* Lecture by Mary Robinson, United Nations High Commissioner for Human Rights, World Bank, Washington D.C., Preston Auditorium, 3 December 2001.

[29] *Indigenous people and their relationship to land, supra* note 3, at para. 123.

[30] *Concluding observations of the Human Rights Committee: Canada. 07/04/99,* at para. 8. UN Doc. CCPR/C/79/Add.105. (Concluding Observations/Comments) (1999). In accord, see, also, *Concluding observations of the Human Rights Committee: Mexico.* UN Doc. CCPR/C/79/Add.109 (1999), para. 19; *Concluding observations of the Human Rights Committee: Norway.* UN Doc. CCPR/C/79/Add.112 (1999), paras. 10 and 17; and *Concluding observations of the Human Rights Committee: Australia.* 28/07/2000. CCPR/CO/69/AUS. (*Concluding Observations/Comments*), para. 8.

[31] Article 27 reads: "In those States in which ethnic, religious or linguistic minorities exist, persons belonging to such minorities shall not be denied the right, in community with the other members of the group, to enjoy their own culture, to profess and practice their own religion, or to use their own language."

[32] The ICCPR has been ratified by 149 States as of December 2002.

[33] Bernard Ominayak, Chief of the Lubicon Lake Band vs. Canada, *Report of the Human Rights Committee,* 45 UN GAOR Supp. (No.43), UN Doc. A/45/40 , vol. 2 (1990), 1. See also, Kitok vs. Sweden, *Report of the Human Rights Committee,* 43 UN GAOR Supp. (No.40) UN Doc. A/43/40; Lovelace vs. Canada (No. 24/1977), *Report of the Human Rights Committee,* 36 UN GAOR Supp. (No. 40) 166, UN Doc. A/36/40 (1981). I. Lansman et al. vs. Finland (Communication No. 511/1992), *supra* note 4; *J. Lansman et al. vs. Finland* (Communication No. 671/1995), UN Doc. CCPR/C/58/D/671/1995; and General Comment No. 23 (50) (art. 27), *adopted by the Human Rights Committee at its 1314th meeting (fiftieth session), 6 April 1994.* UN Doc. CCPR/C/21/Rev.1/Add.5.. Although not decided under article 27, see, also, *Hopu v. France.* Communication No. 549/1993: France. 29/12/97. UN Doc. CCPR/C/60/D/549/1993/Rev.1, 29 December 1997.

[34] Among others, Ominayak vs. Canada, *Report of the Human Rights Committee,* id. See, also, A. Huff, Resource Development and Human Rights: A Look at the Case of the Lubicon Cree Indian Nation of Canada. 10 Colorado J. *Int'l. Enviro. Law and Policy* 161 (1999).

[35] *General Comment No. 23 (50) (art. 27), supra* note 22, at 3.

[36] *Concluding observations of the Human Rights Committee: Australia, supra* note 19, at paras. 10 and 11.

[37] The CRC has been ratified by 191 States as of December 2002.

[38] Human Rights Committee, General Comment No. 24, *Issues relating to*

reservations made upon ratification or accession to the Covenant or the Optional Protocols thereto, or in relation to declarations under article 41 of the Covenant : 04/ 11/94 (1994), para. 8. See, also, S.J. Anaya, Indigenous Rights Norms in Contemporary International Law, 8 *Ariz. J. Int'l & Comp. L.* 1, 15 (1991) and, L.V. Prott, Cultural Rights as Peoples Rights in International Law. In, J. Crawford (ed.), *The Rights of Peoples.* Oxford: Clarendon Press (1988), 93.

    [39] The ICESCR has been ratified by 146 states as of December 2002.

    [40] *Concluding observations of the Committee on Economic, Social and Cultural Rights:Canada. 10/12/98. E/C.12/1/Add.31, at para. 18.*

    [41] Id., at para. 43.

    [42] *Concluding Observations of the Committee on Economic, Social and Cultural Rights : Panama. 24/09/2001. UN Doc. E/C.12/1/Add.64, at para. 12.*

    [43] CERD has been ratified by 165 States as of December 2002.

    [44] T. Meron, *Human Rights and Humanitarian Norms as Customary Law.* Oxford: Clarendon Press (1989), 21.

    [45] *General Recommendation XXIII (51) concerning Indigenous Peoples, supra* note 7.

    [46] P. Thornberry, *Indigenous Peoples and Human Rights.* Manchester: Manchester University Press (2002), at 217-18.

    [47] See, among others, *Report on the Situation of Human Rights of a Segment of the Nicaraguan Population of Miskito Origin* , OEA/Ser.L/V/II.62, doc.26. (1984), at 76-78, 81; *Report on the Situation of Human Rights in Ecuador, supra* note 5, at 103-4; Case 7615 (Brazil), OEA/Ser.L/V/II.66, doc 10 rev 1 (1985), at 24, 31; and, *Third Report on the Situation of Human Rights in The Republic of Guatemala* OEA/Ser.l/V/II. 67, doc. 9 (1986), at 114.

    [48] *Third Report on the Situation of Human Rights in The Republic of Guatemala*, id.

    [49] Case 11.577 (Awas Tingni Indigenous Community - Nicaragua), *Annual report of the IACHR.* OEA/Ser.L/V/II.102, Doc.6 rev., (Vol. II), April 16, 1999, 1067, para. 108 and, See, also, art. XVIII, *Proposed American Declaration on the Rights of Indigenous Peoples,* approved by the IACHR in 1997.

    [50] *Report on the Situation of Human Rights in Ecuador, supra* note 5, at 114-15.

    [51] *Second Report on the Situation of Human Rights in Peru,* OEA/Ser.L/V/ II.106, Doc 59 rev., (2000), at Ch. X, para. 16. See, also, in accord, *Third Report on the Human Rights Situation of Human Rights in Paraguay.* OEA/Ser.L/V/ II.110 Doc.52 (2001), Ch. IX, para. 47.

    [52] Judgment of the Inter-American Court of Human Rights in the case of The Mayagna (Sumo) Indigenous Community of Awas Tingni v. the Republic of Nicaragua Issued 31 August 2001, *Inter-Am. Court on Human Rights, Series C,* No. 79 (2001), at para. 149.

    [53] Id., at para. 151.

    [54] Id., at para. 164.

    [55] Inter-American Commission of Human Rights, *Report N° 75/02,* Case N° 11.140, Mary and Carrie Dann (United States), Dec. 27, 2002. OEA/Ser.L/ V/II.116, Doc. 46, at para. 130. (footnotes omitted) (hereafter 'Mary and Carrie Dann Case').

    [56] Id., at para. 131.

[57] As of December 2002, the following 17 states have ratified ILO 169: Mexico, Norway, Costa Rica, Colombia, Denmark, Ecuador, Fiji, Guatemala, The Netherlands, Dominica, Peru, Bolivia, Honduras, Venezuela, Argentina Brazil and Paraguay. The following states have submitted it to their national legislatures for ratification or are discussing ratification: Chile, The Philippines, Finland, El Salvador, Russian Federation, Panama, and Sri Lanka. Germany has adopted ILO 169 as the basis for its overseas development aid and the Asian Development Bank and the UNDP have incorporated some of its substance into their policies on Indigenous peoples. See, for instance, Asian Development Bank, *The Bank's Policy on Indigenous Peoples*, April 1998.

[58] *Report of the Committee of Experts on the Application of Conventions and Recommendations*, Report III(4A), at 287, International Labour Conference, 75th Session, Geneva (1988).

[59] *Traditional Knowledge and Biological Diversity*, UNEP/CBD/TKBD/1/2, 18 October 1997.

[60] I. Brownlie, *Principles of Public International Law (4th ed.)*. Oxford: OUP (1990) – "The rule universally accepted is that the subsoil belongs to the state which has sovereignty over the surface," at 119.

[61] G.A. Res. 523(VI) and 626(VII), 12 January 1952 and 21 December 1952.

[62] G.A. Res. 837 (IX) 14 December 1954, Recommendations Concerning International Respect for the Right of Peoples and Nations to Self-Determination; 1314 (XIII) 12 December 1958, Recommendations Concerning International Respect for the Right of Peoples and Nations to Self-Determination; 1720(XVI), 19 December 1961, Permanent Sovereignty over Natural Resources; and 1803 (XVII), 14 December 1962, Permanent Sovereignty over Natural Resources.

[63] Among others, see, G.A. Res. 3201 (S-VI), 1 May 1974, Declaration on the Establishment of a New International Economic Order and, G.A. Res. 3281 (XXIX), 12 December 1974, Charter of Economic Rights and Duties of States. The latter reads in article 1: "Every State has and shall freely exercise full permanent sovereignty, including possession, use and disposal, over all its wealth, natural resources and economic activities."

[64] See, Convention on Biological Diversity, article 3, which reads: "States have, in accordance with the Charter of the United Nations and the principles of international law, the sovereign right to exploit their own resources pursuant to their own environmental policies." See, also, Article 22(1) of the CBD, titled 'Relationship with Other International Conventions', which provides that: "The provisions of this Convention shall not affect the rights and obligations of any Contracting Party deriving from any existing international agreement, except where the exercise of those rights and obligations would cause a serious damage or threat to biological diversity."

[65] N. Schrijver, *Sovereignty over Natural Resources: Balancing Rights and Duties*. Cambridge Studies in International Law. Cambridge: Cambridge University Press (1997), 391.

[66] *Principles of Public International Law, supra* note 49, 597 (referring to the right of self-determination as informing and complementing other principles of international law, such as state sovereignty.).

[67] *Sovereignty over Natural Resources, supra* note 54, at 391 and, at 9 – "Various injunctions have been formulated according to which States have to exercise their right to permanent sovereignty in the interest of their populations and to respect the rights of indigenous peoples to the natural wealth and resources in their regions, where 'peoples' are objects rather than subjects of international law."

[68] Among others, J. Crawford, The Right of Self-Determination in International Law: Its Development and Future. In, P. Alston (ed.), *Peoples' Rights*. Oxford: OUP (2001), pps. 7-68, 27 and; E-I. Daes, The Spirit and Letter of the Right to Self-Determination of Indigenous Peoples: Reflections on the Making of the United Nations Draft Declaration. In, P. Aikio and M. Scheinin (eds.), *Operationalizing the Right of Indigenous Peoples to Self-Determination.* Turku: Institute for Human Rights, Abo Akademi University, (2000), pps. 67-84, 76-77.

[69] Article 47 of the ICCPR and Article 25 of the ICESCR, provide that "Nothing in the present Covenant shall be interpreted as impairing the inherent right of all peoples to enjoy and utilize fully and freely their natural wealth and resources."

[70] T. Moses, The Right to Self-Determination and its Significance to the Survival of Indigenous Peoples. In, *Operationalizing the Right of Indigenous Peoples to Self-Determination. supra* note 57, pps. 155-78, at 162-4.

[71] A. Cassese, *Self-Determination of Peoples. A Legal Reappraisal.* Cambridge: Cambridge University Press (1995), at 144.

[72] Among others, The Right of Self-Determination in International Law: Its Development and Future, *supra* note 57. Crawford states that:

> *Just as a matter of ordinary treaty interpretation, one cannot interpret Article 1 as limited to the colonial case. Article 1 does not say that some peoples have the right to self-determination. Nor can the term 'peoples' be limited to colonial peoples. Article [1, paragraph] 3 deals expressly, and non-exclusively, with colonial territories. When a text says that 'all peoples' have a right – the term 'peoples' having a general connotation – and then in another paragraph of the same article, its says that the term 'peoples' includes peoples of colonial territories, it is perfectly clear that the term is being used in its general sense.*

Id., at 27. See, also, Human Rights Committee, General comment 12, *The right to self-determination of peoples* (Art. 1): 13/04/84 (1984), at para. 6 - Article 1(3) "imposes specific obligations on States parties, not only in relation to their own peoples but vis-à-vis all peoples which have not been able to exercise or have been deprived of the possibility of exercising their right to self-determination" (emphasis added) – and, in accord, Committee on the Elimination of Racial Discrimination, *General Recommendation XXI on the right to self-determination* (1996), at para. 5 – "the rights of all peoples within a State."

[73] For an extensive discussion on this issue by a member of the Human Rights Committee, see, M. Scheinin, The Right to Self-Determination under the Covenant on Civil and Political Rights. In, *Operationalizing the Right of*

Indigenous Peoples to Self-Determination, supra note 57, pps. 179-202.

[74] *Concluding observations of the Human Rights Committee: Canada, supra* note 19.

[75] *Supra* note 19.

[76] *Apirana Mahuika et al. vs. New Zealand* (Communication No. 547/1993, 15/11/2000)), UN Doc. CCPR/C/70/D/547/1993 (2000), at para. 9.2. See, also M. Scheinin, supra note 62.

[77] *General Comment No. 15, The right to water (arts. 11 and 12 of the International Covenant on Economic, Social and Cultural Rights).* UN Doc. E/C.12/2002/11, 26 November 2002 ,at para. 7. The Committee added that: "The international financial institutions, notably the International Monetary Fund and the World Bank, should take into account the right to water in their lending policies, credit agreements, structural adjustment programmes and other development projects (see General Comment No. 2 (1990)), so that the enjoyment of the right to water is promoted." Id., at para. 60.

[78] G.A. Res. 41/128 of 4 December 1986, Declaration on the Right to Development.

[79] To date, 53 African states have ratified the Charter.

[80] Article 21 of the African Charter states in pertinent part that: "1. All peoples shall freely dispose of their wealth and natural resources. This right shall be exercised in the exclusive interest of the people. In no case shall a people be deprived of it. 2. In case of spoliation the dispossessed people shall have the right to the lawful recovery of its property as well as to an adequate compensation."

[81] See, among others, R. N. Kiwanuka, The Meaning of "People" in the African Charter on Human and Peoples' Rights, 82 *Am. J. Int'l* L. 80-101 (1988) and; P. Nobel, 'The Concept of `Peoples' in the African (Banjul) Charter on Human and Peoples' Rights.' In, P. Nobel (ed.), *Refugees and Development in Africa*, 9-18, Uppsala: Scandinavian Institute of African Studies (1987).

[82] The Ogoni self-identify as indigenous and have taken an active role in the UN Working Group on Indigenous Populations.

[83] Ogoni Case, at para. 58.

[84] Id., at para. 45 (footnotes omitted).

[85] *Proposed Draft Human Rights Code of Conduct for Companies.* Working paper prepared by Mr. David Weissbrodt. E/CN.4/Sub.2/2000/WG.2/WP.1/Add.1, 25 May 2000, at paras. 14 and 18.

[86] *Indigenous peoples' permanent sovereignty over natural resources. Working paper by Erica-Irene Daes, former Chairperson of the Working Group on Indigenous Populations.* UN Doc. E/CN.4/Sub.2/2002/23, at para. 6.

[87] See, among others, G.A. Res. 41/128 of 4 December 1986, Declaration on the Right to Development.

[88] Id., at para. 7.

[89] Among others, see, *Concluding observations of the Human Rights Committee: Canada, supra* note 19 and; Committee on the Elimination of Racial Discrimination, Decision (2) 54 on Australia, 18 March 1999. UN Doc. A/54/18, para. 21.

[90] *Elwes v. Brigg Gas and Co.* (1886) 33 Ch D 568 – "Being ... in lawful

possession, he was in possession of the ground, not merely the surface, but of everything that lay beneath the surface down to the centre of the earth ...," per Chitty J., at 568, and; *Rowbotham v. Wilson* (1860) HLC 348, at 360; 11 ER 463, at 468 – "There is no doubt that prima facie the owner of the surface is entitled to the surface itself and all below it *ex jure naturae* ...," per Lord Wensleydale.

[91] For US cases, see, among others, *United States v. Shoshone Tribe of Indians* 304 US 111 (1938); *United States v. Klamath and Moadoc Tribes* 304 US 119 (1938); and, *Otoe and Missouri Tribe v. United States* 131 F Supp 265 (1955). Canadian cases, see, *Delgamuukw v. British Columbia* [1997] 3 S.C.R. 1010; and Guerin v R (1985) 13 DLR 4th 321. Australian cases: among others, *Mabo v. Queensland No.2* (1992) 175 CLR 166 and; *Ward on behalf of the Miriuwung and Gajerrong People v. Western Australia* (1998) 159 ALR 483.

[92] Delgamuukw, at 1086.

[93] Among others, *United States v. Northern Paiute Nation* (1968) 393 F 2d 786.

[94] *Sovereignty over Natural Resources, supra* note 54, at 318.

[95] See, for instance, Preambular paragraph 7, Proposed American Declaration on the Rights of Indigenous Peoples, supra note 38, - "Recognizing that indigenous peoples are a subject of international law....".

[96] *General Recommendation XXIII (51) concerning Indigenous Peoples, supra* note 7, at para. 3.

[97] Id., at para. 4(d).

[98] *Concluding Observations by the Committee on the Elimination of Racial Discrimination : Australia.* 24/03/2000. CERD/C/56/Misc.42/rev.3, at para. 9. See, also, among others, *Concluding observations of the Committee on the Elimination of Racial Discrimination : Costa Rica.* 20/03/2002 and, *Concluding observations of the Committee on the Elimination of Racial Discrimination : United States of America.* 14/08/2001.

[99] Mary and Carrie Dann Case, at para. 131.

[100] Id., at para. 140.

[101] Inter-American Commission of Human Rights, Report No. 27/98 (Nicaragua), at para. 142, cited in, The Mayagna (Sumo) Awas Tingni Community Case, Judgment on the Preliminary Objections of February 1, 2000, *Inter-Am.* Ct. H.R. Ser. C, No. 66 (2000). See, also, Case 11.577 (Awas Tingni Indigenous Community - Nicaragua), *supra* note 38, para. 108.

[102] Mary and Carrie Dann Case, at para. 130. (footnotes omitted).

[103] *Concluding Observations of the Committee on Economic, Social and Cultural Rights: Colombia.* 30/11/2001. E/C.12/Add. 1/74, at para. 12.

[104] Id., at para. 33.

[105] The CTC reported to the Working Group four times: proposing methodology, and a draft questionnaire for distribution to Indigenous Peoples (UN Doc. E/CN.4/Sub.2/AC.4/1990/6); a preliminary report (UN Doc. E/CN.4/Sub.2/1991/49); a report focusing on the Americas (UN Doc. E/CN.4/Sub.2/1992/54) and; a report focusing on Asia and Africa, summarizing the findings of all reports and making recommendations "to mitigate the adverse impacts of TNCs on indigenous peoples' lands, and increase indigenous peoples' participation in relevant government and TNC decision-mak-

ing." (UN Doc. E/CN.4/Sub.2/1994/40).

[106] *Report of the Commission on Transnational Corporations to the Working Group on Indigenous Populations.* UN Doc. E/CN.4/Sub.2/1994/40, at para. 20.

[107] *Report of the Workshop on Indigenous Peoples, Private Sector Natural Resource, Energy, Mining Companies and Human Rights.* Geneva, 5-7 December 2001. E/CN.4/Sub.2/AC.4/2002/3, 17 June 2002, at 3.

[108] Study concerning the right to restitution, compensation and rehabilitation for victims of gross violations of human rights and fundamental freedoms. Final report submitted by Mr. Theo van Boven, Special Rapporteur. UN Doc. E/CN.4/Sub.2/1993/8, at 10. See, also, Forced evictions: Analytical report compiled by the Secretary-General. UN Doc. E/CN.4/1994/20, for an enumeration of the various human rights implicated by resettlement; and, Report of the Representative of the Secretary-General on legal aspects relating to the protection against arbitrary displacement. UN Doc. E/CN.4/1998/53/Add.1.

[109] *Resettlement and Development: The Bankwide Review of Projects Involving Involuntary Resettlement 1986-1993.* The World Bank, Environment Department: Washington D.C. 1994, at ¼.

[110] For an extensive overview of the impact on indigenous peoples of relocation caused by dams, see, Dams, Indigenous Peoples and Ethnic Minorities. *Indigenous Affairs,* Vol. 3-4, International Work Group on Indigenous Affairs and Forest Peoples Programme (1999), especially, M. Colchester, Introduction, 4-55.

[111] *The human rights dimensions of population transfer, including the implantation of settlers. Preliminary report prepared by Mr. A.S. Al-Khasawneh and Mr. R. Hatano.* UN Doc. E/CN.4/Sub.2/1993/17*, at para. 101.

[112] Id., at para. 336.

[113] Among others, ILO 107, art. 12, ILO 169, art. 16(2), draft UN Declaration, art. 10, Proposed American Declaration, art. XVIII(6), and Committee on the Elimination of Racial Discrimination, General Recommendation XXIII. See, also, *Progress report prepared by the Special Rapporteur on the human rights implications of population transfer, including the implantation of settlers.* UN Doc. E/CN.4/Sub.2/1994/18, at paras. 24-5.

[114] UN Commission on Human Rights resolution 1993/77 states that the practice of forced evictions constitutes a "gross violation of human rights" and urged governments to undertake immediate measures, at all levels, aimed at eliminating the practice.

[115] *Internally displaced persons, Report of the Representative of the Secretary-General, Mr. Francis M. Deng, submitted pursuant to Commission on Human Rights resolution 1997/39* UN Doc. E/CN.4/1998/53.

[116] *Report of the Representative of the Secretary-General, Mr. Francis M. Deng, submitted pursuant to Commission on Human Rights resolution 1997/39. Compilation and Analysis of Legal Norms, Part II: Legal Aspects Relating to the Protection against Arbitrary Disp*lacement. UN Doc. E/CN.4/1998/53/Add.1, at Sec. IV, para. 4.

[117] *Progress report prepared by the Special Rapporteur on the human rights population transfer, including the implantation of settlers.* UN Doc. E/CN.4/Sub.2/

1994/18, at para. 25.

[118] *Report on the Situation of Human Rights of a Segment of the Nicaraguan Population of Miskito Origin, supra* note 36, 120.

[119] *Third Report on the Situation of Human Rights in The Republic of Guatemala, supra* note 36, at 114.

[120] *Supra* note 22.

[121] *Concluding observations of the Human Rights Committee : Chile.* 30/03/99. CCPR/C/79/Add.104. (Concluding Observations/Comments) CCPR/C/79/Add.104, 30 March 1999, at para. 22.

[122] General Comment No. 4, The Right to Adequate Housing (Art. 11(1) of the Covenant), adopted at the Committee's Sixth session, 1991. In, *Compilation of General Comments/Recommendations supra* note 7, pps. 22-27.

[123] Id., at para. 18. See, also, General Comment No. 7, The Right to Adequate Housing (Art. 11(1) of the Covenant): forced evictions, *supra* note 7, at para. 1.

[124] *Concluding Observations of the Committee on Economic, Social and Cultural Rights : Bolivia.* 21/05/2001. UN Doc. E/C.12/1/Add.60, at para. 21. See, also, *Concluding Observations of the Committee on Economic, Social and Cultural Rights : Panama.* 24/09/2001, *supra* note 31, at para. 12.

[125] General Comment No. 7, The Right to Adequate Housing (Art. 11(1) of the Covenant): forced evictions, *supra* note 7, at para. 10.

[126] Id., at para. 18.

[127] Id., at para. 17.

[128] European Union: Council of Ministers Resolution, *Indigenous Peoples within the framework of the development cooperation of the Community and Member States* (1998) - "indigenous peoples have the right to choose their own development paths, which includes the right to object to projects, in particular in their traditional areas"; Inter-American Development Bank, *Operational Policy 710 on Involuntary Resettlement* (1998), Section IV, para. 4, and; World Commission on Dam*s: Dams and Development: A New Framework for Decision-Making. The Report of the World Commission on Dams.* London: Earthscan (2000) – "The scope of international law has widened and currently includes a body of conventional and customary norms concerning indigenous peoples, grounded on self-determination. In a context of increasing recognition of the self-determination of indigenous peoples, the principle of free, prior, and informed consent to development plans and projects affecting these groups has emerged as the standard to be applied in protecting and promoting their rights in the development process." Id., at 112; see, also, 267, 271, 278.

[129] General principles of international law refer to "rules of customary law, to general principles of law as in Article 38(1)(c) [of the Statute of the International Court of Justice], or to logical propositions resulting from judicial reasoning on the basis of existing pieces of international law and municipal analogies." *Principles of Public International Law, supra* note 49, at 19.

[130] Mary and Carrie Dann Case, at para. 130. (footnotes omitted).

[131] Among others, see, S.J. Anaya, *Indigenous Peoples in International Law* (Oxford and New York: OUP, 1996), at 49-58 and 107; S. Wiessner, The Rights and Status of Indigenous Peoples: A Global Comparative and International

Legal Analysis, 12 Harv. *Human Rights J.* 57 (1999), at 128; R. Torres, The Rights of Indigenous Peoples: The Emerging International Norm, 16 *Yale Journal Int'l Law* 127; and C. Iorns Magallanes, International Human Rights and their Impact on Indigenous Peoples' Rights in Australia, Canada and New Zealand, In, P. Havemann (ed.) *Indigenous Peoples' Rights in Australia, Canada and New Zealand.* (Auckland: OUP, 1999), at 242 — "Further significant international legal developments provide evidence that customary international law has accepted the right of cultural self-determination for indigenous peoples and the consequent autonomous control necessary to achieve that ....".

[132] S.J. Anaya & R. Williams, The Protection of Indigenous Peoples' Rights over Land and Natural Resources under the Inter-American Human Rights System. 14 *Harv. Hum. Rts. J.* 33 (2001), at 55.

[133] The Rights and Status of Indigenous Peoples, supra note 119, at 128.

[134] S.J. Anaya, *Indigenous Peoples in International Law, supra* note 119.

[135] L. Swepston, The ILO Indigenous and Tribal Peoples Convention (No. 169): Eight Years after Adoption. In, C. Price Co*hen, Human Rights of Indigenous Peoples.* New York: Transnational (1998), pps. 17- 36, 34-6.

[136] *Human Rights and Humanitarian Norms as Customary Law, supra* note 33, 21.

[137] *Human Rights Committee, General Comment No. 24, supra* note 27, para. 8.

[138] See, among others, D. Shelton, Environmental Rights. In, P. Alston (ed.), *Peoples' Rights.* Oxford: OUP, (2001), pps. 185-294 and; Kastrup, The Internationalization of Indigenous Rights from an Environmental and Human Rights Perspective, 32 Tex. J. Int'l . Law 97 (1997).

[139] G. Handl, Indigenous Peoples' Subsistence Lifestyle as an Environmental Valuation Problem. In, M. Bowman and A. Boyle (eds.), *Environmental Damage in International and Comparative Law. Problems of Definition and Valuation.* Oxford: OUP (2002), 85-110, at 95 (footnotes omitted).

[140] *Human Rights and the Environment. Preliminary report prepared by Mrs. Fatma Zohra Ksentini, Special Rapporteur.* E/CN.4/Sub.2/1991/8 (1991), at para. 27.

[141] *Human Rights and the Environment. Final report prepared by Mrs. Fatma Zohra Ksentini, Special Rapporteur.* E/CN.4/Sub.2/1994/9 (1994), Annex, at Principle 14.

[142] *Report on the Situation of Human Rights in Ecuador, supra* note 5, at 106.

[143] Ominayak v. Canada, *supra* note 22, 1.

[144] *Case 7615 (Brazil),* OEA/Ser.L/V/II.66, doc 10 rev 1 (1985), 33.

[145] *Report on the Situation of Human Rights in Brazil.* OEAA/Ser.L/V/II.97 Doc 29 rev. 1 (1997).

[146] Id. at 112.

[147] Id.

[148] *Report on the Situation of Human Rights in Ecuador, supra* note 5, at 88.

[149] Id., at 89.

[150] Id., at 92-5.

[151] Id., at 93.

[152] Ogoni Case, at para. 67.

[153] Id., at para. 52.

[154] Id., at p. 13.

[155] Committee on Economic, Social and Cultural Rights, General Comment No. 3, The nature of States parties' obligations (art. 2, para. 1, of the Covenant) (1990). In, *Compilation of General Comments/ Recommendations, supra* note 7, pps. 18-21, at para. 10. The Committee stated that "[i]f the Covenant were to be read in such a way as not to establish such a minimum core obligation, it would be largely deprived of its *raison d'être*." Id.

[156] Ogoni Case, at 62-3.

[157] Id., at 65.

[158] General Comment 14, *The right to the highest attainable standard of health* : 11/08/2000. UN Doc. E/C.12/2000/4, 11 August 2000, at para. 27.

[159] *Concluding Observations of the Committee on Economic, Social and Cultural Rights : Venezuela.* 21/05/2001. UN Doc. E/C.12/1/Add.56, at para. 12.

[160] General Comment No. 12, The Right to Adequate Food (Art. 11 of the Covenant), adopted at Committee's Twentieth session, 1999. In, *Compilation of General Comments/Recommendations, supra* note 7, pps. 66-74, at para. 13.

[161] Ogoni Case, para. 45.

[162] A. Eide, *Promoting economic, social and cultural rights: Obligations of states and accountability of non-state actors.* Paper presented at Second Global Forum on Human Development, Candido Mendes University, Rio de Janeiro, Brazil, 9-10 October 2000, at p. 11-12. Available at: http://www.undp.org/hdro/events/rioforum/eide.pdf.

[163] *Report on the Human Rights Situation in Mexico.* OEA/Ser.L/V/II.100 Doc. 7 rev. 1 (1998), at para. 577.

[164] *Third Report on the Human Rights Situation in Paraguay, supra* note 40, Chapter IX, at para. 38.

[165] Id., at para. 50(8).

[166] Id., at para. 47.

[167] *Second Report on the Human Rights Situation in Peru, supra* note 40, Ch. X, at para. 26.

[168] Id., at para. 39(2).

[169] Id., at para. 39(7).

[170] See, also, the Additional Protocol to the American Convention on Human Rights in the Area of Economic, Social and Cultural Rights "Protocol of San Salvador" (1988), entered into force November 16, 1999, OAS. *Treaty Series*, No. 69.

[171] CEDAW has been ratified by 170 states as of December 2002.

[172] Committee on the Elimination of Discrimination Against Women, General Recommendation No. 24, Article 12 of the Convention on the Elimination of All Forms of Discrimination against Women - women and health (1999). In, *Compilation of General Comments/Recommendations, supra* note 7, pps. 244-51, at para. 6.

[173] World Bank, 2001. Environment Matters at the World Bank, p22. The World Bank Group.

[174] Bank Information Center, 2001. Questions & Answers about The World

Bank's Lending. Toolkits for Activists, issue 5.

[175] See Inspection Panel (2000) *The Quinghai Project: a component of the China-Western Poverty Reduction Project (Credit No.3255-CHA and Loan No.4501-CHA)* Inspection Panel Investigation Report, April 28, 2000, at page xxvi.

[176] OD 4.20 paragraphs 14 and 15.

177 IWGIA, 1990, *Indigenous World 1989-1990*, International Work Group for Indigenous Affairs, Copenhagen.

[178] Griffiths, T and Colchester, M (2000) *Indigenous Peoples, Forests and the World Bank: policies and practice* FPP, Moreton-in-Marsh.

[179] Ibid.

[180] Note that while the OED accepts management's arguments that an Indigenous Peoples Development Plan (IPDP) is only required in projects with potentially negative impacts on indigenous communities under paragraph 13 of the Directive, the World Bank Inspection Panel has ruled that the provision is quite clear that an IPDP is required for all investment projects affecting indigenous peoples – see Inspection Panel (2000) *The Qinghai Project: a component of the China-Western Poverty Reduction Project (Credit No.3255-CHA and Loan No.4501-CHA)* Inspection Panel Investigation Report, April 28, 2000 at page xxvi.

[181] Operations Evaluation Department – OED (2003) Implementation of Operational Directive 4.20 on Indigenous Peoples: an independent desk review January 10, 2003, Country Evaluation and Regional Relations (OEDCR), OED, Washington, DC http://lnweb18.worldbank.org/oed/ocddoclib.nsf/DocUNIDViewForJavaSearch/472DE0AEA1BA73A085256CAD005CF102/$file/IP_evaluation.pdf.

[182] see Bosshard, P., 1999. Energy from Dante's Inferno. Berne Declaration. http://www.ecb.ch.

[183] Idem supra.

[184]For records of 1998-99 consultations, see: http://lnweb18.worldbank.org/essd/essd.nsf/28354584d9d97c29852567cc00780e2a/5e23e566bed37cd6852567cc0077f48d?OpenDocument World Bank (2002) *Summary of Consultations with External Stakeholders regarding the World Bank Draft Indigenous Peoples Policy (OP/BP 4.10)* - last updated 7 October 2002 http://lnweb18.worldbank.org/ESSD/essd.nsf/1a8011b1ed265afd85256a4f00768797/c4a768e4f7c935f185256ba5006c75f3/$FILE/SumExtConsult-4-23-02.pdf.

[185] Tebtebba Foundation (2001a) *Report on the Stakeholders consultation on the World Bank's draft policy on Indigenous Peoples (OP/BP4.10)*, 22 October 2001.

- Tebtebba Foundation (2001b) *Statement of the TEBTEBBA Foundation ((Indigenous Peoples' International Centre for Policy Research and Education) and the Cordillera Peoples' Alliance on the Stakeholder's Consultation on the World Bank's Draft Policy on Indigenous Peoples (OP/BP4.10).*

- Trasparencia (2001) *Mesa de trabajo sobre derechos indígenas: revisión de la políticas 4.20 y 4.10 del Banco Mundial* Oaxaca, agosto de 200.

- Selverston-Scher, M (2001) *World Bank consultation on the revision of the IP policy (OP4.10) - "Andean Region"*, 22-23 October 2001, Cuzco, Peru BIC, Washington, DC.

- Sulyandziga, R (2001) *Discussion on OP4.10 of the World Bank Concerning Indigenous Peoples: information about consultations held in Khabarovsk, Moscow and Nar'yan Mar*, October 2001 Russian Indigenus Peoples of the North Training Centre.

- CONAIE and CONIVE (2001) *Declaración de la Confederación de Nacionalidades Indíegnas del Ecuador y el Consejo Nacional Indio de Venezuela en el marco de la consulta regional andina sobre población indígena del Banco Mundial* 23 de octubre de 2001.

- CORE (2001) *Statement of Core (Indigenous Peoples' Advocacy and Resource Centre for India's North East) external stakeholders consultation on the World Bank's Draft Policy on Indigenous Peoples (OP/BP4.10)*, New Delhi, India, 26 November 2001.

- Declaración de los pueblos indígenas participantes en la 19 Sesión del Grupo de Trabajo sobre Poblaciones Indígenas de las Naciones Unidas sobre las preocupaciones acerca de las políticas del Banco Mundial Ginebra, Julio de 2001.

- Center for Economic and Social Rights (CDES)(2001) Letter sent to World Bank signed by 140 indigenous peoples' organisations, NGOs and individuals, 14 December 2001.

[186] Indigenous Peoples' Declaration (2001) Declaración de los pueblos indígenas participantes en la 19 Sesión del Grupo de Trabajo sobre Poblaciones Indígenas de las Naciones Unidas sobre las preocupaciones acerca de las políticas del Banco Mundial. Ginebra, Julio de 2001.

-Tebtebba Foundation (2001) *Statement of the TEBTEBBA Foundation ((Indigenous Peoples' International Centre for Policy Research and Education) and the Cordillera Peoples' Alliance on the Stakeholder's Consultation on the World Bank's Draft Policy on Indigenous Peoples (OP/BP4.10)*;

-Asian Indigenous and Tribal Peoples Network -AITPN (2002) *The World Bank Defaults on Past Promises: why the World Bank's draft policy on Indigenous Peoples should be rejected* AITPN, New Delhi

-*Indigenous Peoples Declaration (2002) Indigenous Peoples' Statement to a Roundtable Discussion on the Revision of the World Bank Policy on Indigenous Peoples*, 18 October 2002, Washington, D.C.

[187] MacKay, F (2002) "Universal Rights or a Universe Unto Itself? Indigenous peoples' human rights and the World Bank's draft OP4.10 on Indigenous Peoples" *American University International Law Review* 17(3):527-624.

[188] See, generally, *Development and Human Rights: The Role of the World Bank*: Washington DC: World Bank (1998).

[189] Id., at 30.

[190] Advisory Opinion on the Legal Consequences for States of the Continued Presence of South Africa in Namibia, ICJ Rep. 16 (1971), at 31.

[191] *Separate Opinion of Judge Weeramantry, Bosnia and Herzogovenia v. Yugoslavia*, 11 July 1996.

[192] U.N. Charter, Art. 2(7): "Nothing contained in the present Charter shall authorize the United Nations to intervene in matters which are essentially within the domestic jurisdiction of any state ...."

[193] See, among others, *Vienna Declaration and Programme of Action of the UN*

World Conference on Human Rights (1993), Sec. II, para. 2: "The promotion and protection of all human rights and fundamental freedoms must be considered as a priority objective of the United Nations in accordance with it purposes and principles, in particular the purpose of international cooperation. In the framework of these purposes and principles, the promotion and protection of human rights is a legitimate concern of the international community."

[194] J. Isham, D. Kaufmann and L. Pritchett, Civil Liberties, Democracy, and the Performance of Government Projects, 11*The World Bank Economic Review*, 1997.

[195] H.A.Patrinos, *The Costs of Discrimination in Latin America. Human Capital Development and Operations Policy, HCO Discussion Papers.* Washington DC: World Bank. See, also, G. Psacharopoulos & H.A. Patrinos (eds.). Indigenous People and Poverty in Latin America: An Empirical Analysis. Washington, DC: The World Bank. (1994).

[196] *A Proposal for a Comprehensive Development Framework, Memorandum from James Wolfensohn, President of the World Bank, to the Board, Management and Staff of the World Bank Group,* Jan. 21, 1999.

[197] Of the Bank's 181 members, 144 have ratified the International Covenant on Civil and Political Rights, 142 the International Covenant on Economic, Social and Cultural Rights and 179 the Convention on the Rights of the Child.

[198] *Separate Opinion of Judge Weeramantry, Bosnia and Herzogovenia v. Yugoslavia,* 11 July 1996.

[199] Monist legal systems are those in which international law, including ratified international instruments, are considered to be part of an integrated whole together with domestic law.

[200] Dualist legal systems are those which consider international and domestic law to be separate and distinct, the former entering the latter only by way of act of Parliament incorporating international law directly into domestic law.

[201] Article 2(2) of the ICCPR, for instance, "Where not already provided for by existing legislative or other measures, each State Party to the present Covenant undertakes to take the necessary steps, in accordance with its constitutional processes and with the provisions of the present Covenant, to adopt such legislative or other measures as may be necessary to give effect to the rights recognized in the present Covenant."

[202] Interpretation of the Agreement of 25 March 1951 between the WHO and Egypt. International Court of Justice, *Reports of Judgment, Advisory Opinions and Orders.* (1980), at 89-90.

[203] Barcelona Traction, Light and Power Company, Limited, Second Phase, Judgment, ICJ Rep., 32, paras. 33-4, at 33. (1970); *reaffirmed in,* East Timor (Portugal v Australia) *ICJ Reports* (1995), 90 et seq. and, Bosnia Herzogovenia v. Yugoslavia, Preliminary Objections, *ICJ Reports* (1996), 595 et seq.

[204] Id., at para. 34.

[205] Art. 34, Vienna Convention on the Law of Treaties (1969).

[206] A rule in a treaty may become binding on non-parties if it becomes

part of international customary law. Art. 38, Vienna Convention on the Law of Treaties (1969) and Art. 38, Vienna Convention on the Law of Treaties between States and International Organizations or between International Organizations (1986).

[207] I. Shihata, the former General Counsel of the Bank stated that: "Members *obligations* under the UN Charter prevail over their other treaty obligations, including their obligations under the Bank's Articles of Agreement, by force of an explicit provision in the UN Charter (Article 103). The Bank itself is bound, by virtue of its Relationship Agreement with the UN, to take note of the above-mentioned Charter obligations assumed by its members ...."

[208] Agreement Between the United Nations and the International Bank for Reconstruction and Development, Nov. 15, 1947, 16 U.N.T.S. 346.

[209] S. Skogly, Human Rights Obligations of the World Bank and IMF, at 100.

[210] Id., 99-102.

[211] The International Court of Justice recognized the obligatory force of the Charter and Declaration in, among others, *United States Diplomatic and Consular Staff in Tehran* (United States of America v. Iran), ICJ Rep. 3, 42, 1980.

[212] L. Sohn, The Human Rights Law of the Charter, 12 Tex. Int'l LJ 129, 135-36 (1977).

[213] Article 56, Charter of the United Nations.

[214] The World Bank, the IMF and Human Rights, at 63; and, D. Bradlow & C. Grossman, Limited Mandates and Intertwined Problems: A New Challenge for the World Bank and the IMF. 17 *Human Rights Q.* 411, 428.

[215] D. Bradlow & C. Grossman, Limited Mandates and Intertwined Problems: A New Challenge for the World Bank and the IMF. 17 *Human Rights Q.* 411, at note 63.

[216] During a meeting with human rights NGOs in Prague in September 2000, the Bank's President, James Wolfensohn, committed to "making explicit reference to human rights in Bank documents," and "to work with Bank staff to include human rights in their policy documents ...." Human Rights Watch, Press Release, 22 September 2000, 'NGOs Urge Implementation of Wolfensohn Commitment to Human Rights'.

[217] Moody, R. 200 The decade of destruction: How the mining companies betrayed their promised greening. www.minesandcommunities.org/Company/decade.

[218] See for example ' Conclusions and Recommendations' of the Workshop on indigenous peoples, private sector natural resource, energy and mining companies and human rights, UNHCHR, Geneva, December 2001.

[219] Lozano, J. 1997. Mining Act beckons Foreign Firms. Philippine Daily Inquirer, May 8, 1997 and Lozano, J. Taking the Last Stand.) http://humanrights.uchicago.edu/joeylozano/joey03.html.

[220] *Jakarta Post*, February 13, 2003, "Legislators allow exploration in protected forests".

[221] Project Underground, 2002, The Path of Least Resistance: An Assessment of the Compliance Advisor Ombudsman's Handling of the Minera Yanacocha Complaint.

[222] Wilson, R. 2001. How the world mining industry had to dig itself out of a hole. *The Observer*, July 8 2001 .http://www.observer.co.uk/Print/0,3858,4217851,00.html.

[223] Proceedings of the National Conference on Mining May 2002, Tebtebba Foundation.

[224] www.Didipio.com website.

[225] MacDonald, I. 2002. Didipio Case Report. Community Aid Abroad, Mining Ombudsman Investigation.

[226] See for example India, National Convention on Communities Command over Natural Resources, Anandwan, 2001: http://www.mmpindia.org/nc2001.htm. Indonesia, Manado International Conference on STD: http://www.moles.org/ProjectUnderground/drillbits/6_04/3.html Philippines: the Declaration of the International Indigenous Youth Conference held in Baguio: http://www.ayn.ca/news/0208/declaration_iiyc.htm.

[227] Joint OED/OEG Evaluation of World Bank Group Activities in the Extractive Industries Sector Approach Paper. 2001. The World Bank Group.

[228] Ibid page 44.

[229] Ibid page 45.

[230] Ibid p. 45.

[231] Ibid page 47.

[232] Op cit page 43.

[233] Colchester M et al. , 2000, *Undermining the Forests*. Forest Peoples Programme, WRM, PIPLinks, Moreton-in-Marsh. p. 20.

[234] Zorilla, C. 2002 *Minería, Biodiversidad y el Banco Mundial en Ecuador: El Caso del Proyecto Prodeminca*. Presentation to the Regional Workshop, Latin America and the Carribbean, Extractive Industries Review.

[235] Fortytwo directly linked projects around the world.

[236] See for example Philippines: the declaration of the International indigenous Youth Conference held in Baguio, May 2002: http://www.ayn.ca/news/0208/declaration_iiyc.htm.

[237] Barrera-Hernández, L.K., 2002. *The Legal Framework for Indigenous Peoples' and Other Public's Participation in Latin America: The Cases of Argentina, Colombia, and Peru*. Pages 589-628 in Human rights in natural resource development : public participation in the sustainable development of mining and energy resources. Oxford : Oxford University Press, 2002.

[238] In 1993 WMC assisted the Philippine government in conducting a workshop at the annual Asian mining congress where companies were invited to join in the drafting of the revised mining code.

[239] Tujan.A, Guzman. R 1998 , *Globalizing Philippine Mining*, Ibon Books, Manila.

[240] Clark, A.L., 1994, The Philippine Mineral Sector to 2010: *Policy and Recommendations, Report to the Asian Development Bank on T.A. No. 1894-PHI*, East-West Center, Honolulu, Hawaii, 360p.

[241] *Proceedings of the Philippine National Conference on Mining May 6-8 2002* Baguio City, 2002 Tebtebba Foundation.

[242] OED, 2003. Evaluation of the World Bank Group's Activities in the Extractive Industries: Background Paper on Factoring in Governance. Opera-

tions Evaluation Department.

[243] "The Land is Ours", 1997, Stanford, Oxfordshire., *Cordillera Links Briefing No1*. Additional materials from Cordillera Peoples Alliance and Itogon Inter-Barangay Alliance.

[244] See for example, Muntz.B, 2001, *Mining And Community Rights - A Case Study: WMC Resources Ltd. and the Tampakan Copper Project WMC Resources Ltd. and the Tampakan Copper Project* , Community Aid Abroad.

[245] Ibid.

[246] Kirsch.S, 2001 "Mining, Indigenous Peoples and Human Rights: A Case Study of Ok Tedi," Paper presented to the Workshop 'Indigenous peoples, private sector natural resource, energy and mining companies and human rights' organised by the UNHCHR, Palais des Nations, Geneva, December 2001.

[247] Moody.R, 2002, *Partners in Grime: a critique of the bpd natural resources cluster programme*, Nostromo Research, London.

[248] Kirsch.S, 2002, Litigating Ok Tedi (Again) , 2002, in *Cultural Survival Quarterly* , Boston.

[249] *Mining Journal,* 21/2/03.

[250] Johan Peleman, "Mining for Serious Trouble: Jean-Raymond Boulle and his Corporate Empire Project in "Mercenaries" An African Security Dilemma, Pluto Press, 2000: 165-166.

[251] Pratap Chatterjee, Mercenary Armies and Mineral Wealth, *Covert Action Quarterly*, number 62, Washington, Fall 1997, page 36.

[252] Roger Moody, *Out of Africa: mining in the Congo basin in IUCN* The Congo Basin/le bassin du Congoî, Amsterdam 1998, page 137.

[253] (Eds) Abdel-Fatau Musah and J Kayode Fayemi. *Mercenaries: an African Security Dilemma*, Pluto Press, 2000, page 69.

[254] Final report of the Panel of Experts on the Illegal Exploitation of Natural Resources and Other Forms of Wealth of DR CongoS/2002/1146 *Mining Journal* 25/10/2003, MJ 8/11/2002.

[255] See for example, Letter to Emil Salim from Civil Society on The Extractive Industries Review's Consultation Process and the Compilation of Consultation Inputs Working Paper, March 2003.

[256] Vicki Tauli-Corpuz & Danny Kennedy, 2002, Native Reluctance to join Mining Industry Initiatives: Activist Perspectives in Mining Indigenous Lands: Can Impacts and Benefits be Reconciled? Special Issue of *Cultural Survival Quarterly* 25(1).

[257] Letter to Luke Danielson and Richard Sandbrook, of MMSD, August 2000, from Desposito.S et al.

[258] London Declaration, 2001, May: www.minesandcommunities.org.

[259] Private communication from Cordillera Peoples Alliance.

[260] See Roger Moody, *Into the Unknown Regions: the hazards of STD*, SSC and International Books, London and Utrecht, 200I, pages 47-51.

[261] See Roger Moody "Five minutes to Midnight" *Minewatch Briefing*, London, 1995.

[262] Community Leaders of Riverain Communities Affected by the 1995 Omai Cyanide Spill, Letter to Gerald T West, March 18 2000.

[263] IFC SPI, December 14 2001.

[264] IFC internal document, January 2003, page i.

[265] Ibid page ii.

[266] Ibid page ii; see also ibid page 10.

[267] Survival International e-news, 20/2/2003.

[268] IFC ,2003 page 8.

[269] Ibid page 2.

[270] Ibid page 3.

[271] Ibid page 3.

[272] IFC ibid page 13.

[273] Guardian, London 20/2/2003.

[274] IFC internal document, page 17-18.

[275] See FOEI/CED, 2002. *Traversing Peoples Lives*. FOEI. And Nguiffo, S., Breitkopf, S. 2002. *Broken Promises: The Chad Cameroon Oil and Pipeline Project: Profit at any Cost?*, FOEI, Milieudefensie, CED.

[276] Project Underground and FEROCAFENOP, 2001. Complaint Concerning Miner Yanacocha, S.A. submitted to the Compliance Advisor Ombudsman of the IFC.

[277] Ibid.

[278] Ibid.

[279] Project Underground, 2000. Newmont: Why are people around the world so MAD at this company? http://www.moles.org.

[280] Ref MIGA letter of response to Friends of the Earth International dated 28.September, 2001.

[281] Berne Declaration, 1996. Tainted Gold from the Pacific. http://www2.access.ch/evb/bd/lihir.htm.

[282] Berne Declaration, 1996. Tainted Gold from the Pacific. http://www2.access.ch/evb/bd/lihir.htm.

[283] Chatterton, P. 1996. RTZ Dumps on Lihir. Mining Monitor, Feb 1996.

[284] Greenpeace International, 2002. Sea dumping of wastes from the mining industry: the case of the Lihir gold mine, Papua New Guinea. Paper submitted to the London Convention – 24th Meeting (November 2002) and Mineral Policy Institute, 2002. Lihir and International Law. MPI http://www.mpi.org.au/rr/docs/lihir_international_law.pdf.

[285] Moody, op cit.

[286] See E Schwartz , World Bank Backs Russian Gold Venture over some Objections, Bloomberg News Service, USA, August 10 2000.

[287] See, inter alia, S Dennison Smith, Chronicle of a Disaster Foretold: The Omai Gold Mine in *"Mining Issues"*, Number 1, LAMMP, Bromley, Kent, January 1999.

[288] *New Scientist*, London, 23/11/1996.

[289] Comsur press release, La Paz, September 1996.

[290] *Times*, La Paz, 31/10/1006.

[291] *New Scientist* 21-28/12/96.

[292] Motomichi Ikawa, Letter to Pacific Environment and Resource Center, August 16 2000.

[293] Private communication February-March 2001.

[294] Nelson, J. 2002. *Cameroon: Bagyéli struggling to be heard*. WRM Bulletin, no. 62.

[295]Clark, D. 2002. The World Bank and Human Rights: The Need for Greater Accountability. *Harvard Hurman Rights Journal*, Vol 15, p 205-226.

[296] Lawyer's Environmental Assessment Team, 2002. *Assessment Summary of the Complaint Regarding MIGA's Guarantee of the Bulyanhulu Gold Mine, Tanzania*.

[297] International Advisory Group, 2002. *Report of visit to Cameroon and Chad:* October 15 to November 4, 2002.

[298] *The Chad-Cameroon Oil and Pipeline Project : A Call for Accountability*. 2002. Association Tchadienne pour la Promotion et la Défense des Droits de l'Homme, Centre pour l'Environnement et le Développement, Environmental Defense.

[299] Project Underground, 2002. T*he Path of Least Resistance: An Assessment of the Compliance Advisor Ombudsman's Handling of the Minera Yanacocha Complaint*.

[300] Horta, K. 2003. *The Chad/Cameroon Oil & Pipeline Project – Reaching a Critical Milestone*. Environmental Defense Foundation.

[301] World Bank (1992), *Effective Implementation: Key to Development Impact, Portfolio Management Task Force*. World Bank, Washington DC.

[302] World Bank 1992:15.

[303] World Bank 1992: iv and 14.

[304] World Bank 1992: ii.

[305] World Bank 1992: 8.

[306] Coady, P., Statement to World Bank Board Meeting, 23 October 1992.

[307] Rich, B., The Smile on a Child's Face: From the Culture of Loan Approval to the Culture of Development Effectiveness? The World Bank Under James Wolfensohn, Environmental Defense, Washington DC, 1999, pp.6-7. See also: World Bank Memorandum, Human Resources Policy Reform, 6 March 1998 (internal document).

[308] See, for example: World Bank Quality Assurance Group, Portfolio Investment Program: Reviews of Sector Portfolios and Lending Instruments – A synthesis, 22 April 1997 (draft internal report), p.20; World Bank, Operations Evaluation Department, Effectiveness of Environmental Assessments and National Environmental Action Plans – A Process Study, Report No.15835, 29 June 1996, p.37; World Bank, Operations Evaluation Department, Poverty Assessment: A progress Review, Report No. 15881, 7 August 1996; World Bank, The World Bank Procurement Function – Adjusting to Emerging Needs, April 1998; World Bank, Loan Administration Change Initiative – Implementation Strategy paper, 29 June 1998; World bank, Quality at Entry in Calendar Year 1998: A Quality Assurance Group Assessment, July 1999. Such reports highlight the undue optimism of project appraisals; the cynicism with which poverty assessments are regarded; the continuing weaknesses in assessing government commitment, local capacity and the more general risks involved in project implementation; and the insidious institutional effects of the pressure to lend.

[309] The 1998 Loos Memorandum on Indonesia specifically identifies the

pressure to lend as a major factor in corruption: "There is an inherent tension not only between volume/speed of commitments/ disbursements and the quality of our work, but also between these and potential leakages." See: Loos, J., "World Bank Office Memorandum to Mr. Jean-Michel Severino, Vice President, EAP", 19 October 1998.

[310] World Bank Quality Assurance Group, "Portfolio Investment Program: Reviews of Sector Portfolios and Lending Instruments – A synthesis", 22 April 1997 (draft internal report), p.15.

[311] Rich, B., *The Smile on a Child's Face: From the Culture of Loan Approval to the Culture of Development Effectiveness?* The World Bank Under James Wolfensohn, Environmental Defense, Washington D.C., 1999: World Bank, Confidential Internal Document, Summary of RSI Staff Views regarding the problem of 'Leakage' from World Bank Projects Budget, Jakarta, August 1997.

[312] World Bank Operations Evaluation Department, Indonesia Country Assistance Note, 4 February 1999, p.25.

[313] World Bank Operations Evaluation Department, Indonesia Country Assistance Note, 4 February 1999, p.26.

[314] Rich, B., op. cit 13.

[315] Ibid.

[316] *Financial Times*, May 11 2001.

[317] Ibid.

[318] In response to Winter's charges, the Bank's Vice-President for East Asia, Jean Michel Severeno, stated: "This [systematic corruption in World bank lending to Indonesia] is demonstrably untrue. We know exactly where our money is going." Severeno also dismissed the Dice memorandum as "one person's view based on informal interviews." He also falsely argued that a follow up study by Jane Loos had failed to confirm Dice's findings – when in fact it had (see main text). See: Rich, B., The Smile on a Child's Face: From the Culture of Loan Approval to the Culture of Development Effectiveness? The World Bank Under James Wolfensohn, Environmental Defense, Washington D.C., 1999.

[319] Moody, R. (1997), Interview with Lori Weisenberg, Higher Values, number 11, Minewatch, February 1997, p.12.

[320] Quoted in Rich, B., op. cit. 13.

[321] US General Accounting Office, *World Bank: Management Controls Stronger, but Challenges in Fighting Corruption Remain* , GAO/NSIAD-00-73, Washington DC, April 2000, p.21. See also: *The World Bank, Helping Countries Combat Corruption: Progress at the World Bank Since 1997*, Washington DC, June 2000, p.2.

[322] Ibid, p.36.

[323] *The World Bank, Helping Countries Combat Corruption: Progress at the World Bank Since 1997*, Washington DC, June 2000, p.1.

[324] US General Accounting Office, op.cit.23.

[325] Ibid, p.15.

[326] Ibid, p.15

[327] Ibid, p.19.

[328] Ibid, p.20.

329 Ibid, p.15.

330 Ibid, p.15.

331 Ibid, p.5.

332 Rich, B., op.cit.13, p.17.

333 In 1993, for example, the Bank's Financial Reporting and Auditing Task Force reported that "less than 40 per cent of audited financial information is received by its due date, making it inconsequential for project management" and that "Financial statements received by the World Bank frequently are not reviewed by Bank staff or are reviewed by staff without the necessary skills to identify significant problems and initiate appropriate action." See: Rich, B., op.cit.11.

334 World Bank Operations Evaluation Department, Indonesia Country Assistance Note, 4 February 1999, p.20.

335 Tucker, T., Personal Communication, September 2000.

336 LEAT, "Re Assessment Summary of the Complaint regarding MIGA's Guarantee of the Bulyanhulu Gold Mine", Letter to Meg Taylor, Office of CAO, 13 November 2002.

337 CAO, Assessment Report Summary, Complaint regarding MIGA's guarantee of the Bulyanhulu Gold Mine, Tanzania, p. 8.

338 Ibid., pp. 8-9.

339 Ibid, p.9.

340 LEAT, op. cit. 38.

341 CAO, op. cit.39, p. 9.

342 Ibid.

343 LEAT, op. cit. 38.

344 Rome Declaration on Harmonization, Rome, Italy, February 25, 2003.

345 As the chief executive of Britain's Export Credits Guarantee Department notes: "Projects that take full account of environmental and social issues in their design and operation are less likely to fail than those that ignore them...Controversy around projects adds to costs; it is in the interests of exporters and credit agencies to address that as a business issue." See: Brown, V, Speech to Euro 2000 Conference, 2000, reported in Insurance Day, "Environment protection now a factor in securing export credit guarantees", 10 March 2003.

346 Broad, R., Unequal Alliance 1979-1986: *The World Bank, The International Monetary Fund and the Philippines*, Ateneo de Manila University Press, Quezon City, Metro Manlia, 1988, p.11.

347 Ibid.

348 Cray, C., "The World Bank's Revolving Door: Share Program Exchanges, World Bank and Corporate Employees", *Multinational Monitor*, Vol. 21, No.6, June 2000.

349 Rich 1994:148ff.

350 The distinction between private and public sector dam building is not always easy to make. Many dams are built by private companies on 'build, operate and transfer' contracts with government agencies.

351 Hildyard, N., "Snouts in the Trough; Export Credit Agencies, Policy Incoherence and Corporate Welfare", *Corner House Briefing*, 1999.

[352] Australian NGOs recommend the establishment of independently administered funds to ensure resources are available for effective community participation. Such trusts should include both indigenous and company representatives on the Board of Trustees, but the majority of Trustees should not be local people (Gail Whiteman and Katy Mamen, 2002, MeaningfulConsultation and Participation in the Mining Sector: a review of consultation and participation of indigenous peoples within the international mining sector. North-South Institute, Ottawa :39).

[353] Marcus Colchester, Jean La Rose and Kid James, 2002, *Mining and Amerindians in Guiyana*. North South Institute, Ottawa and Amerindian Peoples Association, Georgetown; Whiteman and Mamen 2001 op. cit. ; Viviane Weitzner, 2002, *Through Indigenous Eyes: toward appropriate decision-making processes regarding mining on or near Ancestral Lands*. North-South Institute, Ottawa ; MMSD, 2002, ; Joji Cariño pers. comm. 2 April 2003.

[354] FPP, PIPLinks and WRM, 2000, *Undermining the Forests: the need to control transnational mining companies –a Canadian case study*, Forest Peoples Programme, Moreton-in-Marsh; Whiteman and Mamen 2001 op. cit.

[355] Weitzner 2002:55 op. cit..

[356] Russel Lawrence Barsh and Krisma Bastien, Krisma, 1997, *E f - fective Negotiations by Indigenous Peoples. An Action Guide with Special References to North America.* ILO, Geneva; IFC, 1998, *Doing Better Business through Effective Consultation and Disclosure.* International Finances Corporation, Washington DC; Conrad B. MacKerron and Douglas G. Cogan, 1993, *Business in the Rainforests: Corporations, Deforestation and Sustainability.* Investor Responsibiity Research Center. Washington DC; Amy B. Rosenfield, Debra L. Gordon and Marianne Guerin-McManus, 1997, *Reinventing the Well: approaches to minimizing the environmental and social impact of oil development in the tropics.* Conservation International, Washington DC; Lorraine Ruffing and Judith Kimmerling, 1991, *Socio-cultual impacts of Transnational Oil Corporations in Environmentally Sensitive Areas.* United Nations Centrer on Transnational Corporations, New York; Amy Rosenfield Sweeting and Andrea P. Clark, 2000, *Lightening the Lode: a Guide to Responsible Large-Scale Mining.* Conservation International, Washington DC ; Manuela Tomei, 1996, *Indigenous Peoples and Oil Development: Reconciling Conflicting Interests.* International Labour Office, Geneva; Manuela Tomei and Lee Swepston, 1996, *Indigenous and Tribal Peoples: a Guide to ILO Convention 169.* International Labour Office, Geneva; Anon. 2000, *Canada and the Indigenous Peoples of the Western Hemisphere: putting principles into action in trade and investment. Aboriginal Policy Roundtable*, Canadian Centre for Foreign Policy Development; Brot fur die Welt, 2000, Principles for the Conduct of Company Operations within the Oil and Gas Industry: a Discussion Paper. Stuttgart.

[357] World Bank, 2002, *Evaluation of the World Bank's Activities in the Extractive Industries. Operations Evaluation Department* (draft report) page 20, emphasis in original.

[358] Shelton Davies, 1977, *Victims of the Miracle*. Cambridge University Press, Cambridge; John Bodley, 1982, Victims of Progress. Menlo Park, California.

Colombia:
License to Plunder

Armando Valbuena Wouriyu

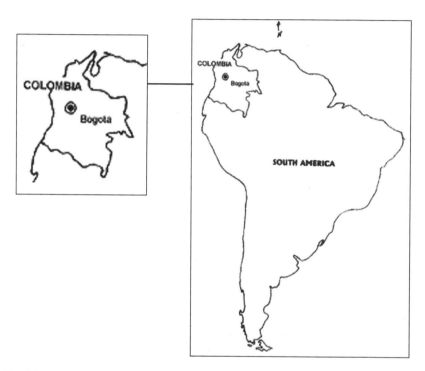

The Mining Code, a very important piece of legislation for the future of the indigenous peoples, was not the product of a dialogue with civil society. On the contrary, the responsibility for preparing the draft Mining Code was given by the government to the Colombian law firm, Martines Cordoba, in February 1999. This law firm was hired to prepare the draft Mining Code in disregard of all rules of procedure for public service contracts. The reason behind this irregular procedure became clear later on. The firm, Martines Cordoba, is the legal representative of the Mexican cement company, Semex, a subsidiary of the Holder Bank, and the oil and gas drilling company Santa Fe, owned at that time by President Pastrana.

A consultation process of the draft was initiated in an attempt to comply with the provisions established by Law 21 (the law that adopted ILO Convention 169 in Colombia). The process was riddled with irregularities and was finally concluded with a unilateral decision taken after some meetings were carried out with indigenous organisations. These meetings however merely informed them about the future Mining Code, and it was suggested that it was not possible to make any change to the draft.

This was made evident by a letter, dated 29 November 1999, to Alberto Henao, sub-director 1 of the Mining Unit, an annex of the Ministry of Mines, by the solicitors of Martines Cordoba. This letter stated that the meeting with the indigenous peoples' representatives had no positive outcome and consequently the draft would not incorporate any new chapter on mining and indigenous territories and would remain the same, thus leaving to the National Congress to make any definitive decisions regarding this issue.

Finally, the Code was approved, against indigenous rights protected and enshrined in the Constitution and in international legal instruments such as ILO Convention 169.

THE MINING CODE

The Mining Code (Law 685, 15 August 2001) came into force not simply to regulate mining activity but, as the first Article states, 'to promote' the exploration and exploitation of the mining resources of 'public and private property'. The aim is to 'stimulate these activities to satisfy the internal and external demand'. While Articles 3 and 4 clearly state that no law can be opposed to this law regarding mining, this directly contradicts many important documents which protect indigenous rights.

Article 5 determines that all mining resources belong exclusively to the State without taking into consideration the property and territory ownership rights of individuals, communities or groups. This goes against the right to indigenous collective property recognised by the Colombian Constitution.

Article 13 declares mining to be of 'public interest', thus consecrating unlimited rights to the State to expropriate any territory with the aim of exploration and exploitation of mining resources. This dramatically affects the right of the indigenous peoples to their territories.

Article 14 establishes a single mining title which does not discriminate between the various mining entrepreneurs, be they indigenous communities undertaking small-scale mining activities in their territories, or transnational companies.

Chapter VII substantially increases the length of a mining concession to 30 years, with two possible situations in which the mining companies could apply for extensions. Read in conjunction with Article 228, which provides that the percentage the mining companies pay in royalties to the Colombian State will be the same for the duration of the contract (up to 90 years), it prevents any control of the state over the profitability of these resources.

Under the title 'Ethnic Groups', Chapter XIV appears to be addressing indigenous concerns. But a reading of its Articles reveals that no right is granted to indigenous communities to oppose a mining concession. This chapter was not presented to indigenous groups for consultation, infringing the provisions for consultation established by the Law 21, 1991 (ILO 169).

Chapter XVI eliminates the differences between small, medium and large-scale mining. This distinction used to allow the State to rule each of such mining activities, with the volume of material moved and the amount of people involved being taken into consideration. With the elimination of this distinction, the law places the small and medium miners and the large scale mining corporations in unequal and forced competition.

Chapter XVII refers to "illegal" mining exploration and exploitation. This illegality however is defined by the lack of formality (i.e. not having a mining title) and does not recognise the economic conditions in which some people perform mining activities. The law is thus defining small-scale or artisanal miners' activities as "illegal" if they do not have a mining title. This means that they can be subject to criminal prosecution. Within the current political situation and the problem of violent conflict in Colombia, this is extremely dangerous. Before the Mining Code, small-scale activities carried out by people without mining titles was not illegal.

Chapter XX addresses the "Environmental Aspects". This is one of the most damaging and dangerous aspects of the law, considering the destructive effects of large-scale mining and the sensitivity of Colombia's environment. Articles 207 and 208 refer to the so-called Environmental License which is the application that mining companies present before starting a project. This application should contain the companies' own environmental assessment of the project for state approval. Once the state has approved the assessment, the license is granted for the *duration of the concession*, without any possibility for environmental authorities to revoke their decision even in case of actions which breach environmental legislation.

Moreover, Article 210 grants mining companies the exclusive right to apply for modifications of the mining license. Article 211 declares that the State *can* (not will) revoke these licenses if there are *reiterative and serious* infringements of the mining companies' environmental obligations (those standards which are set by, and for, the mining companies themselves). Such provisions seem to simply permit anybody to do what they please in the mining sector and with the environment. This law merely shows the State's lack of firm position to ensure that environmental legislation is upheld, as well as its lack of interest in making mining companies accountable for the impact their activities cause the environment.

Finally, the law establishes that 'external environmental audits' be undertaken by the company, Ingeniesa S.A. Public bodies previously performed this function exclusively, but putting it in the hands of a private company opens it to a high risk that the audits may not be impartial and accurate.

Chapter XXII establishes that companies will pay only 0.4% of the production value (royalties) to the State. The very low royalties received by the State and their lack of redistribution to mining regions has made these regions the poorest in the country (as documented by the National Index). We wonder whether it is worth endangering the environment and violating the rights of indigenous peoples when there are clearly no benefits from these activities to be received by the population in the mining regions.

Furthermore, Article 231 forbids the regional and municipal administrations to tax companies for the activities they undertake in their territories.

DAMAGING EFFECTS

The mining legislation has caused various adverse impacts:

- ❐ The presence of armed groups has increased in indigenous areas (mercenaries, paramilitary, guerrilla groups, American military groups). As a consequence there is a higher incidence of acts of human rights abuse.
- ❐ In the areas where mining activities are performed, the lack of institutional security is forcing communities to move because of the increased danger, or they are forcibly removed by armed groups. A clear case is that of the Arauca community, in whose area the Colombian and the US Governments have agreed to implement Plan Colombia. Be-

cause of this the community has been the object of abuse and serious attacks which undermine the peoples' civil and political rights.

- There is more illegal mining now than before because of the impossibility of small and medium scale miners to compete with multinational corporations.
- Applications for mining concessions have increased in an alarming way. There are even companies which have abused this, applying for *12 million hectares* of land for exploration and exploitation.
- The mining companies are pressuring the indigenous communities to choose between only two alternatives: exploit the resources themselves or give them away to be exploited.
- Regarding the elaboration of the legislation, there has been a total lack of ethics in hiring the lawyers of a multinational to prepare such an important piece of legislation as the Mining Code, which fundamentally implicates all natural resources and the environment. This is evidence that the government favours these companies and, in general, all projects funded by the World Bank. This is clearly in violation of our rights as indigenous peoples and destroys the natural environment which is necessary to our physical and cultural survival.
- These lawyers have manipulated the law and removed all protection for indigenous communities, as is clearly shown with the enactment of the Mining Code.
- The conditions of negotiation with transnational companies are always disadvantageous for our country. They are the ones who impose the economic conditions that regulate them. For us, indigenous communities, everything is lost: our land, our capacity to negotiate, our culture, our security. We remain with a damaged environment and depleted natural resources.
- Another important effect is the problem of external debt. This is evident in the case of the Cerrejon Mine, which should have been built with only half of the $3 billion which were eventually spent. This has resulted in the State having to recognise a fictitious debt and given impetus to corruption, with grave cultural and livelihood consequences for the Wayuu communities.
- Transnational companies as well as the World Bank do not make provisions to compensate for the damage their

activities cause the environment and the natural resources, particularly those which are not sustainable.

◻ The environmental impacts are devastating: they extinguish animal and plant species, contaminate our waters, kill our fishes and dry up our rivers. This has happened with the Pamplona River, which has been lost due to mining activities.

RECOMMENDATIONS

In view of the deleterious effects that extractive industries have on our country and our future, we present the following recommendations:

1. The World Bank should not grant funding to the transnational companies which are linked to the preparation of the mining legislation.

2. The World Bank and the investment agencies should withdraw funding to the companies investigated for acts against human rights in our country.

3. The customary norms, livelihoods and modes of living of indigenous communities in their territories should be respected.

4. A total prohibition of mining exploration and exploitation in indigenous territories should be declared.

5. Any legislation related to the use of natural resources should be prepared with the real and meaningful participation of the indigenous communities, and any recommendation should be reflected in the text of the legislation.

Papua New Guinea:
A Guarantee for Poverty

Matilda Koma

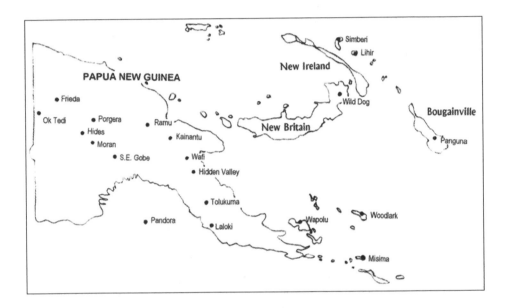

This case study focuses on the Lihir Gold Mine Project in Papua New Guinea (PNG) and how it has affected the Indigenous People who make up virtually the entire population of the country. The mine project was undertaken with the support of the World Bank through the Multilateral Investment Guarantee Agency (MIGA), which provided a huge loan guaranteed by the PNG Government.

New Guinea is the second largest island after Greenland and lies directly North of Australia. The eastern portion of the island is Papua New Guinea and the other portion is West Papua, which is currently a province of Indonesia. Papua New Guinea has a population of around 5.2 million. Geographically, the land comprises steep and rugged forested terrain, low-lying swamps as well as many islands, including the

Lihir Group of Islands.

Papua New Guinea is geologically very rich in minerals. Mining, which has been an integral part of the nation's development, has been the highest revenue generating industry in the country particularly in the late 1980s. However, there was a paradigm shift in the mid-1990s when exploration and mine development - which had for the past decade been carried out side by side - reached a peak, and then began to decline.

Papua New Guinea's population is almost 100% indigenous, having over 800 different local tribes. The people traditionally own about 95%-97% of land, and about 3%-5% is used for other development or government use. Nevertheless, common resources such as minerals and water are state-owned by law. Land ownership is PNG's pride, wealth and asset, and the people say without land there is no life! Developers, however, have in the past found it difficult to deal with land issues in the country, and sometimes refer to these as a hindrance to progress.

EXTRACTIVE INDUSTRIES, INDIGENOUS PEOPLES AND INTERNATIONAL FINANCIAL INSTITUTIONS

Papua New Guinea has vast resources with much of these remaining undeveloped. But its mineral, oil and gas resources have attracted investors in the recent past resulting in their rapid exploitation.

The social and environmental issues associated with extractive resource exploitation became an increasing problem in the late 1980s and early 1990s as mine wastes were directly dumped into rivers and oceans at an alarming rate. Exploration and mine developments began to decline rapidly in the mid-1990s for many reasons. One of these was that mine-affected communities were beginning to challenge the companies and government in a more aggressive and serious manner when they failed to address their concerns. The following presents some of the major issues and the actions taken by these local communities:

□ *1989:* War broke out in Bougainville when landowners and affected communities took control of one of the Panguna mines. It was PNG's largest copper mine, and the controlling company Bougainville Copper Ltd. was 54% owned by the British company Rio Tinto. Between 1972 and the cessation of mining on May 15, 1989, the mine produced copper concentrates that contained an incredible three million tonnes of copper, 306 tonnes of gold and 784 tonnes of silver. The production had a value of PGK5.2 billion which represented approximately 44 per cent of PNG's exports during the period. The war cost the lives of over 20,000 people, partly through a blockade, and even now the struggle for peace has not been fully attained.

❑ *1994:* The controversial issue over ownership of minerals led to the closure of the Mount Victor gold mine owned by Niugini Mining. There had allegedly been over 30 deaths since the mine closed, as local people claimed that the tailings had not been properly neutralised.

❑ *1994:* A rupture occurred on the tailings pipeline in Misima Gold. The local water source dried out in 1996, and a hydrological report from the Environmental Agency confirmed a drop in the water table due to extraction of water by the company via several bores for mill processing.

❑ *1995:* Affected communities within and downstream of the Porgera Gold Mine lodged complaints for compensation, relocation and environmental damage. They are preparing legal documents to challenge the company in court over the mine.

❑ *1996:* A lawsuit was filed against BHP, the company responsible for the Ok Tedi Gold and Copper Mine, for environmental damage. This remains a controversial issue which still has not been satisfactorily settled.

❑ *1997:* At the announcement of the PNG-Queensland gas pipeline, landowners along the pipeline corridor began to organise themselves and negotiate for reasonable compensation. This caused several delays in approval and construction process. Up until now, the project has not yet commenced.

❑ *2002:* Local landowners from a gas development project area disturbed the operations of the Porgera Mine through damage of a power pavilion. This put a halt to operations at the mine for a few weeks, affecting the company's production.

As people became more educated and aware of issues surrounding extractive industries, many of them became vocal on the distribution of benefits and compensation for loss of resources or environmental damage. This was particularly the case where the government had initially failed to address them in a genuine manner.

As these actions became more frequent, they added to the increasing costs associated with exploration and government taxes on the industry. This, coupled with the declining national economy, meant that companies began to lose confidence in further exploration and mine development activities. Therefore, from 1995 to date there have been no new mines. Yet mines continue to dump waste directly into the environment, and thus the pressure from affected communities continues.

As a result of this shift, the PNG government and the mining industry are taking remedial action to revive the ailing industry, as well as tackling the crucial issues that are hindering its progress. Through the Department of Mines, the government has secured a US$10 million Technical Assistance Loan (TAL) from the World Bank for a project entitled: "Papua New Guinea Mining Sector Institutional Strengthening Technical Assistance." The money will be used to strengthen the capacity of the Department of Mining and the Internal Revenue Commission to encourage more exploration and mine development in the hope of "alleviating poverty". A similar US$7 million loan was also provided by the World Bank to the petroleum sector under the "Petroleum Utilisation and Technical Assistance Project" in 2000.

However this report does not intend to look at both these projects in greater detail. The subject of focus is the Lihir Gold Mine, as this is the only private sector mining project supported by the World Bank, through the Multilateral Investment Guarantee Agency, which guarantees loans for political risk insurance. The loan was granted in 1997 when assurance was provided by the PNG government for the consortium to repay the loan.

Environmental and Social Accountability

Environmental destruction and degradation caused by extractive industries, particularly mining, has been a major concern for Papua New Guineans. This is particularly true among the "mine-affected communities". The State owns all minerals at six feet or more below the earth, as laid down in Section five of the 1992 Mining Act. Therefore if local indigenous people own the land there is a conflict of interest with the State's ownership of minerals below it. By law all the water in PNG also belongs to the State. This gives the government the right to issue licenses for the use of water, be it for domestic or industrial use, or for the disposal of waste, for the diversion for industrial purposes or for storage such as dams for hydropower generation.

In the case of the mining industry, all currently existing mines have been allowed to dispose of mine tailings directly into rivers and oceans. Ok Tedi discharges 80,000 tonnes per day and Tolukuma, 300-400 tonnes.

All these mines have been given large stretches of rivers and perimeters of ocean to pollute, using a "mixing zone" concept. Ok Tedi, Porgera and Tolukuma have taken away 200, 150 and 7 kilometers of rivers respectively for dilution of the mine waste. The environmental NGOs in PNG have been campaigning against the double standards that allow multinational corporations to behave in PNG in ways they would not in their own countries.

Compensation for the environmental degradation associated with mining has been a major issue that is usually complex to solve. It is tied in with the land ownership issue, which in itself is also quite complex for a country like Papua New Guinea, whose over 800 tribes have very diverse cultures and customs. Each community has its own unique way of dealing with the issue, and this makes it difficult for any implementing agency to develop general policies and regulatory frameworks that will broadly address the issue. An attempt to register land in order to properly identify landholders failed. Another system used at the moment is the creation of "Incorporated Land Groups", but this system is not yet widespread.

Benefits from the mine are not equally distributed. People located within the Mining Lease Areas get more attention in terms of benefits than those outside and affected by the development of the mine. The industry does not seem to look in broader terms at its impact on the people in the surrounding areas and particularly those that live downstream of their waste disposal sites. Papua New Guineans, and particularly those directly affected by the mines, have become more educated on their effects over the last decade or more.

LIHIR GOLD MINE

Location

The Lihir Gold Mine is located on Niolam Island, in the New Ireland Province of Papua New Guinea, 700 km northeast of Port Moresby. Niolan is referred to as Lihir because it is the principal island of the Lihir Group of islands. Lihir Island is a volcanic seamount that rises steeply from sea level to approximately 600 metres above sea level. At its widest points, the island measures 22 kilometers from north to south and 14.5 kilometers from east to west. The Lihir Gold Mine is considered a large-scale world class mine, and in PNG it is rated the second largest gold mine after Porgera.

Lihir Project

All statutory documentation was completed in 1995 for the opening of the Lihir Gold Mine and the Lihir Gold Pty Ltd. The company was incorporated in Papua New Guinea in August of that year, and is now known as the Lihir Management Company (LMC).

A Special Mining Lease was granted to the project for a term of 40 years. The Environmental Plan for the mine was approved allowing for direct disposal of mine tailings by a submarine tailings (STD) disposal system, at 125 meters depth. Overburden (waste rock) dumping at sea was permitted via a barge within an area covering 1.8 km north and 2.3 km south of Lihir. Low-grade ore is stockpiled by the shoreline in Luise Harbour.

Despite the PNG government granting permission to mine, there was still a drawback — raising public financing for the Lihir project. The project needed about US$300 million to operate. In July 1996 the European Investment Bank announced a 46 million Euro loan for the project. NGOs around the world supported the CEE (Central and East Europe) Bankwatch Network demand that the Bank withdraw support for the mining activities on environmental grounds.

Financing Political Risk

Lihir Gold Limited then floated shares of US$450 million and signed an agreement for a loan of US$300 million which was due to be paid in 2003. The loan agreement contained a long list of potential problems and defaults, including reference to political violence in the country. Regardless of attractive future profits from the mine, international banks from industrialised nations were reluctant to finance mines in PNG following the closure of the Bougainville copper mine. LMC's majority shareholder is the British company Rio Tinto, which also operated the abandoned Bougainville mine.

The European Finance and Insurance Company (EFIC) downgraded PNG to its lowest category, category D. This was done allegedly to add pressure on the PNG government to accept a controversial structural adjustment package. When the government guaranteed the loan repayment by the consortium, MIGA issued guarantees of US$50 million.

Soon after the granting of the loan and making commitments in 1995, the local currency, the Kina, was devalued by 12% and floated on the world market in 1996. Since then the Kina has been falling and is currently worth about 20 US cents, which is about an 80% drop from its original value.

According to the Environmental Manager for the Lihir, Geoff Day, the company had paid off the loan in 2000. The MIGA and the International Finance Corporation (IFC) had been visiting the mine every quarter of the year to monitor performance, as per their policies, until after the loan payment was completed in 2000. According to Day, the company was in compliance with MIGA conditions in terms of governance as well as environment and social accountability. LMC developed policies to regulate environmental, social and economic performances and hence met the requirements of the Bank over the period.

However, the local people of Lihir Island who are shareholders in the mine were not aware that the WB had even been around to monitor the mining project. This raises a question of transparency in the Bank's dealings with the mine.

Mine Equity

Wealth distribution is usually unequal in terms of material wealth: company officials live in and enjoy better facilities than the local people. They are well paid and usually have access to free services like transport, electricity, water, housing, etc. This contradicts the company reports that highlight equity distribution in monetary terms.

The company, Lihir Gold Limited (LGL), is a public company managed and operated by Lihir Management Company, a wholly owned subsidiary of Rio Tinto. According to a report by the Mineral Policy Institute of Australia in 2001, the major Lihir Gold mine shareholders were as follows:

- Southern Gold: 22.9% (owned 75% by Rio Tinto and 25% by Vengold of Canada)
- Nuigini Mining: 17.1%
- ANZ Nominees: 14%
- Mineral Resources Lihir: 8.2%
- Westpac Custodian Nominees: 4.3%
- Chase Manhattan Nominees: 3.4%
- Lihirian Trust (landowners): 8.6%
- Orogen Minerals (PNG Government): 6.8%

The company's 2002 Annual Report states shareholders as follows:

- Institutions and general public: 67.2%

Map of Lihir

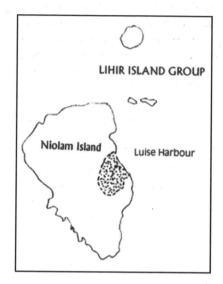

- ☐ Rio Tinto: 16.3%
- ☐ Mineral Resources Lihir (Lihirians): 6.8%
- ☐ Newmont Mining Company: 9.7%

A literature review indicated a continuous slide in the share of the Lihirians from 8.6% in 2001, to 6.8% in 2002 and a mention of 5.2% for 2003. If this is true, it is not clear why this is so.

Local Opinions on WB Funding

This following section is based on the findings of a recent survey conducted by the NGO Environmental Watch Group (NEWG) among the local people of Lihir. The aim was to find out whether the people were aware of the World Bank's involvement in the Lihir project, and if so, to determine the implementation of the Bank's policies on transparency, social and environmental accountability, and poverty alleviation for the indigenous people of Lihir Island.

The survey was conducted in March 2003 through a questionnaire. The respondents of the survey included representatives from the Lihir Area Landowners Association, Lihir Management Company, Nimarmar Development Authority Local Level Government, the local church, local women's group and community leaders. The survey was made possible through the support of the women of Lihir.

Transparency

The research showed little is known about the involvement of the Bank in the Lihir project among the local inhabitants of Lihir Group of Islands. The results indicated that almost 100% of those interviewed did not know anything about the World Bank's involvement. Almost all the people who answered the questions had no idea what MIGA was and what its role was in the project. Thus due to their ignorance on the issue, they were not able to discuss their opinions of the Bank.

Most discussions during a site investigation were mainly on the impacts brought about by the mine. These are briefly discussed below.

Environment

The Lihir area is listed among the country's six high biodiversity areas according to experts with the Worldwide Fund for Nature (WWF) in PNG. It has unique natural surroundings, with reefs that provide -- or rather provided -- habitats for a variety of species of sea creatures, apart from being a magnificent diving spot. Being a volcanic area, the soil is naturally rich, providing good cultivation of crops at both subsistence and commercial values. Unique and valuable cultural sites including graveyards and the shrub-fowl habitat had to be destroyed in order to build the mine.

The mine is pumping 110 million cubic meters of waste, contaminated with cyanide and other toxic chemicals, into the sea each year through a pipeline 125 meters beneath the surface. Another 20 million tonnes of rock waste are dumped each year into Luise Harbour from a barge and stockpiles of low ore grade are heaped in the sea along the shoreline of Luise Harbour.

The responsible parties involved in the Lihir Project had failed to honour their own commitments to the "London Convention", which bans the dumping of waste from ships. It is an international convention, which obliges the countries that have signed it to stop the dumping of industrial waste by barges or ships into the sea. Countries that signed the London Convention include Australia, the UK, and Papua New Guinea. And yet:

- the Australian government Export Credit Agency provided insurance for the Lihir mine which allowed the mine to open;
- the PNG Government gave approval for the project to operate;

NEWG: *How about you? Are you aware of any World Bank involvement in the Lihir Project?*

PWA: *No!, Not at all.*

NEWG: *Well, I'm told that one of the World Bank Group, MIGA financially supports the project's political risk. I thought you might have heard something about (it)?*

PWA: *I have never heard of them and when I asked around here, no-one seemed to know about it as well. Anyway they are also asking what MIGA stands for?*

NEWG: *It stands for Multilateral Investment Guarantee Agency. Could you please ensure leaders at the negotiation of the project particularly church leaders, Landowners Association and even company officials (to) attempt to answer the questions?*

PWA: *All right, I will try to talk (to) the community leaders, church leaders and the company about this.*

NEWG: *Have you had any chance to talk with the company about this?*

PWA: *Yes. In fact we did, we will let you know about all the findings soon.*

◻ and Rio Tinto, a British mining company, owns shares, manages and operates the mine which uses bad environmental management practices.

The LMC, in its recent "Environmental Fact Sheet No. 3", tried to explain what they refer to as the "misconception" on the London Convention, Deep Sea Tailings Placement (DSTP) and the Dumping at Sea Act. They point out that they are not in breach of any of these agreements because they use land-based structures to transport the tailings and that they have been permitted to dump waste into the internal waters of PNG and not territorial waters.

Management and Monitoring

The Natural Systems Research (NSR) are consultants on extractive industries and develop Environmental Plans (EPs) for mining and petroleum projects in the Asia-Pacific Region. They have developed EPs for all the major mines in PNG and have always recommended direct disposal of mine waste into PNG waters, both the river and the sea. This method of waste management recommended by these well regarded experts raises questions on their credibility. The people of Papua New

Guinea are suffering the environmental costs because of the promotion and adoption of this very biased (industry-oriented) management regime.

NSR developed the EP for the Lihir project and recommended the direct discharge of tailings untreated into Luise Harbour, using a Submarine Tailings Disposal System (STD) similar to that in Misima. The mine's tailings are disposed of into the sea. The government (as usual) approved the plan.

The company monitors the waste, and findings are presented to the government (Department of Environment and Conservation) on a periodic basis as a condition of the EP approval. The Department is supposed to evaluate the report but lacks the skills and capacity to do so. Even if it had the capacity, the report usually declares the company is in compliance, and if there was non-compliance they supply a justification. There is no independent review or monitoring of the environment to verify the company's position. Any review would have to be funded independently, to be generally believed as non-biased.

The local people have made numerous complaints of environment pollution but the company always denied the effects saying that it was complying with regulations. There has been little or no independent environmental investigation done to verify this.

Social Challenges

Life on Lihir Island has changed dramatically since the mining began. A rapid transition has occurred in both the physical and social environment.

The troubles of the silent majority are seldom heard, despite what is in their hearts. For some five years or more, a picture has been painted at Lihir of the best mine possible that provided both the necessary services to the local people and the best environmental performance. But this is only one side of the coin.

Besides the boasts of community development schemes, there are increasingly divided classes of people on the island of Niolam, the Lihir Island on which the rich gold mine stands. While it is generally understood that the local people own a bigger share in terms of equity, this does not seem to be the reality. There are definitely two different groups of people on the island – the privileged and the not so privileged.

On the top of a hill in Londolovit sits the Mine Township, overlooking the sea towards the outer Lihir groups of islands, Luise Harbour and parts of Niolam Island where the mine is. This township belongs to the LMC, and it has the best facilities in comparison to those in other areas.

> *The company visits our villages sometimes to tell us about the environment. They give us flashy reports, which many people cannot read. They tell us that there is no problem with the environment. They try to explain the science that nobody on this island really understands or believes. We have naturally grown up here and we believe that we know the environment better. When there is a change, we can tell straight away. We don't necessarily need a scientific explanation. We have been zoned as affected communities and we believe this has been done for a reason. We in Malie would like a very independent monitoring of the environment by an independent institution.*
>
> *This system of waste management only hides the truth about the reality that occurs on the ocean floor beneath the sea. It is the cheapest means that causes massive environmental destruction that is unseen.*
>
> These were the words of a community leader from Malie Island, one of the Lihir Groups of Islands directly facing the mine.

It has sporting facilities, a hotel, national government staff houses and the residence of the Chairman of the Landowners Association (LMALA). The staff houses of mine workers come in different styles, shapes and sizes.

This township has a social club that is only open to the members. Membership fees are PGK150.00 for residents within the township and PGK450.00 for those living outside. The club consists of a barbecue area, swimming pool and other entertainment facilities.

Along the foot of this hill, and barely visible from the hilltop, is the local Lihir township developed by the mine company for the people of Lihir. The town is sparsely populated, with some of the land divided into clan groups. The clans operate small businesses which they brought in with the development of the mine.

The Lihir township has a local marketplace built by the company and managed by the Petztorme Women's Association (PWA). It also has two reasonably big supermarkets and a department store, a community affairs office, a police station, and a few other work shops. The PWA office (newly built without a toilet facility) and a hall "Tutorme" (where LMC embroidery is done) are located right on the waterfront at the foot of the hill.

Having established a special order and delivery system for food and other goods in their camp, the residents of the LMC township hardly go down to shop in the Lihir township supermarkets.

However development has undoubtedly taken place. Through a

Village Development Scheme, local groups and the company have coordinated efforts to build over 500 houses, upgrade and build some local community schools, and assist with the improvement of the health facility. According to LMALA, and the LMC Community Affairs office, much development has taken place over the five years since the mine commenced. There is more development planned, as part of a five-year review. This includes the Integrated Benefit Package, an agreement signed for the people of Lihir in the early stages of the mine, which is going to be reviewed in May 2003.

It is therefore true that many Lihirians are benefiting under the development scheme but there are also negative effects. The livelihood of the majority of Papua New Guineans is based on subsistence farming. They grow and harvest food from gardens, get protein from hunting in the bush, and draw water for their family's consumption. Lihirian people are no exception and lived a similar lifestyle until the development of the mine. People depended on garden food, hunted wild animals, collected srubmegapod eggs and fished in the seas and rivers for fish and prawns. The environment was pristine -- clean waters, clean beaches, clean air, plenty of food, fewer people, less noise, etc.

When the company leased and occupied the land where the mine is now, local communities had to relocate. Their most respected sacred site had to be demolished as it was in the way of the developer. Gold was more important than the significance or cultural value of this scared site. In any case the company had gotten approval for the lease and promised compensation for the losses. This was in the form of cash and building much better permanent houses for the displaced locals.

But do these compensate the real value of the losses? How can we know if what is paid is worth what has been taken away? How can we measure the satisfaction of the indigenous people who don't seem to have much say in the compensation anyway? Let's hear some of the things people of Lihir have to say:

> *I live in Londolovit village which is in the heart of the mining area but I do not benefit at all. Please, don't think that all Lihirians benefit from this mine! Those who are lucky and have a job earn a bit of money to support their family. Those of us living in Londolovit who are not employed are very much affected. When the mine began its development, all our natural creeks were polluted, our sea was polluted, our bush fowls were chased away, our bushes stripped off. We were left here without a thing except for a cheap house and a company water supply facility. We don't believe that what we are getting is worth what the company is making. The gold, the sea, the rivers and our land are God-given gifts (for us, Lihirians) which no*

man should take away from us that easily.

Words of a village church leader from
Londolovit village, Lihir.

Communities were confined to their part of the island, or groups of the islands, despite the natural interactions that occur between communities through family ties and big gatherings such as sports, church and traditional events. The mine has brought a sudden transitional change from subsistence to a monetary-based lifestyle. This has introduced a mixed community of all cultures and races, a more educated community, a shift from the traditional to a modern lifestyle, and increased basic government services.

One thing I find hard to understand is why they (LMC) live in a bigger and differently designed house than I, enjoy the luxury brought about by the gold found in my very own soil. I was given a house without any toilet, showers and kitchen compartments. Why I can't also enjoy that privilege is sometimes what I ask myself. I was relocated from Kapit where the mine now stands. I lost everything, my land and the sea where I used to freely move around and get whatever I wanted. Now I am a prisoner. I got relocated onto a clan land, which means that I cannot use that freedom anymore. Now I am bound by decisions of Clan leaders. It is not the same as when I was on my own land.

My biggest worry now is my children's future! I have lost my land and my children will never own and enjoy that land as I did before. Maybe I was a fool! Even today I have to struggle to meet the school fees for my four children (thank god that a brother helps meet the cost for two), while the company allows their children to go through nearly free education at the cost of my loss.

Words of a relocated Kapit man, Lihir

However, this does not mean happiness has arrived. The Lihirian leaders are preparing for these challenges (not least the eventual closure of the mine) through a program on sustainability, which is focused on agriculture and the development of other resources apart from mining.

Even so, people still feel strongly about the loss of traditional values and their simple way of life.

A matrilineal regime traditionally governed land ownership in

Lihir. Ownership of land is acquired through women. They own land and hence decide on issues relating to it. But were women consulted during the process of negotiations for the mine? Below are comments in relation to this question:

> Lihirians follow a matrilineal society in terms of land ownership. Before the mine this system was well respected. But the mine came into operation on the island, women were never given any space in areas of decision-making. We have little contribution or even nothing at all over land matters today. Our traditional way has lost its true meaning by the introduction of the mine.

Words of a Woman Leader, Lihir

THE ISSUES

Transparency

Conflicts of interest are a result of inadequate awareness, mistrust and corruption. This research indicated a poorly informed society on the involvement of the World Bank or International Financial Institutions in PNG's extractive industries. This clearly shows that there has been a lack of transparency with certain stakeholders. This was especially evi-

> Before we used to go to Londolovit to collect sago leaves, ropes and bamboo for our houses. Through an agreement, a piece of land was provided for Malie people where we could make our gardens as well. Today, the land is a public land. We are now stuck here. We do not know where to go particularly in the future.
>
> Words of a woman from Malie Island, Lihir

dent when local people asked: "What does MIGA stand for anyway?"

In any investment in the country, we hear of stakeholders (be they government, investors/companies or landowners/civil society). It seems the government and the investors work well together but usually do not disclose a lot of information to the third major stakeholder, the landowners. Although this may appear good in terms of protecting the investor, it may not be so in the long run and in many cases, especially as a lack of transparency could lead to corruption or the potential for insurrections against a poorly understood project.

In the case of MIGA, people are not aware of its involvement in the Lihir project. The MIGA and the International Finance Corporation have been closely monitoring the project through regular visits to Lihir, but only company officials knew about this. Only recently have we heard that the loan has been repaid because of good project performance on social, environmental and governance grounds. But has the loan been fully paid or are there still some loans to be paid through the government? If so, can this be explained? Without true transparency how can some of the replies being given be trusted?

On top of these the people still encounter environmental and social problems. The mine on Lihir Island does not affect the people of Lihir alone. The commitment of the PNG government to repay the loan for the project is a matter that all Papua New Guinea citizens should know about. This, we believe, has not happened.

Environmental Problems

Environmental issues, along with inevitably linked social issues, are the key ones the extractive industries have to deal with. In a country like PNG, where solutions to social issues are complex, environmental concerns may be easier to deal with.

We have seen the consultants NSR develop Environmental Plans for extractive industries in PNG, including recommendations to the government on the best technology applicable to projects. It appears the NSR has always advised that the best technology for tailings in PNG is the direct disposal of waste into river systems and oceans.

While this system may be acceptable to the government and the companies, it is not so with those who live with the consequences. New

---

The World Bank's involvement in PNG's mine, oil and gas industries raises some critical questions among different groups of actors; some NGOs and local people describe it a virus, others say it is frightening and others just simply say "we've already sold ourselves as a commodity".

But how can NGOs and indigenous people make such statements when the government is supportive and encourages the World Bank's involvement. There seems to be a conflict of interest.

Maybe we can answer this by asking another question "What do the government and the World Bank know that civil society doesn't know?"

extractive projects that intend to discard untreated waste directly into the environment should not even be allowed to operate in the country. Past and present mines using this technology have greatly harmed people living near such projects.

It is not easy for ordinary citizens, affected communities and informal organisations to have access to information on the environment. A company usually does environmental monitoring and sends the report for evaluation to the responsible government agency, in this case the Department of Environment and Conservation. Whether this report is circulated, and to whom it is circulated, is not very clear. In addition it is believed that the report is naturally biased in favour of the company. The Lihirian people are not satisfied with environmental performances to date, especially when the company frequently reports good performance and yet they see negative impacts all around them.

Expansion

The LMC has also reported recently that exploration on Lihir is showing promising reserves, and thus there is a possibility for expanding the mine. A report by Andrew Trounson of Dow Jones Newswires states: "Papua New Guinea's Lihir Gold Ltd, encouraged by new gold finds near its mine on the tiny Lihir Island, is studying a possible US$200 million to US$250 million expansion of the operation that could increase ore throughput by two-thirds from mid-2006." The report further quotes the Managing Director, Neil Swan, as saying the company is continuing to look at opportunities to diversify beyond PNG and its single reliance on the Lihir mine.

Such expansion could mean more grave environmental consequences if the submarine tailings disposal and the dumping of overburden material at sea are to continue. This will result in the destruction of a large area of marine habitat. In the 30 years of estimated operation at least 104 million tonnes of ore reserves will be exploited, producing 341 million tonnes of waste rock.

The problems of the Lihir project are compounded by the off-shore dumping of waste rock and tailings, which violates the London Convention and the South Pacific Convention. Papua New Guinea is a signatory to both these conventions. Moreover, the mining operation is in a very geologically active area. Seismic activity, extreme geothermal activity and the possibility of active volcanic activity are all characteristics of the mining site.

The region is considered one of the most biologically diverse marine environments in the world. Many aspects of the mine (dumping, land use, gold processing, etc.) threaten this diversity:

- Deep-sea dumping damages coral reefs and marine habitats. The use and disposal of cyanide could also directly harm the species in the area.
- The land that is usurped by the mine includes the breeding ground of the Melanesian Shrubfowl, an endangered species.
- Several culturally and socially important areas such as hot springs, graveyards, and even villages, are being transformed into construction sites to support the mine. The US Overseas Private Investment Corporation declined to support this project on environmental grounds.

World Bank and Technical Assistance Project

The World Bank is now providing Technical Assistance Loans to PNG to strengthen the capacity of the Department of Mines and the Internal Revenue Commission, as well as the petroleum sector. This is to fast-track exploration and mine development in an attempt, they claim, to alleviate poverty. Training provided under the TAL for the staff is commended. But as indigenous people we believe that the World Bank has betrayed us by encouraging mining through a review of the current Mining Act, development of the mining policy and other regulatory framework in PNG.

If it is similarly the PNG government's opinion that it is a means for poverty reduction, then the indigenous communities affected by mining and petroleum projects find this hard to believe. The people of PNG are not starving to death for food and clothing. PNG needs support to upgrade basic services such as health, education and infrastructure development. But promoting extractive industries will not help; in fact in directly affected areas these worsen the situation. The idea of poverty reduction through extractive industries is a kind of reasoning that only justifies the elite's greed and selfishness.

The country's resources are being taken out at an alarming rate, but the benefits are hardly seen, particularly in the rural areas where the companies are temporarily based and where two thirds of PNG's population live. Miners, loggers and their temporary townships are built today and tomorrow are gone with the wind. As they exploit these resources, they also destroy our land, forests, rivers, and ocean; threaten the wildlife and impose unacceptable changes on most of the people's way of life.

The indigenous people affected by mining strongly refute any claims of poverty reduction through the promotion of extractive industries. We realise that our resources have been exploited and misused. We call on our government to rethink its policies and place the needs of the people before the money that this sector will generate out of our resources. Past experience in our country does not warrant and guarantee that we will be any better off.

If we had been given the chance to air our views on this project, we would have asked for diversion of the funds to a more realistic project that will assist in developing Papua New Guinea and thus enable poverty reduction.

CONCLUSION

The World Bank is indirectly promoting extractive industries through Technical Assistance Loans to benefit a few rich people. If it really meant to reduce poverty through this loan, it has made a mistake, at least in the view of the silent majority of local indigenous Papua New Guineans. More mines, oil pipelines and refineries will not bring us any good as our livelihoods are based on the living things of the land, the rivers and the seas.

The government and World Bank should realise that mining in the last decade or more has been more disastrous to people's livelihoods and way of life than anything else. Increasing the number of extractive industries or lowering taxes on the industry cannot alleviate poverty. Mining and petroleum industries are there only for a very few rich people. For the people of Papua New Guinea, this is what it has meant:

- Our rivers and oceans have been polluted. Riverbeds and ocean floors have been destroyed by the deposition of sediments that eliminate aquatic and marine life.
- Our livelihood is in danger as fish numbers decrease rapidly; our water is poisoned so we can no longer use it for drinking, cooking, washing, fishing and other recreational activities.
- Our societies are fragmented. We no longer live and practice our communal Melanesian way of life. Instead we have become self-centred and greedy.
- No mining town today is as cheap as the markets in Port Moresby. Living standards for the overseas workers are

high in mining towns, thus raising prices and causing locals to become poorer than they should be. The class divisions are clear.

◻ Social problems come with the industry as it enters very
remote areas, where the inhabitants have a limited exposure to so-called civilisation. This causes sudden transitional changes that are sometimes detrimental to the
people's traditions and cultures. Respect for elders and
women has disappeared. Womanising, break-up of mar-
riages, new diseases, alcoholism and drug abuse are introduced and on the rise in our innocent communities.

◻ At the end of the day when the developer leaves, we go
back to where we started, only to realise that we had just
been taken for a ride but we have substantially changed.
We have to put ourselves back together again, without the
aid of the companies that have packed up and left.

RECOMMENDATIONS

We, the indigenous communities of Papua New Guinea, therefore recommend the following:

1. The World Bank should ensure that any review, development or changes made to the mining law of PNG and its
   management tools or regulatory framework should be the
   concern of every individual Papua New Guinean. This
   should be done through the engagement of a civil society
   representative on the steering committee of the International
   Development Association (IDA) project or direct engagement with National Umbrella NGOs we are affiliated with.
2. The Department of Mining and the World Bank Team
   should conduct forums and meetings with the widest and
   broadest public participation possible to discuss the
   changes of regulatory framework.
3. Changes in any legal framework should always consider
   the social, environmental and economic concerns from the
   viewpoint of the people.
4. The World Bank should be prepared to fund research into
   problematic projects that it has been a party to in the initial
   stages. It should support and fund an independent environmental monitoring of the Lihir mine, and the monitor-

ing team should stay with local people other than the LMC.

5. No new mines should be encouraged until we are assured that our basic rights have been respected, and that the industry is not going to dump waste directly into our rivers and oceans.

References

March 13 CEE Bankwatch Network letter to EIB President, Philippe Maystadt.

Minerals Policy Institute, Sydney, Australia.

Greg Roberts, *Sydney Morning Herald*, Australia, November 16 2002.

Minerals Policy Institute, Simon Divecha ph: 0428 775 540, advocacy@mpi.org.au.

Greenpeace International Science Officer, David Santillo Ph: 0011 44-1392-263917 d.santillo@ex.ac.uk .

Philippines:
When "Isles of Gold" turn to Isles of Dissent

Raymundo D. Rovillos, Salvador B. Ramo
& Catalino Corpuz, Jr.

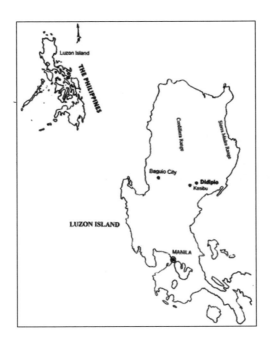

The relationship between the World Bank and the Indigenous Peoples of the Philippines has always been unpleasant, to say the least. This is because projects funded by this international financial institution have caused or threatened the displacement of indigenous peoples from their ancestral domain. The case of the World Bank-funded Chico River Dam Project in the Cordillera has become a nodal point in the history of the region and the entire nation. This and many other cases have engendered a perception among the Indigenous Peoples in the Philippines that the Bank has caused them great suffering.

It is within this historical experience that the case study on the Philippines was undertaken. The study aimed to: a) determine the role of the World Bank in the formulation of the Mining Act of 1995, a law instituting a new system of mineral resources exploration, development, utilization, and conservation); b) assess if adequate effort was made by the Bank to ensure that this legislation would not harm the indigenous peoples; c) analyze the impact/implications of the Mining Act on indigenous peoples/communities; and d) come up with policy recommendation with regard to the mining sector.

This report consists of three parts. The first traces the influence/role of the World Bank and other multilateral bodies in the process of crafting the Philippine Mining Act of 1995. The second evaluates the impact of the Mining Act on the indigenous peoples in general and the third focuses on one indigenous community in northern Philippines to show the impact of the mining policy at the micro level.

PHILIPPINE MINING INDUSTRY

The Philippines is rich in mineral resources. Because of its complex geological history and diverse rock types, it is characterized by a diverse group of mineral deposits.[1] It has one of the leading global reserves in gold, copper, nickel, chromite, iron, bauxite, marble and limestone, among many others.

The country continues to be a major world producer of gold and copper. In 1991 it was 13th in the world in copper production and 11th in gold production.[2] A 1997 survey of major mining firms operating in the Asia-Pacific revealed that the Philippines ranked second only to Indonesia in terms of geological prospectivity.[3]

The Philippines also has abundant deposits of iron, lead, zinc, platinum, manganese, molybdenum, cobalt, aluminum, and mercury.[4] Nonmetallic minerals of economic significance are gypsum, salt, sand and gravel, marble, clay, limestone, feldspar, dolomite, magnesite, phoshate rock, guano, and sulfur.[5]

Gold mining dates back to at least the 3rd Century A.D. when Chinese traders referred to Luzon as the Isle of Gold. However, major commercial mining activity did not begin until the "gold rush" of the 1930s and 1940s when, by 1941, 41 mines were producing approximately 30 mt of gold per year. In 1965 the first porphyry copper deposit was opened by Atlas Mining Company in Cebu, which marked the beginning of modern-day mining in the Philippines.

The decade of the 70s is considered as:

the busiest for the mining industry as old dormant gold mines were reopened, new gold projects developed, existing copper mines ex-

panded and new copper projects undertaken. The deluge of activities seemed to be part investment, part speculative or just "follow trend ventures." An interplay of various factors held promise for the mining industry — one, the brilliant performance of copper and other metals in the world market, the presidential declaration that mining would be the `industry of the 70s' and finally, the stock market boom.[6]

In 1974 there were 18 major copper mines in operation and in 1980 copper production peaked at 304,500 mt of copper metal. In 1980 about 45 operating mines were contributing over 21% to total Philippine exports. It was during this decade that the progressive decline of the Philippine mining industry began.

The Crisis

Since 1985, the mining industry has suffered a "crisis." Copper production drastically dropped by a staggering 90%. Chromite production in 2000 was only 5% of that two decades ago. The drop in copper production can be attributed to the closure of mining companies. The main reason was the financial crisis, which was aggravated by other incidents.

Atlas Mine, once Asia's largest producing copper mine, was closed due to the financial crisis (1994); Marcopper mines due to the infamous tailings spill incident (1996); Dizon mines after a massive erosion caused by a typhoon (1998); and Maricalum in view of operational and financial problems, including failures in its tailings dam, and the shift by Manila Mining (this too stopped after two tailings spills and poor community relations) and Lepanto Consolidated Mining Company (LCMC) to gold production (2001).[7]

In 1993 the Philippine Chamber of Mines reported that "out of the 39 mining companies in the early '80s only 16 have remained active in production today."[8] Gold managed to increase production due to the contribution of gold rush areas, notably the Diwalwal gold rush area in southern Philippines. Since the mid-90s, production from these gold areas has accounted for about 50% of total Philippine gold production. Nickel production also increased due to fairly stable metal prices.[9]

The slowdown in the mining industry was felt by the national economy. From 1970 to 1974, mineral exports accounted for an annual average of 21.7% of total exports, mainly due to favorable world prices. This contribution declined to 16.1% from 1975 to 1985, with a brief comeback (21.3%) in 1980. Since 1986, the average value of mineral exports per year has been equal to only 7.3% of the total foreign exchange earnings.[10]

Various groups offered different explanations for the crisis in the mining industry. The Philippine Chamber of Mines attributed it to three reasons: first, the absence of a new mining code that would "provide for a production sharing structure with government and local and foreign investors… a situation that has discouraged new investments into the industry"; second, the excessive (5% then) taxes imposed on the gross receipts of mining companies; and third, the fact that "the operating mines on the average are extracting generally low grade ore."[11]

The Asian Development Bank (ADB) also argued that the decline in mineral production was due (in addition to downsizing of major operations) to the fact that "additional foreign investment in the mineral sector has all but ceased as a result of the investment climate in the Philippines, which is perceived by the worldwide mining industry as negative." The ADB report adds:

> The Philippines ranks 98th overall (below China and Vietnam, two major regional competitors for foreign investment in the mineral sector). Similarly when the Philippines was compared with other ASEAN nations in terms of its overall investment climate (not minerals specifically) it did not receive a superior rating in any 18 rating categories.[12]

By "good investment climate," the ADB meant an open economy, where foreign investors are offered competitive fiscal incentives and guarantees. The ADB specifically proposed that the 60-40 provision* of the 1987 Constitution be corrected and the mining companies allowed full access to mineral lands and resources. It added that mining companies be given tax holidays, full repatriation of profits, and other incentives. All these, ADB ultimately suggested, should be protected by a new mining code for the Philippines.

It should be noted that both the Chamber of Mines and the ADB focused on the production aspect when they explained the crisis in the mining industry. Both institutions did not pay much attention to the consumption side and the overall global crisis affecting the industry. From the perspective of the ADB and the mining companies, expansion

---

*Section 2, Article XII of the 1987 Philippine Constitution stipulates that…. The state may enter into co-production, joint venture or production sharing agreements with Filipino citizens or corporations or associations at least 60% of whose capital is owned by such citizens.

of mineral production will and shall happen only when the Philippine mining industry is opened up for infusion of huge amounts of foreign capital.

Towards a Mining Code

The problem confronting the mining industry is not purely local in origin and character. Indeed, the past two decades have seen the slowdown in mineral production due to the global economic recession. Slow economic growth means that less people are buying jewelries and other products made from mineral products. The low demand is also due to more and more companies using substitutes for metals in their production processes.

Still, key industry actors such as the World Bank and its regional counterpart, the Asian Development Bank, the United Nations Development Program (UNDP), United Nations Department of Technical Cooperation and Development (UNDTCD), the local Chamber of Mines and (later) the Philippine Government agreed that the crisis could be solved once the policy fundamentals were in place.

These policy fundamentals, these institutions prescribed, should result in an improved "investment climate" that the ADB cited in its final report. These various actors played distinct roles and their relationships were characterized by dynamism. As they engaged in other "policy dialogues" they were guided by the same principles of free market and export-oriented development framework. Thus in the end, their distinct as well as coordinated efforts finally resulted in the Mining Act of 1995.

These above-mentioned studies however never mentioned nor considered the possible impact of mining on indigenous peoples. The ADB technical assistance did recognize the social dimension of mining but, according to its final report, this was something that should be studied by academic research institutions.

Role of World Bank

The role of the World Bank in policy reform development of the mining industry in member countries is succinctly captured in the following statement:

> The World Bank contributes to the process of developing policy responses to development issues in the minerals sector by collecting and disseminating knowledge about topical minerals development

issues. It does this, not only through its involvement with member countries in its operations, but also by participating in and sponsoring seminars, conferences, and industry roundtables.[13]

In 1989 the World Bank participated in a seminar organized by the United Nations Department of Technical Cooperation and Development. The seminar was themed "Prospects for the Mining Industry to the Year 2000." The Philippine Government was represented by then Director of Mines and Geosciences Bureau (MGB), Guillermo R. Balce, and Michael V. Cabalda. During this seminar, World Bank Senior Industrial Specialist Felix Remy shared the perspectives of the World Bank on mining policy. He explained the nature of the Bank's "problem" thus:

> *The first set of sector-specific problems that we find in our mining sector work are the 'mining law' issues, that is, the constraints arising out of the existing mining legislation. The issues that we encounter most frequently in the mining legislation of our borrowers are: problems of inadequate or difficult access to land and mineral rights by the productive agents of the sector; restrictions to foreign investment which are specific to the mining sector; the existence of 'sector-specific taxes' which can take the form of royalties, production, sales or export, taxes; and legislation of discretionary nature.*[14]

The World Bank pushed for giving high priority to the public availability of mineral lands and reasonable taxes. It also suggested an institutional set-up that would provide the mining sector with quality services. The World Bank then proposed that "an institutional strategy that responds to existing legal framework in a given country and that will make good use of it must be developed, and the role of World Bank is to provide support for this."[15]

Also in the late '80s, the World Bank launched a Mining Policy Study in the African region. According to John Strongman, the Principal Mining Officer of the World Bank:

> *While the study focuses on African mining policy, as a first stage the findings of the suggested survey are meant to be expanded in such a way that **conclusions can be reached on policy initiatives that have the greatest potential for improving mining sector performance in different countries**, and the relative emphasis that should be given to: (i) opening up the sector to encourage new private sector participation; and (ii) improving the efficiency and competitiveness of mining enterprises. (underscoring added).*[16]

Unfortunately, these studies did not seek to identify the issue of indigenous peoples as an important policy concern (i.e., the possible negative impact of mining on indigenous peoples and the poor), despite the wealth of knowledge and experience on indigenous peoples that were already available to the World Bank at that time.

The findings and recommendations of this World Bank study are quite instructive of its role in the crafting of national mining codes not only in Africa but also in other parts of the world including the Philippines. It reiterates WB policies of deregulation, privatization and liberalization of the mining industry.

The main finding of the report is that the recovery of the mining sector in Africa will require a shift in government objectives towards a primary objective of maximizing tax revenues from mining over the long term, rather than pursuing other economic or political objectives such as control of resources or enhancement of employment. The study further recommends that this objective will be best achieved by a new policy emphasis whereby governments focus on industry regulation and promotion and private companies take the lead in operating, managing and owning mineral enterprises.[17]

The study further recommended that countries wishing to attract foreign investments to support mineral development should develop or support:

▫ A legal framework that adequately defines the investor's rights and obligations;
▫ Security of tenure to give the investor assurance of the fruits of success;
▫ A fiscal package that shares the rent of profitable production equitably between the government and the investor; and
▫ Guarantees of access to foreign exchange at market rates for repayment of debts, repatriation of capital and profits, and purchase of essential inputs. Without these essential conditions, new investment is unlikely.[18]

The study also proposed that an effective mining code should: 1) apply equally to all investors; 2) clearly specify the ownership of mineral resources; 3) contain explicit criteria for the allocation of rights and allows them to be transferable and saleable; 4) ensure that land is either actively explored and worked or relinquished; and 5) prescribe procedures for settling disputes in the courts or by arbitration.[19]

This set of conditions is indeed biased for the mining companies and against the interests of the indigenous peoples. For example, there was no requirement whatsoever to secure the rights of indigenous peoples as a prior condition. Therefore, the entry of mining corporations would inevitably add to the insecurity of tenure of indigenous peoples over their lands.

That the prescriptions for an ideal mining code have strong similarities with the Philippine Mining Act of 1995 is no coincidence. An official document reports that in 1988 "a joint effort of government, the mining industry, professional associations, and academe, with some input from United Nations advisers, has resulted in a new draft Mining Code."[20] The same document explicitly states that representatives of the UN Department of Technical Cooperation for Development were directly involved in the formulation of the Mining Code.

These initiatives drew their data from and were supported by several mining and geological studies conducted by different international/multilateral agencies. Some of these were: the German Development Institute (GDI), *Development Perspectives of the Philippine Mining Sector* (August 1980); United Nations Department of Technical Co-operation for Development, *Strengthening The Government Capability In Gold Exploration* (1987); US Agency for International Development (USAID), *Detailed Policy Guidelines For Mine Tailings Disposal*; ADB, *Mineral Sector Study* (1994).

MINING ACT OF 1995

On March 6, 1995 President Fidel Ramos signed into law Republic Act 7942 or the Philippine Mining Act of 1995. On August 15 of that year, the Department of Environment and Natural Resources (DENR) issued the Act's Implementing Rules and Regulations (IRR).

On one side, the law was hailed by the Philippine Chamber of Mines as a landmark legislation, a fruit of their years of persistent lobby in Congress.[21] On the other side, environmentalists, social activists and indigenous peoples' organizations opposed it.

The law is based on Article XII of the Philippine Constitution that mandates the State to manage the country's mineral resources as owner and administrator, and to control and supervise their exploration, development and utilization. It reiterates the Constitutional provision that only the government may grant mining rights to individuals and corporations.

Under the new Mining Act, the government may grant three major kinds of mining rights:

□   Exploration Permit (EP) grants the exclusive rights to the permittee to explore a tract of land based on an approved work program. If a mineral deposit is delineated and found to be technically and economically feasible to be developed, the permittee has the right to enter into any type of mining right with the government.[22]

□   Mineral Agreement grants the contractor the right to conduct mining operations within the contract area for a period of 25 years, renewable for another 25 years. This agreement has three types: Mineral Production Sharing Agreement (MPSA), Joint Venture, and Co-Production Agreement. It allows 40% foreign equity.[23]

□   Financial or Technical Assistance Agreement (FTAA) is a contract involving large-scale mining operations with an investment of not less than $50 million. It allows the entry of 100% foreign-owned mining corporations which possess the qualifications set forth in the law and its implementing rules and regulations. This agreement has a term of 25 years, renewable for another 25 years.[24]

The FTAA provision drew strong criticisms from civil society organizations. The Legal Rights and Natural Resource Center-*Kasama sa Kalikasan* (LRC-KSK, Friends of the Earth) believes that the FTAA is unconstitutional. They cite Article II, Section 2 of the 1987 Constitution which provides that the FTAA is an agreement for mere assistance, either technical or financial, in the development of mineral resources. "The FTAA contemplated by the Constitution is not a mineral agreement or a contract for the exploration of minerals. Nowhere in this provision does the Constitution allow foreign corporations to actually control, manage or engage in full mining operations."[25]

But the Philippine Mining Act of 1995 allows 100% foreign control over large-scale mining operations, through the FTAA. Other militant organizations have accused the government of selling the patrimony of the Philippines to foreign capital.[26]

To attract foreign investors through the FTAA, the Philippine government, through the Mining Act of 1995, offers a package of fiscal and non-fiscal incentives such as those provided for by the 1987 Omnibus Investment Code (this includes income tax holiday for four years for non-pioneer and six years for pioneer projects; tax and duty free importation of capital equipment); pollution control devices; income tax-carry forward of losses; and income-tax accelerated depreciation.

The Mining Act also offers investment guarantees, such as: repatriation of investment; remittance of earnings, remittance of foreign loans and obligations from contracts; freedom from expropriation, freedom from requisition of investment and confidentiality.

The law professes to respect the rights of indigenous peoples by containing a provision on Free and Prior Informed Consent (FPIC). It also includes provisions on environmental safeguards. Critics however view these as token provisions or lip service to sugar coat the primary motivation of mining corporations, that is, the maximization of profit. Community experiences on the use of the FPIC provisions tend to validate the skepticism of civil society and non-government organizations (CSO/NGO) of the sincerity of mining companies on their pronouncements of concern for the social and environmental impacts of mining.

Finally, the Mining Act grants mining corporations, both foreign and local, the rights to use water and forest resources. It grants easement rights, which means the right to "ease out" any impediment to mining operations. "Effectively, the government has granted mining corporations the right to dislocate and displace farming, fishing and indigenous communities."[27]

IMPACT OF MINING ACT

One immediate result of the Mining Act was the flurry of mining applications in the Philippines. In 2002, 43 FTAA applications were under process, covering around 2.16 million hectares or some 8% of Philippine territorial land.[28] It is interesting to note that six FTAAs had already been filed even before the Senate had approved the Mining Act. This may be attributed to the substantial promotional campaigns the government conducted with the support of UNDTCD and UNDP.[29] These campaigns gave assurances that the proposed mining code would soon be approved by Congress.

Since the enactment of the law, the government has approved: 180 Mineral Production Sharing Agreements; 70 Exploration Permits; 126 Industrial Sand and Gravel Permits; and 5 Special Mineral Extraction Permits.[30] This does not include the two Financial and Technical Assistance Agreements and Mining/Placer/Lode Lease Contracts granted under previous mining laws. Collectively these mining rights cover an area of 850,000 hectares or about 2.8% of the total Philippine land area.[31]

On May 6-8, 2002 several indigenous peoples' organizations, and non-government and peoples' organizations* held the "National Conference on Mining" in Baguio City. Some 131 representatives of various national, regional and community-based peoples' organizations participated, including indigenous peoples/communities directly affected by mining. The conference highlighted the impact of the Mining Act of 1995 and the adverse effects and actual and potential threats of what they called TNC (transnational) mining in their communities. Below are some of these effects as articulated by the affected community people themselves.[32]

Divided Communities

The most glaring impact of the Mining Act of 1995 has been the disunity engendered in indigenous and local communities. This has been caused mainly by the "divide-and-rule" tactic employed by mining corporations.

In Southern Mindanao the Australian-owned Western Mining Corporation (WMC) was reported to have organized "Tribal Councils" that turned out to be non-representative of the indigenous communities concerned. Genuine tribal councils, such as the Lugal Tribal Association organized by the B'laans long before the WMC came, were pitted against the company-organized tribal council, dividing the ranks of Lumads or indigenous peoples.

On the island of Mindoro in southern Luzon, Mindex, another Australian mining company, has caused community conflicts among Mangyans. The company organized its employees into the pro-company *Lupaing Ninuno Mangyan Inc.* (Mangyan Ancestral Domain Inc.) to undermine the opposition representing the legitimate indigenous *Alangan and Tadyawan Mangyan* organizations.

In the Cordillera, Lepanto Consolidated Mining Company's prospecting activities in Mainit village, Mountain Province employed similar tactics of using one family against others. The LCMC management convinced the Chaloping family, who had long been residing elsewhere, to stake their ancestral land claims in the village. From these claims, the family applied for a Mineral Production Sharing Agreement which they used to negotiate for a mining project in partnership with LCMC.

---

*Tebtebba (Indigenous Peoples' International Centre for Policy Research and Education), Philippine Indigenous Peoples' Links, Legal Rights and Natural Resource Center, BAYAN (New Patriotic Alliance), DCMI (Diopem Committee on Mining Issues), KALIKASAN, Center for Environmental Concerns and Cordillera Peoples Alliance

Sham Consultation of Indigenous Peoples

Companies have abused and misused the principle of Free and Prior Informed Consent to get the approval and participation of indigenous communities. They have employed various means, ranging from deception, cooptation to coercion, to get the supposed consent of indigenous peoples.

The most revealing example of a company's misuse of the FPIC is again seen in the case of Western Mining Corporation in Southern Mindanao. Nestor Horfilla, an anthropologist and the executive director of Davao City-based Kaliwat Performing Arts Cooperative (KPAC) and convenor of *Panagtagbo*, a Mindanao-wide forum of non-government and peoples' organizations, claims that WMC "dealt with, short of literally bribing, individual leaders to accept (and sign agreements with) Western Mining."[33]

Juanito Malid of the Salnaon Banwu, an indigenous B'laan settlement, disclosed that his father, Majon Malid, was promised a big house, other infrastructure and livelihood projects in exchange for his signature on the agreement with WMC. The agreement, signed on February 17, 1995, binds the B'laans "to support and will make no objection to the grant of an FTAA to WMC and acknowledge and confirm the WMC's exclusive right to conduct mining activities."

The young Malid was forced to sign the documents, too, to prevent fighting among the clan members. The company, he added, employed other "forms" of pressure on the B'laans to sign the agreement. Prior to his father's signing, clan members were brought by two WMC employees into what Juanito simply called a "hotel" in General Santos City. Juanito described the scene thus: *"There was dancing, nude women, lots of food and drinks, and women for partners."*

Juanito narrated another incident when leaders from the B'laan community of Denlag were also brought to the city. *"There were 10 of us; for two days we were billeted in a hotel, four in each room well stacked with food and drinks."* At the hotel, Juanito quoted a man named Patricio as saying: *"The military will come if you oppose. The project has been approved by the government."*[34]

In Zamboanga, Toronto Ventures, Inc. (TVI) employed deception, prompting the local people to sign a blank sheet of paper during a meeting and later using this as "proof" of endorsement of its mining project. Boy Ano, a community leader, said: *"TVI gathered some students, including myself, prodded us to affix our signatures on a paper with a TVI letterhead, and declared that we have permitted the company's operation in our communities."*[35]

Displacement from Ancestral Domain

Massive legalized land grabbing by mining transnational corporations through the new Philippine Mining Act has deprived indigenous peoples of their ancestral domain rights. Narratives of actual and potential displacement have reverberated throughout the country since the mining industry was liberalized.

Since 1994 TVI has been forcing its way into a territory that is within the 6,523.7-hectare ancestral domain claim of the indigenous Subanen people in Zamboanga. The government has recognized the Subanen's ancestral territory under a Certificate of Ancestral Domain Claim (CADC).

In Zamboanga del Sur, big companies had applied for one FTAA and six MPSAs in the 27,000-hectare town of Midsalip. The town, inhabited by Subanens, still has 1,500 hectares of virgin forests, 1,000 hectares of second-growth forests, and 500 hectares of reforested land. The biggest FTAA applicant is CRA/Rio Tinto, with an FTAA covering 100,000 hectares.

In Southern Mindanao, the FTAA application of Western Mining Corporation was one of the first two FTAAs approved by the government. The WMC FTAA covers 99,400 hectares of the area-boundary provinces of South Cotabato, Sarangani, Sultan Kudarat, North Cotabato and Davao del Sur. The entry of the project (now operated by Saguitarius Indophil) will displace indigenous peoples -- Tagakaulo, B'laan, and Manobos -- from their ancestral domain.

In Mindoro, the Mindex-Crew got a permit from the Mines and Geosciences Bureau to conduct mine exploration. The Exploration Permit covers areas that include the ancestral domain claims of the Mangyans. In fact, the government, through the National Commission on Indigenous Peoples (NCIP), granted the Mangyans a CADC over the same area on February 26, 1996, almost a year before the Mindex-Crew's exploration permit was granted.

Thousands of indigenous peoples have also been displaced from their ancestral lands due to militarization that usually accompanied mining exploration.

Repression, Violence and Militarization

Dr. Rodolfo Stavenhagen, the United Nations Special Rapporteur on the Rights of Indigenous People, in his report on his mission to the Philippines on December 2-11, 2002, observed:

Serious human rights violations have been reported to the Special

Rapporteur regarding the implications for indigenous communities of economic activities such as logging, mining, the building of dams, commercial plantations and other development projects. Of particular concern have been the long-term effects on the environment and the livelihood of indigenous peoples of open-pit mining and the expansion of existing mining operations.[36]

Dr. Stavenhagen was not wrong in his observation. The following testimonies are just some of the stories of repression and violence being experienced by indigenous peoples nationwide.

In Guihulngan, Negros Oriental, fanatic groups, elements of the paramilitary Citizens Armed Force Geographical Unit (CAFGU) and military troops terrorized communities where Western Mining Corporation has staked mining claims. In a fact-finding mission conducted by Kilusang Magbubukid ng Pilipinas (KMP, Philippine Peasant Movement) on April 1-3, 2002, it was found that rights violations were due to militarization, which intensified with the entry of mining on the island. WMC applied for an 88,000-hectare FTAA spread over 14 towns where 300,000 villagers live.

A campaign was initiated by KMP-Negros against the entry of WMC, land grabbing and militarization. The KMP accused the government, through its military machinery, of being the company's virtual security guard. The military set up detachments in three villages where farmers had strongly protested against mining. They also helped organize fanatic and paramilitary groups, which stalked poor farmers who asserted their rights to land and who questioned the planned entry of the WMC to their island.

In Siocon, Zamboanga del Norte, military checkpoints became part of the community's terrain after Toronto Ventures Inc. entered the Subanen's ancestral domain. These served as a tool by the company to harass the local people. These barred the residents from bringing home food supplies, which the company and the soldiers claimed were being given to communist insurgents.

TVI hired goons and mobilized the police to intimidate traditional small-scale miners who had been in the area long before the company came. In one instance, company goons hurled a grenade and indiscriminately fired upon a group of small-scale miners.

On March 6, 2003 a company of the Philippine Army's 50th Infantry Battalion conducted operations in villages of Quirino and Cervantes in Ilocos Sur province allegedly to flush out communist rebels. They entered several villages purportedly to act as a blocking force because of a reported encounter between Army troops and New Peoples Army guerillas.

Dinteg, an alternative indigenous law center in the Cordillera, belied the claims. It dismissed the Army reports of encounters to justify deployment of troops and the recruitment of CAFGUs and paramilitary forces in the area. The villages in Quirino and Cervantes, along with several towns of Benguet and Mountain Province had recently launched a campaign against Lepanto Consolidated Mining Company's operation and expansion. The villagers claimed that LCMC's mine tailings dam has adversely affected farm production, destroyed the fertility of their lands and contaminated irrigation water from the Abra River.[37]

In the province of Aurora, in the northwest portion of the country, residents report that they are now facing the consequence of their anti-mining campaign with the increasing presence of military and paramilitary troops in upland communities. Some 51,000 hectares of Aurora province, larger than the actual size of the province, have been granted to three FTAA applicants, namely Omnigroup, BHP and Chase Mining Ltd.

It is clear from these testimonies of indigenous peoples and farmers that they are not only against the Mining Act of 1995. They are also opposed to TNC mining or any other kind of extractive industry activities on their ancestral domains/territories.

Indigenous peoples lament that decades of mining on their lands have only resulted in massive ecological destruction and wanton exploitation of the natural resources. Mining corporations, protected by state legislation, have displaced them from their ancestral domain. This has meant the loss of livelihoods, thereby worsening poverty in indigenous communities.[38] Indigenous peoples also claim that the entry of mining has led to the destruction of their rich cultures, as it has introduced and made rampant decadent values and practices such as drinking, gambling and prostitution.

Further TNC mining has impacted indigenous women disproportionately. For instance, as the water dries up due to mining operations, women have to fetch water from a farther distance and their worries increase when their children fall ill because of lack of water. The closure of mining has also increased the multiple burden of women. They take on the role of breadwinners as their husbands are deprived of a livelihood.

From a brief rendering of the national experiences vis-à-vis the Mining Act of 1995 (and mining in general), we present the particular experience of a local/indigenous community in northern Philippines. This amplifies the issues presented above and illustrates the specific impacts that the World Bank-supported mining industry has brought to one community.

CLIMAX ARIMCO PROJECT IN NUEVA VIZCAYA:
A CASE OF BEST PRACTICE?

The development of the Dinkidi ore body is socially acceptable. It conforms to all material criteria specified by the World Bank, to 'world's best practice' principles adopted by all major mining groups in Australia and North America and to the particular requirements of the government of the Philippines.[39]

This was the assessment of the Climax Arimco Mining Corporation (CAMC) about the community participation and social acceptability of its mining project in Didipio, Kasibu, Nueva Vizcaya in northeastern Philippines.

The paper cites the role of the World Bank in this project:

The project funding arm of the World Bank, International Finance Corporation (IFC), independently audited the proposed development plan. In approving the plan, the IFC consultant stated that the acceptance by the host community of the development plan represented the best case of prior informed consent he had ever witnessed. Steffen Roberts and Kersten (SRK) independently reviewed and approved the community development plan on behalf of potential members of the international banking syndicate.[40]

These claims are challenged by the people who are directly involved and adversely impacted by CAMC's mining activities.

The Project

On June 20 1994, the Philippine government granted CAMC a Financial or Technical Assistance Agreement covering 37,000 hectares in Nueva Vizcaya and Quirino provinces for mining exploration and development. The CAMC project was the other of two FTAAs granted before the enactment of the new mining law in 1995.

The Didipio Gold/Copper Project, which covers about 1,500 hectares, was established out of CAMC's FTAA. It is a mineral development project subjected to a feasibility study on the Dinkidi deposit, one of a number of mineralized bodies located in the Didipio Valley. The project has reached the "advance stage of exploration having substantially completed geological mapping, stream sediment geochemistry, geophysical induced polarization surveys and sub-surface drilling."[41] The same project was granted an Environmental Clearance Certificate (ECC) on August 11, 1999.

Registered on July 5, 1990, Climax Arimco is owned jointly by two Australian mining companies, Arimco NL and Climax Mining Limited. Through CAMC, Climax holds an aggregate 92% interest in the FTAA. Philippine investors hold the remaining interest. The CAMC project is expected to operate for a period of 12 years, three 3 years for the development aspect and nine years for operation.

According to the people's organization, Didipio Earth Savers Multi-Purpose Association (DESAMA), the Didipio Gold/Copper Project "aims to extract as much as 1,200,000 ounces of gold and 99,000 tons of copper metal. The open pit and cave-block mining process is expected to produce 4,550,000 tons of waste rock."[42]

CAMC estimated a budget outlay of $138 million to develop the project, which it has drawn from various funding sources in Asia and Europe.

Didipio - land of plenty and opportunity

The pioneers of Didipio are indigenous Ifugaos who came from Hungduan, a municipality of Ifugao province in the Cordillera region. In the 1950s they came to the valley in waves in response to government's offer to open up frontier areas (homesteads) for resettlement.[43]

The new settlers encountered Ilonggots or Bugkalots, another indigenous group in the area, who were hunters and food gatherers. It was from them that the Ifugao settlers heard of the word 'Kasibu', which means 'place where people settle their differences'. Finding it a fitting word, they adopted it to name their place of settlement.

Didipio is one of 30 barangays (villages) of the town of Kasibu. Today, it is home to approximately 1,500 individuals belonging to 250 households.[44] Didipio is a fertile valley, whose base is planted mainly to rice grown in terraced plots as well as to other crops and vegetables cultivated for domestic consumption. Clusters of mostly wood and concrete houses dot its sides as well as the school, churches and multi-purpose halls where the community occasionally gather.

The valley is endowed with rich natural resources. Its forests provide wild game, timber for houses, and waters that feed the Camgat and Dinauyan rivers, which flow into the Didipio River. These bodies of water supply the irrigation that sustains agricultural production and fish source for the local people.

The lands yield various crops for subsistence. The Ifugao settlers started clearing lands through slash and burn, taking over lands earlier cleared by a logging company, the Luzon Loggers Inc, reportedly owned by a political clan in nearby Quirino province. Gradually they built permanent terraces and irrigation canals. They continued to practice their traditional land and resource management practices such as the *muyong*¯* to protect the watershed. They have managed to preserve the fertility of the soil, taking pride in the fact that up to now they do not need to use chemical fertilizers, herbicides and pesticides to increase production.

In areas where water is scarce, the farmers cultivated citrus, bananas and other fruits. This proved to be a lucrative endeavor but in 1995 the banana plants contracted *tungru,* a fungus-based disease. Antonio Dingcog, the Barangay Chairman, attributes the fungi to CAMC, saying the bananas were infected with the fungi after a CAMC plane flew over Didipio in 1995 to survey the area. While this anecdote needs validation, it is a clear expression of the low esteem and lack of trust the local people have for the mining company.

Other members of the community engage in small-scale mining to supplement their income. Some others raise farm animals like chickens, hogs and goats as an additional food source.

The community used to be close-knit, living in peace and harmony. They settled their differences amicably with the active intervention of the elders. While they no longer perform the rituals that their kin in Ifugao continue to do, they have retained some of their useful cultural practices. Community folk for instance engage in the practice of *batarisan* or *ammoyo*. This is pooled work voluntarily offered by neighbors to anyone who needs to finish certain jobs like building a house, making an irrigation canal, planting or harvesting.

This was Didipio, a simple, economically subsistent community, idyllic and peaceful. The people lived in harmony with one another and with nature. A perfect picture indeed -- until the CAMC came.

Enter the Giant

In 1989 mine prospectors arrived in Didipio, sampling the lands. Community folks were surprised, but as is common with them, remained friendly and accommodating. The visitors assured them that nothing extraordinary was happening, and then left, later to return. They did this several times until they established a more permanent camp in 1994.

Without the people's knowledge, a foreign company named Climax Arimco Mining Corporation had already secured the approval of

---

¯*Muyong* is a clan-owned forest in Ifugao. The Ifugaos still observe customary laws with regard to the use and management of this common resource.

then President Fidel Ramos to explore and eventually mine Didipio. Feeling deceived and betrayed, they protested this transgression on their hospitality. But the company went on to hire local hands to lay the groundwork for the project.

CAMC plans to establish a small open pit mine and later to excavate underground through the block caving method. It will build a diversion tunnel, processing facilities, and a tailings dam to contain the waste. The needed engineering and construction equipment includes: large hydraulic excavators, blast hole drills, haul trucks, bulldozers, load, haul and dump units, ventilation shafts, crushers, conveyors, feeders. The project promises to generate jobs, projected at 745 employees during the development stage and 555 employees during the operations stage.

In compliance with the Mining Act of 1995, the CAMC conducted an Environmental Impact Statement (EIS). The company also prepared an Environmental Protection and Enhancement Program (EPP) and submitted it to the Department of Environment and Natural Resources. Local opposition to the project however was mounting, and in response, CAMC in 2000 revised its mining proposal to make it more socially 'acceptable.' The new proposal was called Yawanoo Concept Study [*See Table 1*].

Table 1: *Comparison between Previous Proposal and Yawanoo Concept Study.*

	Previous Proposal	**Yawanoo Concept Study**
Reserve	17 mt	3 mt
Mining Method	Small open pit Block cave (underground)	Small open pit Cut and fill
Construction period	Three years	One year
Production rate	2 mt year	.3 to .5 mt year
Mine life	Nine years	Eight years extendable
Design	6 km drainage tunnel, diversion tunnel, large tailings dam	No drainage tunnel, no diversion tunnel, small tailings dam
Capital	US$150 million	US$32 million
Government share	60% net revenue	60% net revenue
Community share	1% operating costs	1% operating costs

Source: Didipio Gold/Copper Project - Climax Arimco, *Building the Philippine Future through Responsible Mining*, undated.

The Concept Study also attempted to point out its advantages over the previous proposal [*See Table 2*].

Table 2: *Advantages of the Yawanoo Concept Study*

Advantages of Yawanoo Concept Study	Disadvantages of Previous Proposal
- low initial capital cost at US$32 million - one-year construction period - low environmental impact - small tailings dam - fewer tailings - tailings also used as underground stope backfill - 6 km drainage tunnel not required - use of pumps for dewatering - pumped water can be distributed for agriculture and irrigation purposes - no diversion tunnel required - new tailings dam location - fewer people.	- cut and fill is a high cost mining method - more labor intensive - extract only a portion of the orebody: various pillars are required for ground support like stope pillars and crown pillars - less gold and copper produced

Token consultations

It took three years before CAMC publicly acknowledged its intention to mine in Didipio. In 1997, three years after the government granted it an FTAA, the company conducted its first public consultation. This was later followed by several other consultations.

Upon learning of the CAMC mining project, the local people staged protest activities in the barangay as well as in the town and provincial centers and the national capital of Manila. They expressed their outrage through petitions, resolutions and even on the walls of houses and rocks around Didipio, which bore messages of dissent. They also engaged in dialogues with barangay and national government leaders. However, the people were not satisfied with the manner in which the consultation meetings were conducted.

In one of these supposed consultations called by CAMC, community folk said company representatives only listened to pro-company elements and dismissed the protests of those against the mining project.

The testimony of a community leader, Peter Duyapat, was disturbing:

> *The official documentor would deliberately switch off a tape recorder when I presented the community's position. He would record only the company representative's statements.*[45]

In the earlier cited "National Conference on Mining", similar testimonies were given:

> *The people found out that even before a dialogue, the Mines and Geosciences Bureau and the company had already agreed on what they would like the dialogue's outcome to be. The company and the MGB also went to the extent of deceiving people, saying they would not use any chemical in separating gold from the ore.*[46]

Often CAMC dismissed local dissent as plain sentimentalism and anti-development views. For the indigenous peoples of Didipio, CAMC's only goal is apparently to pursue its profit-making project at all cost. This is what they say.

Dinaon Cut-ing may be an old woman but she has vowed to join the other members of her community to protest CAMC's insistence to go on with the project:

> *Even if I am an old woman, I will fight them…*[47] *With land, even if it is small, if you are industrious, you will be able to eat. There is kamote (sweet potato), gabi (yam) and rice. If you plant vegetables, you will have food. That is plenty to live on. Even if you have a lot of money, but you don't have rice, would you be able to chew your money?*[48]

The youth of Didipio believe that their voices too should be heard on the issue. Julian Inlab, who lives in *sitio* (a unit of the barangay) Surong said: *"There is nothing it will bring us in terms of long-term livelihood."*[49]

Sixty-seven year old Andres Lumatic, who lives in the same sitio, protested the destruction the tailings dam would bring to his land:

> *I have not seen (any) mines, but I know that the threat is what they refer to as the proposed tailings dam. This land is our life. If they do build the tailings dam, where will we get what we will live on? That's why mines are destructive.*[50]

Lumatic also expressed his sentiments about CAMC, having once worked with the company:

> I observed that there was favoritism towards certain workers. They did not give equal treatment. (This would indicate) that when they begin operations, they will not give equal treatment to our community.[51]

Didipio's farmers have raised the issue of the mine's effect on the community's water resources. Alfredo Cul-hi lamented:

> I know why we do not want it. This is because I know that this area gives us life like a wellspring where we get our water. So if they go and bore holes in it or do open pit (mining), what will happen to our place? We know that our water will be the first to dry up, no matter how much planning is done; whatever small terraces we have built will dry up. Then from where will we get our sustenance?[52]

Benny Ansibey, another youth from Surong, agreed and expressed his fears on the ecological impact of mining:

> I believe that mining will only pollute the water, destroy our land and become a source of misunderstanding within the community. I believe sustainable development can only be obtained if we are industrious, if we work hard. ...like in Barangay Malabing (which) has proven this by planting citrus and other crops. (T)hey became prosperous. Mining can only teach us to be lazy because people become dependent on what the mining company can provide.[53]

Carrots for the taking

The CAMC did not fail to emphasize the benefits that the mining operation would bring to the community. It dangled a package of benefits to the people in exchange for their consent. It promised better roads, communication facilities, electricity and jobs. It promised more and better schools, as well as hospitals. It also promised income generating projects, compensation and relocation. For the local government, it offered more income through taxes.

The mining company needed to win the support and endorsement of the Didipio Barangay Council, a strategic sector, being the duly elected leaders of the community. The Barangay Council then was initially staunchly opposed to any mining activity in their area. But most of them changed their tune after the Company's aggressive cooptation campaign. The Manila-based Legal Rights and Natural Resource Center observed that *"(b)arangay officials were offered jobs in the CAMC bunkhouse until all of them, save for one kagawad (councilor), had acquiesced to the operation of CAMC."*[54] Those opposed to the CAMC project added that these officials received regular, and arguably illegal, payments from the company, in exchange for their active support.

The offers were indeed tempting. Peter Duyapat, the only Councilor who did not fall into this trap, testified: *"I have been offered by the company a 20-hectare farm in Bayombong, also in Nueva Vizcaya, a sum of money that I could not spend in my lifetime, a house and lot and a Pajero land cruiser."*[55]

This practice of providing 'aid' to gain acceptance or concessions is as relevant at the community as it is at the national level. In Didipio, a health center was built for the community in the early '90s. Supposedly paid for by the Australian government, it is now being heralded as a project of the mining company. The St. Patrick Catholic Parish in Kasibu, which assisted in maintaining the health center, attempted to move for its fiscal independence but this has not been received positively.[56]

Mary Bajita, a midwife in charge of running the clinic, confirmed that, indeed, CAMC made it appear it owned the project by paying the salaries of two staff members. This was a commitment the company made under a Pre-Development Memorandum of Agreement signed with the majority of the Barangay Council and leaders of local pro-CAMC organizations in 1999. The Agreement signified concurrence to the mine project and contained a package of benefits and assistance the company would provide the community. Bajita claimed that CAMC reneged on one of these commitments when it stopped giving the staff's salaries.[57] Also part of the promised assistance under the Pre-Development MOA was the remuneration of three contractual teachers. This similarly ceased when the mine project was suspended.[58]

The CAMC did not leave any stone unturned. It made sure it had its own coterie of supporters from all sectors in the community, in addition to the support of the local government unit. Benny Ansibey, DESAMA's vice chairperson, observed:

> The company organized and assisted in the activities of sectoral organizations of women, youth, the religious sector, a farmers' cooperative and others. From these organizations, the Barangay Development Council (BDC) was organized to pursue commitments made in the MOA. But the BDC functioned more as a spokesman and an apologist for the company, effectively parrying public outcry against CAMC and its mining project.[59]

And now the Stick

As early as 1994, a unit of the Philippine Army was deployed in Didipio to secure the operation of CAMC. In 1997, an irate farmer whose land CAMC employees trespassed on, shot at a helicopter flying over Didipio, killing the company's Canadian consultant. Following this incident more government soldiers were deployed to the barangay.[60]

Recently able-bodied youth from Didipio, mostly from the pro-mining ranks, were recruited into the Citizens Armed Force Geographical Unit. It was only in Didipio that the CAFGU was organized in the entire town of Kasibu. The CAFGU unit, with about 20 members, joined up with three regular forces of the Army and armed with high-powered rifles like M16 and M14.[61]

The CAFGU is notorious for human rights violations throughout the country. Didipio residents reported that "the CAFGU would quarrel with one another after getting drunk. They would enter houses without a search warrant, and scatter things in the house. They would steal food and livestock. This went on until the people complained."[62]

The people of Didipio also complained about harassment and other abuses committed by elements of the CAFGU and the Army. The story of Tony Pinkihan was one such incident.

> In November 2001 at around 6 pm, a certain Primo Duhalngon, a member of the Citizens Armed Force Geographical Unit approached me. He was armed with a caliber .45 pistol. Duhalngon was a staunch supporter of the pro-mining organization and received an allowance from CAMC. Mr. Duhalngon poked the gun at me and said 'you anti mining, what do you think of yourself, a tough guy? Do you want me to shoot you?' I reported the incident to Barangay Councilor Simeon Ananayo, who is also an active member of the pro-mining organization. Until now such complaints have not been acted upon.[63]

Lorenzo Pulido, another resident of Didipio, testified:

> I was approached by Oscar Nicano, Community Relations Officer of CAMC, compelling me to issue a certification against those who signed a petition against the mining operation in Didipio. He instructed me to state in my certification that those who made the petition were not residents of Didipio. I did not issue a certification because they are residents of the barangay.
>
> Because of my refusal to issue a certification, Nicano got angry,

threatened to slap me and inflict bodily harm. I was also verbally abused. Nicano instructed the pro-mining supporters not to load my harvest including the harvests of other anti-mining supporters on the truck that usually delivers our products to the market. As a result, our harvests were left to rot which resulted in financial hardships for me and my family as well as the others.[64]

Lopez Dumulag cried for justice:

I am an owner of a small piece of land in Dinauyan. In 1995 a staff of CAMC entered my property without my consent. They conducted clearing activities, which included cutting trees, digging holes, removing crops. They conducted the activities without my consent and against my will. I was not compensated.

When I demanded compensation, the CAMC Community Relations Officer informed me that I would be compensated with 5 trucks of gravel. In exchange, I would agree to allow the use of my land for the construction of the road. They only delivered one truckload of gravel. Until now the promise of the CAMC has not been fulfilled.[65]

One sorry impact of CAMC's intrusion into Didipio is the breakdown in relations among relatives, friends and kinfolk. The once united community is now divided into pro-mining and anti-mining camps, and even the children have been dragged into the conflict.

Here is the testimony of Eduardo Ananayo, father of Adelina, 13 years old:

My daughter was in good terms with her classmates and childhood friends. After the arrival of the mining corporation, the relationship was severed. Every time my daughter passed in front of the houses of the pro-mining group, the children (would) curse her… (t)hey would point a finger at her, followed by a statement: 'so you are the daughter of Eduardo, the anti- mining (fellow)?'[66]

And this polarization in the community may persist. CAMC has continued to secure legitimacy for its mining operations even in the face of local protest. It used the Pre-Development MOA to secure another important document, an Environmental Compliance Certificate, from the Department of Environment and Natural Resources to push forward its mining project.

The anti-CAMC sector of the Didipio population demanded their barangay officials to revoke the MOA, but the latter refused. They thus decided to organize the Didipio Earth Savers Multi-purpose Association to initiate a campaign against the mining project. DESAMA subsequently submitted a petition to the Commission on Election (COMELEC) on July 16, 1999 invoking their power of initiative.

The local initiative is a mechanism embodied in both the 1987 Constitution and the Local Government Code to allow the recall of certain officials and laws deemed detrimental to the interest of the people. To date however the COMELEC has not set a date for a referendum to satisfy the local initiative for recall. But this has not dampened the people's spirit. In fact other groups have joined in to support the protest.

Outpouring of Support

The Roman Catholic Social Action Commission has stood by the people of Didipio on this issue, mobilizing support in many forms, including organizing and assisting in mass campaigns. The local bishop was also very supportive as were civil society organizations. The Legal Rights and Natural Resource Center responded with training, researches and legal actions, among others.

In June 2001 DESAMA joined the Cordillera Peoples Alliance (CPA), a federation of indigenous peoples' organizations in the Cordillera. The CPA took up DESAMA's struggle against the intrusion of CAMC in Didipio. A 30-man delegation of DESAMA had earlier joined other Cordillera peoples and their supporters in the celebration of Cordillera Day held in the mining town of Mankayan, Benguet. The CPA-led event provided an opportunity for them to bring more awareness on their problems in Didipio.

DESAMA also attended national conferences such as the "National Conference on Mining" and the "Dapitan Initiative", another forum on mining issues organized by people's and non-government organizations. These occasions gave the Didipio people a wider network of support as well as a broader arena for their struggle.

Various local government units supported the local opposition to the CAMC project, expressed in numerous resolutions. The Cagayan Regional Development Council (RDC), comprised of line government and provincial officials among others, issued in 2000 a resolution rejecting CAMC's proposal to operate the Didipio Gold/Copper Mining Project. The resolution declares:

> ... *The body was convinced that the harmful effects of the project to environmental integrity of the project areas in the provinces of Quirino and Nueva Vizcaya and other rivers and watershed areas in*

Region 02 outweigh the projected economic and social benefits that may be derived from the implementation of the project.[67]

All 70 members of the RDC later reaffirmed their decision not to support the mine project. An article in the *Mining Monitor* (July 2001) reported, *"While Climax had planned to start mine construction in January 2001, its representative was reported to be disappointed when the proposed mine was rejected again."*[68]

Shortly after on October 11, 2001 CAMC operations were suspended. Then DENR Secretary Heherson Alvarez issued a Notice of Suspension of Exploration Activities to CAMC on the following grounds: "1) the Project has not secured Social Acceptability; and 2) the Project is located inside the Addalam River Watershed."[69]

Secretary Alvarez ordered CAMC to refrain from conducting exploration in the FTAA area until the issues were resolved and until the Provincial and Municipal Councils had favorably endorsed the project.[70] The Secretary's action, which directly contradicted that of the International Finance Corporation, which hailed the Didipio project as a best case of prior informed consent, was apparently a political accommodation. Alvarez is a leading political figure in the Cagayan Region.

Other barangay officials of Kasibu similarly criticized the proposed mine project, citing as one reason its non-acceptability by the community. The town's 30-member Association of Barangay Captains urged the Municipal Council not to endorse the Didipio Gold/Copper Mining Project of CAMC and to spare the entire municipality from any mining application.[71] Their resolution states:

..... *(W)e believe that Kasibu is best suited for agriculture as it is the fruit and vegetable bowl of the province ... Mining will destroy the agricultural lands which is the main source of livelihood in the area; ...... (T)he CAMC project is not socially acceptable to the community.*[72]

The Barangay Council of Didipio however continued to endorse the CAMC project and get it broader support. On March 1, 2002 it sought the favorable endorsement of the Municipal Council for the CAMC project. The resolution they issued was supported with the signatures of 311 residents and local organizations which openly favor the mine project. In response the Environmental Committee of the Kasibu Municipal Council conducted on June 13 a signature validation in Didipio. The result was to serve as a basis for the Municipal Government to decide whether to endorse the CAMC project or not.

The validation of signatures revealed the following: a) some retracted their signatures on the endorsement; b) some were neutral; c) some claimed they were not the ones who signed the endorsement; d) some were below 15 years old. [73] Based on these results, the Environmental Committee recommended non-endorsement for the proposed Didipio Gold/Copper Project, which the Municipal Council adopted. [74]

The subsequent resolution passed by the Council cites that "the project is not acceptable to the people of Didipio as shown in various petitions and resolutions from DESAMA and other groups." [75] This was a reiteration of its earlier resolution, supporting the call by the Regional Development Council to reject the CAMC proposal to operate the mine project.

The Municipal Council further recommended that a 'consensus election' be held, but the new Didipio Barangay Council, which had then just been elected, promptly rejected this. The latter passed a Barangay Resolution on September 12, 2002 stating:

> *The findings of the Municipal Validating Team on the endorsement of the Pre-Development MOA that was entered into by the previous Barangay Council with Climax Arimco Mining Co., are enough basis to determine the validity or non-validity of the endorsement;...If the referendum that was earlier proposed did not materialize, why should we submit the barangay this time for a Consensus Election?...The result of the July 15, 2002 Barangay Elections is one manifestation of the support of the community.* [76]

Indeed the result of the Barangay Elections earlier in July bolstered the contention of those critical of the mine project that the Didipio community is against the CAMC project. Save for two, all newly elected Barangay Council members ran on an anti-mining platform. The highest number of votes (333) was garnered by an anti-CAMC candidate. Reelected Barangay Council member Peter Duyapat also won by a wide margin — 233 votes against the little more than 100 votes of the most popular pro-CAMC candidate. The electoral exercise provided the people of Didipio the legal opportunity to boot out their old officials, who were serving more as agents of CAMC rather than serving the interests of the community.

Opportunities and Threats

Recent developments have clearly made it difficult for CAMC to proceed with the project, especially in light of the current Barangay Council's decision to oppose it. The Council however is now challenged to come up with community projects since those supported by CAMC ceased with the suspension of its operations. For a start the barangay officials have moved to bring electricity to the community. They have successfully negotiated with the Nueva Vizcaya Electric Cooperative (Nuvelco) to have transmission lines installed in Didipio. Jointly with their counterparts in other barangays, they have also improved a connecting road linking Didipio to an adjacent village.

They have further assisted the earlier cited three elementary school teachers on CAMC's payroll whose salaries were cut off in July 2002. Not wanting to plead with CAMC to resume the payments as this would compromise their anti-mining stance, the new barangay officials sought assistance elsewhere. They received this from other government offices and leaders who agreed to pay the teachers' salaries from July to December 2002.

But the CAMC is not yet out of Didipio. It continues to fire the enthusiasm of its hired supporters to drumbeat the virtues of mining and its purported new image. It is waiting and hoping for the national government, its biggest ally, to make good its promise of full support to the mining industry.

The government apparently will make good its promise. In December 2002, President Gloria Macapagal-Arroyo announced in a policy statement that the government will prioritize the development of the mining sector to boost revenues amid a worsening budget deficit. The President asked the DENR Secretary to fast track the consultations on a new National Minerals Policy (NMP). The NMP, which looks biased for the mining industry, removes all stumbling blocks to the full exploitation of the country's mineral resources.

CONCLUSION

Over the past decade, a powerful bloc of institutions led by the World Bank has been pushing obstinately for the development of the mining industry. The World Bank has, in various ways (directly and indirectly), influenced the crafting of national mining codes primarily within the framework of liberalization, privatization and deregulation. It believes that these policies create a good investment climate to attract foreign invsestors, thus catering mostly to the interests of Transnational Mining Corporations.

The World Bank created in the Philippines and other countries an impetus for mining legislation reform and liberalization. Its influence also led and even financed other agencies (such as UNDP, NTCD, ADB) to support such programmes. Yet in so doing the Bank neither consulted indigenous peoples nor researched the impacts on them or required any adequate safeguards.

The role of the World Bank in the formulation of the Philippine Mining Act of 1995 may not be as conspicuous as in other countries (e.g. Africa). However, its influence over Asian Development Bank, UNDTCD, and the MGB-DENR, institutions that had a direct hand in the formulation of the Mining Act, cannot be denied. In this study, we have tried to show the relationships and connections between and among these actors, towards the final enactment of the law.

The impact of the Mining Act was felt immediately by the sectors who were to be directly affected by mining activities — the indigenous peoples and farmers. Even in the initial stage of mining exploration, conflicts mainly over ownership and access to land already emerged throughout the country. This is because, in almost all instances, the areas being targeted for mining are the same areas being claimed by indigenous peoples as their ancestral domain. The latter are in fact supported in their claims by a more recent law, the Indigenous Peoples' Rights Act (IPRA) of 1997.

Besides conflict over the lands, the Mining Act also engendered social tension and conflict within the indigenous/farming communities. Mining companies used the provision of the Mining Act to seek the "Free and Prior Informed Consent" especially of indigenous communities. However, local testimonies from practically all communities where the FPIC was supposedly employed reveal rampant violation of the real intent, principle and methodology of the FPIC. We have documented various violations in this study.

The expansion of mining activities is also vehemently opposed by indigenous peoples/local communities on account of actual and potential threats to biodiversity and sustainable development of their territories. For indigenous peoples, no amount of well-packaged Environmental Impact Assessments — approved by the DENR — will cover up for the damage that TNC mining would bring into their ecosystems. History and experience validate these fears.

In light of strong civil society protests against TNC mining, proponents and apologists for mining are now talking of "sustainable mining." The government has started conducting regional and national consultations on its National Minerals Policy. This policy substantially discusses the environmental and social costs and implications of mining. However this is still within the framework of growth-driven, profit-motivated, export-oriented industrialization as encoded in the Philippine Mining Act of 1995. This is the main reason why indigenous peoples' and civil society organizations in the country are skeptical of the National Minerals Policy of the present administration.

RECOMMENDATIONS

In the course of the debate on the Mining Act and the mining industry, indigenous peoples' organizations have always reiterated their pro-active positions. They have said time and again that they are not against mining or development. In this final section we put forward their recommendations:

1.   *Scrap the Philippine Mining Act of 1995 and its Implementing Rules and Regulations and all anti-people mining laws.*

Effect a moratorium on the opening of new large mines and the expansion of existing ones until such time that a new mining law is legislated. A new mining law should be crafted within the framework of national industrialization and supportive of advancing agriculture in order to contribute to food security, jobs and job security, and just wages.
The new mining law should also:

   a.   Uphold the social, economic, civil and political rights of all democratic sectors of Philippine society vis-à-vis the threat that mining poses to the exercise of these rights.
   b.   Recognize and respect the rights of indigenous peoples to their ancestral domain, to their ancestral lands, and to self-determination.
   c.   Uphold and recognize declarations by Local Government Units for a mining moratorium or mining-free zones in their towns/provinces.
   d.   Recognize the right of the people to veto a mining project.
   e.   Ban open pit mining, submarine mine waste disposal methods and other destructive mining technologies.
   f.   Ban mining where the ecosystem is fragile.

2.   *Cancel all Financial or Technical Assistance Agreements, Mineral Production Sharing Agreements, Exploration Permits, and other instruments, licenses, or contracts issued to foreign mining companies and their domestic counterparts in large mining:*

   a.   Declare a moratorium on the processing of large mining

applications.
b. Companies with a bad record regarding indigenous peoples should not be promoted.

3. The historical baggage against mining companies could only be overcome if they establish confidence-building measures, such as:

a. Guarantee adequate separation pay and benefits for workers retrenched from mining operations that have been discontinued as a result of the cancellation of mining contracts.
b. Guarantee justice and indemnification for all victims of mining — including disabled workers; dispossessed peasants; displaced communities; persons who have suffered diseases caused by mining operations; and persons who have been harmed and have suffered death in their families from the violence that has surrounded the mining projects.
c. Rehabilitate the land and other resources ravaged by mining operations, including mined-out areas. Mining companies should be responsible for these.
d. Rehabilitated land and other resources should be returned to the people in order that they can make use of these productively.

Notes and References

[1] Antonio Tujan Jr. and Rosario Bella Guzman, *Globalizing Philippine Mining*, (Manila: IBON Foundation, Inc., 2002) 9.

[2] Minerals Policy Program, East-West Center, "The Philippine Mineral Sector to 2010: Policy and Recommendations," (Manila: Asian Development Bank, 1994) xxvii.

[3] Clark Allen, L. 1997, cited in Tujan and Guzman, 2002.

[4] Chamber of Mines in the Philippines, Mining Investment Opportunities in the Philippines,   1991:9.

[5] Ibid.

[6] Salvador Lopez, *Isles of Gold: A History of Philippine Mining* (London:

Oxford University Press, 1992) 264 and 265.

[7] M.V. Cabalda, M.A. Banaag, P.N.T Tidalgo and R.B. Garces, Sustainable Development in the Philippine Minerals Industry: A Baseline Study. This report was commissioned by the MMSD project of IIED, February 2002, 8. www.iied.org.

[8] Toti E. Reyes, "Mining Industry Facing Extinction," *The Critical Years Of The Philippine Mining Industry 1993-1995*, (Pasig City: Chamber of Mines of the Philippines, 1995) 4.

[9] MGB-DENR, A Situationer On The Philippine Minerals Industry. Unpublished document, 2002.

[10] Bangko Sentral ng Pilipinas, records from 1970 to 1st semester 1997, cited in Tujan and Guzman, 2002. 22-33.

[11] G.H. Brimo, "Chamber of Mines of the Philippines Position Paper," A Paper read at the January 11, 1994 Senate Public Hearing on the Mining Act, published by the Chamber of Mines, 1995.

[12] ADB Mineral Sector Study, T.A. No. 1894:PHI, 1994, xxviii.

[13] The statement continues: "Examples of conferences and roundtables which the World Bank has cosponsored include a 1994 Seminar on Coal Industry Restructuring; a 1994 Mining Legal Roundtable; a 1996 Clean Coal Initiative Roundtable; a 1996 Artisanal Mining Roundtable; a 1997 Conference on "Mining - The Next Twenty-Five Years,"; and a 1997 conference on "Mining and the Community." William Onorato, Peter Fox and John Strongman. "World Bank Group Assistance for Minerals Sector Development and Reform in Member Countries," www.worldbank.org.

[14] Felix Remy, "Mining Policy: A Perspective From The World Bank: Frequent Issues In The Mining Sector Of The World Bank," *Prospects for Mining To The Year 2000* (United Nations, 1992) 11.

[15] Ibid.

[16] John Strongman, "Mining Policy Study," *Prospects for Mining*, p. 14.

[17] William Onorato, Peter Fox and John Strongman, "World Bank Group Assistance for Minerals Sector Development and Reform In Member Countries," www.worldbank.org.

[18] John Strongman, "Strategies to attract new investment for African Mining," www. worldbank.org.

[19] Ibid.

[20] The Philippines: A Prospectus for the International Mining Industry. January 1992. This prospectus was prepared by the Mining Journal Ltd for the Philippines Mines and Geosciences Bureau and the United Nations Department of Technical Cooperation for Development (UNDTCD) under the minerals investment promotion project funded by the United Nations Development Programme (UNDP).

[21] See for instance the message of thanks from the President of the Chamber of Mines, in The Critical Years, 1995, p. 26.

[22] Sections 20-25, Republic Act No. 7942, "An Act instituting A New System Of Mineral Resources Exploration, Development, Utilization and Conservation," in LRC-KsK, *A Compilation of Laws on Natural Resources and Indigenous Peoples' Rights: A Field Handbook*, vol. 1, (Quezon City, LRC-KsK,

1997), pp. 128-129.

[23] Sections 26-32, R.A. 7942.

[24] Sections 33-4, R.A. 7942.

[25] Marvic Leonen and Francelyn Begonia, eds. *Mining: Legal Notes and Materials*, (Quezon City: LRC-KsK), pp. 52-53; Also see LRC-KsK, Supreme Court Mining Petition, (LRC-KsK, February 1997).

[26] Catalino Corpuz, "Selling Our Patrimony," *Cordillera Currents* (Baguio City: Cordillera Resource Center, December, 1996).

[27] Tujan and Guzman, *Globalizing Philippine Mining* , p. 84.

[28] Ibid.

[29] Chamber of Mines of the Philippines, in cooperation with UNDTCD and UNDP, Mining Investment Opportunities in the Philippines, 1991; Chamber of Mines of the Philippines, The Philippines: A Prospectus for the International Mining Industry, 1992.

[30] MGB-DENR, "A Situationer On The Minerals Industry," p. 11.

[31] Ibid.

[32] This section is based largely from the conference proceedings written by Maurice Malanes, *Proceedings of the National Conference On Mining*, (Baguio City: Tebtebba Foundation, 2002).

[33] Joey R.B. Lozano, "Tribes Bite The Mining Carrot," *Philippine Daily Inquirer*, May, 1997.

[34] Ibid.

[35] Maurice Malanes, *Proceedings of the National Conference On Mining*, Baguio City: Tebtebba Foundation, 2002.

[36] Rodolfo Stavenhagen, Debriefing Statement, UN-SR country mission to the Philippines, December 10, 2002.

[37] "Rights Group Hits Army For Unit of Terror in Ilocos Sur Town," Northern Dispatch, March 7, 2003.

[38] See, for instance: Raymundo D. Rovillos and Jennifer Curry, Globalization and Women in the Mines, a research report under Cordillera Studies Center, University of the Philippines College in Baguio, 1997.

[39] eirdocs/wbdidipio.html

[40] Ibid.

[41] Environmental Impact Study, November 28, 1997

[42] Documentation on the Climax – Arimco Mining Corporation (CAMC) Didipio Gold-Copper Project by DESAMA submitted to the UN Special Rapporteur on Indigenous Peoples Rights Dr. Rodolfo Stavenhagen during the Luzonwide Dialogue conducted in Sta. Catalina Convent, Baguio City on December 5, 2002.

[43] *Nueva Vizcaya Socio-Economic Profile*, 2000

[44] Estimated figures were provided by Didipio Barangay Captain Antonio Dingcog in an interview on January 30, 2003

[45] "Nueva Vzcaya: Peoples Initiative Against Mining," *Proceedings of the National Conference on Mining*, May 6-8 2002 in Baguio City, Tebtebba

[46] Ibid.

[47] Rina Corpuz, "Dissent in Didpio," *Tam-awan*, Sept.-Oct. 1999

[48] Ibid.

[49] Ibid.

[50] Ibid.

[51] Ibid.

[52] Ibid.

[53] Excerpts from the affidavit of Benny Ansibey submitted to the UN Special Rapporteur on Indigenous Peoples Rights, Rodolfo Stavenhagen, during the Luzonwide Dialogue held in Baguio City on December 5, 2002

[54] Rina Corpuz, "Dissent in Didipio" , Tam-awan, Sept.-Oct, 1999

[55] Testimony of Peter Duyapat, as cited in the Proceedings of the National Conference on Mining.

[56] Andre Gerard Ballesteros, "Mining Mates, Mining Might" Tam-awan, October 1998.

[57] Personal Interview with Mary Bajeta, January 29, 2003.

[58] Data provided by the newly elected Antonio Dingcog, Barangay Captain of Didipio.

[59] Personal Interview with Benny Ansibey in Didipio on January 29 2003.

[60] Ibid.

[61] Ibid.

[62] Testimony of Peter Duyapat to the Luzonwide Dialogue with the UN Special Rapporteur of Indigenous Peoples Rights, Rodolfo Stavenhagen held in Baguio City on December 5, 2002.

[63] Excerpts from the affidavit of Tony Pinkihan submitted to the UN Special Rapporteur on Indigenous Peoples Rights, Rodolfo Stavenhagen, during the Luzonwide Dialogue held in Baguio City on December 5, 2002.

[64] Excerpts from the affidavit of Lorenzo Pulido submitted to the UN Special Rapporteur on Indigenous Peoples Rights, Rodolfo Stavenhagen, during the Luzonwide Dialogue held in Baguio City on December 5, 2002.

[65] Excerpts from the affidavit of Lopez Dumulag submitted to the UN Special Rapporteur on Indigenous Peoples Rights, Rodolfo Stavenhagen, during the Luzonwide Dialogue held in Baguio City on December 5, 2002.

[66] Excerpts from the affidavit of Eduardo Ananayo submitted to the UN Special Rapporteur on Indigenous Peoples Rights, Rodolfo Stavenhagen, during the Luzonwide Dialogue held in Baguio City on December 5, 2002.

[67] Regional Development Council 02 Resolution 02-34-2000, Rejecting the Proposal of Climax Arimco Mining Corporation to Operate the Didipio Gold/Copper Mining Project.

[68] Peter Murphy, " Climax Flounders while Opposition Mounts," Mining Monitor, July 2001.

[69] DENR document, Notice of Suspension of Exploration of Activities, October 11, 2001.

[70] Ibid.

[71] Association of Barangay Captains of Kasibu Resolution not to Endorse the Didipio Gold/Copper Mining Project of CAMC and to spare the Entire Municipality from Any Mining Application, undated.

[72] Ibid.

[73] Committee Report by the Committee on Environment and Natural

Resources, Validation of the Submitted Resolution No. 12 Series 2002 by the Barangay Council of Didipio dated March 1, 2002 with Attachment of Signature Campaign by Individual Endorsement, DFIA Endorsement, DIMCO Endorsement, BARO Endorsement, SK Endorsement and DWMCP Endorsement Regarding the Proposed Didipio Gold-Copper Project of Climax Arimco Mining Corporation Located at Didipio, Kasibu, Nueva Vicaya, undated.

[74]Ibid.

[75]Kasibu Municipal Council Resolution 156, S-2002, Denying the Request of the Sangguniang Barangay of Didipio, Kasibu, Nueva Vizcaya for the Endorsement of the Proposed Didipio Gold-Copper Project of Climax Arimco Mining Corporation Located at Didipio, Kasibu, Nueva Vizcaya", dated November 11, 2002.

[76] Office of the Barangay Council, Resolution No. 3, Series of 2002, Resolution Rejecting the Proposed Consensus Election to be Conducted by the Sangguniang Bayan at Barangay Didipio, September 21, 2002.

Bibliography

A. Books/Published Reports

Cabalda, M.V., Banaag, M.A., Tidalgo, P.N.T., and Garces, R.B. *Sustainable Development in the Philippine Minerals Industry: Baseline Study*. IIED and WBCSD: 2002.

Leonen, Marvic, and Begonia, Francelyn, eds. *Mining: Legal Notes and Materials*. Quezon City: LRC-KsK, undated.

Lopez, Salvador P. *Isles of Gold: A History of Philippine Mining*. Oxford University Press, 1992.

LRC-KsK. *A Compilation of Laws on Natural Resources and Indigenous Peoples' Rights: A Field Handbook*. Quezon City: LRC-KsK, 1997.

Malanes, Maurice. *Proceedings of the National Conference on Mining*. Baguio City: Tebtebba Foundation, 2002.

Rovillos, Raymundo D. and Moralles, Daisy. *Indigenous Peoples/Ethnic Minorities and Poverty Reduction*. Manila: Asian Development Bank, 2002.

Tujan, Antonio Jr. and Guzman, Rosario Bella. *Globalizing Philippine Mining*. Manila: IBON Foundation, 2002.

UNDTCD. *Prospects For Mining To The Year 2000*. New York: United Nations, 1992.

B. Newsletters/Brochures/Pamphlets

Ballesteros, Andre Gerard G. "Mining Mates, Mining Mights," *Tam-awan*, 1:1 Quezon City: LRCKsK, 1998.

Chamber of   Mines of the Philippines. The Critical Years of the Philippine Mining Industry. Pasig City: 1995.

Chamber of Mines of the Philippines, with MGB-DENR and UNDTCD, Mining Investment Opportunities In The Philippines. 1991.

Chamber of Mines of the Philippines. *The Philippines: Investment Opportunities for International Mining Companies.* 1992.

Corpuz, Catalino. "Selling Our Patrimony," *Cordillera Currents.* Baguio City: Cordillera Resource Center, December 1996.

LRC-KsK. Supreme Court Mining Petition. Quezon City: LRC-KsK, 1997.

Murphy, Peter. "Climax Flounders While Opposition Mounts," *Mining Monitor*, July 2001.

Corpuz, Rina, "Dissent in Didipio," *Tam-awan*, Sept-October, 1999.

C. Unpublished Reports/Briefing Papers

Corpuz, Catalino Jr. "Comments and Recommendations on the National Minerals Policy Framework. *Briefing Paper No. 11.* Tebtebba Foundation, February 8, 2003.

Environmental Impact Statement, 1997.

German Development Institute (GDI). Development Perspectives of the Philippine Mining Sector. August, 1980.

Kasibu Municipal Profile, 2003-2007.

Mineral Policy Program, East, West Center. *Philippine Mineral Sector To 2010:Policy and Recommendations.* Final Report. Asian Development Bank Mineral Sector Study. T.A. No. 1894-PHI.

Mines and Geoscience Bureau-DENR. A Situationer On The Philippine Minerals Industry. 2002.

Nueva Vizcaya Socio-Economic Profile, 2000.

UNDP-United Nations Department of Technical Cooperation for Development. Strengthening The Government Capability In Gold Exploration Bureau of Mines and Geo-Sciences, Department of Environment and Natural Resources. *Technical Report No. 5: Geology and Mineralization in the Baguio Area, Northern Luzon.* Manila, 1987.

D. Internet

Onorato, William, T., Fox, Peter, Strongman, John E. "World Bank Assistance for Minerals Sector Development and Reform in Member Countries." www.worldbank.org.

Strongman, John. "Strategies to attract investment for African Mining," www.worldbank.org.

World Bank, "Strategy for African Mining: Executive Summary." *World Bank Technical Paper Number 181.* Africa Technical Studies Departmental Series Mining Unit, Industry and Energy Division. 1992. www.wordbank.org.

Climax Mining Ltd, "Community Participation and Social Acceptability." www.worldbank.org

E. Interviews/Affidavits

Ananayo, Eduardo. Luzonwide Consultation with the United Nations Special Rapporteur. December 5, 2002.

Ansibey, Benny. Didipio. January 29, 2003.

Bajeta, Mary. Barangay Health Office. January 29, 2003.

Dumulag, Lopez. Luzonwide Consultation with the United Nations Special Rapporteur. December 5, 2002.

Duyapat, Peter. Barangay Councilman, Didipio, Nueva Vizcaya. January 28, 2003.

Pinkihan, Tony. Luzonwide Consultation with the United Nations Special Rapporteur. December 5, 2002.

Pulido, Lorenzo. Luzonwide Consultation with the United Nations Special Rapporteur. December 5, 2002.

THE RUSSIAN FEDERATION: DESPOILED LANDS, DISLOCATED LIVELIHOODS

Rodion Sulyandziga & Vladimir Bocharnikov

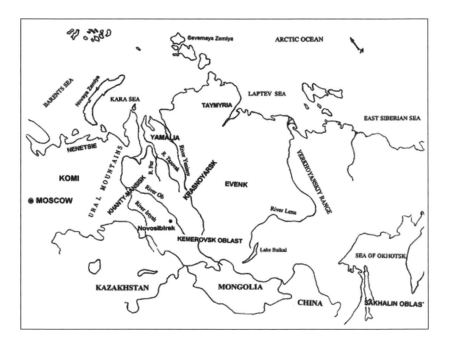

The third millennium could be the last for mankind. The reasons for this grim scenario are well known. The requirements of civilisation are rapidly growing, while the potential resources are decreasing just as quickly. Simultaneously, the health of human society is deteriorating while the health of the natural environment is faced with multifarious problems.

Financial resources are becoming the basic engine of fundamental changes in world politics, economics and society. The providers and distributors of these resources are largely oriented towards financial organisations, including the most influential, the World Bank Group (WBG).

At the beginning of the 21st century, up to 20% of their portfolios consisted of investments in industrial development in various parts of the world. A fifth of these resources are being directed towards oil and gas projects. These priorities will remain the same for a long time. In its special review[1] the WBG notes that, in the next 20 to 30 years the role of oil, gas and mineral extractive industries in the world will go on growing, with a corresponding growth in the number of client countries making demands upon the financial assets of the WBG.

In the future the Bank will be more actively involved in distributing funds and monitoring the results of these projects. Analysts at WBG warn that the need for a general solution to the problem of ecological and social impacts has come into sharp focus in the last 10 to 15 years. Thus, the WBG leadership is forced to pay much more attention not only to the creditors but also to the areas where projects are taking shape.

While the most complicated problems are arising in this particular context, it is noticeable that the consequences of industrial development vary widely across regions. General trends are fairly well understood. In densely populated territories and in all developed countries priority is given to the development of economic efficiency, reliable ways of resolving social problems and guarantees of ecological safety. It therefore follows that in remote, sparsely populated regions of the world where similar industrial developments are increasing, more attention must be paid to supporting the local population, preserving biodiversity, protecting the integrity of often unique natural complexes and searching for non-traditional ways of achieving a balance of social, economic and ecological interests. The WBG also sees advantages and problems linked to the development of oil, gas and mineral extractive industries in such places.

A principal aim of WBG is to build a mechanism to widen responsibility for the development of the extractive industries. A whole series of interested parties is listed under this head: governments, the local population, the private sector, civil society, international development organisations, bilateral agreements and partnership links, codes and principles.

The main priority of this review is an examination of the rights of indigenous peoples exposed to the most immediate impact of the development of the extractive industries.

POLICY ON THE INDIGENOUS PEOPLES

The World Bank is now preoccupied with the way in which sustainable growth is achieved in the world. It recognises that the principles involved must lie at the heart of the fight for economic growth and the maintenance of the health of the environment.

The development and implementation of a framework for the situation in the extractive industries is one of many ways of achieving sustainable growth. One of its major concerns is to know whether the WBG should invest money in the extractive industries.

This specific question, in turn, flows from one of the key positions of the sustainable development paradigm — *Can natural wealth be used to support sustainable development and to a decisive fight against poverty in countries rich in natural resources?* Where large-scale extractive industries projects are in progress or might be implemented, it is envisaged that there will be intensified consultations with the local population as part of a wide spectrum of measures. It is important to note the precise direction of exploratory development and the particular nature of the questions that must be elicited in the process of consultation with the local population [*See below*].

The direction of this study is not accidental. It stems from the fact that WBG states that work with the indigenous peoples of the world is one of its priorities, although the review process which was started in 1998 has not yet been completed.

Despite numerous meetings and consultations, there remain a whole series of unresolved questions. For example, representatives of indigenous peoples assembled at the 19th session (March 2001) noted a range

---

Were programmes for the development of local housing construction successful in raising the standard of living significantly and improving social conditions?

Was the local population consulted before, during and after the completion of projects (did the local population have access to precise and accurate information)?

Was the local population compensated for the losses suffered (was the compensation just)?

Are there sufficiently high standards for protecting the health of workers and the population, safety norms and emergency measures for coping with ecological catastrophes and accidents?

---

of difficult questions, in particular:

 ◻ A positive language for the negotiation of existing political and economic problems has not been found, established or promoted;

- ☐ The ongoing process of preparing a document does not allow for the inclusion of key recommendations put forward by indigenous peoples in the course of preceding consultations;
- ☐ The discourtesy of certain principle clauses substituting unnecessary consultations for meaningful participation by indigenous people was noted;
- ☐ The impossibility of obtaining guarantees on the protection of the resources and territory of indigenous peoples;
- ☐ The inability to acknowledge rights (the right to free prior and informed consent);
- ☐ The impossibility of eliminating the involuntary resettlement of indigenous people as a result of the continuing process of industrialisation;
- ☐ The incompatibility of existing and newly adopted international standards on human rights and sustainable growth;
- ☐ The lack of progress towards international standards on ways of involving indigenous peoples in the process of sustainable development.

Considering a similar situation, the choice of a list of basic questions from the ADP[2] handbook on visits to places where WBG projects have been implemented seems logical [*See next page*].

This version of the policy is clearly too brief and incomplete to yield adequate information for the analysis of existing problems. This is one of the basic conditions for achieving an effective information policy and establishing a mechanism for cooperation between the local population and participants in large scale projects in extractive areas.

The spectrum of questions under examination must be widened. It requires the receipt of such data on a regular basis. It needs an expert coordinating body and a mediator in this very difficult process. Four strategic elements in the new policy of the WBG on protecting the environment[3] are presented, thus:

- a. Inclusion of nature conservation considerations when evaluating all projects.
- b. Support for ecologically oriented projects in all sectors.
- c. Inclusion of nature conservation aspects as basic elements in the regional and country strategy and operations in the course of technical collaboration.

> ▫ Does the participation of WBG in a given project exhibit a generally positive influence?
> ▫ How are predicted ecological and sociological problems solved? Should consideration be given to the question of whether experience was acquired in the implementation of a given project?
> ▫ Were all the preliminary conditions of WBG financing of a given project observed? Were the recommendations on the preparation of the technical-economic basis fulfilled?
> ▫ What impression of the given project was received from the local population: unofficial and official dialogues with groups of different interested parties, such as business circles, local inhabitants and society, companies, local and central state authorities, and the leaders of non governmental organisations?

    d. Creation of partnerships to resolve regional and global ecological problems.

World experience shows that genuine consultations with the community are one of the most widely acknowledged methods of raising the quality of projects. Cooperation with non-governmental, ecological and international organisations is hailed as a way of shortening the route to solving complicated social, economic and ecological problems. The working group of the non-commercial organisations (NKO) of the Europe and Central Asia region (ECA) acts as a de facto mediator in this work.

THE WORKING GROUP

The basic element in achieving effective information policy, communication and cooperation of the NKO group with World Bank is the principle that the working group must play the role of mediator in Europe and Central Asia region. Frameworks using instruments and channels of change between the working group and the WBG should be introduced to understand the role of this important undertaking.
    These include[4]:

> ▫ Raising the level of transparency and accountability in the WBG operation in the ECA region.

- ◻ Strengthening and deepening of community participation in the early stages of development and implementation of WBG projects and policies.
- ◻ Encouraging the use of the principles and procedures of multilateral negotiations on the environment when WBG loans are being set up and implemented.
- ◻ Establishing working relationships with in-country representatives of WBG.
- ◻ Increasing the volume and quality of information exchange with WBG across the whole spectrum of socially and ecologically sensitive projects.

CONSEQUENCES OF OIL EXTRACTION

Extractive industries play an important role in the economy of Russia. The international financial community, particularly the WBG (the International Bank for Reconstruction and Development – as well as the separate European Bank for Reconstruction and Development) has a big influence on the work of requesting and receiving large-scale international loans. The breadth and multi-faceted nature of this field attracts the keen attention of many interested parties. Amongst the very active traditionally are the ecological, non-governmental organisations. It is worth noting certain developments arising from their work that make possible a firm presentation both on WBG policy and on the consequences of projects in the oil, gas and mineral extractive industries.

In Russia during the Soviet period, the fundamental emphasis in the oil and gas sector was on a short-term increase in production volumes. This resulted in huge damage to the environment which was largely ignored. The process of oil and gas extraction in the post Soviet period was even less ecologically oriented. Mechanisms for a conservation policy became ineffective. This took place during a simultaneous and steady growth in the flow of foreign investment in the development of new fields. In critically examining the ability of Russia to independently solve its economic and political problems in this field, the adverse ecological consequences of implementing projects in Siberia and in the Far East of Russia must be examined in the context of the present and future involvement of WBG.

The aims declared after changes to WBG policy can be achieved by: generating accurate knowledge of existing ecological and social problems; exposing the weaknesses in the policy on procedures and instructions for achieving the Banks' environmental assessment policy; encouraging the application of international standards by Russian companies and establishing dialogue with local inhabitants, particularly indigenous peoples.

We now survey the work illustrating the impact of oil and gas projects on the environment in Russia, to which the international financial community, International Bank for Reconstruction and Development (WBG) and the European Bank for Reconstruction and Development have some relationship[5].

The Russian oil and gas industry has inherited a multitude of ecological problems from former times. These problems were either tackled half-heartedly or not at all. In this context it is usually very difficult to distinguish how much adverse influence can be attributed to a particular project or to an interval of time. Measured by the amount of damage inflicted upon the environment, that very same fuel oil and energy sector is in the lead in Russia. Seventy percent of all emissions in the entire country are due to it. This includes wastage from oil and gas, occurring from the use of obsolete infrastructures that contribute 25 million tons per year of discharge into the atmosphere. This discharge is due primarily to the use of such traditional methods as burning natural gas during the extraction of oil. More than 3.5 million cubic metres of natural gas is burned off on oilfields every year. There are diverse consequences of this process. They include changes in the macro-climate and biological systems, processes occurring unnaturally in much of the ecosystem, mass death of birds during seasonal migrations and change in the atmospheric make-up.

Another consequence is the inevitable presence in the Russian interior of industrial waste that leads to the degradation of natural resources. Very often, unprocessed wastes (a mix of water, oil and other polluting materials) flow directly into geological cavities and not into specially prepared and isolated depositories. Such a negligent, indeed criminal, attitude leads to the discharge of boring liquid, diluted to a certain concentration and containing hydrocarbons and harmful chemical substances that pollute local soils and underground waters. According to many evaluations the degree of pollution in the Arctic and the concentration of hydrocarbons in all river samples taken from the rivers of Western Siberia, significantly exceed the norm. This pollution is spread in the soil along the banks of all connected waterways. It is concentrated in plants and accumulates in the tissues of animals used as food by the local population. The consequences of this for the health, not only of individuals, but also of whole peoples, are very clear.

The adverse effect distributed over a huge territory shows that the Russian oil industry received a very doubtful "legacy" after the fall of the Soviet Union. A multitude of oil redevelopment undertakings are using up to 20-30% of national power. A vast network of pipelines is not being exploited. The number of unemployed in settlements built during the period of intensive opening up of oilfields in Siberia continues to grow. These are exacerbating the exhaustion of the oilfields and most of those in Western Siberia are more than half exploited. The proportion of water in the end product is constantly growing, reaching 90% or more almost everywhere.

The condition of the infrastructure is another big problem. The Soviet Union created a pipeline network unique in its extent and scope. Today the network consists of warped pipes, eaten away by corrosive rust, where there is a lot of leakage and spillage of oil. This is a real catastrophe, comparable in its effect with major accidents, as for example in Komi, where in only six months about 100,000 tons of crude oil was released into the environment. Pipelines damaged by corrosion annually give rise to the loss of 8-10% of all spilled oil (20-50 million tons depending on the volume of extraction).

This problem arises from the fact that most of the large oilfields on Russia's territory are situated in remote northern areas, where the restoration of ecosystems takes place extremely slowly. The felling of the forest, construction works and the installation of drilling equipment in northern regions leads to the displacement or complete destruction of the upper layer of peat protecting the natural isolation of the permafrost. This disrupts the thermal balance and results to irreversible changes in these ecosystems. Toxic components are retained in the soil for up to 30 years (five times longer than in a temperate zone).

Felling occurs on a significant scale. In the North Eastern quadrant of Siberia alone, the destruction of vegetation constitutes not less than 2500 square kilometres. This is only within the boundaries of gas and oil fields themselves and along the routes of the main pipelines. The standard area of impact is only surmised to be a strip 400 metres on either side of the pipes under construction. This is obviously an insufficient measurement for a correct evaluation of that impact. In publicity promotions and glossy literature much mention is made of the effect of the presence of thousands of drilling men and geologists in the field. Nothing is mentioned on the role of scientific investigation. But the effects of this influence are extremely varied: fires, felling of the forest for firewood and building, and massive poaching.

It is important to understand that the psychology of the "temporary man", characteristic of oil and gas workers, is in sharp contradiction to the traditional ideas of aboriginal peoples. Indigenous peoples had secured a truly harmonious coexistence with nature. On the other hand, incomers think that resources are inexhaustible and that nature is at the disposal of man only as a source of sustenance and material riches. This logic makes for a large scale, uncontrolled shooting and taking of game, uncontrolled harvesting of fish (often actually in spawning areas), and using barbaric ways to harvest a range of valuable non-wood and medicinal products.

The consequences of exploitation last much longer than the oil and gas industry itself. The roads, houses and stores already constructed facilitate penetration into remote areas and unemployed workers still living in collective, temporary villages spend their time in large scale poaching. Very often, this takes place in the territories of traditional habitation and economic activity of indigenous peoples. In Siberia and the Far East the network of railways, roads and ports constructed by the oil and gas companies is widely used by commercial loggers. This exacerbates the combined damage inflicted by the oil and gas industry.

There is no definite answer to the very complex question of how to restore ruined areas. Unwanted equipments, structures and materials are often discarded on site, where they rust, poisoning life over time. Although it is standard practice to use special settling tanks, which are covered and enclosed in a special way, in Russia the practice is rarely used. Small animals are dying in huge numbers in these places, allowing entry of alien species into the territory which are aggressive to local varieties of flora and fauna. This process begins from the moment of prospecting when technology and material is often brought in from distant regions and countries, where exotic species are also being harmed.

Industrial noise and light pollution is another significant pressure. Apart from the direct and massive loss of nocturnal animals -- birds, moths and other types of nocturnal insects, the pressure has a prolonged and little understood direct effect upon the state of many animals. An extremely negative effect in the waters of North Sakhalin is that marine mammals are being frightened away from breeding grounds and seasonal feeding places. Numerous publications have reported that the local population of grey Pacific whales are being threatened with extinction.

It may be concluded from this review that the ecological situation in all regions of Russia where gas and oil fields are being opened up needs serious attention. A scientific approach is traditional to western society. Yet it is also important to understand local knowledge. The most critical situations of this kind may come to light because of appeals from the indigenous peoples of Russia, who come together and study in the Association of Numerically Small, Indigenous Peoples of the North, Siberia and Far East of the Russian Federation (RAIPON) [hereafter referred to as "the indigenous peoples of the North"].

Below, we will examine the most common examples of problems encountered. This may provide the basis for answering many of the key research questions by the Extractive Industries Review (EIR) and the Working Group of NKO ECA.

THE EFFECTS OF INDUSTRIAL PROJECTS ON INDIGENOUS PEOPLES IN RUSSIA

Under clause 69 of the Constitution of the Russian Federation, the rights of indigenous peoples are guaranteed in accordance with the universally recognised norms. One of the fundamental questions in this area of rights is the right to land.

The indigenous peoples of the North live on the territories of many of the subjects of the Russian Federation. Their environment since time immemorial may extend over a number of contiguous administrative areas. This makes the resolution of problems of land use and natural resource use much more difficult to solve. Management problems are complicated by the difficulty of coordinating the interests of various departments and administrative subjects. The needs of various sections of society and the legal position on similar questions differ considerably in different parts of the Federation. As a result, practical questions such as creation of communities, territories reserved for the traditional use of natural resources (TTP), allocation of lands, conclusion of agreements on the use of resources and so on, have to be forged with each of the regions.

Following are examples illustrating conflicts between indigenous inhabitants, mining companies and authorities.

Members of family cottage industry groups (communities) "Kosvino" in Osharovo in the Evenk Autonomous Okrug appealed to C.H. Khariyuchi, President of the Russian Federation AKMNSS and DV [The Association of Indigenous Peoples of the North]. They requested help in protecting an ancient area of habitation from the arbitrariness of the geological company OOO [Limited Liability Company] "Evenkiya-Geophysica" and the authorities of the Evenk Autonomous Okrug. The latter's operations led to a tangible loss in the value of natural resources of the Evenk peoples. The statement noted the following consequences of prospecting work:

◻ Defilement of an ancestral Evenk sacred place (a forest grove where, according to legend, the spirits of their ancestors

live) which was felled to make way for a future drilling rig
platform.

❑ Defilement and total destruction of a burial place of Evenk
ancestors dating from the turn of the 19th/20th centuries.

❑ Complete destruction of the spawning ground of valuable
species of fish (grayling, trout and dace) in the upper
reaches of the River Kosvino.

❑ Destruction and looting of work implements (traps and
snares) and also of hunters' trails (paths) and nomadic
routes.

❑ Hunting structures and winter huts belonging to members
of the community turned into storage accommodation and
used by workers of this company, leading to the shooting
and taking of animals without a government licence or
permission.

❑ All valuable game and rare species have completely disappeared and landscapes formerly almost untouched have
been turned into lifeless areas of countryside, disfigured
by people and machinery.

These examples are not isolated cases. According to information
from A.I. Pankagir, Deputy to the Legislative Assembly (Suglan) of the
EAO [Evenk Autonomous Okrug], the number of indigenous peoples in
the region decreased by 42% between 1995 and 2002. The consequences
are wholly predictable. Indigenous peoples' traditional occupations such
as hunting, reindeer breeding and fishing are rapidly falling.

The Evenk people work primarily in clan communities (48 in the
region) and reindeer breeding (27 of them). This economic activity is
considered by some as unprofitable. Thus, while there were more than
50,000 reindeer in the Soviet period, today the entire herd number no
more than 2,000. These conditions are aggravated by the connivance of
federal and local authorities. The indigenous peoples cannot effectively
resist the illegal activity of industrialists because of lack of coordination.

Incidents involving major mining companies (for example UKOS)
exacerbate the situation. The impossibility of conducting industrial extraction in the Arctic and northern taiga, contributes to the desertifica-
tion of the northern territories.

Another different, but equally typical kind of situation was noted
in the Nenets Autonomous Okrug. The Association of the Nenets People
"Yasavei" presented a written appeal to the President of the Russian
Federation, V.V. Putin. In this letter, attention was drawn to an uncontrolled situation taking shape in areas of the NAO [Nenets Autonomous

Okrug] linked to the intensive opening up and exploitation of natural resources. Experts indicate that authorities are not carrying out their functions in the course of operations by various oil companies. As a result, there are massive violations of ecological legislation. The consequences of this can be seen across wide territories where it has become impossible to carry out traditional activity.

Apart from earlier individual meetings, the local people attempted to negotiate with the oil companies. One of the positive results of this was the institution of round table discussions.

This measure resulted in a resolution in which the parties set out their intentions and planned the stages of future work to secure a rational and ecologically sustainable use of natural resources. It gave rise to the hope that there would be a favourable ecological situation, not only in areas untouched by the oil industry but also in those sectors where prospecting for hydrocarbons was taking place.

Fulfilment of company obligations is complicated by the fact that different companies adhere to different standards in their work. This delays the process of regulation in contentious situations. It is even worse in situations where conflicts arise between local inhabitants and company workers. Many of these conflicts could have been settled at the local level but are prolonged, drawing in many state and commercial structures. The situation in the Surguts region of the Khanty-Mansisk Autonomous Okrug is a typical example of this.

On 14 September 2000, the famous writer Yuri Ivasyeda went with some foreign guests to his ancestral homeland. His granddaughters, who were going to meet with their friends to take part in a school celebration, went with them. On the way to the Khapleyut region local inhabitants and guests were stopped by workers of the "Lukoil – Western Siberia" company, who were dismantling a bridge across the river, making it impossible to cross or to get to their ancestral homeland. Dispute with the company workers ensued. The local authorities blamed local inhabitants, even as the latter were the main losers, since it became impossible for them to maintain the costly transport infrastructure.

Many breaches were covered up when official documents were being put together as the basis of legal action by the indigenous peoples. Following legal advice, it was established that "economic agreements" concluded in the Surgutsk region (i.e., on the allocation of natural wealth for refining and industrial exploitation) should be recognised as invalid. Judicial and legislative problems of this kind arise when industrial prospecting takes place in lands where natural resources are used in a traditional way. Ancestral lands, hunting grounds, fishing areas and reindeer pasture lose their productiveness in these conditions. They suffer from grave ecological damages. Families of Khants, Mans, Nenets and Shurts have to leave the graves of their forebears and ancestral places that had sustained them since the earliest times.

An appeal of the Association of the Teluit people "Enye Bayat" to C.H. Khariyuchi, the president of AKMNSS and DV, revealed a very disturbing situation in the Kemerovsk Oblast. The Teluits are one of the most ancient peoples in the Russian Federation. Already by the 5th century AD they had their own education system. By the 8th century, their territory was about 330,000 square kilometres. Now it has been contracted to 90 square kilometres. The remaining fifth of this land is under great pressure from mineral extraction, metallurgical and other industrial undertakings. Scientific investigation undertaken in the Kemerovsk Oblast in the last 3-4 years has shown that:

- Pollution of the environment has repeatedly exceeded the maximum permitted norms and the degradation of the biology, soil and plant life associated with open cast coal mining has become irreversible.
- In the Teluit population, especially amongst children and young people, there has been a sharp increase in genes in the body that give rise to adverse mutations and threaten with physiological degradation and physical degeneration of their ethnicity.
- Activity of the Teluit national production association is severely limited by the arbitrariness of the authorities and large mining undertakings.

In the case of Kemerovsk Oblast, one of the large projects of WBG in Russia, the Coal Sector Restructuring Implementation Assistance Project No P045622, operational until 31 December 2003, relates almost entirely to the coal mining enterprise in Kuzbass. Other WBG projects, such as Oil Rehabilitation No P008809, Emergency Oil Spill Recovery & Mitigation Project No P040409, Second Oil Rehabilitation Project No P008805 and certain others were implemented on land occupied by the indigenous peoples of Russia. In the interest of justice, they should be directed towards the mitigation of adverse consequences in regions of intense industrial development. However, it will be very difficult to calculate the actual effect of their implementation.

Mining companies do not usually take the initiative to conduct community hearings in Russia, even in cases when they impinge directly on the interests of the local population. The demands of indigenous peoples are simply ignored. Managers pay no attention to recent complaints about the reduction in the number of animals, fish, wild birds and medicinal plants. Company leaders demand officially certified information of a kind that is usually impossible for the community in the regions to obtain.

Lacking this information, local population often resort to demonstrating soil and waterway pollution, ruined trees and so on, even to high ranking managers of companies. The arguments about light and noise pollution, the unsanctioned construction of roads, poaching, the violation of ancestral shrines and the misappropriation of property, are completely ignored.

Company representatives try to buy the rights to oil extraction or to build a pipeline on ancestral lands in exchange for building materials, fuel for the old equipment of the inhabitants or simply for a water tank. The often calamitous social and economic position of indigenous inhabitants, problems with their health, the possible consequences of the spread of alcoholism, reveal the amoral way that business is conducted.

There are cases when an illiterate old man or of a young person, is deceived into signing an official document that is passed off as insignificant bits of paper. In "signing" the documents, local people are made to agree to the development of oil extraction in their vicinity or even to their own eviction to another territory. No less confusing are the situations with local authorities and the link between nature conservation organisations and the large companies.

We will now try to emphasise positive forms of cooperative relationships between aboriginal peoples and mining companies. Four basic questions arise when dealing with such problems.

In the first case, where there is official use of legislation on the indigenous peoples of the North of Russia, it is essential to take into account the difference between those who lead a traditional way of life and those who do not. Different ways of arriving at a solution should be applied, based on the legal rights of indigenous peoples.

The concept or use of natural resources is another important aspect. In such cases the Land, Water and Forest Codes of the Russian Federation, the Federal Law "On the animal world" and other Federal laws on the use of natural resources should be the overriding authority. So far, the question of coordinating the laws on the use of natural resources with the Federal Law "On guaranteeing the rights of the indigenous peoples of the Russian Federation" has not yet been fully worked out. In practice questions relating to the allocation of land to aboriginal peoples are often very badly resolved.

The third point is that indigenous peoples have peculiar views on economic activities such as reindeer herding, fishing and others. These traditional economic activities must not be equated with agriculture and other sectors of the Russian economy that function in accordance with other rules. For example, reindeer breeding, compared with another type of agricultural production, may not have a discernable advantage or gain, except those perceived by the producer.

If reindeer breeding is recognized as part of the traditional agricultural activity, then all the standards directed towards implementing the rights of indigenous peoples must be applied in full. In practical terms, Federal laws guaranteeing the rights of communities of indigenous peoples in the North, Siberia and Far East are largely incomplete and need to be more precisely defined. They may require changes to give more valuable guarantees of the rights of indigenous peoples in Russia.

This broader explanation of the rights of the indigenous peoples of Russia leads to a better understanding of the problems with mining industry projects and their pressures on indigenous peoples.

There could be more points of contact if new forms of evaluation of the pressures in indigenous territories could be worked out. It is especially important for indigenous peoples themselves to get timely expert advice on all projects that may affect their life and territory.

GOVERNING PRINCIPLES

Evaluation of pressure on culture

In the process of conducting evaluations of cultural impacts, questions that have significance to cultural aspects should be emphasized. Examples of are: beliefs or religion, traditional practices, forms of social and communal organisation, systems of natural resource use, including plans for land use, places of cultural significance, shrines and ritual ceremonies.

Conditions that protect local languages are defined. This should be considered, together with generally accepted systems of administration and supporting unwritten laws, original political instruments, hierarchies and local customs. It is essential to secure respect for custodians and holders of traditional knowledge and to preserve and protect that same knowledge. The evaluation must encompass all aspects of likely pressure on all aspects of culture, including the preservation of sacred sites (sanctuaries).

Evaluations of pressure on the environment

To make an effective evaluation of pressure on the environment, it is essential to analyse the following concerns: areas valuable for the preservation of biodiversity, ecologically restraining factors, geographical aspects of natural resource use and the potential for sustainability of the process of pressure and the transformation of ecosystems.

The consequences of direct and indirect pressure on the condition of places of biodiversity must be evaluated. In the context of those ecosystems, the following should be accounted for: species and genetic resources used by local inhabitants as the means of their sustenance; the satisfaction of other vital material or spiritual needs or the acquisition of other products important for life and essential for a sustainable and lengthy life in the given territory. Conditions for the implementation of a project must be carefully examined with the view of the possible introduction of undesirable biological items harmful to the local biosphere.

Evaluations of pressure on the socio-economic situation

Effective evaluation of the socio-economic consequences of proposed projects require the completion of a workplan that evaluates demographic factors, the presence of habitation and housing conditions, employment, the availability of essential infrastructure and utilities, expected incomes and their distribution, traditional production systems, and also educational needs, technical skills and financial consequences.

Projects must be evaluated from the point of view of securing real benefits to the community such as the creation of jobs , steady incomes (including income from appropriate payments and compensation), facilitating access to markets and diversification of incomes for small business. When predicted consequences may lead to a change in the traditional practice of food production or to local inhabitants switching to the cultivation and procurement of a narrow range of species or species dissimilar to earlier commercial wild plants, all alternatives must be evaluated. Commercial cultivation and collection of the harvest should prevent the destruction of the natural resource potential.

To clarify the situation and predict socio-economic consequences, indicators of social development must be worked out. While supported by science, these indicators should take into account the ideas of indigenous peoples/local inhabitants. They must also allow for the examination of such questions as gender aspects, the breakdown of generational links, health, the safety of foodstuffs, security of the essentials of life, and other possible effects on the protection and preservation of the social unity of society.

There is already some experience in the Russian Federation of this kind of work. In the Yamalo-Nenets Autonomous Okrug, the Ministry of Food Reserves of the Russian Federation issued a licence to the ZAO [joint stock company] "Gazprom" subsidiary OOO "Gazflot" to undertake research and evaluation work in the region of the Ob and Tazovsk bays. These bays are noted for their exceptional biological productiveness. For centuries, they have supported the lives and welfare of indigenous peoples across the wide expanse of the Ob-Irtyshk and Pur-Tazovsk basins.

Before work started in these waterways, indigenous peoples and the local population generally were not informed about the project. The consequences of this project could be very serious. Two thirds of the world reserves of white fish live in this region. Even drilling reconnaissance threatens their spawning grounds with destruction, lowers the productiveness of the food base of commercial marine mammals and degrades the whole ecological situation. Local inhabitants understand this situation very well. In all community hearings in 2001 inhabitants of the settlements in the Nadyiminsk, Tazovsk and Yamalsk regions spoke out categorically against it. The Association "Yamal-potokam" took action "For the protection of the waters of the Ob and Tazovsk Bays", gathering and signing letters of protest. Unfortunately, this did not have the effect that it should have had. Hence, it was decided to bring in specialist ethnological expertise.

In Russia, ethnological expertise is sought to evaluate the potential influence of search/reconnaissance work or programmes of industrial development on the territories of traditional habitation and economic activity of indigenous peoples. This serves as a component of the sustained development of ethnic groups. With the help of AKMNSS and DV a group of experts was organised for the Yamala territory that prepared its conclusion in March 2002. The experts established that there was a risk that the implementation of the ZAO Gazprom programmes in the waters of the Ob and Tazov bays could inflict long-term damage on fish reserves in the basins of the rivers Ob and Taz.

These risks are unacceptable in the light of the current demographic and socio-economic position of the indigenous populations and the inadequate guarantees of the ecological safety of research/reconnaissance work given by Gazprom. This practical success allows one to hope that a special monitoring system could be created in Russia to control the influence of large-scale projects. Considering the need to strengthen the role of the indigenous peoples of Russia in evaluating consequences, it is proposed to bring about in the near future:

- ❑ Development of an information system that integrates scientific evidence of the biological and ecological trend with the traditional knowledge of the indigenous peoples of Russia for effective protection and sustainable use.
- ❑ Development and creation of a computer system to provide expertise on the consequences of pressure on the state of biodiversity in the most important territories (that is, in regions designated for the creation of OOPT [specially protected natural sites], in places where there are sanctuaries belonging to the indigenous peoples of Russia and in territories rich in biological resources that are most important for traditional use).

THE EUROPEAN BANK FOR RECONSTRUCTION AND DEVELOPMENT PROJECTS

If only briefly, we would like to note some results of EBRD activity in Russia. The International Bank for Reconstruction and Development (EBRD), developed and finalised their ecological policy over a number of years. Thus, from the very beginning, the EBRD had an ecological mandate that obliged the Bank to promote sustainable development in all of its operations.

Considering the fairly wide spectrum of completed projects, we may single out one of the largest, long-term oil and gas projects of Russia, "Sakhalin 2". We will not list here the arguments set out in many publications prepared on this theme in Russia, limiting ourselves to quoting the fundamental arguments that were laid out in the survey[6].

In Russia the EBRD, in financing the "Sakhalin 2" project, did not fulfill certain requirements that could seriously affect the ecological situation, namely:

1. The project envisages throwing the waste from drilling work (worked out drilling mixes, sludge, emulsified water) into the sea, which breaches Article 96 of the Water Code, Article 54 of the "Law on the protection of the environment", Article 37 of the Law "On inland marine waters, the territorial sea and the adjacent zone of the Russian Federation"; GOST [Federal Standard] 17.01.02-77.
2. According to Russian legislation, the financing and conduct of work on a large scale at "Sakhalin 2" can only be done after the actual completion of a state environmental

assessment. However, preparatory works on the installation of the drilling platform "Molikpak" began on the Sakhalin shelf long before the "Sakhalin 2" project received the result of the GEE. The seriousness of the position is evident from rumours that the choice of location for construction of the drilling platform was a failure, primarily because of Arctic conditions. There are also fundamental arguments about the inadequacy of financial guarantees because during the transport of oil and in the event of spillage, the financial liability of "Sakhenergy" ends as soon as a tanker casts off from the terminal. The consequences of the accident with a tanker on the coast of Spain are still fresh in the memory and they have not yet been remedied or even completely understood.

3. It has been noted that there is poor preparation to react quickly in the case of an oil spill accident (there is an absence of courts and of both sea and land based equipment, there are poor communications and inadequate or nonexistent roads along the north eastern shore of Sakhalin).

4. Opening up oilfields on the Sakhalin Shelf is inextricably linked to the construction of a surface pipeline to the south of the island and on the mainland, which is fraught with many consequences for the fishing industry, the ecological situation across a wide area and the interests of the indigenous peoples who live in this area.

Our evaluation of the possible effects of the construction of a pipeline in the south of Sakhalin could lead to the conclusions (set out below) on the condition of game and commercially valuable animals important for maintaining the traditional life systems of KMNS [Sakhalin indigenous peoples] in two northern regions - Okhinsk and Nogliksk.

In the Okhinsk region oil and gas exploration has been going on for more than half a century. The primary areas of economic interest suffered important changes in both qualitative and quantitative terms. However, the consequences of this became apparent in very different ways. A large part of the taiga in the territory is crisscrossed by geophysical exploration tracks. Oil production has long been conducted in many parts and the main sections of transformed landscape are now contiguous to the coast.

Many hunting grounds were changed a fairly long time ago. Within their present day boundaries an almost natural cycle of growth has already been established. In recent years, serious changes to the state of hunting grounds have taken place because of fires in the Nogliksk region. Therefore it is no accident that along the main road to the north of the area up to the Piltun Gulf there are often traces of the consequences of fire that become less noticeable further north.

One of the fundamental particularities of the Nogliksk region is that three quarters of the hunting economy is supported by aboriginal occupations – hunting, fishing, mining and partial processing of fish products. Field investigation of part of the most intensively transformed hunting grounds (between the rivers Chachma and Dzhimdan and up to the summit of the Daga Ridge) shows that the indigenous deciduous and evergreen forests of the feature have been completely transformed in large areas. As a result of this pressure the qualitative characteristics of the places where sable live have been completely changed. There has been a sharp drop in the population density of mouse like rodents.

The long-term extraction of mineral resources (oil and gas), which started a fairly long time ago in the Soviet era, has greatly influenced the quality of local sectors. Analysis of territorial characteristics showed that all these circumstances profoundly changed the structure of hunting grounds, sharply reducing their overall productivity. On the basis of just a preliminary count, the general productivity of sable hunting grounds has contracted in the order of 12-15 fold. Many economically valuable areas in the Nogliksk region have retained only a limited importance in the period of migration of the northern reindeer and the autumn breeding season of the brown bear, when berries ripen en masse on the slopes of the hills. Hunting grounds scorched by fire offer open shooting areas so that the reindeer in their wanderings are easy pickings for poachers.

Deterioration in the quality and corresponding productivity of hunting grounds provoked a widespread refusal of rent in areas assigned as actual national economic assets. The effective "no man's" status of these territories has affected the standard of protection so that poaching has come to prosper, which has a destructive effect on the dwindling numbers of northern reindeer in Sakhalin. In this situation the habitation and the traditional activity of indigenous peoples is very problematic. We will look at some arguments put forward by the investigator Emma Wilson from the Scott Institute for field studies at Cambridge University[7].

In the Nogliksk region of the Sakhalin Oblast the officially recognised proportion of representatives of indigenous peoples is only about 7.4% (1086) of the entire population. Of them, 205 live in villages, 17 shepherds wander with their reindeer all the year round and 15 catch fish. These are peoples' main source of income. Indigenous people who live a traditional way of life do not receive tangible support either from local inhabitants or from local authorities.

Recently, the extent to which the local administration depends heavily upon the oil industry has come to be understood. This was reinforced after the breakdown of government enterprises and changes in state municipal and social subsidies. Now the region exists largely on a subvention from the "Rossneft-Sakhalinmorneftegaz" [contraction of "Sakhalin Sea oil and gas"] company that is noted for the pollution of the lands taken by them. In this company there are frequent oil leaks during pumping, shaking during transport and disturbance in storage. Old, worn out equipment, inadequate infrastructure and outdated technology are the main reasons for this.

Mining companies do not provide suitable jobs for local inhabitants, either in basic production or in the accompanying services. Indigenous inhabitants adapt badly to new conditions. There is widespread alcoholism and unemployment.

Fishing is the main source of income for many, but this source does not support reasonable living conditions. The effect on salmon fisheries, which are a basic link in the ecosystem of mountain and coastal rivers, have a bearing on this. Fish are caught with signs of poisoning by phenols or by oil fumes. Spawning grounds and riverside vegetation are degraded.

There are neither sufficiently good programmes for monitoring the numerous salmon rivers nor methods of adequately calculating the number of losses from industrial activities.

This analysis of work on the completion of the "Sakhalin-2" project shows that Stage 1 of the project has turned out to be ineffective, that is, it is an UNPROFITABLE [author's capitals] project ("Sakhalin-2" project, Stage 2, OVOS materials, November 2001). The second stage of the "Sakhalin-2" project will only be profitable if there is a functioning plant with both technological lines of 9.6 million tons per year. A low social return is noted:

- The first stage of the "Sakhalin-2" project only provided a few hundred jobs, the second stage proposes 3000 jobs during the period of construction and about 300 new jobs in the period of exploitation.
- Notwithstanding the "huge investment" in the economy of the Oblast, wage indebtedness persists and the price of heating oil, electric power, community services, goods and food has risen swiftly. More than half the population of the Oblast is below the official poverty line. On an island

with huge reserves of oil, gas and coal thousands of people are wintering in unheated apartments.

The ecological problems are:

- Pollution of the waters of the north eastern Sakhalin shelf by drilling wastes and emulsified waters.
- The death of 5000 tons of herring in 1999 around the "Molikpak" platform,
- A sharp decline in the catch of navaga [small member of the cod family] and other species of fish over the last four years in the bays of North East Sakhalin.
- Deterioration in the physical health of the grey whale population.
- Severe danger of oil spills.
- Huge discharge of poisonous substances into the atmosphere in the event of the construction of a plant.

The acute nature of the existing problems is also underlined by a quotation from an appeal to V.V. Putin, President of the Russian Federation, by students at the DVO RN [Far East Academy of Science] Institute of Marine Geology and Geophysics:

> *The criminality of the Sakhalin-2 agreement lies in the creation of a precedent which will be the basis of subsequent agreements on the allocation of work (SRP). The State Duma of the Russian Federation has already taken a decision on the development of the largest gas condensing fields (approximately 1 trillion cubic metres) under the terms of SRP as part of the Sakhalin-3 project. If it comes about under the former conditions of Russia the available base of hydrocarbon raw materials on the Sakhalin shelf will be completely lost...*

In concluding our review we try to equate the situation of the indigenous peoples of Russia and their relationships with the extractive industry with what is happening in the world. In the Extractive Industries Review (EIR) there is discussion of how experience accumulated during the project "Mining, raw material and sustainable development" for Latin America shows that the pressures of industrial development create great difficulties.

The World Bank must accept as the basis for its operations the triangular relationship between civil society, government and industry. It should also take account of economic, social and ecological influences. The Bank must ensure that revenue received by the mining industry reaches those communities who suffer the effects of these projects.

The World Bank can avoid some adverse consequences by increasing the transparency of consultations, recognising the right of indigenous people to exert a veto on mining activity and promoting the social responsibility of producers.

It is doubtful whether the World Bank could ensure that projects are carried out properly or whether investors can manage poverty. At the same time, if the World Bank abandons this sector, then the fight against poverty, the improvement of social conditions and guarantees of the rights of indigenous peoples will get harder.

INDIGENOUS PEOPLES OF THE NORTH OF THE RUSSIAN FEDERATION, THE EXTRACTIVE INDUSTRIES AND THE WORLD BANK

The Nenets Autonomous Okrug is situated in the north of the European part of Russia. In administrative-territorial terms it is part of the Archangel Oblast, although it is an independent subject region of the Russian Federation. The overall total of the population is *around 30,000 people, including about 5,000 Nenets, one of the indigenous peoples of the Russian Federation.* [Author's italics]

Characteristics of these people are: a close attachment to places of historic settlement and the natural resources of their territory; ethnic self consciousness (designating themselves as a particular ethnic community); a native (Nenets) language; a traditional community structure and production (reindeer herding, hunting, fishing, collecting wild plants) that is fundamentally oriented towards a natural economy. Reindeer breeders who lead a traditional way of life are at the heart of the Nenets people. Pasturing reindeer is a tradition for a large proportion of Nenets reindeer breeders. They drive reindeer between the forest tundra and the tundra itself depending on the season.

This kind of reindeer breeding economy corresponds very well with the natural migration cycle of the northern reindeer and its natural instinct. An overwhelming proportion of the reindeer herdsmen wander all year round with the herds. Each reindeer-breeding group is allocated a plot of land, the so-called reindeer breeding passage where breeders can wander and pasture their animals. The present day location and boundaries of these passages were introduced in 1974 under a land tenure commission plan. Since then they have not changed, at least officially.

The Nenets Autonomous Okrug is the northern part of the Timano-Pechorsk oil and gas rich province. Intensive prospecting for, and extraction of, oil began there in the 70s. From the beginning of the 90s a new phase in the development of the oil fields began in the Okrug. That was the operation of giant national and foreign oil companies. The joint undertaking (CP) "Polar Light," registered with the Finance Ministry of the Russian Federation in 1992, was a pioneer in opening up oil fields in the Nenets Autonomous Okrug. Its constituents were the American company "Conoco" and the Russian "Arxangelskgeologiya" [contraction of "Archangel geology"]. The joint undertaking received a licence to develop the "Ardalinsk" field in 1993.

As part of the "Polar Light" project, which received World Bank credits, it was proposed that 22 boreholes should be made and that 13,000 oil workers should construct a pipeline 67 km long. The industrial extraction of oil from the Ardalinsk field began in 1994. In 2002 the "Polar Light" joint venture changed its organisational-legal status in accordance with Russian legislation, becoming OOO "Polar LightS".

As in the Nenets Autonomous Okrug, other foreign and Russian companies joined in the development of oil fields (Lukoil, Total, Exxon and others). A real struggle began between them, which drew in the administration of the Okrug. The particularities of mutual relationships between the local authority and oil company led inevitably to the aggravation of its relationships with other companies. "Polar Light" came into direct collision with this phenomenon.

Criticism aimed at the company began to be heard ever more frequently in the pages of the local press and in the executive branches of authority. The main claim came down to the fact that "Polar Light" enjoys a privileged financial regime. The company pays 5% royalties despite the norm, established by Russian law, of 6-16%.

For a period of six months the governor of the region did not sign a licence for the joint undertaking, on the basis that it is paying too little tax and has too low a level of royalties. Meanwhile, CP "Polar Light" is one of the main tax contributors to the regional budget. Difficulties in mutual relationships with the local authorities and certain other reasons led to a stable and profitable company beginning to experience problems. In the first quarter of 2002 "Polar Light" showed, for the first time, serious losses rather than a profit.

Problems in relationships with the administration and a significant part of the population of the Okrug are also characteristic of other companies. The elections in 2000 clearly showed the strains that had arisen in the community with the arrival of large oil producers in the Okrug. This was particularly so in the case of the relationship with "Lukoil", whose relationship with the regional administration became worse. The population was divided between those who support "Lukoil" and those on the side of the administration.

Those who support the administration fear the usurpation of power by oil oligarchs and are indignant about meagre payments to the regional budget. They hope that smaller, particularly more localised companies would take more account of the interests of the local population. Others think that more jobs will become available if "Lukoil" is present, that there will be more development of the infrastructure and that life will get better.

Authority in the Nenets Autonomous Region is likewise divided in two. One part is against "Lukoil" opening up a field. Their basic proposition is that smaller companies mean more taxes in the region, there will be no corporate price on the oil and so on. Opponents of this point of view prefer to talk about ecological risks, about how smaller companies, having taken out part of the oil, could disappear. In the interests of the region a complex should be opened up, at least as "Lukoil" has proposed. Federal structures always try to maintain a neutral position. The stand off has been going on for about three years. This has effectively frozen development of the region.

It is also feared that each company will build its own oil pipeline, covering the whole of the eastern part of the region with a network of oil pipes owned by different companies. How then will negotiations with them be conducted, how will the oil extraction process be controlled, how will ecological requirements and the interests of the indigenous peoples of the region be observed?

Such is the overall situation in the Nenets Autonomous Okrug as far as the exploitation of its oilfields is concerned.

The indigenous population has its claims on the oil companies. It is well known that extractive industries exert pressure on the traditional economy in two ways:

◻ They destroy the ecological basis of traditional production.
◻ They change the socio-economic situation, which inevitably modifies the social organisation and value of the traditional economy.

The ecological element of the pressure of oil extraction on reindeer breeding manifests itself primarily in the destruction of the reindeer pasture ecosystem, in its pollution by extractive products and in disturbance of the top level of the soil. Apart from that, the construction of oil pipelines and improved canals and roads constitute obstacles to the migration of reindeer. Many pastures have become inadequate for reindeer breeders. Reindeer cannot graze close to oil installations because they become frightened and run away.

Such claims are not groundless. Many companies do not observe ecological standards and they violate work standards in Arctic conditions. There are many claims against the Kalmyik oil company, ZAO "Lukoil-north", ZAO "Severgeoldobyicha" [contraction of "northern geological extraction"] and others. There is a particularly serious situation in the south east of the Nenets Okrug. Here there are periodic oil spills and disturbance of the topsoil during the summer. The slogan "Oil at any price!" is not acceptable in the Okrug, especially as there are already examples of a more careful approach to Arctic nature in the Nenets Okrug on the part of a number of oil companies such as Total Fina Elf and Sever TEK. OOO "Polar Light", working in the Okrug in cooperation with the "Environmental Assessment" Operational Directive of the World Bank (OD 4.01), is particularly significant in this regard. The Ardalinsk field company is ecologically safe.

Aside from ecological infringements, the shooting of reindeer by oilmen is the subject of a never-ending dispute between reindeer breeders and companies, as is the drunkenness of young people and many other adverse social consequences stemming from an increase in an incoming population with the psychology of temporary workers. At the same time, the indigenous population is well aware of the advantages that oil extraction brings. The most obvious for the reindeer breeders is that the development of the oil industry and a growing number of oil workers creates favourable conditions in which to sell reindeer products. It allows traditional economic activity to expand, it raises the profitability of traditionally valuable areas and it improves the social conditions of life.

The indigenous population is not the irreconcilable enemy of industrial development in the Okrug. The results of a sociological opinion poll conducted in the region are interesting in this context. These polls [sic] indicate that people perceive oil companies primarily as subjects of economic life. They expect that oil companies working in the region will make full and timely payments of tax to the regional budget (69.6% of those questioned), create new jobs (46.8%), have a caring attitude to nature (45.8%), deliver goods and foodstuffs at moderate prices (38.1%) and guarantee cheap heating for residents (34%). Other expectations (increasing the extraction of oil, respect for local traditions and customs, rendering charitable and sponsorship assistance and so on) are not so immediate.

Attempts by a series of companies to exert an influence on the political life of the Okrug were regarded as wholly unacceptable by those who took part in the poll. According to experts, the active participation of a number of companies in the electoral contest for the seat of a deputy in the State Duma and governorship of the Okrug seriously undermined trust in the oilmen. Such statements as: "If they're in the oil business, let them stick to it, they shouldn't sneak into power", "If they grab power, wages will be cut straight away", "They only care about themselves, so they'll sneak into power and the region can go to hell" and so on, are significant.

The image of the oil companies as demonstrated by the results of polls, depends as much on the degree of their influence on the political life of the Okrug as on their attitude to problems more worrying for the inhabitants. The undoubted leader in the loyalty rating amongst oil companies is "Polar Light." Almost half of all those interviewed expressed a preference for it and its partner, Arxangelskgeoldobyicha [contraction of "Archangel geological extraction"]. Their attractiveness index (the relationship between the number of loyal inhabitants and the number of those knowledgeable about a given company) is 0.57 and 0.51 respectively which significantly exceeds that of all other companies.

Amongst the most attractive features of "Polar Light" people most often list the following: high wages, better working conditions and respect for people, safe working practices, concern for the environment and conscientious payment of taxes.

Insofar as the World Bank is demonstrating its involvement in the oil industry of the Nenets Autonomous Okrug through "Polar Light", it suggests that the Bank's operational policy and procedures on indigenous peoples, ecological evaluation and cultural heritage, which "Polar Light" has had to follow during the course of its work in the region, on the whole demonstrate a positive influence on the oil companies. As experience of the work of "Polar Light" shows, such companies are considering the concerns of the indigenous population more carefully and drawing indigenous inhabitants into the process of social modernisation, without violating their traditions and customs.

However, this completely successful outward appearance does not always reflect the true state of affairs. Being the main contributor to the regional budget and of specialised funds for the support of indigenous peoples, where the regional administration is the basic manager, the company is promoting a lack of clarity and effectiveness in the delivery of resources intended for the needs of indigenous peoples. It is essential to draw the organisation of indigenous peoples (the "Yasavei" Association) into a closer cooperation and real partnership.

Endnotes

[1] General review. Operation of the World Bank Group in the extractive industry. 29 August 2001.

[2] Analysis of the position in the extractive industry. Regional conference on Eastern Europe and Central Asia. Budapest, Hungary, 18-22 June 2002.

[3] New publication of policy on protecting the environment. Document 7419R-O.

[4] Information policy and policy on cooperation of the NKO working group in the ECA region. Prepared by L. Proskuryackovoi and O. Malakhovoi.

[5] I.A. Baronova. *Oil extraction and environmental problems in Russia. The role of the World Bank and European Bank of Reconstruction and Development.* Kiev, 2001. p72.

[6] Targulyan O.U. *The dark pages of "black gold": ecological aspects of the operation of oil companies in Russia.* M.:OMNNO "Soviet Greenpeace", 2002. p80.

[7] Wilson E. Traditional natural resource use and oil extraction in North East Sakhalin // World indigenous peoples. *The Living Arctic.* No 4, 2000. pp 40-45.

CHAD-CAMEROON:
PUSHED BY THE PIPELINE

Jeanne Nouah, Joachim Gwodog, Félix Devalois Ndiomgbwa,
Armand Noahmvogo, Constant Félix Amougou Mbatsogo,
Belmond Tchoumba & Adrien Didier Amougoua

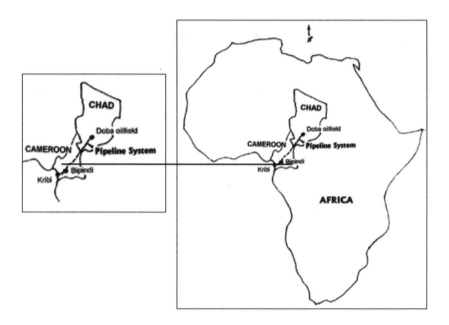

The main objective of the Chad-Cameroon Pipeline project is the construction of an oil pipeline for the transportation of crude oil from the oilfields of Doba in Chad, crossing through Cameroon, to the coastal slopes of Kribi. The pipeline measures 1070 kilometres, 890 kilometres of which is located on Cameroonian territory, and has a 30-metre wide route (cf. Michel Gallet; 2002). The total cost of the project is about 2 500 billion CFA francs. It benefits from a World Bank contribution of 10% through two loans guaranteed by its agencies.

One loan is from the International Development Association (IDA) of about 72 billion CFA francs to finance Chad and Cameroon's participation, and the other is a direct investment from the International Finance Corporation (IFC) of about 150 billion CFA francs, a loan to a consortium of oil companies. The consortium is composed of Exxon, an American company that is the major player (40%), Shell, a Dutch company (40%) and Elf, a French public company (20%). Two companies were created by these partners to manage the implementation phase of the project. They are the Cameroon Oil Transportation Company (COTCO) and the Chad Oil Transportation Company (TOTCO).

The construction work of the oil pipeline is drawing to a close and has led to the destruction of plant cover and the stripping of soils along the route. Apart from the disturbance of the ecosystem, the work involved in this extensive project has also led to socio-cultural imbalances in the agricultural systems and the way of life of the communities living alongside it. The World Bank recommends that any project likely to affect the environment should have as a constraint the preservation of a balance between the requirements of the environment and the economic needs of the parties concerned. In order to reach these objectives, the project should as much as possible, avoid causing negative impacts on the environment.

For situations where these negative impacts cannot be avoided, the project should put adequate mitigation measures in place. Similarly, the World Bank requires and ensures that the development process favours the complete respect of the dignity, fundamental rights and the socio-cultural specificity of indigenous peoples. It defines guidelines to ensure that indigenous peoples, ethnic minorities or other groups that, due to their economic and social status, do not have all the means to highlight their interests and assert their rights to the land and to other productive resources, benefit from development projects and that potentially negative effects on these peoples are mitigated or non-existent.

It is within the framework of the follow-up of the World Bank Operational Directives that a preliminary study was conducted to identify whether the rights of the Bagyéli - indigenous people from Southern Cameroon, who live along the final route of the oil pipeline - to land and other natural resources have been respected and their interests safeguarded during the construction of the Chad-Cameroon pipeline.

The specific objectives of this study are to:

◻ Identify and locate the Bagyéli villages in relation to the final route of the pipeline.
◻ Evaluate the level of involvement of the Bagyéli before and during the implementation phase.
◻ Identify the impacts after the implementation phase in the report "Man and his living environment".
◻ Determine the number of people and heads of families that

have had paid employment during the work of constructing the pipeline.
◻ Evaluate the Bagyéli's level of knowledge of FEDEC.
◻ Evaluate the compensation given to the Bagyéli by the
builders of the pipeline.
◻ Identify the level of application of the World Bank Operational Directives.

METHODOLOGY

The objective of the Chad-Cameroon Pipeline project is the transportation of crude oil from the oilfields of Doba in Southern Chad to the coastal
slopes of Cameroon, in order to export the crude oil to international
markets. The implementation of this project caused undoubted loss to
the people living nearby, in particular, the Bagyéli Community of Bipindi-
Kribi.

The study was conducted in the Bagyéli villages located at least 2
kilometres from the pipeline route in the Bipindi-Kribi region of Southern Cameroon (cf. Chad export project, Dames and Moore, Figure 9-4).
There are 26 villages located in the Bipindi and Kribi areas at least 2
kilometres from the pipeline route. Twenty (20) of these villages were
visited but only 15 interviews were conducted due to the movement of
the Bagyéli to hunting camps that were not well-known. Eight (08) interviews were carried out in the Bipindi area and seven (07) in the Kribi
area, therefore a total of 15 villages were covered by the interviews.

Data collection was carried out through semi-structured surveys
using a questionnaire targeting the village's population (focus group).
Data was collected in village meetings organised in 15 of the 20 Bagyéli
villages that were visited by a team of three (03) interviewers and two
(02) translators.

After a meeting to explain and understand the questionnaire, the
team was divided into two sub-teams. During the interviews at the
community meetings held in the Bagyéli villages, the two sub-teams
took photographs and made audio recordings intermittently. Field visits were carried out from two bases, namely Kribi and Bipindi.

Bibliographic research enabled us to complete the data that we
were unable to collect on the ground.

DATA PRESENTATION

Settling of Bagyéli Villages

Table 1 demonstrates the fact that the Bagyéli have very old villages. The Bagyéli, who were semi-nomadic in times past, living off hunting and gathering, have today become sedentary and practice subsistence agriculture linked to hunting, from which they get the animal protein neces-

Table 1: *Characteristics of the villages where interviews were conducted*

N°	Name of village	Number of inhabitants	Distance from pipeline route (in m)	Number of persons employed	Years Community settled
01	Log Ndiga	15	700	02	More than 30 years
02	Ndtamayo	08	700	01	More than 15 years
03	Nloundabele	13	150	01	4 years
04	Makoro Ndzong	68	400	02	More than 02 years
05	Maboulou	29	800	02	More than 30 years
06	Mandtoua	42	800	None	07 years
07	Bitoumbo	12	500	01	More than 50 years
08	Bandevouri	40	1900	04	More than 30 years
09	Sum Mimbo	08	200	None	More than 50 years
10	Angoua Mbvoule	18	400	None	More than 50 years
11	Bidou	36	1800	06	About 15 years
12	Bissiang	17	1200	None	2 months
13	Bilolo	16	300	None	More than 30 years
14	Kourmintoum	27	1500	01	More than 20 years
15	Nkoundou Nkoundou	67	1900	None	More than 50 years

sary to their diet. At the same time, this generates income from wildlife and other non timber forest products that they sell to the Bantu people and other foreigners.

Therefore, the term camp is incorrect for a site that has been occupied for more than 10 years as a point from which one carries out all one's movements. Their culture and way of life has created a deep attachment between the Bagyéli and their ancestral lands and the natural resources of these territories. This signifies that any displacement from the environment they occupy, no matter how much time is taken to implement it, represents a violation of their rights.

Distance of the villages from the pipeline route

All the Bagyéli villages where the interviews were conducted are located less than two kilometres from the pipeline route, according to the project's study report drafted by Dames and Moore. Sixty-six (66%) of the villages are situated less than 1 kilometre from the final pipeline route, out of a population of 229 inhabitants. These people are exposed to numerous risks linked to the pipeline passing close to their homes. Table 2 shows the villages in relation to the final route.

Active Involvement of the Bagyéli in the Project

Active involvement in the project relates to the entire process, from preparing the site, to carrying out impact assessments, right to the implementation of the project. Out of the fifteen (15) villages where interviews were conducted, we counted a population of four hundred and sixteen

Table 2: *Location of the villages in relation to the final pipeline route*

Distance from the pipeline route	Village		Number of inhabitants		Number of people employed
	Number	%	Number	%	
Distance less or equal to 1000 m	10	66.6	229	55.05	09
Distance more than 1000 m	05	33.4	187	44.95	11
Total	15	100	416	100	20

(416) inhabitants. From this total number, only 20 people were employed by the project, that is about 5% of the overall population was affected.

It was revealed several times that the Bagyéli had been informed of the safety conditions to be observed around the pipeline during the construction operations. They had been requested to stay far from the pipeline route during the construction operations. Nevertheless, the fact that they gave evasive responses such as "the pipeline is a pipe that will transport oil and we are going to work there in order to develop ourselves", shows that the information was not properly conveyed.

Out of 15 Bagyéli villages surveyed, six (06) did not have anyone who had been employed during the different stages of implementing the pipeline project. Does this mean that the Bagyéli were incapable of undertaking the so-called simple tasks that the Bantu had?

When one refers only to the distance from the pipeline route, out of 416 inhabitants, the Bagyéli should have been entitled to more positions, since this was only for jobs that did not require any qualifications. Paradoxically, they were the most marginalised.

It is likely that this will also be the case with the FEDEC, whose activities do not really take account of the demands or the expectations of the Bagyéli. Their concern here is not only to be involved in the FEDEC's programmes at the base, but also to control its operations, and their implementation. The FEDEC structure was established, as a result of the controversial nature of the construction of the pipeline, in order to take charge of implementing the compensation plan in favour of the Bagyéli. Yet only one Bagyéli sits on its management structure, and consequently does not have much of a voice.

The Spin-offs

The pipeline's exploitation period is 30 years, hence substantial benefits for the two parties, i.e. Cameroon and Chad. Table 3 next page shows the benefits anticipated by Cameroon and Chad during the project's exploitation period.

These benefits go into the State's coffers and have neither direct nor immediate effect on the Bagyéli, the indigenous people of Southern Cameroon in the Bipindi-Kribi region.

Consumer goods

In the majority of Bagyéli villages where we conducted interviews, the inhabitants had received consumer goods under the IPP, such as small agricultural implements (machetes, files, hoes); medication; foodstuffs

Table 3: *Benefits expected in 30 years*
(Source : Esso Chad, cited by CED 1998; figures in billions of cfa f).

Country	Benefits in 30 years	In 1 year
CHAD	- Direct income............ ....3 000 - Indirect income......... ....2 100 - Total................................5 100	170
CAMEROON	- Direct income ....300 - Indirect income ....240 - Total..................................540	18

Direct income: Taxes paid by the consortium to the government concerned
Indirect income: Taxes, salaries of nationals, etc.

(rice, fish, salt, …); and school supplies.

These supplies were indeed distributed, but the Bagyéli children of the Foyer Notre Dame de la Forêt, which houses the largest proportion of Bagyéli children in the region, received no school supplies or medicine.

A few bags of rice, a few kilos of fish, and a bit of salt distributed here and there in a sporadic manner do not really represent anything in the process of sustainable development which is a fundamental need of the Bagyéli community. On the contrary, the model of development simply renders them more dependent, rather than providing bases for sustainability. It is not occasional aid that is needed, but sustainable programmes.

In certain villages, support to the residents is evident (with the establishment of official rooms), but in others, notably Bilolo and Bissiang, there has been none. After having paid their individual contribution of 1,000 CFA francs, since 29 October 2002, the date when the identification fees were to be paid, the people are still waiting for the identification team's visit.

Sustainable goods

Only one head of family of the village of Nloundabélé received a house with four (4) rooms following the destruction of his manioc field.

In addition, it was established in the framework of regional compensations for the Bagyéli and Bakola pygmies that houses would be built.

Negative Impacts

When this point is raised with the Bagyéli, it results in total distress

Table 4: *Occurrence of the consumer goods cited*

Consumer goods cited	Number of times occurred	%
• small agricultural implements	15	100
• medication for the huts serving as health facilities (NB: the medication left in the health huts is made payable to the Bagyéli	15	100
• schooling (school supplies)	12	98
• foodstuffs	15	100
• support to residents	15	100

because the people are tired of always being questioned on the disadvantages arising from the construction of the pipeline, whilst nothing is done about compensation and the pipes are already laid. Table 5 shows some of the points that are often raised during the interviews conducted in the different Bagyéli villages.

The Bagyéli are accustomed to hunting. Today, following the work of the pipeline, they are forced to go further into the forest in search of game. This has resulted in the increase of hunting time and effort since the distances to be covered have become longer than before the pipeline was built. The case of destruction of property without compensation was also raised. This was the case of a woman from Sum Mimbo whose house had been destroyed because the first pipeline route passed inside her house whilst the other route was 300 metres from the other huts in the village. With regard to this negative aspect the Bagyéli feel that their attachment to their ancestral land could have been taken into account so that they could be compensated with new hunting land, since theirs is now in peril. Overall, they feel that their way of life is changing as a result of the building of the pipeline.

Compensation

In order to compensate for the disruption caused by the work of constructing the pipeline, and in accordance with the commitments made within the framework of the project's compensation plan, COTCO began a process of community and regional compensation (cf. CPSP letter no. 2 of January 2002). The compensation should consist of social projects, chosen by the people living near the pipeline, who would benefit from being provided with health and/or school infrastructures, village water systems, etc. The distribution of the money allocated for this would be done by the affected village. All these possibilities remain

Table 5: *Importance of the disadvantages cited by the Bagyéli*

Main disadvantages cited	Number of times occurred	%
• Destabilisation of their food/income, disturbance and destruction of hunting grounds (NTFP)	15	100
• Destabilisation of their health, destruction of the Strophantus « neeng », a plant with a great deal of power, and other forest products, both timber and non timber.	15	100
• Destabilisation of water resources	13	86.66
• Imbalance of man and his environment	15	100
• Degradation of inter-community relationships	08	53.66

more favourable to the Bantu people than to the Bagyéli.

However, in what concerns individual compensation, only one Bagyéli from Nloundabélé village benefited from a four-roomed hut (03 bedrooms and a living room) after the destruction of his field of food crops (compensation would be evaluated at 650 000 cfa francs, the cost of the house would be 500 000 cfa francs and the rest of the money would be handed over to the person concerned). The management of these funds would be the prerogative of COTCO. The house has already been built. Moreover, we heard that, after the survey team had left, MINTON Gaston received one hundred and sixty thousand three hundred cfa francs (160 300cfa f), four (04) padlocks, one paraffin lamp, five (05) litres of oil and one packet of matches.

On the other hand, the latter deplored the fact that he had not received compensation after the destruction of two of his brothers' graves. The graves were in the middle of the route of the pipeline, on the old site of the village. He believes that he has the right to compensation when a grave is destroyed, since this was the case for his Bantu neighbours. This state of affairs thus leads to tensions between the two communities.

To date, no real compensation has been paid to the Bagyéli based on all the losses they have suffered. All the same, a community compensation programme is planned - there have been promises to build a 03-bedroomed hut with a living room in each village to serve as a model, and the rest of the community should receive building materials to continue the work.

The process is such that by the end of the Bagyéli/Bakola training for house construction, the eligible individuals will be able to start receiving the support of COTCO for the construction of their own house. In step with the rhythm of construction of each beneficiary's house, COTCO will provide the following materials:

◻ Some nails and a hammer after the collection of the various stakes, lianas and bamboos.
◻ Sheet metal and nails for this after the installation of the house.
◻ Prefabricated doors and windows after the establishment of the roof and the filling of the walls with earthen mortar.
◻ It should also be noted that the elderly would be the priority beneficiaries of this programme.

ANALYSIS

The survey we conducted enabled us to identify and locate the Bagyéli villages along the final pipeline route, to evaluate the level of involvement of the Bagyéli communities before and during the implementation phase, to ascertain the impacts after the pipeline's implementation phase in the report "Man and his living environment" and to evaluate the compensation awarded to the Bagyéli.

1. Consultation of Bagyéli communities and Working Approach used in the pipeline's implementation process.

Information campaigns and consultations linked to the Chad-Cameroon pipeline project were organised. It seems obvious that the Bagyéli community was not sufficiently prepared to receive the project into their environment. When you are given an evasive response like the pipeline project is " the transporting of fuel in pipes and we will be working there to develop ourselves", this shows that very little time was set aside to adequately explain the project and all its risks to the Bagyéli people.

Throughout the awareness-building and information campaigns, flyers, brochures and posters were distributed. This communication was held without taking account of one another's peace of mind. What is more, the Bagyéli peoples are 98% illiterate. Oral tradition being the customary mode of communication in this community, it would have been wiser and more appropriate to use an approach that lent itself to this state of affairs.

2. Choice of Main Line of Work Devoted to Compensation.

The IPP (Indigenous Peoples Plan) was put in place through FEDEC where four (04) projects were retained in the short term. These are:

◻ The supply of national identity cards;
◻ Medical diagnosis of pulmonary ailments;
◻ Assistance in the area of education;
◻ Agricultural extension services and distribution of seed.

It is clear that the Bagyéli are responding to a concern for their practical basic needs, whilst in regard to their status as vulnerable and marginalised people, they can present their ideas in a way that demonstrates their strategic interests and their priorities for their lives. Therefore, any approach that would prove effective for them must take account of their strategic interest.

3. Analysis of the notion of property to be compensated.

Such an analysis was made without taking into account the specific characteristics of each community. In this analysis, it was only the system of assessing the value of property that was taken into account. This situation further favoured the neighbouring Bantu community. At the end of the 2nd quarter of 2002, the project had paid more than 5,6 billion CFA F (8,6 million dollars) in compensation in cash and kind to the users of individual land (cf. Chad-Cameroon Development project, Report n° 07 2nd quarter 2002.). On the contrary, the Bagyéli have a different perspective of the advantages of economic property which means that they do not favour the system of assessing the value of property. Rather, they attach their beliefs to natural and cultural elements such as the forest. It was not they who planted the latter and consequently, the registration system did not consider the effects and losses to be compensated.

Furthermore, the World Bank, through the Operational Directives, recommends that any programme of this nature should take account of the social structure, religious beliefs and ways of using resources that is particular to the local population.

4. Organisational Bodies and Structure of the Project.

By way of compensation for the community, an Indigenous Peoples Plan — IPP was drafted, and should be implemented through FEDEC. This plan comprises the following projects for the benefit of the Bagyéli communities in the project area:

- A list of agreements linked to the Bagyéli/Bakola's rights to land and the improvement of their living conditions;
- Provision of national identity cards;
- Organising free access to health care and information campaigns in this regard;
- Diagnosis for tuberculosis;
- Assistance in the area of education;
- Agricultural extension services and distribution of seed.

During different field visits by different teams involved in executing the project, the Bagyéli peoples were informed of the pipeline activities and of the different structures. Nevertheless, in general, they were unable to retain what they were told. In some places, the name of a structure could be cited, but without the person knowing the exact role of that structure and its area of intervention. The FEDEC's role is not well known, since the IPP that it is supposed to direct remains unknown to the Bagyéli. There was undoubtedly information given and awareness raised, yet the approach used did not take account of the specific case of the Bagyéli.

Violation of the Operational Directive (OP 4.20) of the World Bank

The Bagyéli community has an oral-based culture in which it is believed that all the elements of nature function in osmosis. The community relies entirely on the forest, and the latter was not planted by them but is inherited from their ancestors; the forest is their soul. When the system of compensation only takes into account the principle of monetary value, this lead to individual compensation in nature and in money to be given to their Bantu neighbours and the Bagyéli only receiving some paltry consumer goods, and the proportion of these remain to be seen! This is the evidence once again of the violation of one of the World Bank's directives (c.f. OD 4.20 paragraph 6).

The FEDEC's programmes have only shown token public participation, because when a FEDEC agent presents a farming implement to a Bagyéli, which is to be paid for, the latter believes it is a deception, whereas if the FEDEC took to the time to explain and involve the Bagyéli in the elaboration of its programmes and operational planning, these cases would be isolated. This is also evidence of the violation of one of the World Bank's directives (c.f. OD 4.20 paragraph 15 (d).

The Campo Ma'an National Park

The Bagyéli were left with a bum deal, it is said, in the region of Kribi-Lolodorf in terms of the compensation for the destruction of the biodiversity they rely upon. In order to compensate for the overall loss of biodiversity caused by the pipeline, the region of Campo Ma'an was chosen to establish a National Park. This region is also inhabited by Bagyéli peoples who once again will suffer the negative effects (collateral damages) of the pipeline, despite their living at a great distance of the pipelines route.

The Bagyéli community living in the Campo Ma'an National Park only hold "user rights" (for the exploitation of the plant and animal resources and other non timber forest products) rather than ownership or tenure rights. It appears however that to this day, even these user rights are being denied to the Bagyéli. This is due simply to the fact that a forest exploitation company established in the Campo Ma'an National Park has obliged the Bagyéli community to leave their hunting, fishing and gathering territories.

CONCLUSION

The work involved in the construction of the Chad-Cameroon pipeline is nearing completion, at least the implementation phase in the area where the study was carried out. The peoples living along the pipeline, notably the Bagyéli, have paid a great price, for it is no secret that it is from the forest that they obtain the bulk of their livelihood. When the forest is on the verge of destruction (stress on the flora and fauna), they no longer know to which saint they should pray.

If you enter a Bagyéli village today and talk about the pipeline, you see anger, sadness, desolation, broken dreams: "the pipeline has come and gone!" -- That says everything.

The system of assessing the value of property having been the only one that was taken into account for the purpose of compensation meant that the Bantu were favoured over the Bagyéli who are more attached to the natural elements that constitute the basis of their culture. Moreover, concerning the advantages linked to the pipeline, we noted that there was a smaller number of Bagyéli people recruited during the pipeline operations and this despite their proximity to the pipeline route. In addition, their rights to their ancestral lands and other natural resources that were destroyed were not respected.

The question of land access rights and of land ownership in favour of the pygmy peoples is even more acute in this case, since the demography of their neighbours is ever increasing, with all that implies in terms of exploitation of the land. The public authorities, the national and the international community should act in a pragmatic way in order to establish real rights to land ownership of the Bagyéli community in order to ensure sustainable development for them.

THE BAGYELI'S RECOMMENDATIONS

As a consequence of the pipeline, the Bagyéli community has suffered many losses,. This issue can be seen in terms of the destruction of our living environment, maginalisation/discrimination in the awarding of compensation and discrimination in recruitment or distribution of jobs. Furthermore, the demographic growth of the Bantu is increasing the exploitation of the land where we practise hunting and gathering of Non Timber Forest Products. Moreover, we are gravely concerned to see all this land reducing in size, or else of being banned from it in the very near future, apart from token concessions here and there. This situation will definitely increase our dependence/semi-slavery vis-à-vis the Bantu.

Armed with the extent of these issues, *we request the World Bank to facilitate consideration of the question of Access to/Control of the land in favour of the Bagyéli so that definitive and sustainable decisions are made.*

In addition, we request that the World Bank, both now and in the future, see to it that:

- ◻ Our administration, through its local representatives and traditional chiefs, consider a Bagyéli person as being Cameroonian through and through, a person who should enjoy their rights:
  - The right to own our land;
  - The right to access our hunting and fishing territories.
- ◻ The concrete realisation of FEDEC programmes is a product of the real needs and strategic interests of the Bagyéli community. This supposes the capacity building of our community in tools of analysis for setting objectives and choosing activities.
- ◻ All the promises made within the context of the pipeline project be fulfilled, such as :
  - Building houses;
  - Supplying national identity cards;
  - Assistance in the area of education;

- Medical diagnosis of pulmonary ailments;
- Agricultural extension services and distribution of seed;
- etc.

❑ The consultation system be more relevant, adapted to our culture and to our peace of mind so as to better enable us to make our own choices as to what is best for our community.

❑ The education system for the Bagyéli children is strengthened in order to guarantee their improved integration into socio-economic life.

Bibliography

Pipeline Tchad-Cameroun, *Bulletin trimestriel*, N°2002 – 01/février 2002.

La Lettre du CPSP, N° 02 janvier 2002.

Projet de développement Tchad-Cameroun, *Rapport N° 07*, 2ème trimestre 2002.

Manuel opérationnel de la Banque Mondiale, septembre 1991 O.D 4.04, P. 1-6.

Rapport du Groupe Externe de Suivi de la Conformité Environnementale (ECMG), 4è visite, janvier 2002.

Synthesis Paper - Indigenous People, Forest and the World Bank : policies and practice, Thomas Griffiths and Marcus Colchester, Forest Peoples Programme 1c Fosseway Business Centre, Stratford Road, Moretun in Marsh. GL 569 NG, (England).

Workshop on Indigenous Peoples, Forest and the World Bank Policies and Practice, Washington D.C., 9-10 May 2000. Delegates Room, Embassy Suites Hotel, 1250 22nd Street NW, Washington D.C., USA.

Restauration Durable de l'Environnement des Ecosystèmes Forestiers dans le Cadre de la réalisation du Pipeline Tchad – Cameroun, Wilbros, SPIE Capag (JERSEY) ltd, GEO CONSULT.

Draft report on the IPP Consultations Conducted in the Kribi – Lolodorf. Area, September 2001.

Françis Nkoumlele Sociologist, COTCO.

Geogius Koppert, Nutritionnist, Antropologist.

Dr Godefroy Ngima Mawoug, Dr, Sociologist, GEPFE.

Le projet pétrolier Tchad-Cameroun : Pipeline de l'espoir ou tuyau de la misère? Brochure produced at Yaoundé in March 1998 by :
  - Centre pour l'Environnement et le Développement (CED)
  - Réseau Foi et Justice Afrique-Europe, Antenne Yaoundé
  - Service Oecuménique pour la Paix (service Humanus).

INDONESIA:
PARTNERSHIP FOR DEVELOPMENT?

Pius Erick Nyompe

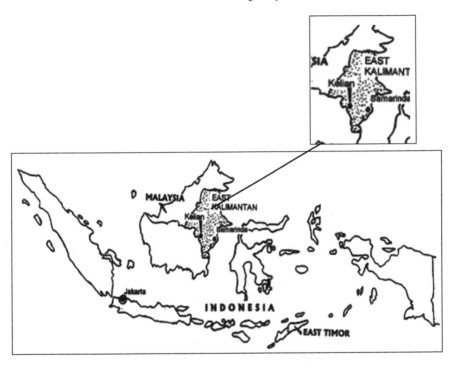

Kelian Equatorial Mining (PT KEM) is a mining company registered under Indonesian law. It is 90% owned by Anglo-Australian mining company Rio Tinto (the biggest mining company in the world) and PT Harita Jayaraya Inc (10%) — an Indonesian company. KEM signed a Contract of Work with the Indonesian government in 1985 for a 286,233.5 hectare concession. This agreement[2], signed by the (then) president Suharto, allows KEM to explore for and mine gold in the Kelian area of Kutai[3] district in East Kalimantan province.

The primary gold ore deposits are on the slopes of Prampus Barat and Prampus Timur. The mineable ore is estimated at 53.5 million tons with a gold content of around 1.97 grammes/ton. KEM started production on July 1st 1991. At that time, the mine was thought to have a lifespan of 9-10 years (ending in August 2002) with production levels at 6 million tonnes of ore processed per year (approx 23,000 tons per day). On average, about 15 tonnes of gold and 13 tonnes of silver are produced each year.

This part of the eastern part of the island of Borneo is largely rugged hills and mountains covered with tropical rainforest. This area is the watershed for the many streams and rivers which drain into the River Mahakam -- East Kalimantan's major river. The indigenous (Dayak) community have traditionally depended on clearing some forests to cultivate rice and vegetable crops. When soil fertility drops, this land is used to grow long-term crops such as rattan, various types of fruit trees and palms. After a number of years, this agroforestry system is cleared and replaced by rice farming for several seasons. Under customary law, some forest is never cleared but left intact for spiritual reasons as well as for protection of watersheds and wildlife. People collect a range of forest products for their own needs and for sale such as honey, damar resin and medicinal plants. They also used to hunt for bushmeat.

HISTORY OF COMMUNITY MINING

The community gold mining which is going on around the KEM mine is not the result of the recent discovery of gold in this area by the company. The local community has long known that there was gold in these hills. Stories of gold have been passed down through the generations. Even today the remains of pits and tunnels constructed hundreds of years ago can be found by local people who know where to look.

In 1949, a visiting group of Penihing Dayaks came to the village of Muara Kelian to ask Lung Bulan, the traditional leader of that community, for permission to collect rattan up the River Kelian and to put up some simple shelters at Gah Balui. It happened that when they were washing themselves in the river after a day's work, they noticed that the sand on their bodies was black and shiny like iron filings. They guessed that this sand might contain gold because they had seen local people panning for gold at Danum Biang, near Long Pahangai. So they took a metal plate from their canoe and tried panning themselves. The men soon found tiny grains of yellow metal. By the end of a week they had filled an old lemonade bottle with the yellow metal which they took down river to Long Iram. There, two Chinese goldsmiths[4] examined their find and immediately bought the gold for Rp10 per gram[5].

News spread that gold had been discovered at Kelian and people rushed from surrounding areas (and eventually from neighbouring islands) to pan for gold too[6]. A small-scale mining industry quickly grew up along the whole length of the Kelian River[7]. Initially, all newcomers only mined with the consent of indigenous community leaders. The population of the Kelian area has obviously increased and become more ethnically mixed since the 1950s. However, families of different ethnic origins share common interests and experiences, so the Kelian community has not experienced the inter-ethnic conflicts which have afflicted other parts of Indonesia in recent years.

KEM COMES TO KELIAN

PT Rio Tinto Indonesia first came to the area in the early 1970s and carried out explorations along the River Kelian at Prampus. The company followed this up by drilling bore holes to take further samples in the Kelian area in 1985. Rio Tinto Indonesia and Buana Jaya Raya Indonesia (a Jakarta-based company) formed PT Kelian Equatorial Mining before applying to the Indonesian government for a concession to explore further and exploit their finds.

From the start, the company claimed that there was no genuine community mining at Kelian. This was a means to avoid paying compensation for the loss of local livelihoods. KEM went on forcibly to evict local inhabitants from Muara Bayaaq to Kampung Baru in 1987. The company forbade local people from gold mining, agroforestry or cultivating fields in the area around the mine site because this was all part of KEM's concession. This ban provoked a strong response from the community (in the form of demonstrations in 1988) who opposed the company's position. KEM responded by bringing in two helicopter loads of security forces. There were a number of other serious human rights violations during the next ten years. [*See Appendix*]

The communities' grievances against KEM's operations in Kelian at that time included the following:

- Local people are not allowed to carry out agroforestry or to farm their customary lands which lie within KEM's concession.
- The community is gradually getting poorer because they were forced off their land and prevented from mining within KEM's concession.
- There is pollution in the Kelian River. In 1991, there was an incident when 1,200 drums of chemicals for KEM fell into the river. Local people believe they contained cyanide.

Most of the community complained of itchy areas of skin which became swollen then turned into open sores. Other negative indications were mass fish deaths along the Kelian River from Gah Macan to Muara Kelian.

◻ KEM's trucks and heavy equipment cause air pollution due to the large amounts of dust they stirred up when they pass people's homes on unsurfaced roads.

◻ KEM's security guards had harassed, beaten up and shot at local people mining in and around the Kelian River within the mine concession. They did this even though East Kalimantan's governor had issued an edict which allowed community mining within 50 metres from the banks of the river[8].

◻ Local people had been evicted from their cultivated lands, homes and small-scale mining sites without any prior consultation.

◻ Some graves were destroyed when the main mine site and access road were established.

◻ Some local women suffered sexual harassment by KEM staff on and off the mine site and there were a number of rape cases – some involving girls under the age of consent.

COMMUNITY'S DEMANDS

Local people's concerns about KEM generated the following demands:

1. Compensation for land for which the company had never paid;
2. Compensation for land where the company had only made inadequate payments;
3. Compensation for the loss of community miners' livelihoods;
4. Compensation for homes and shelters which had been destroyed with no payment;
5. Reduction of dust pollution caused by mine traffic along roads through settlements;
6. Measures to tackle environmental problems[9];
7. Redress for human rights violations[10];
8. Honour the promises made by KEM to the community about the provision of clean drinking water supplies, electricity, 2 hectares of land for cultivation and new housing[11].

LOCAL PEOPLE'S ATTEMPTS TO FIGHT FOR THEIR DEMANDS

The community have tried various means to press KEM to meet their demands including:

1. Putting their grievances in writing and sending letters to various relevant authorities such as:
   a. The Long Iram sub-district head and the district administrator's assistant at Melak, with copies to the National Commission for Human Rights, government ministers and the Indonesian President;
   b. The East Kalimantan governor (who passed it on to the Kutai district administrator);
   c. The National Commission for Human Rights who responded by sending a letter expressing concern to KEM.
2. Presenting their grievances to the legal aid office in the provincial capital, who wrote three times to KEM and the district and provincial governments.
3. Getting government and customary (*adat*) bodies at village level to send supporting letters to the authorities to settle disputes.
4. Taking community grievances straight to Jakarta: to the National Commission for Human Rights, Indonesian Parliament and the Ministry of Mining and Energy.
5. Raising the profile of the community's case through NGO fora, such as the workshop in Banjarmasin (1995) and the 'Peoples' Meeting' in Jakarta (1997).
6. Campaigning in Australia with Australian mining unions and NGOs.
7. Holding a series of demonstrations locally.

All these pressures finally resulted in discussions between LKMTL and KEM in early May 1998 and an agreement about negotiations to settle the community's demands[12]. Six rounds of discussions were held between KEM (supported by its parent company Rio Tinto) and LKMTL (supported by the NGOs WALHI and JATAM[13]) during 1998-9. However, the mining company reneged on agreements reached through these negotiations on several occasions and in various ways. In 2000, the negotiation process reached deadlock and the Kelian community responded with large-scale demonstrations outside the mine site and in local villages [*See Box 1*].

The negotiations were only resumed in March 2001 after a new

Protocol on procedures was reached and KEM had a new chairman. This 'peace deal' was brokered by the chairman of the Indonesian Commission for Human Rights, Asmara Nababan, and Amar Inamdar of the Oxford-based consultancy Synergy[14]. Australian High Court judge Marcus Enfield and Indonesian Supreme Court judge Artidjo Alkostar were chosen as arbitrators. The Protocol – between LKMTL representing the community and the mining company KEM - was witnessed by WALHI and Rio Tinto.

CLOSURE OF KEM MINE

KEM intends to close its Kelian mine in 2004. It will rework some of the lower grade stockpiled ore and possibly some of the tailings before leaving the site in 2007. In order to prepare for this, the mining company established a Mine Closure Steering Committee (MCSC). This comprises representatives of KEM, Rio Tinto, local government and central government[15], academics[16], the local Customary Council[17] and LKMTL (for the community).

Four Working Groups support the MCSC by more detailed planning and technical discussions on:

- Waste-retaining dams;
- The environment;
- Disposal of assets;
- Community empowerment and regional planning.

A brief outline of the mine closure plans (focusing on the environmental aspects), is as follows:

- All the waste containment areas (primarily Nakan and Namuk) and the main mine pit will be filled with water. The long-term safety of this method, which KEM calls 'wet cover', is questionable as a means of environmental protection. It is by no means certain that this will guarantee the stability of the dangerous materials remaining in the waste dumps and effectively prevent their mobilisation into the broader environment. The community must have some guarantee of environmental security from KEM to cover the period after the company has left the area. In the long-term, KEM must take responsibility for any pollution incidents which damage the local community and the Indone-

Box 1: *Police violence and company complicity*

◻   By 1 May 2000, negotiations between KEM and the community organisation LKMTL over the community's demands had broken down. The company had broken the terms of its agreement with LKMTL by involving local government officials. Tempers were running high – one official had a heart attack at an earlier meeting.

◻   Yohanes Nyomung, a community leader from Melapeh Baru village, was arrested in early May for 'fomenting dissent' and sentenced to seven days in prison. In July, the police threatened to rearrest him on the original charge. His family and other villagers had to spend Rp50 million in payments to the police, prosecutor and judge to get him released again.

◻   Meetings between KEM and LKMTL were held over a day's journey away from the mine site 'for security reasons.' In early May, a squad of police and soldiers surrounded the hotel wherein LKMTL's negotiating team were staying for the next meeting and kept all 15 of them overnight in the cells at their headquarters. This was because the local police chief had decided that a splinter group (backed by the company and the district administrator) were the rightful representatives of the community - LKMTL.

◻   By that time, local people were engaged in mass demonstrations and blockades at various villages in protest about the breakdown in negotiations. At Kebut, a couple of hours from the mine near Barangtongkok, several hundred people had put large pieces of timber across one of the main roads to stop workers and materials reaching the mine site. But the protest was peaceful. People were camping under tarpaulin shelters in the front yards of villagers' homes.

◻   On 26 May 2000 at around 6 am, three busloads of Mobile Brigade forces and a pickup of plain clothed police suddenly appeared in Kebut. They fired into the air several times and then ordered the protestors to disperse.

◻   People fled in terror as the police tore down their shelters and chased them through the village. The police trampled their belongings and confiscated any large knives (essential traditional farming equipment) and blowpipes (local hunting equipment). A substantial amount of money (over

Rp1 million), and some identity cards and clothing were stolen.

- ❐ The police, who numbered around 100 men, warned the villagers that if they had not removed the blockade by mid-day, they would return and take even stronger action. Six people were taken away by police and held in custody.

- ❐ At that time KEM made regular payments to the local authorities to protect the mine site, in addition to its own security guards (some of whom were ex-police) and paid the transport costs of the police/military to break up demonstrations and take 'suspects' down river to police headquarters. It is not known if this practice continues.

sian state.

- ❐ Each waste dump will be confined by retaining dams. KEM must be certain that these structures are stable and able to contain all the waste.

- ❐ Waste water from the Nakan dam will be drained into the mine pit and, from there, into a 30-40 hectare 'wetland system' before eventual discharge into the River Kelian. The scientific basis of the effectiveness of this waste disposal method must be questioned to ensure that water discharges into the River Kelian are genuinely safe. The company must be absolutely certain that this method is safe as the River Kelian flows into the Mahakam – the main river of east Kalimantan on which many hundreds of thousands of people depend.

- ❐ Waste rock and other spoil heaps which do not contain toxic materials are to be dealt with by the 'dry cover' method. These artificial hills will be covered with clay and topsoil and then planted. Once again, KEM must be absolutely certain that this method is effective in preventing acid rock draining in the long-term.

- ❐ It is intended that the local community will be able to use the artificial lakes created by flooding some tailings dumps for fishing. This option must be reconsidered since the 'lakes' contain toxic wastes. These substances can accumulate in fish through the food chain and, if eaten, could endanger human health. Long-term safety factors must be the prime concern in any alternative option.

- ❐ Other areas are to be replanted or reforested.

❏   All KEM's assets and responsibility for the area will be handed over to the Indonesian government in the post-closure period.

LKMTL is also concerned that once the company has left, small-scale gold miners will return to the area to rework tailings and to explore for gold elsewhere. Although KEM claims that the mine is no longer commercially viable, there is sufficient gold in remaining deposits to give small-scale miners a reasonable profit. Given that the contaminated waste is only going to be covered over and there will also be a huge water filled pit, the dangers are obvious — both to these 'illegal miners' and to the broader community as rainwater will carry toxic wastes into local rivers.

LKMTL'S INVOLVEMENT IN THE MINE CLOSURE STEERING COMMITTEE

In the case of the approaching closure of Kelian in Kalimantan, Rio Tinto has joined the World Bank Business Partners for Development Programme. This brings together the private sector, civil society and government under the convening authority of the World Bank. The idea is to progress situations in which all three partners have an interest but limited chance of success on their own[18].

This quote clearly shows that KEM was already planning for mine closure by 1998. However, the first time the community knew of this was when KEM sent BPD/World Bank consultant Amar Inamdar and Ramanie Kumanayagam[19] (from Rio Tinto London) to talk with LKMTL. It was assumed at the time that his role was to help settle the differences between KEM and the community over compensation demands and human rights abuses, since this was precisely at the time negotiations were deadlocked. They did also discuss mine closure plans.

In September 2000, LKMTL recommended (via KEM's anthropology consultant Michael Hopes) that Niel Makinuddin[20] should be a facilitator in the Mine Closure Steering Committee. KEM also proposed Amar Inamdar as a facilitator. LKMTL hoped that the presence of these two facilitators — one from the community side and one from the company's — would maintain some equality between the two parties' struggle to promote their own interests. Nevertheless, only the community's facilitator stuck to the agreement to be neutral. In private, he explained that he had been pressed by KEM not to be biased in favour of the community. The other facilitator did not seem to be under the same obligation and clearly favoured the company in all discussions.

The first meeting of the Mine Closure Steering Committee was held in February 2001 at the Dusit Hotel in Balikpapan[21]. It was agreed that meetings would be held thrice a month.

LKMTL chose five people to take part in the mine closure discussions: one for the Steering Committee and one for each of the Working Groups. As the process went along, LKMTL began to feel that its recommendations were not being taken seriously by the company. Local government representatives always sided with the company, so the community was usually 'outvoted'. Furthermore, LKMTL's four Working Group representatives were no longer included in meetings from March 2002 onwards with no explanation from the MCSC secretariat. Representatives from other parties on the Working Groups continued as before. So, despite the way that KEM always claims that the community is fully involved in discussions on mine closure and are equal partners, this is not the case. Eventually, on 19 March 2003, LKMTL decided to withdraw from the MCSC because it was dissatisfied with the process[22].

The two processes -- settlement of outstanding disputes and mine closure -- which should be quite distinct, are actually connected in many subtle ways. This becomes more complicated as some of the same figures (including consultants) are involved in both processes. There are suspicions that KEM has deliberately dragged out the compensation and dispute settlement process in order to make sure that the community were part of   the mine closure process. Rio Tinto and KEM have tried to promote the Kelian closure plans as a model of good practice for mine closure elsewhere in Indonesia and worldwide. Obviously, they do not want any public discussion of unresolved charges of human rights abuse or environmental pollution.

FURTHER KEY ISSUES

There remain some major outstanding issues, from the community's perspective (apart from those explained in the March 19th letter).

- MCSC and KEM/Rio Tinto's management has never been open about the profits it has made through exploiting this area of community natural resources.
- The salaries of foreign and Indonesian staff or contractors are not the same (i.e. there is discrimination against Indonesian workers).
- There remains a difference between LKMTL and KEM in their long-term views of the issues. For example, KEM looks

more at the potential short-term negative impacts, whereas LKMTL focuses on the long-term impacts of the tailings for the whole Kelian watershed and the communities living along the Kelian river.

◻ The issue was raised that KEM could 'sterilise' the mine, by processing remaining alluvial gold and the tailings (which have a significant gold content). The profits could be deposited in a trust fund to pay for the education of people whose lives had been so adversely affected by the Kelian mine. However, this idea has been dropped without any proper consideration.

◻ KEM/Rio Tinto did not support the involvement of LKMTL in spreading information about the outcomes of the MCSC and gathering inputs – positive and negative – from the community. KEM/Rio Tinto have established their own system and say that they have only received very positive responses to the mine closure plans.

Appendices

Appendix 1: *Human rights violations suffered by the Kelian people*

Time	Incidents
1949	A group of Penihing Dayaks visit Muara Kelian and discover gold in the R. Kelian.
1972	Exploration by Rio Tinto Indonesia.
1976	Exploration by PT Buana Jaya Raya Mining Company (BJR).
1982	Local gold panners told to leave their sites by Long Iram sub-district head to secure the area in preparation for BJR/Rio Tinto's operations.
1982 – 1991	Forced eviction of hundreds of local miners and burning of their shelters/homes at Gah Macan, Gah Bujang, Gunung Runtuh, Gah Panjang, Loa Tepu, Sungai Tukam, Gunung Runcing, Gah Ekong and Gah Punan.
1985	KEM's Contract of Work signed.

1985 – 1989	The frequency and severity of conflicts between local miners and KEM increased. Evidence for this is: • The number of complaints from local people to LKMTL and WALHI[243] about cases of houses or shelters being burnt down, intimidation, evictions, brutality and sexual violence by company employees or local military/police • The number of cases where KEM accused local people of theft of illegal mining within the concession area.
1990-92	Construction of processing plant and mine site buildings.
July 1991	KEM mine starts pilot production
20 December 1991	Daniel Paras and his family evicted from their home at gunpoint
1992	KEM mine starts commercial production
19 December 1992	Local people demonstrate with 7 banners
22 December 1992	Number of demonstrators increases to 200
24 December 1992	400 people demonstrate demanding fair land compensation.
26 December 1992	9 people invited to a meeting with Kutai District Administrator but were held in police custody instead.[24]
28 December 1992	H. Ridwan detained by police.
29 December 1992	5 more people held in detention
31 December 1992	200 people demonstrated at Tutung and were confronted by the security forces. KEM agreed to settle compensation claims, but the local government was slow to act.
5 January 1993	Eduard Tarung died in police custody (aged around 80).
1987 – 1997	Detention, torture of local people and confiscation of their mining equipment and other belongings at Gah Macan, Gunung Runtuh, Gunung Runcing, Gunung Gundul, Muara Nakan, Camp Prampus, Gah Punan, Gah Sadiah, Rodah Lampung, Gah Donggo and Gah Ekong.

1990 – 1997	Repeated thefts of equipment from KEM mine site.
1997 – 1998	Inhabitants of Gah Donggo (at edge of mine site) blamed for thefts and suffer intimidation from KEM and local police.
6 February 1993	Mukidin Anshori is drowned in Nakan tailings dam after being pursued by KEM security guards.
1989 – 1994	10 cases of violence against women.
1994 – 1997	7 more cases of violence against women.

Appendix 2: *The community representation's withdrawal from the Kelian mine closure process*

19th March 2003

From: The Association for the Welfare of the Mining Community and Environment (Lembaga Kesejahteraan Masyarakat Tambang dan Lingungan – LKMTL)

Re: LKMTL'S WITHDRAWAL FROM THE MINE CLOSURE STEERING COMMITTEE (MCSC)

Melapeh Baru, Kutai Barat District, East Kalimantan, Indonesia

To: Chairman of the Mine Closure Steering Committee of Kelian Equatorial Mining
President Director, Rio Tinto Indonesia
President Director PT Kelian Equatorial Mining

Dear Sirs:

As part of PT KEM's mine closure plans, LKMTL has been involved in the Mine Closure Steering Committee team, both as a member of the Steering Committee and its Working Groups, as the representative of the community around the PT KEM mine. Based on our observations gained during nearly two years of participation in meetings to discuss the post-mine phase, we are sending this letter to put forward some of the community's suggestions and requests relating to the environmental and social conditions after the mine has closed. We do not think the MCSC has given these and other points serious attention and consideration.

1. Requests for the Contract of Work document for PT KEM/Rio

Tinto have been ignored; we have still not been given a copy. We find this surprising since this contract is very important as evidence of PT KEM's programme, concession area, mine plans and the basis for the mine closure programme. LKMTL and the community should be able to examine this document in all discussions and meetings with the MCSC. The contract is also important in that the community should know what the company's responsibilities are in managing the mine.

2. LKMTL has suggested in MCSC meetings that there should be an independent expert in the mine's laboratory monitoring pollution levels both now (in the short term) and when the mine closes. It appears that there was little response to this suggestion – it was just noted in the MCSC and Working Group minutes. This is an extremely important matter for us: that the community has access to reliable information about the levels and dangers of pollution.

3. LKMTL has requested that PT KEM should take responsibility for the recovery of the community economy post-mine closure for a period twice the length of the production period or the company's Contract of Work. This is intended to guarantee the revival of a healthy local economy once PT KEM ceases its operations in Kutai Barat district.

4. LKMTL has requested that environmental restoration is carried out in such a way that the community's safety is fully protected, both during mine production and after its closure. This means environmental rehabilitation; filling in the pits and lakes left by excavation; ensuring that the waste disposal site (Namuk Dam) will not cause future pollution problems by leaking or collapsing. The PT KEM mine site and surrounding concession area should be replanted.

5. LKMTL has requested that PT KEM/Rio Tinto gives some sort of guarantee or insurance to the whole community surrounding the mine in the event of pollution resulting from PT KEM's operations which endangers people's health either during production or after mine closure.

6. LKMTL has requested that PT KEM builds a free hospital for the community around the mine; this could monitor local people's health. The need for this is also supported by accusations made by the inhabitants of Batu Apoi (Letter 02/BA/2003; dated 10th Jan 2003) who suffer various complaints which they suspect are caused by pollution of the River Namuk.

7. LKMTL requested that PT KEM/Rio Tinto explain what their responsibilities are for various problems that might arise after the mine closes.

8. LKMTL requested that PT KEM gives an honest account of the cases of the deaths of Abdul Rahman and Arifin within the

mine site. This is necessary so that the community understands the dangerous consequences of panning for gold in the mine tailings (Namuk dam) and parts of the mining location which may have been contaminated by chemicals.

On the basis of these facts which, in our opinion, have not received serious attention through the process of MCSC meetings and the various contributions relating to the post-mine period made by members of the community - either in these meetings or directly to PT KEM, LKMTL has decided to withdraw from the MCSC and its Working Groups with immediate effect.

Thank you for your attention.

Yours sincerely

Pius Erick Nyompe
Executive Director LKMTL

Endnotes

[1] *Lembaga Kesejahteraan Masyarakat Tambang dan Lingkungan (LKMTL)*, the Association for the Welfare of the Mining Community and Environment.

[2] The Contract of Work B-06/Pres/1/1985 was signed on 21st February 1985.

[3] The area is now part of the new district of Kutai Barat (West Kutai) created when regional autonomy was introduced in 2000.

[4] Atjip died some years ago, but Tjien Bie still lives in the provincial capital, Samarinda.

[5] At current rates of exchange US$1 is worth around Rp10,000.

[6] Initially by traditional panning methods, but later the system of pit mining and tunneling was reintroduced. Nowadays most small-scale miners use high pressure hoses to wash ore-bearing soil from the river banks or use suction pumps to bring up larger amounts of gravel and mud from river beds and sand banks.

[7] Gold mining sites include: Gah Pahang, Gah Biru, Gah Cincang, Gah Busra, Gah Tukul, Gah Lalang, Gah Pal, Gah Sadiah, Belengyan River, Batu Mak, Batu Bidawang, Gah Batang, Muara Buang, Gah Donggo, Gah Panjang, Gah Kubur, Muara Nakan, Prampus, Gah Sombin, Gah Bujang, Gah Macan, Loa Tepu, Gah Ekong, Gah Punan, Gah Kenyah, Sungai Jiu and Sungai Kelian Hulo.

[8] SK Gubernur Kalimantan Timur No.545/3346/Proda/83.

[9] These include forest destruction and pollution of water courses due to acid rock drainage.

[10] These include intimidation, threats and eviction at gunpoint of people

from their homes and small-scale mining operations plus the sexual harassment and rape of local women (some of whom were under age).

[11] Unwritten commitments made by Alan Hawkes, a senior manager at KEM.

[12] In mid-May 1998, shortly before Suharto's 33 year autocratic rule came to an end, an LKMTL representative attended Rio Tinto's AGMs in London and Melbourne and (later) discussed the community's case with senior Rio Tinto executives.

[13] JATAM is a Jakarta-based NGO mining advocacy network.

[14] This consultant's role in mine closure and dispute settlement is far from clear to the community.

[15] Kutai Barat district government and the Department of Energy & Mineral Resources.

[16] Including from Bandung Institute of Technology (ITB) and UNMUL - the state university in the provincial capital, Samarinda.

[17] A government-backed organisation of traditional representatives.

[18] Rio Tinto 1998 Annual Review, p15.

[19] It is hardly surprising that local people are confused about the roles of various consultants. Ms Kumanayagam first appeared at Kelian as 'an independent anthropology student', who then worked for Rio Tinto and is now with the World Bank. Amar Inamdar appeared on the scene in March 1999 accompanied by senior Rio Tinto staff in Jakarta when he was introduced as a World Bank consultant.

[20] Then director of the respected Samarinda-based natural resources NGO, Plasma.

[21] A large coastal city which is Rio Tinto's Kalimantan base: one and a half day's journey by public transport from Kelian or a 45 minute helicopter ride for company staff.

[22] See letter No. 22/LKMTL/MB/III/2003 in Appendix 2.

[23] WALHI is an NGO network: Indonesia's 'Friends of the Earth'.

[24] Fifteen people were detained at Kutai district police station, a day downriver from the mine site, over the Christmas-New Year period as follows: Dither Tarung (10 days); Eduard Tarung (10 days); M. Tolla; M. Baluk (5 days); M. Nurung (5 days); Salire (5 days); Sutarji (5 days); Likupan (5 days); M. Ginting (5 days); H.Ridwan; Mahran (2 days); M. Londit (2 days); Sidik (2 days); Truni (2 days); Edi (2 days).

INDIA: BREAKING THE TRUST

Bineet Mundo

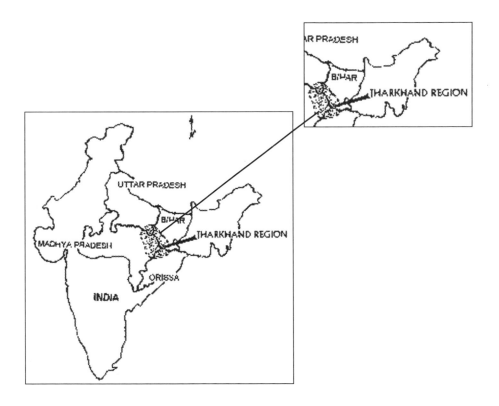

We dream of our land.
Everything that we see, that we walk on, that we feel through our
body, it belongs to our land.
We need the land to think about ourselves, to know who we are.
We are no people without our land.
The government should understand this.
This is not negotiable.
Land cannot be compensated.

Gregory Bahla, Displaced
from the Rourkela industrial region

GENERAL OVERVIEW OF EXTRACTIVE INDUSTRIES
AND THEIR IMPACT ON INDIGENOUS PEOPLES

What the industrialisation process has brought to indigenous peoples' territories today for the benefit of other peoples raises serious questions. The development method introduced in their territories has been an experience of betrayal for the indigenous peoples. This report presents a general overview of the Extractive Industries and their impact on the indigenous peoples, focusing on the World Bank-funded Coal India Ltd.'s (CIL) East Parej Project in Hazaribag district in Jharkhand. Central Coalfields Ltd. (CCL), a subsidiary of CIL, operates the project.

The problem with extractive industries operating in indigenous peoples' areas and territories worldwide is that their impact is more indirect than direct. The indirect impact is long term such that without a deep analysis, it would not be possible to understand the link between the opening up of extractive industries and the degradation of the life of the indigenous peoples.

To understand this process we need to look into India's industrial policy. India has accorded great importance to mining in its industrial development and overall growth. Mining and a policy on the management of mineral resources were part of India's industrial policy and initial five-year plans, both in the non-Scheduled and Scheduled Areas. The latter are areas specified by the India Constitution as having an indigenous population. Land here cannot be owned by non-indigenous persons unless it is for 'public purpose' and other such uses.

In these areas, massive industrial programmes were carried out in the 1950s and 1960s, enabling the industrial sector to fuel development in other sectors. Enormous sums were invested in large projects such as irrigation and power installation, steel plants and mines. This massive industrialisation not only put tremendous pressure on the mineral resources of the country, but also on the traditional lands and resources of Adivasi/indigenous communities in India.

Extractive industries like oil, gas and coal need certain infrastructures like a highly developed network of transportation which requires the building of road networks, rail heads, linkages to ports among others, and all this means erosion of indigenous peoples' rights over land, forest, and their livelihood resource base. These industries not only require capital in the form of money but also sophisticated machines. Hence these require other ancillary industries for repair and maintenance of sophisticated technology. This kind of investment is required simply to put up an extractive industry and run it.

Certain other requirements also have to be met, of which three are most important: 1) skilled labour, 2) management and 3) scientists and technical personnel. Briefly put, for an extractive industry to function it is necessary that a technically skilled population of non-indigenous people are brought in. Thus by definition, setting up of an extractive industry implies not only a curtailment of rights of the indigenous peoples to land and forest resources but also of putting them in a radically subordinate position vis-à-vis a non-indigenous group with an urban orientation. This is so because indigenous peoples, with an agrarian and traditional way of life, usually perform only the manual and unskilled tasks. The non-indigenous population provides the bulk of skilled and technical staff.

As far as the loss of rights to resources is concerned, there is only a limited understanding about what constitutes fair and just compensation for grave losses, which have a devastating impact on human welfare and cultural integrity. But on the whole, the protection of the indigenous peoples from this subordination to non-indigenous people, who are technically qualified and understand the dynamics of the extractive industries, is also a serious problem.

Since Indian independence in 1947, mining and manufacturing activities in the industrial Jharkhand region have undergone massive change. These brought rapid urbanisation, with centres chiefly concentrated in the Damodar and Subarnarekha basins which are the main mining and manufacturing zones of the region. The ancillary industry is small scale, for which there are no strict policy guidelines, and sometimes these are not even available.

The small-scale industry's other activity is distribution for the network of extractive industries — these are transportation, coal loading, and gas pipeline contract systems of subcontracting, which are dominated by the local mafia. In this whole exercise, Adivasi/indigenous people's identity is further eroded.

Urbanisation, and the attendant dependence on the market and the rise of consumerist values, work against the indigenous peoples' ways of life and values. These bring indebtedness to tribal communities which results in: 1) debt servitude -- i.e. bonded labour; and 2) alienation of land. The long-term dependency on cash, the Adivasis being low-skilled communities, leads to migration. This brings about the collapse of self-sufficiency.

But among the biggest impacts on indigenous peoples is dislocation. The extent of displacement in the process of industrialisation is illustrated by the following historical cases. For instance, the TATA Iron and Steel Company, established in 1907, initially acquired 3,564 acres of land comprising villages at the cost of Rs. 46,332. No one knows about the condition of those displaced. The construction of Rourkela Steel Plant in 1956 caused the displacement of 32 villages consisting of 2,465 families of which 70% were Adivasis. Only 1,200 of these families have been rehabilitated in the two settlement colonies at Jhalda and Jhirpani in Orissa.

The Heavy Engineering Corporation, established at Ranchi in 1958, acquired 9,200 acres of land from 25 villages. As a result, 2,198 families or a total population of 12,990, mostly Adivasis, were displaced. Forty-six villages were acquired for the construction of Bokaro Steel Plant, displacing 12,487 families, 2,707 of them Adivasis.

PROJECT CONTEXT

In India, Jharkhand state alone contains approximately 51 billion tonnes or 27% of India's coal reserves. The mining operation in this region is done by Central Coal Fields Ltd. CCL operations are spread over Palamau, Hazaribagh, Ranchi, Bokaro and Giridih districts, with its headquarters in Ranchi.

There are 11 coalfields within its area of operations: Giridih, East Bokaro, West Bokaro, Ramgarh, North Karanpura, Daltonganj, Auranga, Hutar, Jayanti and Sherghati. The total area of these coalfields is approximately 2,700 sq kms, but only 1,750 sq kms are good for coal mining.

CCL has 69 collieries and five coal washeries under revenue production, 30 mining projects, 20 non-mining projects and one washery under development construction. The existing manpower of CCL is 92,816 which includes 3,313 executives.

Open cast and underground mining

There has been an ongoing shift from underground to open cast mining in the last few decades. In the 1970s, 80% of the total coal production was from underground mines. In 1990, underground mines produced 40% of the total output, and open cast mines, the remaining 60%.

In the CCL mines, 82.8 % of the mining in 1990–1991 was open cast, and this is expected to increase further. All of its new projects in the last decade in the east and west Bokaro coalfields, Ramgarh and North Karanpura were open cast mines..

The land used in open cast mining is considerable, most of it originally being forest and agriculture land. The requirement for open cast mines varies with reserves of coal per unit area, stripping ratio, the type of excavating equipment and the method of dumping waste.

In an open cast mine in CCL, with a reserve of 345 mt. and designed to produce about 10 million tonnes per year, the area of land required is about 1,602 ha. for quarries and around 2,281 ha. for magazines, colony, industrial site, etc. This works out to about 7 ha. per million tonnes of reserves.

The India Coal Sector Environment and Social Mitigation Project

The India Coal Sector Environment and Social Mitigation Project (CSESMP) was initially conceived as a component of the Coal Sector Rehabilitation Project (CSRP) of the World Bank. It was then taken up as a separate project called the *Indian Coal Sector Environmental and Social Mitigation Project*. Its objective was to assist the Coal India Ltd. in making coal production more environmentally and socially sustainable.

Specifically the project aimed to: a) enhance CIL's institutional capacity to deal more effectively with environmental and social issues; b) implement policies for environmental and Rehabilitation and Resettlement (R&R) mitigation of affected people; and c) help CIL develop its policies for R&R, Community Development, Environmental Management.

These objectives were to be achieved by means of :

a. Rehabilitation Action Plans (RAPs) for 14 mines where people were to be resettled
b. Indigenous Peoples Development Plan (IPDP) in 25 mines for the villages within a 1 km.-radius of the mines
c. Capacity building and institutional changes in CIL (appointment and training of Rehabilitation and Resettlement officers, Public Information Centre)
d. Appointing NGOs to facilitate the RAPs and IPDPs
e. Formation of Village Working Group
f. "Self-employment" as the main strategy for economic rehabilitation.

Employment in the Company (the traditional means of economic rehabilitation) was radically curtailed. An International Development Association (IDA) credit of $63M was granted in May 1996, which was originally due to end on June 30, 2001. However on this date, $24M of the loan remained undisbursed, so this was extended to June 30, 2002.

The Coal Sector Rehabilitation Project

The Coal Sector Rehabilitation Project of the World Bank was formed with the objective of financing the purchase of mining equipment for modernisation and maintenance of 24 CIL open cast mines, chosen on the basis of larger profitability. This would increase the total output of the mines from 78.6 million to 104.6 million tonnes/year. The loan would also contribute to the overall modernisation and profitability of CIL. Coal India Ltd., which is the recipient on the Indian part, is a holding company for 7 subsidiaries, who are owners and managers of the 25 mines of the project. East Parej is one of these mines. The Environment Impact Assessment (EIA) estimates that by the end of 2004, the project would thus boost Coal India Ltd's annual production to about 320 million tonnes, as compared to the 240 million tonnes without the project.

The World Bank Board approved the loan for the CSRP in September 1997. This loan was due to expire in June 2003. However, for reasons this study has been unable to ascertain, the second phase was cancelled on 24 July 2000. At that time International Bank for Reconstruction and Development (IBRD) loan disbursements had totalled $235.7M, and IDA credit disbursements had reached $1.41M. Japanese Bank for International Cooperation (JBIC) disbursements were the equivalent, which were also cancelled.

Reasons for cancellation of the loan's second phase are rather ambiguous. According to the official version, the revised demand made by the Department of Coal indicated that coal demand would not grow as fast as initially estimated, and hence with the main equipments brought in the first stage of the loan, the second phase would not be necessary. There seems to be more. *Business Line* (June 24, 2000) indicated that the Government of India has done little to reconstitute the domestic coal sector which the Bank has made a conditionality. This would include amending the Coal Nationalisation Act, opening the mining industry to the private sector etc. It is acknowledged that the failure of income restoration to resettled communities is also a factor.

According to the CSESMP Staff Appraisal Report (No.15405-IN, April 24 1996), the following are some figures on land to be acquired, number of people to be affected by these mines, number of indigenous peoples among the total population etc. As this paper focuses on the Parej East case it has specified it among the 25 mines. [*See Table on p. 303*]

WORLD BANK, GOVERNMENT, AND PRIVATE SECTOR CONSULTATIONS AND DEALINGS WITH AFFECTED COMMUNITIES

"You ask us if we have been consulted or how we have been treated by the management ? .... (W)e people here have been crippled. The land is gone, (it) is like amputating one leg. Our forests are gone, (it) has amputated our other leg. We have no jobs and have to depend on casual labour of truck loading which you don't get, (it) is like amputating an arm. Then you come up with some project plan. The money for compensation is like a slap on our face. You may call it development, but our life is ruined. The project has given us more trouble then we had before. We people are tired of you all coming here, taking photos of us, interviewing us and then what happens. Our situation is deteriorating still."

An activist working in the project area
for more than five years

Consultations

There have been 18 World Bank visits. The Bank representatives were always assisted by Central Coalfields Ltd officials, on whom they depended for translations of what the people in the project area said. Because of this language problem, the CCL officials took advantage of it. For instance, in one of the visits to the Pindra rehabilitation site, World Bank officials interviewed the people who had to relocate there. CCL

Total land acquired in these 25 projects: 1,827 ha
Land Acquired for Parej East project: 237 ha

Total number of persons affected by the project: 17,632
Total number of people affected in Parej East: 1,172

Total number of Tribal persons affected: 4,619
Total number of Tribal persons affected in Parej East: 487*

Total population of this area: 185,811
Parej East's total population: 2,913

---

* These figures are misleading because the project actually affects communities in 11 villages and from this figure one is made to believe that the number of Adivasis is very small. The figures can be distorted; however the project fails to show that the damage is not just contained in Parej East alone or that the problem has intensified further.

officials presented Mr. Ashok Ganjhu as Arjun Turi's brother. They asked him, "Are you happy here?" and he said "Yes". But team members of the Chotanagpur Adivasi Sewa Samiti (CASS), a local organisation, protested, saying he was not Arjun Turi's brother nor was he displaced or residing in Pindra. CCL officials also quoted a Sathal man belonging to the host community in Pindra saying he was happy there. But the man they were referring to had died two years ago.

How can the WB say that they have consulted the people when in actual fact the people were angry and shouted at them. The CCL officials had never made an effort to gather the people and inform them that WB representatives were coming, and that they could tell them their grievances. People saw cars arriving in front of the offices of Xavier Institute of Social Service (XISS), the facilitation NGO in Peraj East; and a crowd gathered to voice out their complaints, i.e. jobs, drinking water, etc. The CCL officials literally had to chase them away because they were angry and had a lot of problems to air.

There have been other numerous cases when the people's problems were ignored. It has been five years since nine Turi families were displaced. Recently, Rameshwer and Bisheshwer Turi went to the East Parej Project Officer, Mr. Gopal Singh, at his residence which is adjacent to theirs, to share their grievances. But the Project Officer got annoyed with them and shouted, "I don't know who you are." He also got angry with his driver for allowing them in. But before Rameshwer was displaced, the CCL went to him, pleading for land.

In Jogwa Tola, another Santhal hamlet that was displaced, the people wanted to collect their last Mahua fruits, a minor forest product of that season, as they were eventually to be relocated. But pressure was placed on them to leave immediately. When queried, the General Manager, Mr. Tarsem Kumar said, "The people have agreed to move." There was no dialogue, as few of the men had jobs in the company (and they were later laid off) . The women were not consulted either, as the general manager was only concerned with the heads of the family (apparently meaning those men who had jobs in the coal company).

As mining started coming closer to the people's homes, the means used by the company became more and more frightening. The company called in the police and people were arrested. Rameshwer Turin was beaten up by the police in front of his family. Teklal Turi was arrested in a raid and incarcerated. He subsequently died in jail.

Consultations happened in this oppressive and intimidating environment, brought on by the company. Because of this, the people were unfairly compensated for their houses and lands. Cash is a medium that Adivasis (Turis are also considered a part of the Adivasi community, though listed as Scheduled Caste) cannot handle, and this form of compensation is totally inappropriate. As a consequence, many of them have been ruined and impoverished.

Many Adivasis tried to go into business, like Shikari Manjhi who opened a *Gumti* shop near the coal dump but it failed. Merilal and Kallu started poultry farms, but these too failed. Beniram bought a tracer (an 8 to 10 seater jeep normally used as a shared taxi) with the compensation money he got, but he was forced to sell it at a low price, because it didn't work. Dhaniram bought a car which is sitting in his garage. Mehilal Murmu started a bicycle repair shop, but it didn't work; he has ended up raising pigs. Anil Hembrom from Lopongtandi started a grocery shop but he is hardly there.

In March 2002, when Mr. Asgher Christein visited Pindra, he was pleased to see some houses in the Pindra rehabilitation site. He said they were similar or better than what they had in the old site (the site acquired by CCL before consulting the Project Affected Persons [PAPs]/ oustees). But in actual fact, most of the houses there had used asbestos, a banned material, in their houses. What was unfortunate is that he failed to go beyond the facade, i.e. he failed to see their loss of income, loss of community support, and loss of a meaningful structure where social conflicts could be resolved.

Even on income restoration there was no meaningful interaction on work alternatives even though the mines had started in 1993. It was only in 1998 when Ms. Jelena Pantelic came that the people were finally told that jobs were not possible in the mines. She was deputized by the World Bank as Task Manager in 1996 for the Environmental and Social Mitigation Project to look into the income restoration and income generation programmes for the PAPs. She got Colonel Bakshi involved and a Rehabilitation and Resettlement officer from the 24 mines visited Turi Tola to talk to them about income generation schemes. This resulted in cane basket making which initially was quite successful, as Turis are traditionally basket weavers.

But today due to bureaucratic problems the people have been left high and dry. With the help of Col. Bakshi the company agreed to supply the cane and buy the finished products usually used for manual loading of coal. A few stocks were supplied. The Turis made the baskets and supplied these to the company; some baskets were taken, some were rejected. Gradually most of the baskets were rejected, but not necessarily for their quality. The cane supply from the company became irregular when contractors came in. The basket weaving thus failed as a substitute livelihood for the Turis. They lost confidence in the company, and Col. Bakshi too gave up further efforts, disheartened with the company's management of this economic activity.

The Government's attitude has also been biased for the company. An example is the authentication of land titles. Once the land is given on lease, the government refuses to authenticate it. If a man whose name is on the land document has died, his heir has to get a succession certificate which involves a lengthy court process. On the other hand, in the case of Borwa Tola which did not want rehabilitation, the company got the local administration to bring the police and evict the people. The reason the Deputy Commissioner gave was that World Bank machines were lying unused. The people are thus caught between the Indian government and the World Bank. And the World Bank is supporting this dirty business.

From early 1996 there has been constant interaction between the NGOs in the field, international level management and the World Bank. [*See Table, p. 308*]

Issues put forward by Inspection Panel

The Inspection Panel was created in September 1993 by the Board of Executive Directors of the World Bank to serve as an independent mechanism to ensure accountability in Bank operations with respect to its policies and practices. In the case of East Parej the request for inspection was submitted on June 21, 2001 by the Chotanagpur Adivasi Sewa Samiti on behalf of villagers who requested anonymity. The management response on 20 July 2001 mentioned that it had received the complaint. The Panel recommended an investigation after reviewing Management's response and visiting the project area. The Board approved the Panel's recommendation for inspection on September 7, 2001.

The Inspection Panel visited the site in December 2001 and submitted its report to the Board on November 25, 2002, nearly a year after. The following are some issues that came out from the Inspection Panel's report on the East Parej Project:

- Gap between Bank Planning Documents and Ground Realities: The Inspection Panel found that "Management's failure to ensure that the original Rehabilitation Action Plan reflected reality on the ground resulted in many problems (Paragraph 13 of the executive summary of the Inspection Panel report)."
- While proclaiming "poverty alleviation", the Bank funding of 24 large open cast coal mines for mechanisation has led to the retrenchment of 87,000 mineworkers, and new

jobs that have been contracted out in the mines in Orissa have less job security.

◻ Despite Bank claims to have introduced best international practices, it made no effort to press the Government of India to ratify the International Labour Organisation (ILO) Convention on health and safety in mines. (Frontline July 2001) The Inspection Panel findings confirm what many people know or have suspected about the World Bank's ability and interest to seriously consider the social and environmental aspects of its loans.

◻ To mine a village, its lands and commons, and expect a mitigation project like CSESMP to compensate for the destruction of the life-giving natural resource base of the village is to be out of touch with reality.

◻ The Panel cited that this project was one of the most supervised World Bank Projects ever. The Bank undertook 21 supervision missions between 1996 and 2001. However, the Panel found that "the supervision team's knowledge of ground realities was limited, and for that reason, their efforts to resolve problems had virtually no impact on the ground" (paragraph 458 in the main text of the Inspection Panel report). People have long argued that the Bank indulges in 'check-box' appraisal and supervision of its loans, adding lists of new criteria but not following through to ensure that these are rigorously adopted and enforced. [*See Annex for other specific issues raised in the Inspection Panel's Report*]

IMPLEMENTATION OF WORLD BANK'S SAFEGUARD POLICY FRAMEWORK

Involuntary Resettlement

Only 12 families opted to move to Pindra Rehabilitation site, a place that had been prepared for 290 families. Most of them were those who had been forcibly evicted in 1999 in the cold month of December. Even Dhaniram Manjhi, an Adivasi village headman, is among them because he wanted to escape the harassment of CCL officials.

In Turi Tola the company started an eviction case against the people, which went on for a long time and concluded in a compromise that to date has not been implemented. Agaira Tola is the East Parej Project

Interaction of NGOs with World Bank and Other Agencies

25.02.96	"Comments": initial communication of Indian NGOs to the World Bank.
20.04.96	"Report on the East Parej Opencast Project" by CASS.
26.04.96	"Mainstreaming Sustainability" by Berne Declaration.
30.04.96	"Environmental Arguments" by Mine Watch.
13.05.96	World Bank (Pollak) reply to "Mainstreaming".
15.05.96	"NGO rejoinder" to WB response to "Mainstreaming".
09.06.96	"Memorandum" by Indian NGOs on occasion of Task Manager Pollak's visit.
13.09.96	"Benchmarks" submitted by 13 NGOs.
04.10.96	NGO discussion of Benchmarks with the Bank's India Department, Washington.
29.10.96	Letter to Chaoji "Arrest & beatings".
01.11.96	WB response (Vergin) to Benchmarks.
12.12.96	D.Marsden "Update Concerns".
07.02.97	"Outstanding Issues".
27.02.97	J Panelic "issues to new TM.
05.04.97	Local NGO Meeting with CCL Ranchi.
16.04.97	Meeting in Washington between northern NGOs and WB.
25.04.97	WB response (Drysdale) to Outstanding Issues.
27.04.97	CASS letter to Bauer.
30.04.97	Second meeting in Washington, northern NGOs and WB.
30.04.97	Meeting with Marsden at Charhi.
06.05.97	Pantelic to Bossard.
09.05.97	Consultation in Paris, World Bank and northern NGOs.
13.05.97	Bossard re Delhi NGO Meeting.
13.05.97	Bossard to Gerber.
14.05.97	K Singh to Bank re Delhi NGO Meeting.
14.05.97	CASS to Pantelic re Delhi NGO Meeting.
15.05.97	WB proposed NGO consultation in New Delhi.
20.05.97	Letter to WB President Wolfensohn (42 NGOs from 12 countries).
04.06.97	Response by Wolfensohn.
12.06.97	"Output Indicators" proposed by NGOs.
30.09.97	WB response (McKechnie) to Output Indicators.
03.02.98	CASS to Patnelic.
19.05.98	CASS to TM (A Christensen).
01.09.98	CASS to A Christensen.
12.12.98	CASS Letter (and 24 NGOs) to World Bank.
14.02.99	WB response (C Asger) to CASS.

Mid-99	Efforts by CASS and Minewatch to obtain mid -term Review.
24.07.99	CASS to Mohan.
08.09.99	Asger to CASS.
04.01.00	Letter on Borwa Tola evictions.
27.01.00	To Md. Hasan.
08.02.00	WB response to CASS on Borwo Tola evictions.
11.02.00	From Md.Hasan.
22.02.00	CASS reply to World Bank of 8.2.001.
4.08.00	Wall St Journal article in which World Bank virtually admits failure of Environmental and Social Mitigation Project (ESMP) project.

IPDP (resettlement) village, but mining is going on right next to it. The people's water resources have been badly affected. The *Maddai* where they worshipped ancestors has been bulldozed by TISCO, which was also mining in the same village. CCL has no health services for the people there and so far 11 have died due to various illnesses.

The Inspection Panel has touched almost all points as defined in the World Bank's Operation Directive (OD) 4.30 on Involuntary Resettlement. There were only six counts of compliance as compared to 31 counts of non-compliance (including Operation Directive 4.20 on Indigenous Peoples, OD 13.05 on Project Supervision and Operation Policy Note (OPN) 11.03 on Management of Cultural Property).

In the area are several other open cast mines: TISCO (West Bokaro), Jharkhand mine, Liayo mine, Kedla mine, Tapin North and Tapin South, Pundi Project. With all these mines, the people in the East Parej Project area, which has a total of four revenue villages, were made to believe that by letting the project come in they would be given jobs. The notification for acquisition of the land for this project is also unclear. People in general had no idea about the project. It only came to their notice when they were invited to inaugurate the project with songs and dances, and following talks of "development" by the officials.

The CCL office has the tape of the formal announcements in the villages where some elders of the project-affected villages, and the Mukhyas, Netas were present. After that the heavy machines started coming in and digging in the forest area west of Parej village. With the company's assurance that development would improve their lives, people looked forward to the project. East Parej had 1,095 jobs in its project span of 27 years. For the oustees there would be 17 hired from the first village Parej, which would be displaced in the first five years of the project.

The project was implemented without the people being fully informed of the potential direct and indirect negative impacts. In particular consultations failed to fully explain key issues relating to choice of sites for relocation. In short, the consultation provided incomplete and inaccurate information to the affected communities, which prevented them from making informed decisions about resettlement and development options. Out of fear for their jobs, those who were employed in the company could not also be more assertive. The movement of people to resettlement sites became involuntary or forced because they rejected the sites chosen for their relocation.

With the displacement of Dhaniram Manjhi, the tribal chief (*Manjhi Haram*, as he is called), to Pindra; of Bablu Murmu, who was the *Pranic*, to Dogdagia; and of Mehala Manjhi, the *Jogwa*, to Chenaro, the social structure of the Adivasis has fallen apart. Dhaniram's authority/ headmanship is over and in the rehabilitation site he now has to submit to the social structure of the host community of which he is no longer the head.

Participation

The World Bank guidelines provide for a Village Coordination Committee whose role is to inform the Management of the grievances of the project-affected persons and help it take appropriate action. But the people for a long time did not know that Simuli Turi was on such a coordination committee. Inclusion of the name Simuli Turi sounded as if the committee was also representative of the Turis. The villagers have no knowledge how this committee was formed. There has also been no participation on how their resources have been computed and compensated, e.g. trees, domestic animals, and cultural property.

Special reference must be made of the extent to which women were able to participate in the negotiation process. It was only when officials suddenly turned up in a village and the women happened to be home that they met these concerned officials. Among the ten members in the Village Coordination Committee only one was a woman. She is the wife of an influential person whom the company considers as their man.

Three women have died since displacement, and they were from those families that moved to Pindra at the time of the forcible relocation in December 1999. At Pindra, Phulo Manjhi (sister of the village headman -- *Manjhi haram* -- his elder son is Dhaniram Manjhi) has also expressed concern that the land that CCL has given them does not have a legal title.

With the coming in of financial institutions, women's role in Adivasi societies has been neglected and they are relegated to the home and to being labourers. Decisions are being made for them with regard to alienation of land, home and forests. Women are nowhere in the discussions. As it is, negotiations with the people start only at the implementation stage. As Matio Tudu shares, "We thought that the mines would give us 'Rozgar' (livelihood)". Today the women in East Parej have no job, no land, no land title, and no rehabilitation package.

Forestry

In 1993 mining in East Parej started in the forest. It was inaugurated by the company, with dances and songs by the Adivasis. We feel this was done on purpose as people could not say any thing about it. After the forests were destroyed, mining started in their *Gair Majurwa* land.* The people then started questioning.

They pointed out the fact that for the villagers the forest is a source of food, medicine, fodder and shelter. It has very valuable trees like *Sarjom* (sal), *Mahua, Keyond, Pyaar* and *Karam*. These trees are meaningful for the Adivasi way of life, livelihood and culture. These forests have been replaced by *eucalyptus* and *acacia*, mostly around the overburden and generally around the mines to bring some "greenery"; these do not have any social, medicinal or economic uses. This has brought a very drastic transformation for the Adivasis. There is already a water crisis and planting both *acacia* and *eucalyptus* intensifies the problem. The trees the projects destroyed for these plantations were very old, strong, and useful, and held a historical and sacred importance for the Adivasis.

Cultural Heritage

According to the Adivasi world view, land, forest, and rivers are all cultural heritage sites. We find that the World Bank does not have a clear policy on cultural sites, even if it has a theoretical policy. The implementation of this is unclear since all the festivals of the Adivasi community are linked to the forests, rivers and land. How will they celebrate them when all these are destroyed. In fact the life cycle of the Adivasis revolves around this entire natural environment. Here the land is turned into a huge pit, forests are no longer forests, and most of it continues to be

---

*This is land which is for common use. If one farms on this land for more than 7 - 12 years and has some documentary proof of his use, he can apply for authentication in his name. He then becomes a legal holder of this land.

destroyed.

The East Peraj mining started when the mining activities encroached into the *Gair Majurwa* and revenue land. During the project's inauguration, the local Adivasis were invited to perform traditional dances and songs for the occasion. The project presumably was to bring "prosperity and development" for the people in the area. How could the Adivasis know that what they were singing and dancing for would change their lives.

Sacred groves are patches of virgin forest that are left by the Adivasi community where they worship their ancestors. There are three such sacred groves in East Parej, but one of these is now destroyed. According to our understanding, the sacred grove in question could have been left untouched, and after the backfilling of the other sites, the patch where the sacred grove stood could have become part of the ecology around. This would have allowed the protection of certain species in the vegetation of the old virgin forest. The Bank seems to be unclear about the protection of sacred groves.

According to OPN 11.03 that deals with Management of Cultural Property, the project should not have been financed. The Bank applies two standards. If you are a vocal people then the company will not destroy your property. For instance in East Parej there is a Muslim graveyard near where the coal company tried to make a drain; the people got angry and as a result the company was forced to build a wall around it. The Adivasi community is not of a similar temperament, so the company deals with them in another manner -- by not giving them respect.

The Adivasis are generally peace loving, not demanding or complaining by nature, open and accommodating, unlike other communities where, being market-oriented, the sense of insecurity is more pronounced. This makes the two groups different from each other in many ways. The other communities have to take out the best from what they have, whereas the Adivasi communities count upon nature and depend on the natural environment. It is also their language that has contributed to their not being very vocal.

Environmental Assessment

In and around East Parej, there were already several environmental problems even before mining started in 1993 due to two coal washeries. One operated by TISCO and the other by CCL at Basatpur, both of these have polluted the Chutwa Nala and the Bokaro River. As a consequence, the waters have turned black. All forms of life in the river have died. Due to the East Parej Project there are also two work shops, two dispensaries, a store, employees' colonies, which all contribute to environmental problems in the area.

From the work shops, untreated wastes are released down to the Bokaro River. From the employees' quarters plastic bags are thrown all over the forest areas. Cattle from the adjoining villages eat the plastic and die. Dispensary waste is sent into the streams of Lopongtandi village. Besides all these, huge quantities of coal dust are inhaled by the villages especially those living close to the road where thousands of trucks, loaded or overloaded with coal, pass by the hamlets. Environmental assessment must be done by an independent agency other than the Central Mine Planning & Design Institute Ltd. (CMPDI), which is also a subsidiary of Coal India Ltd., like CCL.

REASONS FOR FAILURE OF THE PROJECT

When the Turis in Turi Tola, the first village to be evicted, were charged with an eviction case and taken to court, there were added false criminal cases against them for which they appealed. The court gave the judgement in favour of the Turis. This followed a compromise with CCL, which included the following provisions:

1. The nine Turi families would get manual coal loading work in the dump every working day.
2. Basket weaving work will be given to them and the cost will be borne by the CCL.
3. Suresh Turi, son of Rameshwer Turi, will be given a job against 2.08 acre land.
4. Bhola Turi, son of Taklal Turi, on compassionate grounds, shall get a temporary job in CCL until there is a vacancy in future.
5. The false criminal case on Turis will be withdrawn.

Even with a compensation and rehabilitation package, the Project Affected Persons who have been displaced from their original territories feel they are broken and powerless. The court order in their favour also has less or no meaning today.

The earlier cited basket weaving income restoration initiatives taken up by retired Colonel Bakshi with the Project Affected Persons of East Parej in 1998 is no longer operational. Also the agreement letter from the court which said that the oustees should be given priority in manual loading of coal in the dump is of no use. When Rameshwer went to the

Project Officer to ask for the manual coal loading job as they were deprived of it by the coal dump committee, the Project Officer refused to recognise him and told him to get out of his office. On insisting that he had the court agreement paper for it, the Project Officer's reply was "I will then see you in court. Let them call me". The electricity supply has also been cut off from the houses in Prem Nagar. There is no water supply there anymore.

Rameshwer Turi in Prem Nagar was robbed some six months ago. The family's belongings, marriage jewels/ornaments were all taken away. Rameshwer says, "We had informed the police. They came to see but nothing happened after that."

The man who used to live with so much self-confidence and self-respect when he was on his own land, in his house, with his family, who would be open to invite guests even when he didn't have much to give - - today he is a wretched man. Seeing some people whom we knew after five years or so of their being displaced and "relocated", we saw visible changes in their person. For Biseshwer Turi, Rameshwer Turi, Arjun Turi, and others, *there was a sense of insecurity, loss of confidence, loss of selfhood.*

NGOs as CSESMP Implementing Sub-contractors

During its interview in East Peraj, the Inspection Panel was able to confirm ESRP's finding that CCL treated the NGOs it had engaged like hired hands. They had to deliver, without room for critical comment, "plans and data at regular intervals for its [CIL's] reporting to the World Bank and wide range of consultations engaged with ESMP."

As the Environmental and Social Review Panel said, this "further moved the programme from one which was to be tailor made for each local community, towards a more generic and less flexible format, which again made it easier for [CIL's World Bank Project Division] to report on." Instead of the villages being the NGO's clients, the client now was Coal India Ltd.. (Id., 2001 Report, pp.17-18) (Paragraph 321 from the main text of the Inspection Panel report)

Broken Commitment

The Sectoral Environmental Impact Assessment (SEIA) (on the basis of which the project is approved) gives an unambiguous commitment to reclamation of mined land (From paragraph 354 of the main text, IP report). Yet CCL's senior mine manager made it clear to the Inspection Panel that they had no intention of reclaiming the land for post-mining use, (From paragraph 372 of the main text, IP report) nor was the Inspection Panel able to find any evidence of such reclamation (363, 364). We are faced here with the hard reality of commitments made (by both CIL and the Bank) at the planning stage (to get project approved), and yet wilfully ignored at the implementation stage. This raises questions:

    a. About the credibility of such commitments in any other context; and
    b. If there is not a legal possibility of challenging such breaking of commitments.

One disturbing feature is the use of misinformation in planning documents. By this are meant the inflated, unfounded or partly true claims, not grounded on fact, that form an important part of project planning. Examples are:

1. The Bank's Staff Appraisal Report of April 1996 stated that "implementation of Environment and Social Mitigation Project will safeguard the rehabilitation of 9,260 people and the proper resettlement of about 10,000 people. The implementation of the Indigenous Peoples Development Plan will improve the lives of about 186,000 of which 56,900 will be tribals." The basic defect in the project is that from the beginning there has been heavy "oversell" of its capabilities. Such oversell is found in the planning documents (Cf SAR 1.8, 1.9, 2.2, 2.11, 1.24, 4.2), almost appearing to exaggerate the value of the product in the hope that it will be approved by the board. Such exaggeration, when accepted, has allowed the mining to go ahead, with the goals of environmental and social rehabilitation virtually impossible to achieve.

2. Another example is the claim in the environmental management plan for the East Parej mine. This suggested that only about half of the 253-hectare mine area would be reclaimed for agriculture land after mining, while the rest would be left to fill up with water. This water, it was argued, "will help the local population, as a source of irrigation, drinking or industrial demand". The Panel concluded, however, that the water would be inaccessible, as it would be "tens of meters below the countryside and separated from it by vertical quarry rock faces" (357). It would be very costly to pump it for irrigation and impossible to use it for drinking as it would be poisoned by contact with coal seams.

Concluding on transparency, the Panel notes that many of the villagers participated in a baseline survey. "But beyond these interviews there is nothing to indicate that the PAPs in Parej East were systematically informed and consulted during preparation of the resettlement plan about their opinions and rights" (as is called for in the Bank's

Involuntary Resettlement policy). The Panel found "no evidence" that documents such as the Sectoral Environmental Impact Assessment were available to local NGOs for their review. The Bank claimed that the report of the mid-term review of the project could not be released unless authorised by Coal India.

3. A local Public Information Centre was established, but suffers from a number of flaws. Documents can only be consulted with supervisory (Coal India) staff present and it is not possible to study documents in private or photocopy them. The Panel expressed surprise that despite the low level of literacy among PAPs, all information in the Centre is in technical written documents. The Panel was surprised to see "no pamphlets, or simplified information material, or sketches, photographs or visual materials to depict the Project, its sequence and effect on people (403)"

It also noted that "the location of the Centre in the office of the Resettlement and Rehabilitation Officer, in the gated CCL mine headquarter's compound, does nothing to facilitate information being provided 'in a timely manner and in a form that is meaningful for, and accessible to, the groups being consulted', as required by the Bank's Environmental Assessment Operational Directive. On the contrary, for poor, vulnerable and dependent people, it is clearly intimidating to approach an officer in that location, let alone walk in and freely request information, register complaints and engage in dialogue." (Paragraph 408 of the main text of the IP report)

RECOMMENDATIONS

The Chotanagpur Adivsasi Sewa Samiti has drawn up its own Action Plan which it wants supported by the World Bank. The Action Plan, agreed to by the displaced communities, sets out ways to address the livelihood restoration of the project affected people. They urge the Bank's Executive Board to agree to fund and secure its full implementation when it considers the Inspection Panel's report in mid-January.

Towards an Action Plan

Policy Change

The Inspection Panel points to areas where changes need to be made at the level of Policy. These concern legal changes, CIL Rehabilitation and Resettlement policy and current implementation policies with CIL.

a. Policy Change

On Customary Held Land:

❑ Make legal provisions so that Gair Majurwa land can be settled in the names of those in possession (170, 179,478).

On Land Reclamation (top-soil preservation, backfilling, and re-vegetation):

❑ Land reclamation should be required by law (372);

❑ Financial remuneration/incentive be created to enable CIL to reclaim the mined land (372);

❑ For planning new mines, CIL should explore possibilities of utilisation of available backfilling to maximise the area restored to productive land use (373);

❑ CIL should improve reclamation of mineland, being fundamental to its future environmental and social performance (376);

❑ Each subsidiary of CIL should be required to prepare and implement an Environmental Management Strategy (377);

❑ CIL should improve planning system for new mines, with particular reference to land use issues and reinstatement of mined areas for agriculture use (377);

❑ CIL should lobby the government to amend existing legislation to allow for the eventual transfer of reclaimed land (377).

On consultation:

❑ A post mine audit should be conducted;

❑ Improve relations with civil society;

❑ Use bottom up approach (349);

❑ In formulation and implementation of plans (EIA, EAP, RAP, IPDP), consultation of affected groups should be made mandatory under Indian environmental legislation. (417).

b. R&R Policy changes

On Resettlement site:

❑ Size of the plots should be sufficient for second generation growth (110);

❑ Provide health and education services, not just infrastructure (126);

❑ Provide potable water (117);

❑ Give titles to plots (145, 468);

❑ Evidence of eligibility (158).

 c. Policy: current implementation within CIL

On Compensation for Land:

❑ Compensation be taken on rates of date of payment, not on date of notification (59,71); at replacement cost, not at market rate (66); by direct negotiations with oustees (70);

❑ Reform tribunal process (74);

❑ Itemised breakdown of compensation be given (76).

One Time Cash Grant:

❑ An audit should be made to assess the long term results of cash settlement approach (887);

❑ Review the change of R&R policy which gives a one time grant payment (88).

Compensation for houses:

❑ Make public the rate of house measurement (85).

Planning:

❑ The baseline survey should recognise and accurately record the dependence of tribals on natural resources vital to their subsistence. (194, Ex Sum 44).

Access to natural resources:

❑ The RAP should ensure continued access to natural resources vital to their subsistence (44, 204);

❑ All documents (EIA, EAP, RAP, and CDP) have to be location-specific. It was damaging to this project that they were repeatedly non-specific, general in nature (313, 324).

Consultation:

❑ NGOs should not be treated as inflexible implementers (321) to serve people not the company (321);

❑ For adequate information, key documents (EIA, EAP, RAP, etc.) be made accessible at a public place to affected groups and local NGOs for their review and comments, in a form and language meaningful to the groups being consulted. (394);

❑ Set up system of genuine consultation with a) PAPs, b) host communities, c) NGOs. These systems must a) go beyond information giving to actual consultation, b) bypass manipulating *dalals* (middle men), and c) represent especially the weaker sections who tend to be dominated. (410-448)

General:

❑ Need to change attitude and approach in CIL towards social issues, strong leadership, satisfactory and timely internal and external measures, employment of appropriate expertise, significant changes in career incentives (472).

◻ World Bank should make good its promises to continue monitoring the social issues after the project closes.

Income Restoration

◻ Income restoration of PAPs should be ensured. It touches the right to livelihood, "shares benefits of the project", and is the test for aims of the project and of those who make them.

◻ If there is no employment in the company, and large numbers are displaced, then the affected peoples should be given alternative jobs (227).

◻ Change the current field practice of company people interacting with the indigenous people (now still widely practiced in new mining areas, of building up hopes of *naukri* [jobs]).

Follow-up for Coal India Ltd.

◻ Posting and training of R&R officers, the opening of a Public Information Centre, the formation of village working groups, in general, a wider understanding of the need for good R&R.

◻ Check continuing violations related to preparation and appraisal of the original RAP and IPDP. Most urgent is the restoration of income to the PAPs who have not received it and of further urgency is the issue of backfilling as the mining progresses.

◻ Inspection Panel's recommendation on CIL's standard practices on Rehabilitation (concerning plot size, land title, basic services, potable water, host community) have to be seriously considered by CIL.

◻ An Independent Monitoring Committee should be set up. In the case of the similarly controversial Singurali National Thermal Power Corporation loan, such a committee composed of three well-respected Indian nationals, produced some useful recommendations.

Guidelines for Mining Companies

◻ Local people must be the target of the project, rather then production alone.

- ❏ Inform local people about what the mines will do and how useful it will be to their life. Then take their consent.
- ❏ If they are willing to give land, dialogue with them many times, not once, and give them time. *Culturally appropriate* consultation must be a step-wise process.
- ❏ Baseline surveys must be done carefully.
- ❏ What is valuable to the indigenous peoples must not be touched because those same things are valuable to the human race as well, e.g. *Sarna,* the sacred grove.
- ❏ After mining, land must be returned to the original owners - the Adivasis/indigenous peoples, after refilling and making it fit for agriculture.
- ❏ A serious concern are the influx of outsiders into the area and the replacing of valuable trees like *keond, mahua, bahera, Pyaar, kusum,* and *sarjom* by *Acacia,* and *Eucalyptus.*
- ❏ Land for land must be done on a priority basis.
- ❏ *Cash Compensation* is not fit for indigenous people.
- ❏ Whatever land is being given for the project-affected peoples must be with legal *Patta.*

We need to rethink whether mining is sustainable for us or not. Can we not think of developing renewables? For how long will we go on flattening mountains and making mountains of overburden?

Annexes

Other Issues Raised in Inspection Panel's Report: Extent of Compliance with Operation Directive 4.20 on Indigenous Peoples

Indigenous Peoples Development Plans (IPDP)

It appears that experience did not result in much change. In its 2001 report, the ESRP observes that subsequent revision to the original IPDP "followed the lead of the first plan[s], adding a little here, subtracting a little there, but essentially repeating the form and substance of initial work plans, year after year." And they conclude that "What was originally meant to be a series of location-specific plans, arrived at through local consultation, tailored to the needs of villages, quickly grew into a rigid, inflexible and largely unresponsive exercise." Its own lack of success was built right into the design, in the very genes of the project itself" (paragraph 322 of the main text of the IP report)

In its review the Panel found that each year entire sections of the annual IPDP for Parej East are repeated verbatim, including the one indicating the community's 'felt needs'. Each year there appears to be a 'one size fits all' plan for each of the 11 communities, regardless of specific needs. The description of every hamlet begins with the same qualitative paragraph, and the plan ends with the same recommendations (and the same costs) such as "Bleaching Powder Distribution", Fruit Tree Distribution, Mahila Mandals' (self-help saving schemes) etc." (Paragraph 324 of the main text of the IP report.)

On the Issue of Resettlement

The Panel finds that the original Rehabilitation Action Plan (RAP) of Parej East did not reflect the actual situation in Parej East and was not location-specific as required by Management when it approved Coal India Ltd.'s R&R policy. In the Panels view, Management's failure, during appraisal, to ensure that the original RAP reflected reality on the ground resulted in many problems that are at the root of the Requesters complaints. In light of this, the Panel finds that Management's appraisal of the Parej East RAP was not in compliance with paragraph 30 of OD 4.30. (Paragraph 13 of the executive summary of Inspection Panel -IP report)

It seems evident that Project Affected Persons (PAPs) in Parej East were not consulted in the selection of the Pindra site as required by OD 4.30. In light of this, the Panel finds that Management was not in compliance with paragraph 8 of OD 4.30 (Paragraph 96 of the main text of IP report).

The Panel viewed the barracks besides CCL Headquarters and observed that the conditions are pathetic, as the Requests claim: they are hardly fit for human habitation, especially for families. Even so, it would now appear that the seven PAFs (Project Affected Families) regard remaining there a better alternative than building a house in Pindra because of the proximity of the barracks to casual labour opportunities and the informal economy at the mine site. The Parej East RAP limited its discussion of casual labour opportunities for resettlers at Pindra to mentioning some future nearby industrial development. "The panel could not find any report of a professional analysis to the pre and post reallocation (casual) labour market" Those who have moved in Pindra thus have superior physical accommodation but lack access to formal and informal labour opportunities at mine site. Thus in neither case have these PAPs regained their former standard of living. (Paragraph 102 of the main text of the IP report)

Management accepted Coal India Ltd's R&R policy on the clear understanding that it would "have to receive each RAP to be sure it contains the obligatory requirements for a successful RAP" The Parej East RAP simply repeated CIL's R&R Policy in respect of the size of plots (100m2) and did not provide for second generation growth or land for animals. The panel therefore finds that Management's appraisal of the Parej East RAP was not in compliance with Paragraphs 13 and 19 of OD 4.30. However, in practice, Management recognised this flaw, and in response to CASS insistence, CCL allocated plots twice the size of that provided for in the RAP. In addition, since implementation commenced, management has continued to press Coal India Ltd. to change its policy. (Paragraph 110 of the main text of the IP report)

It is clear that the question of title transfer should have been identified and dealt with when the Parej East RAP was prepared, as required under OD 4.30. CCL had already purchased the Pindra resettlement site by that stage. Now up to four years after affected people have been involuntarily resettled they are still suffering the harm that results from lack of title, including a sense of insecurity and an inability to borrow for self employment restoration schemes. (Paragraph 144 in the main text of the IP report)

As provided for in paragraph 15 (c) of OD 4.30 the RAP states that the Pindra resettlement site will provide equivalent access to the forest, but it fails to support this statement with any details about the adjacent forest including whether the forest will support the same income earning opportunities for 227 families originally expected to move there, or whether the host community is prepared to share the resources. The Panel found no evidence that during appraisal, Management ensured that access would be available, or the access to that forest besides Pindra would provide PAPs who moved there with equivalent compensation for loss of their access to forest products. Because of this, the panel finds that Management was not in compliance with paragraph 15 (c) of OD 4.30 during Preparation. (Paragraph 204 of the main text in the IP report)

Complaints not met with in OD 4.30 on Involuntary Resettlement

Adequacy of planning, RAP -- The Panel finds that the original RAP for Parej East did not reflect the actual situation in Parej East and was not location-specific as required by Management when it approved CIL's R&R policy. In the Panel's view, Management's failure during appraisal to ensure that the original RAP reflected reality on the ground resulted in many problems that are at the root of the Requesters complaints. In the light of this, the Panel finds that Management's appraisal of the Parej East RAP was not in compliance with paragraph 30 of OD 4.30. (Paragraph 13 of the executive summary and also see paragraph 56 & 57 from the main text of the IP report).

Adequate compensation for land -- When affected land holders are not satisfied with compensation decided by CCL and the district authorities, they may seek a decision to increase the amount from a special tribunal, constituted under section 14 of the Coal Bearing Areas Act. In this regard, the Panel considers it revealing that, in all cases so far finalised in Parej East, the tribunal has awarded increased compensation to those PAPs able to lodge an appeal. In the Panel's view, it is not appropriate that PAPs should have to go through lengthy and costly judicial processes to get compensation, especially since not all PAPs can afford the direct costs of an appeal process and, even if they could, they would end up losing, unless the cost of the appeal were added to their award. Even then, the delays and uncertainties associated with the process could result in tangible harm, especially since the awards are subject to future appeal by CCL. It is unfortunate to note that CCL is appealing all these decisions. In light of this, the Panel finds that Management was not in compliance with paragraph 3 (b) of OD 4.30. (Paragraph 16 of the executive summary also see the main text paragraph 74 & 75 of the IP report)

Compensation process to be transparent -- There is another problem: the lack of transparency in the compensation process. In the Panel's view, it is clear that, as the Requesters claim, the compensation process in Parej East was and is not transparent. In light of this, the Panel finds the Management is not in compliance with paragraph 8 of OD 4.30 (Paragraph 17 of executive summary, also see the main text paragraph 78 of the IP report)

Consultation in selection of resettlement site -- Concerning the choice of site, the PAPs generally complain that they had never been consulted in their selection. They were guided to a pre-selected site and told to move there. The Panel finds that the PAPs in Parej East were not consulted in the selection of the Pindra resettlement site as required by paragraph 8 of OD 4.30 and the Management was not in compliance with the OD in this respect. (Paragraph 22 of executive summary; also see the main text paragraph 96 of IP report)

Resettlement site, second generation expansion -- Concerning the size of the plots offered to the PAPs, OD 4.30 provides that planning for shelter, infrastructure, and service should take into account population growth. Management accepted CIL's R&R policy on the clear understanding that it would have to review each RAP to be sure it contains the obligatory requirements for a successful RAP. The Parej East RAP simply repeated Coal India's R&R policy in respect of the size of plots, and did not provide second-generation growth or land for gardens and animals. The Panel therefore finds that Management's appraisal of Parej East

RAP was not in compliance with paragraph 13 and 19 of OD 4.30. However, in practice, Management immediately recognised this flaw, and in response to CASS insistence, CCL allocated plots twice the size of that provided for in the RAP. In addition, since implementation commenced, Management has continued to press CIL to change its policy. (Paragraph 25 of executive summary, also see the main text paragraph 110 of IP report)

Potable water for resettlement site -- Concerning potable water, based on the Panel's review of the records available, it seems clear that the date set for the families to move in Pindra, December 15, 1999, was dictated by the scheduled mine experience and that they were moved without establishing whether potable water was available at Pindra. For failing to ensure access to potable water before the PAPs were moved to the Pindra resettlement site, the Panel finds the Management was not in compliance with Paragraph 19 of OD 4.30 (Paragraph 26 of executive summary, also see the main text paragraph 117 of IP report)

Educational services at resettlement site -- Concerning schools, in December 1999, the PAPs from Borwa Tola were involuntarily relocated some distance away to Pindra. There they found a school building with no teacher, despite OD 4.30 and promises to the contrary. The Panel therefore finds that Management was not in compliance with paragraph 19 of OD 4.30 in this respect. (Paragraph 28 of the executive summary, also see the main text paragraph 126 of IP report)

Arrangement for legal title deeds -- It is clear that the question of title transfer should have been identified and dealt with when the Parej East RAP was prepared under OD 4.30. CCL had already purchased the Pindra resettlement site by that stage. Now, up to four years after affected people have been involuntarily resettled they are still suffering the harm that results from the lack of title, including a sense of insecurity and, as Management itself had stated, an inability to borrow from self-employment income restoration scheme. The Panel finds that management was not in compliance with paragraph 13 (c) and 14 (a) of OD 4.30 when the RAP for Parej East was prepared. (Paragraph 35 of the executive summary, also see the main text paragraph 145 of the IP report)

Legal recognition for customary held land -- The Panel finds that Management was not in compliance with paragraph 17 of OD 4.30 and paragraph 15 (c) and 17 of OD 4.20, in connection with the preparation of the Parej East RAP. At the same time, the Panel recognises that after this flaw was raised by CASS and international NGOs, Management acknowledged the problem. It raised the issue to the level of a cross conditionality under the CSRP loan. And since, it had worked with persistence to try to get the matter resolved. (Paragraph 40 of the executive summary, also see the main text paragraph 177 of IP report)

Compensation for customary held land -- The Panel questioned Management on this and received a response in mid October 2002. The Panel notes that there are two villages in Parej East and Durukasmbar. With respect to Durukasmbar village, the Management response is clear and no PAPs have yet been relocated. For the village of Parej, the Management response appears to deal only with one of the existing hamlets of Parej, namely Borwa Tola. This hamlet no longer exists so clearly every PAP has been relocated. Apparently six tribals from Borwa Tola claimed they were cultivating Gair Majurwa Khas -GMK land. Of these, two claims were rejected. Of the four claims approved two were paid compensation before relocation, one not paid before relocation due to bureaucratic error, and one had died but their heirs have not been informed of the claim. This response informs that 18 non-tribal PAPs apparently from Borwa Tola claimed they were cultivating land under customary rights.

The response does not state whether compensation was paid, before their relocation, to the seven whose claims were authenticated. Of the 11 whose claims were rejected, Management could not discover the status of the appeal lodged by eight of them, so it would appear that they have relocated before a decision on their appeal. Finally, all three times Management has addressed this question in its response; it mentions that for Parej village a total of 8.17 ha out of 59.5 ha have been authenticated and that claims regarding the other 42.44 ha remain to be settled. None of the answers provide any further information on this, so the Panel does not know how many PAPs are involved, which hamlets of Parej village they are from, and whether or not they have been relocated. For the above reasons, the Panel notes that Management has failed to provide the Panel with evidence that it has complied with the OD 4.30 with regard to the compensation of PAPs who own land under traditional or customary rights, prior to their relocation. (Paragraph 41 of executive summary; also see the main text paragraph 179 of IP report)

Access to equivalent natural resources -- (Forest Products). As provided for in paragraph 15 (c) of OD 4.30 the RAP states that the Pindra resettlement site will provide equivalent access to the forest, but it fails to support this statement with any details about the adjacent forest including whether the forest will support the same income earning opportunities for the 227 families originally expected to move there with equivalent compensation for loss of their access to forest products. Because of this, the Panel finds that Management was not in compliance with paragraph 15 (c) of OD 4.30 during Preparation. (Paragraph 44 of the executive summary; also see the main text paragraph 196 & 204 of the IP report)

Improve former livelihood standards -- (Income restoration). In the light of the above, the Panel finds that, as Management itself recognises, it is not in compliance with paragraphs 3(b) (iii) of OD 4.30, and since, according to the April 2000 Management Response, the income of at least 21 percent of PAPs in the Parej East sub-project has not been improved, much less, restored. (Paragraph 48 of the executive summary, also see paragraph 210, 211 & 212 of the main text of the IP report)

Feasibility of rehabilitation arrangements -- In Panel's view, it is quite understandable that PAPs who opted for jobs in June 1994 should naturally expect to receive those jobs. Nor is it surprising that those who owned less then two acres continued to demand and expect jobs for land. It must have been a shock for them to discover otherwise when finally presented with the reality of their situation in early 1997. The Panel finds that Management was not in compliance with paragraph 30 (e) of OD 4.30 during preparation and appraisal of the Parej East RAP. (Paragraph 51 of the executive summary; also see the main text paragraph 227 of IP report)

Preference to land-based resettlement strategies -- Under the Bank's policy the land for land option is not mandatory, but it is clearly preferred wherever possible. Under CCL's Parej East RAP, CCL was to offer assistance to PAPs to find replacement land. According to Management CCL received no request for such assistance. But in the RAP some 117 opted for this assistance and 115 qualified. Management also indicated in its Response that a large number of PAPs found replacement land, indicating that, with effort, it could be obtained. The Panel finds that Management was not in compliance with paragraph 4 of OD 4.30. (Paragraph 53 of the executive summary; also see the main text paragraph 235 of IP report)

Failure of self -employment -- The Panel finds that Management failed to ascertain the adequacy or feasibility of the self-employment income rehabilitation strategy in the Parej East RAP during appraisal and, after the Market Survey was finally conducted in March 1998, it failed to ensure that the recommended follow-up measures were taken. In the light of this, Management was not in compliance with paragraph 24, 29, and 30 of OD 4.30. (Paragraph 55 of the executive summary; also see the main text paragraph 243 of the IP report)

Failed to improve, or at least restore livelihood standards -- During the project preparation and appraisal, Management relied almost entirely on off-farm self-employment as the strategy to regain standards of living, without assessing its feasibility for income restoration in Parej East. As a result, many PAPs in Parej East have failed to restore their living standards and incomes to their previous levels and consequently have suffered and continue to suffer harm. In the light of the forgoing, the Panel finds that Management was not in compliance with OD 4.30 in this respect. (Paragraph 57 of the executive summary; also see the main text paragraph 258 of IP report)

Self employment unrealistic for regenerating livelihood -- In the Panel's view it was a major planning flaw for the Bank not to have recognised that it was unrealistic to expect that the PAPs in Parej East could become entrepreneurs in five years. In accordance with paragraph 30 of OD 4.30 the feasibility of Parej East PAPs regarding their livelihood through self employment should have been reviewed when the RAP was appraised. (Paragraph 62 of the executive summary; also see the main text paragraph 267 of the IP report)

Assistance during transition period -- Management provided no data as to whether PAPs have received the Subsistence Allowance (Part B of 3.4.4). The Panel notes that Management's response of April 2002 asserted that "no PAP has received a subsistence allowance because the eligibility criteria have not been met." The R&R budget for Parej East, however, contains a line item for subsistence allowance/grant for the years 1998- 2002. Management has provided no explanation concerning the disposition of the monies for the subsistence allowance/grant, nor concerning the reasons why the PAPs were regarded as ineligible for their benefits, nor the procedures followed to arrive at this determination. The supervision report made available to the Panel finds that Management has failed to demonstrate that it has complied with paragraph 3 (b) (ii) of OD4.30 that requires that displaced persons "be supported during the transition period in resettlement site." (Paragraph 68 of the executive summary, also see the main text paragraph 284 of IP report)

IPDP not responsive to local needs -- In the panel's view, as recognised by the ESRP, the Parej East IPDP should have been responsive to local needs. It was not. Moreover, Management clearly erred in ignoring a local NGO report on the IPDP, especially since it did not itself review the latter. However failing to revive the Parej East IPDP, Management could not have assessed whether it was in compliance with paragraph 18 of OD 4.20 during appraisal. The Panel finds that Management did not ensure that the original Parej East IPDP was prepared in compliance with paragraph 18 of OD 4.20. (Paragraph 77 of the executive summary, also see the main text paragraph 316 of the IP report)

Inflexible -- The Panel found that each year entire sections of annual IPDP for Parej East are repeated verbatim, including the one indicating a community's "felt needs." Each year there appears to be a "one size fit all" plan for each of the 11 communities, regardless of special needs. (Paragraph 80 of the executive summary, also see the main text paragraph 326 of IP report)

Not informed and consulted systematically -- But beyond these interviews, there is nothing to indicate that the PAPs in Parej East were "systematically informed and consulted during preparations of the resettlement plan about their options and rights." In light of this, the Panel finds that Management was not in compliance with paragraph 8 of OD 4.30 (Paragraph 102 of the executive summary, also see the main text paragraph 433 of IP report)

Consultation of host community -- The evidence is clear that the host community for the Pindra resettlement site was not consulted during project preparation and, in light of this, the Panel finds that Management was not in compliance with paragraph 9 of OD 4.30. (Paragraph 103 of the executive summary, also see the main text paragraph 434 of the IP report)

Complaints met with in OD 4.30 on Involuntary Resettlement

Formally in compliance with the Grievance Mechanism -- Since a grievance mechanism was established in Parej East and appeals process described, the Panel finds that Management is formally in compliance with paragraph 17 of OD 4.30. However Bank staff was unable to confirm that any independent person was on the grievance committee. The Panel is also concerned that it was unable to establish whether or not PAP members are elected democratically, or are selected by authorities (Paragraph 37 in the executive summary of the IP report)

PAPs interviewed during Baseline Survey -- The Panel recognises that Management ensured that the PAPs in Parej East were interviewed during the process of the Baseline Survey preparation and, to the extent that this provided inputs for the RAP, finds that management was in compliance with paragraph 8 of OD 4.30 (Paragraph 101 of the executive summary of the IP report)

Systematic consultation and involvement by facilitating -- The Panel notes that, after the RAP was prepared, consultation with PAPs and PAP participation in resettlement process was to be undertaken entirely through the implementing NGO, but also observes that in Parej East, the implementing NGO XISS, set up an office in Parej East only in July 1997. During the three years that elapsed since the RAP had been preparing there is scant evidence of consultations on planning for displacement except occasionally at the insistence of CASS. The Panel, finds however, that once XISS began work, there was systematic consultation and involvement of the PAPs, on behalf of CCL, and therefore finds Management in compliance with paragraph 8 of OD 4.30 (Paragraph 104 of the executive summary of the IP report)

Did Indigenous Peoples benefit from the Project?

Land-for-land

The Environmental and Social Review Panel (ESRP) visited some mines, including the CCL mines, in 1997. They noted that part of the Coal India

Ltd. policy were a source of much discontent and confusion. They observed that, contrary to Bank Policy, "this [land for land] option has never been offered in any of the subsidiaries visited. Partly as result, the question of the adequacy of compensation paid for land is an important source of discontent with land owners" (Paragraph 231 of the main text of the IP report)

Under the Bank's policy, the land-for-land option is not mandatory, but it is clearly preferred wherever possible. Under CCL's Parej East RAP, CCL was to offer assistance to PAPs in finding replacement land. According to Management, CCL received no requests for such assistance. But in the RAP some 177 PAPs opted for this assistance and 115 qualified. Management also indicated that a large number of PAPs found replacement land, indicating that, with effort, it could be obtained. The Panel finds that Management was not in compliance with paragraph 4 of OD.30 (Paragraph 235 in the main text of the IP report)

Land Compensation

Basic principle of OD 4.30 is that "[d]isplaced persons should be (i) compensated for their losses at full replacement cost prior to the actual move ..." In the light of the above, the Panel finds that, in Parej East, many of the displaced PAPs have not been and are not being compensated at full cost, with the result that many of them have suffered harm. (Paragraph 14 is from the executive summary and paragraph 72 from the main text of the IP report)

In the Panel's view it is difficult, if not impossible, to reconcile the Bank's aim of development with a one time cash grant for acquisition of home and land. Presenting a poor oustee, whose previous source of survival included a small patch of land with a check may be a legal way of getting them to move on, but it should not be confused with development. The Panel highlights that the ESRP has recommended that the Bank commission a post-Project audit to assess the long term results of the cash settlement approach. (Paragraph 20 from the executive summary of the IP report)

During the project preparation and the early stages of project implementation, at least through late 1996, the record indicated that the East Parej PAPs were led to expect a mine job. In February 1997, the mine has expanded to within a few hundred yards of the hamlet of Turi Tola where the PAPs resisted relocation. At this point, the Bank supervision team noted the discrepancy between what the PAPs expected and the eligibility criteria in the RAP. They reported that the previous mine manager had given promises of jobs to PAPs with less then two acres of land.

In the Panel's view, it is quite understandable that PAPs who opted for jobs in June 1994 should naturally expect to receive these jobs. Nor is it surprising that those who owned less then two acres continued to demand and expect jobs for land. It must have been a shock for them to discover otherwise when finally presented with the reality for this situation [no job] in early 1997. The panel finds that Management was not in compliance with paragraph 30 (e) of OD 4.30 during preparation and appraisal of the Parej East RAP. (Paragraphs 50 & 51 from the executive summary of the IP report)

Traditional Land Rights (Land held under Customary Title)

In June 1997, after the NGOs had raised the issue a number of times, the Bank team, under a new Task Leader, admitted that although Coal India Ltd's R&R policy stipulates that the tribals cultivating land under customary tenure arrangements are entitled to full compensation under package A, Coal India Ltd. admits that this is at present not possible because there is no legal framework to accommodate this. The R&R policy is in this respect ineffectual unless the required legal provisions are created. To achieve this CIL accepts an additional cross-conditionality for the CSRP.

The agreed minutes of the CSRP negotiations held in July 1997 state that: "the Bank team expressed its concerns that compensation for land held under customary tenure has not been uniformly provided by all Coal India subsidiaries. The Indian delegation assures that these issues will be addressed to the satisfaction of the Bank. In the supplemental letter to CSRP Loan Agreement, signed in March 1998, "CIL Obligations Relating to Resettlement Action Plans" was attached. The "Agreed Action" for Parej East lists the need for a "Record of Right" for all land held under tenure forms such as *Ghai Mazurwa Aam*, *Gair Mazurwa Khas*, *Bhudan* and *Bahamian* and states that there were a total eligible 382 PAPs in Parej East.

The letter shows that there were a total of 3350 PAPs at eight mines in need of a "Record of Right" and figures were to be provided for other six mines. The ESRP concluded that the CIL R&R Policy was contrary to Operation Directive (OD) 4.30! (158). The Panel reports that CIL informed management in 1998 that necessary title recognition applies to "3359 PAPs at eight mines… and figures were to be provided for other six mines. (Paragraph 170 from the main text of the IP report)

The above account in Parej East of Traditional Land Rights reveals a serious failure to comply with the relevant Bank policy provisions. In proceeding with the CSESMP, Management expected (and Coal India Ltd. agreed) that the tribals would be treated in accordance with the Bank ODs 4.30 and 4.20. Yet, it appears that the laws of the state of Bihar (now Jharkhand) precluded such treatment without documentation. The Panel finds it difficult to understand how, at the time of preparation,

Management could be unaware of this when the Bank has been involved in resettlement projects in India for some years. Furthermore, based on the foregoing, it seems clear that, during preparation, Management did not raise any question about the possible lack of legal recognition or the process required to ensure compensation for tribals cultivating traditional land without title or documentation. (Paragraph 174 of the main text of IP report)

Legal recognition of traditional land rights is a serious problem. In Bihar (and now Jharkhand) authentication by state authorities is required. During its field visit, the Panel was told that this process was and is not on the District Administration's priority list, so it continues to be delayed, with the resulting serious consequences for the PAPs. Nearly eight yeas after adoption of the CIL (R&R) policy and the RAP for Parej East about 150 ha out of the total of about 167 ha claimed by tribals (indigenous peoples), and under traditional rights have not been settled. This is extremely serious and need immediate action. (Paragraph 176 of the main text of the IP report)

Income Restoration

A basic principle of OD 4.30 is that displaced persons should be compensated for their losses at full replacement cost prior to the actual move. The Panel finds that, in Parej East, many of the project displaced affected persons have not been and are not being compensated at full replacement cost, with the result that many have suffered and continue to suffer harm. (Paragraph 14 of the executive summary of the IP report)

The Panel finds that this suffering and harm comes as a result of a failure to:

- ❏ Be transparent in how existing land and housing was measured.
- ❏ Value existing land and housing realistically.
- ❏ Offer a choice of resettlement site.
- ❏ Provide jobs or effective income generation schemes.

During Project preparation and appraisal, Management relied almost entirely on non-farm self-employment as the strategy to regain standards of living, without assessing its feasibility for income restoration in Parej East. As a result, many PAPs in Parej East have failed to restore their living standards and income to their previous levels and consequently have suffered and continue to suffer harm. In the light of the foregoing, the Panel finds that Management was not in compliance with OD 4.30 in this respect. The Panel finds that the Management failed to

ascertain the adequacy or feasibility of the self-employment income rehabilitation strategy in the Peraj East RAP during appraisal and, after a
Market Survey was finally conducted in March 1998, it failed to ensure
that the recommended follow-up measures were taken. In the light of
this, Management was not in compliance with paragraphs 24, 29, and
30 of OD 4.30. (Paragraph 55 of the executive summary, paragraph 243
of the main text of the IP report)

Non-farm based Self Employment

The Panel finds that the Management failed to ascertain the adequacy or
feasibility of the self-employment income rehabilitation strategy in the
Peraj East RAP during appraisal and, after a Market Survey was finally
conducted in March 1998, it failed to ensure that the recommended follow-up measures were taken. In the light of this, Management was not in
compliance with paragraphs 24, 29, and 30 of OD 4.30. (Paragraph 55 of
the executive summary; also see 243 of the main text of the IP report)

In the Panel's view, it is difficult, if not impossible, to reconcile the
Bank's aim of development with a one time cash grant for acquisition of
house and land. Presenting a poor oustee, whose previous source of
survival included a small patch of land, with a check may be a legal way
of getting them to move on, but it should not be confused with development.... (Paragraph 20 of the executive summary of the IP report)

Counts of Compliance

IP No.	Oper. Dir.	Issue
129:	ODN 11.03	Discussion on cultural issues.
152:	OD 4.30 para 17	Grievance mechanism, formally in compliance.
299:	OD 4.20	To include all vulnerable people in framework plan...
432 :	OD 4.30 para 8	PAPs interviewed during base-line survey.....
440:	OD.4.30 para 8	Systematic consultation and involvement by....
473:	OD 13.05	Major problems, doing best to translate efforts into outcomes.

Further commendations

291:	"for recognizing that a land-based income restoration option was essential..."
340:	"recent efforts by Management...in some progress..massive shift of institutional culture.... "
466:	"made significant effort to overcome some of the problems."

Counts of Non-Compliance

IP Rpt	Oper. Dir.	Issue
57:	OD 4.30 para 30	Adequacy of the planning, RAP.
75:	OD 4.30 3(b)	Adequate compensation for land.
78:	OD 4.30 para 8:	Compensation process to be transparent.
96:	OD 4.30 para 8:	Consultation in selection of resettlement site.
110:	OD 4.30 paras 13,19	resettlement site - second-generation expansion.
117.	OD 4.30 para19	Potable water at resettlement site.
126.	OD 4.30 para 19	Educational services at resettlement site.
145:	OD 4.30 paras 13(c), 14(a)	Arranging for legal title deeds.
177:	OD 4.30 p.17, OD 4.20: 5c,17	Legal recognition of customary held land.
179:	OD.430	Compensation for customary held land.
196*:	OD 4.20 para 15(a)	Tribal dependence on /access to natural resources.
204:	OD 4.30 para 15(c)	Access to equivalent natural resources.
212:	OD 4.30 para 3(b)(iii)	Improve former living standards.
227:	OD 4.30 para 30(e)	Feasibility of rehabilitation arrangements.
235:	OD 4.30 para 4	Preference to land-base resettlement strategies.
243:	OD 4.30 para 24, 29, 30	Failure of "self-employment" to improve, or restore.
258*:	OD 4.30	Failed to improve, or at least restore living standard.
267:	OD 4.30 para 30	Self-employment unrealistic for regaining livelihood.
284:	OD 4.30 3(b) (ii)	Assistance during transition period.
304:	OD 4.20 para 18	Review of IPDPs before appraisal.
316:	OD 4.30 para 18	IPDP responsive to local needs.
326:	OD 4.30	Inflexible IPDP.
331:	OD 4.20 para 14(a), 18	Consultation during preparation of IPDP.

341:	OD 4.20 para 15(d)	IPDP non specific to community needs.
394:	OD 4.01 p. 21, BP 17.50 p.12	Inadequate disclosure of information.
409:	OD 4.01 p. 21, BP 17.50 p.12	Inadequate accessibility to information.
425:	OD 4.01 p. 20, BP 17.50 p.12	No meaningful consultation on EIA preparation.
433:	OD.4.30 para 8	Systematically informed and consulted.
434:	OD.4.30 para 9	Consultation of host community.
448:	OD 4.01 para 19	Consultation of local NGOs.
457:	OD.13.05	Bank supervision unsatisfactory.

* 196 omits important point of Ex Sum 44,
* 258 omits important point of Ex Sum 57.

INDIGENOUS PEOPLES' DECLARATION ON THE EXTRACTIVE INDUSTRIES

Oxford, United Kingdom
15 April 2003

PREAMBLE

Our futures as indigenous peoples are threatened in many ways by developments in the extractive industries. Our ancestral lands -- the tundra, drylands, small islands, forests and mountains -- which are also important and critical ecosystems have been invaded by oil, gas, and mining developments which are undermining our very survival. Expansion and intensification of the extractive industries, alongside economic liberalisation, free trade aggression, extravagant consumption and globalisation, are frightening signals of unsustainable greed.

Urgent actions must be taken by all to stop and reverse the social and ecological injustice arising from the violations of our rights as indigenous peoples.

We, indigenous peoples, welcome the initiative of the World Bank to carry out an extractive industries review. We note that the purpose of this review is to assess whether, and under what circumstances, the extractive industries can contribute to poverty alleviation and sustainable development.

We note that 'sustainable development' is founded on three pillars which should be given equal weight if such development is to be equitable namely environmental, economic and human rights. We note that this issue has already been addressed by the Kimberley Declaration of Indigenous Peoples to the World Summit on Sustainable Development and by the Roundtable between the World Bank and Indigenous Peoples held in Washington in October 2002. We also draw attention to the findings of the Workshop on Indigenous Peoples, Human Rights and the Extractive Industries organised by the Office of the High Commissioner for Human Rights in Geneva in December 2001.

We, indigenous peoples, reject the myth of 'sustainable mining': we have not experienced mining as a contribution to 'sustainable development' by any reasonable definition. Our experience shows that exploration and exploitation of minerals, coal, oil, and gas bring us serious social and environmental problems, so widespread and injurious that we cannot describe such development as 'sustainable'. Indeed, rather than contributing to poverty alleviation, we find that the extractive industries are creating poverty and social divisions in our communities, and showing disrespect for our culture and customary laws.

KEY CONCERNS

Our experience of mining, oil and gas development has been one of:

◻ Violation of our basic human rights, such as killings, repression and the assassination of our leaders.

◻ The invasion of our territories and lands and the usurpation of our resources.

◻ By denying us rights or control over our lands, including subsurface resources, our communities and cultures are, literally, undermined.

◻ Many of our communities have been forced to relocate from their lands and ended up seriously impoverished and disoriented.

◻ Extractive industries are not transparent, withholding important information relevant to decisions affecting us.

◻ Consultation with our communities has been minimal and wholly inadequate measures have been taken to inform us of the consequences of these schemes before they have been embarked on.

◻ Consent has been engineered through bribery, threats, moral corruption and intimidation.

- Mines, oil and gas developments have ruined our basic means of subsistence, torn up our lands, polluted our soils and waters, divided our communities and poisoned the hopes of our future generations. They increase prostitution, gambling, alcoholism, drugs and divorce due to rapid changes in the local economy.
- Indigenous women have in particular suffered the imposition of mining culture and cash-based economies.
- Extractive industries are unwilling to implement resource sharing with indigenous peoples on a fair and equal basis.

These problems reflect and compound our situation as indigenous peoples. Our peoples are discriminated against. Those who violate our rights do so with impunity. Corruption and bad governance compound our legal and political marginalization. We find that the extractive industries worsen our situation, create greater divisions between rich and poor, and escalate violence and repression in our areas.

RECOMMENDATIONS

In view of this experience and in line with precautionary principles:

- We call for a moratorium on further mining, oil and gas projects that may affect us until our human rights are secure. Existing concessions should be frozen. There should be no further funding by international financial institutions such as the World Bank, no new extractive industry initiatives by governments, and no new investments by companies until respect for the rights of indigenous peoples is assured.
- Destructive practices such as riverine tailings disposal, submarine tailings disposal and open pit mining should be banned.
- Moreover, before new investments and projects are embarked on, we demand -- as a show of good faith -- that governments, companies and development agencies make good the damages and losses caused by past projects which have despoiled our lands and fragmented our communities. Compensation for damages encompasses not only remuneration for economic losses but also reparations for the social, cultural, environmental and spiritual losses we

have endured. Measures should be taken to rehabilitate degraded environments, farmlands, forests and landscapes and to restitute our lands and territories taken from us. Promises and commitments made to our communities must be honoured. Appropriate mechanisms must be established to address these outstanding problems with the full participation of the affected peoples and communities.

◻ Once and if, these conditions are met, we call for a change in all future mining, oil and gas development. All future extractive industries development must uphold indigenous peoples' rights.

◻ Equally, international development agencies must require borrower countries and private sector clients to uphold human rights in line with their international obligations. The international financial institutions and development agencies, such as the World Bank, must themselves observe international law and be bound by it in legally accountable ways.

◻ By human rights, we refer to our rights established under international law. We hold our rights to be inherent and indivisible and seek recognition not only of our full social, cultural and economic rights but also our civil and political rights. Respect for all our rights is essential if 'good governance' is to have any meaning for us.

◻ In particular we call for recognition of our collective right as peoples, to self-determination, including a secure and full measure of self-governance and control over our territories, organisations and cultural development.

◻ We demand respect for our rights to our territories, lands and natural resources and that under no circumstances should we be forcibly removed from our lands. All proposed developments affecting our lands should be subject to our free, prior and informed consent as expressed through our own representative institutions, which should be afforded legal personality. The right to free, prior informed consent should not be construed as a 'veto' on development but includes the right of indigenous peoples to say 'no' to projects that we consider injurious to us as peoples. The right must be made effective through the provision of adequate information and implies a permanent process of negotiation between indigenous peoples and developers. Mechanisms for redress of grievances, arbitration and judicial review are required.

- Education and capacity building are needed to allow us to be trained and informed so we can participate effectively and make decisions in our own right.

- Before projects are embarked on, such problems as marginalisation, insecure land rights, and lack of citizenship papers must be addressed. Indigenous Peoples' Development Plans (IPDPs) must be formulated with the affected communities and indigenous peoples should control mechanisms for the delivery of project benefits.

- Voluntary standards are not enough: there is a need for mandatory standards and binding mechanisms. Binding negotiated agreements between indigenous peoples, governments, companies and the World Bank are needed which can be invoked in the courts if other means of redress and dispute resolution fail. Formal policies and appeals procedures should be developed to ensure accountability for loan operations, official aid, development programmes and projects. These accountability measures should be formulated with indigenous peoples with a view to securing our rights throughout the strategic planning and project cycles.

- Independent oversight mechanisms, which are credible and accessible to indigenous peoples, must be established to ensure the compliance by all parties with agreed commitments and obligations.

- Companies seeking to invest in mining, oil and gas ventures on our lands should also be obliged to take out bonds as guarantees of reparations, in the case of damages to our material and immaterial properties and values, sacred sites and biological diversity.

- We recognise that many mining, oil and gas investments have their origins in national, regional and international policy agreements, which often facilitate relaxation of laws, fiscal reforms, encouragement of foreign investment and accelerated processes for handing out concessions to extractive industries. International agencies, such as the World Bank, promote such changes through adjustment and programmatic lending, through technical assistance interventions, country assistance strategies and sectoral reforms. Our experience is that often these policy and legal reforms ignore, override or even violate our constitutional rights and our rights and freedoms set out in national and international laws. Often the impacts of these developments on indigenous peoples are ignored during national planning.

□ We demand our right to equal and effective participation in these planning processes and that they take full account of our rights. Given the country-wide embrace of these national strategies, we demand that the agencies such as the World Bank give equal attention to the application of existing laws and regulations which uphold our rights in policy and country dialogues and financial agreements. Development agencies should give priority to securing our rights and ensuring they are effectively implemented before facilitating access to our lands by private sector corporations such as extractive industries. Mining laws which deny our rights should be revised and replaced.

□ The World Bank must encourage member states to fulfil their obligations under international human rights law and existing national legislation on indigenous peoples' rights. Consistent with the call for "Partnership into Action" by the UN Decade for Indigenous People, we call for equal participation by indigenous peoples in the formulation of general Country Assistance Strategies and particularly in Indigenous Peoples Development Plans.

□ Poverty alleviation must start from indigenous peoples' own definitions and indicators of poverty, and particularly address the exclusion and lack of access to decision-making at all levels. Rather than being merely lack of money and resources, poverty is also defined by power deficits and absence of access to decision-making and management processes. Social and ecological inequalities and injustice breed and perpetuate the impoverishment of indigenous peoples.

□ Independent and participatory environmental, social and cultural assessments must be carried out prior to the start of projects, and our ways of life respected throughout the project cycle, with due recognition and respect for matrilineal systems and women's social position.

□ As indigenous peoples, we do not reject development but we demand that our development be determined ourselves according to our own priorities. Sustainable development for indigenous peoples is secured through the exercise of our human rights, and enjoying the respect and solidarity of all peoples. We are thus empowered to make our contributions and to play our vital role in sustainable development.

A CALL FOR ACTION AND SOLIDARITY

We call on the international community and regional bodies, governments, the private sector, civil society and all indigenous peoples to join their voices to this Indigenous Peoples Declaration on the Extractive Industries.

We call on the World Bank's Extractive Industries Review to uphold our recommendations and to carry through their implementation in the World Bank Group's policies, programmes, projects and processes.

We also recommend a discussion on this theme at the upcoming meeting of the United Nations Permanent Forum on Indigenous Issues. We call on the Permanent Forum to insist on respect for our human rights by companies, investors, governments and development agencies involved in the extractive industries. The Permanent Forum must promote understanding of the negative impacts of the extractive industries on the economic, cultural, social and spiritual well-being of indigenous peoples and appropriate safeguard policies. The World Bank, as part of the United Nations family, should report to the Forum on how it proposes to amend its policy on indigenous peoples, in conformity with international law and the recognition of indigenous rights.

We also propose that further discussions on this theme of 'Indigenous Peoples, Human Rights and Extractive Industries' are held at the UN Working Group on Indigenous Populations (UNWGIP) with a view to developing new standards on this matter, in conformity with the Working Group's mandate.

We call for democratic national processes to review strategies and policies for the extractive industries towards a reorientation to secure sustainable development.

We enjoin all indigenous peoples to unite in solidarity to address the global threats posed by the extractive industries.

The Authors

Adrien Didier Amougoua is from the Planet Survey Yaoundé-Cameroon.

Vladimir Bocharnikov is affiliiated with RAIPON, the Russian Association of Indigenous Peoples of the North.

Emily Caruso is the Campaigns Assistant of the Forest Peoples Programme (FPP) and is the main author of "The Extractive Industry Review", "The World Bank's Policy on Indigenous Peoples"; and a contributory author of "A Record of Institutional Failure" of the *Synthesis Report*.

Marcus Colchester is the Director of the Forest Peoples Programme and the main author for the the introductory section, "Definitions of Indigenous Peoples", "From 'Best Practice' to Binding Standards", "Conclusions and Recommendation" of the *Synthesis Report*; and this book's *Introduction*.

Catalino Corpuz Jr. is the Campaigns Officer of Tebtebba.

Joachim Gwodog is a Bagyéli from the Log Ndiga community.

Nick Hildyard of The Cornerhouse is the main author of "A Record of Institutional Failure" of the *Synthesis Report*.

Matilda Koma is from the NGO Environmental Watch Group (NEWG) based in Port Moresby, Papua New Guinea.

Fergus MacKay is the Coordinator, Legal and Human Rights Programme of the FPP and the main author of "Indigenous Peoples' Rights and Resource Extraction" and "The World Bank and Human Rights" of the *Synthesis Report*.

Constant Félix Amougou Mbatsogo is a Permanent Consultant, Planet Survey.

Bineet Mundo is a freelance indigenous researcher from India.

Félix Devalois Ndiomgbwa is a reporter of the Bubinga newspaper, CED.

Geoff Nettleton of the Philippines Indigenous Links is the main author of "The World Bank Experience" of the *Synthesis Report*.

Armand Noahmvogo is a specialist in the management of Local Co-operatives and Development Associations, Planet Survey.

Jeanne Nouah is a a Bagyéli from the Bandevouri community.

Pius Erick Nyompe is the Executive Secretary of the *Lembaga Kesejahteraan Masyarakat Tambang dan Lingkungan (LKMTL)*, the Association for the Welfare of the Mining Community and Environment based in Indonesia.

Salvador Ramo is with the Special Projects Desk of Tebtebba.

Raymundo Rovillos is the Research Coordinator of Tebtebba.

Rodion Sulyandziga is the Deputy Project Coordinator of RAIPON.

Belmond Tchoumba is from the Bubinga newspaper, CED.

Armando Valbuena Wouriyu is from the Organización Nacional Indígena de Colombia.